Published by:
Cambridge House Press
New York, NY 10001
www.CamHousePress.com

Library Congress Cataloging-in-Publication Data

The Book your church doesn't want you to read : or synagogue, temple, mosque... / edited by Tim C. Leedom and Maria Murdy.
    p. cm.
  Includes bibliographical references.
  ISBN 978-0-9787213-8-1 (hardcover : alk. paper)
  1. Religions. 2. Religion. I. Leedom, Tim C. II. Murdy, Maria. III. Title.

  BL41.B66 2007
  200--dc22

2007011078
Second Edition.

10 9 8 7 6 5 4 3 2

Printed in the United States of America.

The book your church*

doesn't want you to read

*(or synagogue, temple, mosque..)

Edited by
Tim C. Leedom
and
Maria Murdy

CAMBRIDGE HOUSE PRESS
NEW YORK § TORONTO

"Most people would rather feel comfortable than know the truth. Well I'm going to make you uncomfortable by telling you the truth."

Robert F. Kennedy

CONTENTS

Contents

VI DOCTRINE

VII THE CATHOLIC CHURCH

Contents

VIII FUNDAMENTALISM

IX ARCHAEOLOGY AND SCIENCE

Contents

X NEW TAKES, NEW CONSEQUENCES

XI REVELATIONS

Preface

The book you are holding is the second edition of a very popular book entitled *The Book Your Church Doesn't Want You to Read*. *The Book* first came out in 1993 at book signings in Newport Beach, CA that featured many of its authors, including Steve Allen, Dr. Robert Eisenman, Dr. Gerald Larue, Bill Edelen, Dr. Alan Snow and Jordan Maxwell. It debuted amid much controversy and publicity and was favorably reviewed in *The Los Angeles Times* and *The Orange County Register*. It was covered by Southern California television stations and of course attacked as heresy by many churches who never took the time to read it. *The Book* started to make people think; which was the expressed goal of its editor and authors.

Since 1993 *The Book* has become a best seller and was praised by many as a "must read." Over a half a dozen printings later, it has been used as a textbook by universities and seminaries from Northern Alabama College to Berkeley. It has been featured at the American Booksellers Association Convention and front paged by the Whole Life Expos.

The Book has been upgraded and expanded. A few mistakes have been corrected. Unlike fundamentalist religions, we are not afraid to admit mistakes, and thus change; after all there have been new discoveries in science and technology over the last 13 years, so we've updated as well. The major religions cling desperately to non-original stories, unverifiable evidence and legends which continually prove disastrous for the human race. Creationism is now being taught to our children in science classes. Our current President routinely quotes the Bible even in matters concerning U.S. military aggression.

We have expanded *The Book* to include all major world religions, their commonalities and the reasons for their insane conflicts with each other. The examination of stellar worship, the sacred feminine, paganism and the development of Hinduism puts many current issues in the right perspective.

The second edition includes contemporary scholars, researchers and writers such as national correspondents Bill Moyers and Chris Hedges, Bishop John Shelby Spong, Joseph Campbell, Judy Chicago, *Village Voice* writer Rick Perlstein, Thomas Doyle, and David Stannard. Like the first edition, the second still encourages people to think for themselves and look for proof. We want our readers not to rely on answers given by ancient texts and philosophies that were myths then and are absurd today. The foundation of *The Book* is the spirit of free inquiry, from the ancient Greeks — Protagoras, Socrates and others — through the Renaissance humanism of Erasmus and Spinoza, followed by the Enlightenment — Voltaire, John Locke, Thomas Paine, Thomas Jefferson — to the present secular culture of great scientific achievements. All through these times, those who thought for themselves, who explored new questions and found new answers, had to contend with the repressions of religious orthodoxy. This was inevitable, since their work was a mortal challenge to old ways of thinking. We who stand on their shoulders thank them. The scholars or theologians who have contributed to *The Book* aren't naive to the point of believing that this anthology will create "Rapture" in reverse. Knowing the reaction of established religion in the past to critique and examination, we anticipate another strong response by those who won't even read it. These leaders and followers continually take the attitude of "don't bother me with facts; I've already made up my mind."

The Book sets its tone with Robert Ingersoll and Thomas Paine. It does not back off from the challenge and exposure of the Bible and religion. The mere mention of pagan origins, astrotheology and mythology always brings howls of protest and denial from the church. *The Book* makes more than mere mention: it shows religion for what it is. You will not find the uniformity of belief that you find in a religious tract. There are some lively disagreements among our authors. This is fitting in a book meant to challenge.

Discovering the truth of the evidence of other saviors and of stories identical to many in the Old and New Testaments, which appeared one thousand years before Jesus, will be unsettling, as will the exposure of modern-day abuses and policies in the name of God. To be sure, just as many will be shocked by these facts, many will be surprised by the number of intelligent, patriotic, sincere and kind men and women who do not embrace the God of the Bible. A final word. This is not an anti-religious book. The search for the meaning of life started long before Moses, Jesus, Mohammed or organized religion. *The Book* is a reference book that is meant to be challenging and informative. Many religious people are kind, peace-loving and good. Many are not. Whether it is the belief system that molds them or their nature, it is hard to say. Most are woefully misinformed and underexposed to material that could change them for the better. But literacy takes reading, change takes effort and enlightenment takes courage. In the end, "Ye shall know the truth, and the truth shall make you free" (John 8:32).

– Tim C. Leedom, Editor

About the Editors

Tim C. Leedom *was educated at the University of Kansas, completed his studies at the University of Hawaii, and was the recipient of several fellowships in journalism and political science. He served as an administrative assistant to both the Governor and Lt. Governor of Hawaii, and was an administrative aide in the Hawaii State Legislature in the 1960s and '70s. Tim has authored or edited five books, including a best seller and an award-winning children's book,* The Light Side.

Maria Murdy *has been working for Tim C. Leedom as a Research Assistant in the areas of religious studies and freethought for eight years. She has worked in production and design on several media ventures including an upcoming educational documentary she co-produced with Tim.*

Introduction

There seem to be three subjects which are among the most important things in life: politics, sex and religion. However, along the way, some wise sage coached the general population that these three subjects should never be discussed. I suggest to you that those sages — the politician and those who wanted to put someone (generally a spouse or sexual partner) in some kind of sexual bondage, and the religious leader — were the very ones who would profit most from a lack of discussion on any of those subjects.

I do not want to address the subject of politics or sex here, but rather what is commonly referred to as religion. I grew up in central Texas in one of the most fundamentalist Christian regions in America. One positive thing it provided was a respect for forces greater than man, a respect for history, and certainly a respect for some very basic concepts of interpersonal behavior. But it did little more, other than to demonstrate vividly that there is no connection between the evolution of the spirit of man and his adherence to ritual, ceremony and rote memory as dictated by some religious organization's edict.

The relationship between you, your spirit and the Creator of the Universe is a deeply personal matter. There can be no middle-man in this relationship. Not your parents, not your minister, not a bishop, nor any other self-appointed representative of God, such as the Pope and his phalanx of underlings. How absurd to think that another human being could be the representative of the Creator of the Universe, for us humans living on this planet!

Let us look at some vital facts:

Because of religion, more human beings have been murdered, tortured, maimed, denigrated, discriminated against, humiliated, hated and scorned than for any other reason in the totality of the history of man.

Today the only wars under way are religious wars. Arabs are killing Jews and vice versa. Ethnically religious groups are killing ethnically religious groups in the aftermath of the demise of the Soviet Union. Arabs of one religion are killing Arabs of another. Catholics and Protestants are killing each other in Ireland and the British Isles. There is an endless list of clashes in Africa and the emerging nations of Southeast Asia.

Religion, more than politics and economics, kills and cripples humankind. There has never in all known history been a genocide of any kind which was not fueled by religion. Every religious organization on Earth is designed to gain economic and political power for those in the religion. Look at it closely and you will see for yourself.

I look at my family and friends in those fundamentalist religious organizations in central Texas. They are bound by ideas which are not true. They believe in myths as if they were fact. They grow old early in life. The wonderful personal resources available to them are stifled and lost. Their lives become boring and non-productive unless they free themselves from the concepts imposed upon them by their religions.

In this book, you will find that the story of Jesus and the "crucifixion" has been played out sixteen times over the last ten thousand years. You are also going to find ideas about religion that the Pope and other religious leaders don't want you to read or understand. Because if you do read and understand, you will no longer be a part of their group. What this means is that you will no longer provide them with funds, and you will no longer be a number to give them political clout.

There are three major changes under way now in the affairs of all mankind. First is politics. We have seen the demise of Communism, and other such non-humane political concepts will fall as well. We are beginning to see the end of a long-established economic tyranny, which for centuries has gripped the affairs of nations, including ours. To these we add religion, the most crippling detriment of them all to the evolution of humankind. All of these changes are coming as we enter the "new age," now upon us. This work addresses itself most admirably to this vital effort.

– Bill Jenkins, former ABC talk show host

I

Origins of Religion

Religion, Where it Began

Hanging on the wall of my study is a remarkable map. It is about three feet wide and six feet long. It shows the history of religious evolution starting about 180,000 years ago and ending at the bottom in 1966. The title is THE HISTORY MAP OF RELIGIONS. It is in eight colors, with each color representing the flow of mythologies, and concepts, from one religion to another. For instance, if you follow the color 'blue,' you can see the mythological diffusion, or continuity, from Zoroastrianism and Mithraism into Christianism. It is quite an educational experience to stand in front of the map and study the overall evolution of religions from the third (warm) interglacial period; the Lower Mousterian Culture of Neanderthal man in Europe to the religious picture of Earth today.

We ask: "Where did it all begin, this behavior that we call 'religious'?" How far back do we go to find the origins of some of our beliefs, like life after death, or the belief in supernatural beings and spirits? Anthropologists believe think that religious behavior can easily be found in the Neanderthal period of 135,000 years ago. The Neanderthal people buried their dead with great sensitivity and care. Flowers were put into the graves. Artifacts were buried with the dead. Artifacts were either to take with you into another life following death, or have them for an offering to the gods or goddesses. We ask: "What led them to believe in an after-life, or supernatural beings?" The answer that I am most comfortable with is "fear" and "dreams."

We all know what fear can do, and when you realize that the Neanderthal people could not possibly have had an explanation for lightning and forest fire, earthquake and storm, thunder and gale, what else would they think but supernatural beings behind it all and had to be placated, worshipped and feared? Fear must have played a major part in the development of ideas concerning supernatural beings. For what know that today, even in our own time, it is fear that drives millions to churches and to their knees, either begging or asking the gods for forgiveness of one thing or another. Today, millions live filled with fear of what is going to happen to them after death. Still today, it is fear that is one of the primary religious motivators of our species, Homo sapiens.

As for life after death beliefs, I like the "dream" theory than any other. We all know how vivid, alive, real and moving dreams can be, to such an extent that when we awaken, we are surprised it was a dream. My father died thirty years ago, and yet from time to time, my dreams of him are so sharp and clear it is staggering. What would you think, if you were a member of the

Neanderthal group, and you knew that your friends long, long ago and yet, last night, in a vivid dream once again you were with him, hunting? He was alive! But how could that be? You buried him many moons ago. Last night he was alive and hunting with you. Why, your friend is not dead at all. He lives on after death in some other place.

From such a beginning, thousands and thousands of years ago, there developed and evolved basic ritualistic behavior patterns, and mythological motifs, or themes, that have spread by a process or diffusion from, at least, the Neanderthal from Cro-Magnon caves, and into the Christian churches and cathedrals of twentieth century America. One of the more obvious is the "sacred meal" or ritualistic cannibalism. We still practice this ritual today in a symbolic form in the Protestant and Roman Catholic communion, where we eat the body and drink the blood of the divine leader.

– William Edelen

William Edelen *has his Masters degree in Theology from McCormick Seminary, on the campus of the University of Chicago. A former Marine Corps pilot and ordained Congregational minister, he has written regular weekly columns for many Western newspapers including* The Desert Sun *of Palm Springs,* The Chieftain *of Pueblo, Colorado,* The Idaho Statesman *of Boise, Idaho,* The News Press *of Santa Barbara, California,* The Press Democrat *of Santa Rosa, California and others. He is the author of four books of his essays* Toward the Mystery, Spirit, Spirit Dance *and* Earthrise. *His books, and other essays, are available on his website:* www.williamedelen.com.

Mithraism

During the first century of the Common Era, the Roman worship of Mithras began to influence the Roman Empire. It originated as a Persian Mystery religion which began around the seventh century B.C.E. It reached a peak in the third and fourth centuries when many of the followers were Roman soldiers. Highly secret, Mithraic doctrine could only be obtained from other initiates. Women were prohibited from joining the cult. It began to die out around 325 C.E. after Christianity began to take hold. By the year 400 C.E., it had disappeared.

As a result of such secretive traditions, there is almost no literary evidence that Mithraism ever existed. Fortunately, the archeological evidence is plentiful. Ruins of Mithraic temples are scattered all through the former Roman Empire. Stone sculpture, sculpted stone relief, wall painting, and mosaic can be found, as well as dedicatory inscriptions and iconographic representations of Mithras. More than 100 such inscriptions and 75 sculpture fragments have been found in the city of Rome.

A Tauroctony is the place of honor in every Mithraic temple. This can be recognized by a representation of Mithras killing a sacred bull; although, this is now believed by some to be a symbolic representation of the constellations (Ulansey, 1991).

– The Catholic Encyclopedia, Volume X, The World Encyclopedia

Tauroctony Statue, Vatican Museum

Religious Illiteracy

Fourteen organizations in this country, ranging from People for the American Way to the National Education Association, have issued a document that informs parents and teachers that public schools can be a proper place to teach Comparative Religions as an academic discipline. Such a course of study could make a major contribution toward erasing much of the religious illiteracy in this nation; it could also make a major dent in the bigotry, prejudice and religious superstitions that exist everywhere. But now, when this issue is proposed locally, some will say, "Oh, but we do not need or want our young people to be exposed to the other great religious traditions. All they need is Jesus Christ. That's where truth is, for it was Jesus who said, 'I am the Way, the Truth and the Light.' That's all our young people need."

What people taking this position do not know — and this is a mark of their own religious illiteracy — is that practically every religious leader or hero has said exactly the same thing. Zoroaster used exactly the same words, saying, "I am the Way, the Truth and the Light." The Buddha used the same language, as did Lao Tzu of Taoism. The vast majority of the mythological formulas attached to Jesus were borrowed from Mithraism, Zoroastrianism, Egypt, Babylon and the Greek Mystery religions.

A perfect example is Mithraism (sixth century B.C., Persia and India). Mithras was born of a virgin, with only a number of shepherds present. Mithras was known as "the Way," "the Truth," "the Light," "the Life," "the Word," "the Son of God" and "the Good Shepherd." He was pictured carrying a lamb on his shoulders. Sunday was sacred and known as "the Lord's Day" centuries before Jesus. On December 25th, there were magnificent celebrations with bells, candles, gifts, hymns; and "communion" was observed by the followers. From December 25th until the spring equinox (Estra or Easter) were the "40 days" which later became Christian Lent. Mithras was finally placed in a rock tomb called "Petra." After three days he was removed with giant celebrations, festival and great joy.

Petra, the sacred rock, centuries later would become Peter, the mythological foundations of the Christian church. (Matthew 16:18: "Thou art Peter, and upon this rock I will build my church.") Christian mythology is quite obviously saturated with Mithraism.

The followers of Mithras believed that there would be a "day of judgment" when non-believers would perish and believers would live in a heaven or "paradise" (a Persian word) forever and ever. All of these mythological formulas were absorbed centuries later by the Christian cult into their rituals. Paul, who never even knew Jesus, took all of these mythological themes and attached them to Jesus, building his Christ mythology. He took Jesus out of Judaism and borrowed the Mithraic Sun-day instead of the Hebrew Sabbath. All of the Mithraic holy days were used to fill in this mythological construct – Christmas, Easter, Lent, and the spring resurrection festival. The Christian "Mass" was, and is, basically the old sacrament of the Mithraic "taurobolia" (a symbol of a divine sacrifice and of the saving effect of blood).

Well, enough of an illustrating example. My thesis stands: the study of Comparative Religions in high school could make an enormous contribution toward erasing religious illiteracy, which in turn would be a giant step forward in reducing religious bigotry, prejudice and the superstitions that so cripple the human spirit.

– William Edelen

" *To those searching for truth — not the truth of dogma and darkness but the truth brought by reason, search, examination, and inquiry, discipline is required. For faith, as well intentioned as it may be, must be built on facts, not fiction — faith in fiction is a damnable false hope.* "

Thomas A. Edison

Across a Void of Mystery
and Dread

L ong before sagas of ancient tribes were recorded, religions arose all over
the world. Wise men and poets, seers and soothsayers, medicine men
and researchers of magic, chieftains and kings sought answers to perplexing
questions. They tried to solve the mysteries of life and death. The religious
rites they created reflected a desire for knowledge about their own origin
and their destination. The ancient peoples yearned for assurance that life had
purpose and death was not the end. As they confronted human existence
they experienced awe, sometimes fear, often exultation.

This was the beginning of religion; the efforts made men to accept and
to adapt themselves to the world about them. Their environment was, for the
most part, puzzling and unpredictable, hostile and at times destructive. Yet it
might be full of beauty and joy; it might bring a measure of comfort and, in
certain seasons and places, an amazing abundance. Life could be cruel and
hard and was apparently meant to be brief; but above all else it was uncertain. Man could not control the elements of the sea and sky, forest and field.
He might kill wild beasts, catch huge fish, vanquish old enemies, conquer a
nearby tribe; but in the world about him and in the life he so precariously
lived, disasters came swiftly, without warning. Forces and powers over which
he had no sway triumphed and seemed always to be ultimately victorious.

Primitive man thought that by observing a fetish — performing some
ritual or allowing a medicine man, the shaman, to intercede for him — he
might propitiate the hostile spirits. By offering thanks to benevolent spirits
he might encourage them to grant more favors.

The earliest among primitive men seemed to have believed in spirits that
were either hostile or neutral; later there developed a belief that spirits were
benevolent and brought good, and men then began to hint at the idea of
gods. At the same time, primitive men resorted to the device of hiding from
what they considered to be veil forces or spirits.

In our day we may feel we have progressed far beyond primitive beliefs;
in reality the customs and outlooks that mold our beliefs often originated in
times before history. There is, however, a difference between then and now;
we look upon religion as the conduct which indicates our belief in, our reverence for, and our desire to please some divine power. By rites and observances we accord recognition to a higher power which has control of our destiny
and to which we owe reverence and obedience. We construe religion to be

the general moral and mental attitude which results from such beliefs and which affect both the individual and the community. We interpret religion as the forms of faith and worship which urge devotion to a principle or an idea that seems most worthy and demands a measure of fidelity to an ideal; we approve of such feelings and attitudes as standards for either a person or an entire nation in the practical struggle for survival.

These conceptions of religion in our own era differ to a great extent from the religious views and practices of long ago, some of which we now examine.

Foremost among the regions from which the earliest religions appear to have emerged was the Fertile Crescent, the semicircular area of cultivable soil which stretches northwest from the Persian Gulf, around the valley of the Tigris and Euphrates rivers, then southwest down along the Levant into Syria, Lebanon, Jordan, Israel, and the Nile valley of Egypt. Between the Tigris and the Euphrates several important groups lived in antiquity; the Sumerians, the Babylonians, the Hittites, and the Assyrians. In their earliest centuries these peoples had been nomads, rovers believing in a number of gods, some of whom were thought to demand not only the first fruits of the herds and flocks, but also the sacrifice of human beings. The devotees of these early religions glimpsed only dimly the ideas of good versus evil, of justice in contrast to inequity and exploitation. Such ideas were secondary to the immediate purpose of their religious rites; to stave off hostile spirits and to gain favor from friendly gods. They adhered to the *lex taliones*, the retribution law which allowed "an eye for an eye and a tooth for a tooth."

Among these peoples of Fertile Crescent in the second and first millennia B.C., the Babylonians were perhaps the most enterprising and creative, drawing on the heritage left them by their Sumerian predecessors and making contributions and in several significant areas of thought. Famed in part for the magnificence of their temples and tombs and the vast amount of their religious literature, the Babylonians are also remembered for their ethical standards. Centuries before the Israelites, Babylonian writings contained their own vivid versions of the creation, a flood, the expulsion of Satan from heaven and his descent into hell. The Code of King Hammurabi (1728–1686 B.C.) was unique in its comprehensive nature and its establishment of laws on a high level of justice and ethics. On the whole, the Code was humanitarian and protected the weak, the helpless, and the less fortunate.

The Assyrians (named after their chief god, Assur) never attained the higher ethics of the Babylonians; nor did they desire to do so. They seemed to be a fierce people who excelled in cruelty and savagery. Few ancient tribes could equal their bestiality; to them war gods were absolutely essential. Their religion affirmed no belief in a judgment after and had therefore little influence on a man's conduct, certainly none to render him more humane and kind.

In contrast to the Babylonians and the Assyrians, the Hittites are far more obscure in history. It is known that they flourished from the twentieth century B.C. to about the thirteenth. In recent decades archeologists have unearthed enough evidence to show that this once powerful nation, a potent cultural force in Western Asia, had an eclectic religion wherein beliefs of many kinds and from different backgrounds prevailed; many gods were adopted from Babylonians and Assyrian patterns of culture.

To the south and west of the Tigris and the Euphrates region lay the land of Egypt, revealing to the world an odd mixture of the worship of the sun and nature, of animals and ancestors, along with what may have been a rather advanced form of belief in a godhead. In its earlier history of the third millennium B.C., Egypt was an isolated, self-contained country; it had not only two major sectors — the kingdom of the Nile Delta, Lower Egypt, and the kingdom of Upper Egypt. Extending to the First Cataract — but it was split up into "nomes," that is, a large number of autonomous districts with their own units and gods, usually portrayed as animals, to guard and protect them. As the nomes merged and eventually formed the two kingdoms, these became antagonists with a rivalry that lasted many centuries. Later they united to become a nation of great strength and considerable influence.

The Egyptians looked upon animals as possessing remarkable power and conveying wisdom, fertility, and strength to men. In time they were symbolized in human form with the heads of animals, among those the most memorable was the ram Amon.

The ancient Egyptians worshipped the Nile River and the sun — Osiris, the god of the Nile, his sister and wife, Isis, their son Horus, the god of darkness, Set, and Re, the sun god who had as his symbols the pyramid and the winged sun disk. Worship of Osiris encouraged the worship of ancestors, for in the popular legend Osiris was killed by the god of darkness, Set, and was subsequently resurrected by the love and the mourning of Isis; this drama highlighted by the Egyptians' belief in immortality.

Kings, thought of as divinities, built pyramids of rare beauty and great size to entomb themselves. They left orders for their bodies to be mummified and supplied with food, weapons and clothes. The Book of the Dead, with its formulas to bring the soul to Osiris' judgment hall, granted an ornate burial to both rich and poor, ruler and ruled. Osiris judged the soul by the morality of a man's life, a new interpretation that made more than a mere ritual as it directed men's minds toward the just and the moral.

Into this complex of beliefs that existed in the early part of the fourteenth century B.C. came Amenhotep IV. He is known also as Ikhnaton ("Spirit of Aton" or "Profitable to Aton") and is remembered as a sensitive, gentle, but courageous ruler who put aside Amon and all other gods to make Aton, "sun" or "light," the All Father or omnipotent God:

> Thy dawning, O living Aton, is beautiful on the horizon…O Beginning of
> Life, Thou art all…and Thy rays encompass all…Thou art the life of life;
> through Thee men live.

In this famous "sun hymn" was embodied the highest development of Egyptian religion.

Soon, however, Ikhnaton's reforms with revoked. Upon his death the priests of Amon quickly regained control and destroyed Ikhnaton's architecture, literature, and art. A reaction set in. the eventual results were decay and corruption for the religion, the country, the land and the people.

During the two millennia or more that these four peoples — the Babylonians, Assyrians, Hittites and Egyptians — waxed and waned in their power and influence, developments in religion were under way in the Grecian peninsula and islands which would make themselves felt throughout the world down to this very day. Here men no longer groped blindly toward the light; they began to be illuminated by it. The ancient Greeks refined beliefs and rites in the centuries from about 1,000 B.C. to almost the beginnings of the Christian era and with their signal contributions in thought and conduct had an incalculable effect on the western world.

When the Indo-Europeans poured down from central Europe to fuse their destiny with the Minoans and Aegean civilizations around 2,000 B.C., they helped to create a host of native deities. The Indo-Europeans, of obscure origins had practiced primitive forms of religion and had the usual array of gods and goddesses; these invaders from the northern regions brought to the superstitious people of the Greek plains and valleys a newer sect of gods, some fresh terms to describe godly attributes and failings, and a hearty gusto in celebrating both the virtues and the vices of the gods and goddesses.

Confusion reigned. The Minoans and Aegeans had revered sea-gods and river-gods, fertility-gods and goddesses. Now there prevailed a bewildering complexity, a mélange of old deities and new deities merging and then proliferating, vanishing and later re-emerging. More order and more unity began to develop, but pagan habits were hard to cure; polytheism and magic, recourse to superstition and oracles were still strong and unrestrained.

All the gods resembled human beings. The only difference between gods and men lay in the superior strength greater beauty of gods; these endowments entitled them to their immortality. Even here there was discrimination; only the most heroic of men and the most favored among the gods were chosen for the Elysian fields, Greek mythology's paradise for the virtuous after their death; the vast majority of men, joined by some of the gods, went on to a spirit world which was dreary, dank, and dark. Life after death, it should be noted, did not assume as much importance among the Greeks as it had, for example, among the Egyptians.

During the long centuries that Greek mythology prevailed, Mount Olympus was the home of the gods; and in the pantheon of the Olympic gods, Zeus stood supreme as the father of all mankind. He was the god who reigned over humanity and, at the same time, over all the gods and goddesses, among whom were the twelve great gods; himself, Hera, Poseidon, Demeter, Apollo, Artemis, Ares, Aphrodite, Hermes, Athena, Hephaestus, and Hestias.

Zeus was not, however, the All Supreme, for he had to bow before destiny or fate. The gods might be supra-human, but they "lived and moved and had their being," just as did men, within the history of framework and nature. Such forces as death and strife and terror, humor and error and folly, operated with Fate's spell to men's — and the god's — joy and woe, success or failure.

Religion in Greece took a new turn in the eighth and seventh centuries B.C. with the Athenian festivals and the mystery religions. In the mystery religions the Greeks sought personal salvation and the assurance of immortality by means of an emotional religion. The gods on Mount Olympus were remote, and the rites to honor and propitiate them, too formal and unemotional.

The most notable contribution of Grecian civilization, however, was that of the philosophers. Many of them were profoundly religious in their thinking as they sought a unifying principal behind all phenomena. As a study of ultimate reality and the causes and principals which underlie all thinking and being, Greek philosophy differs from theology by ignoring all dogma and by dealing with speculation, not faith. The pre-Socratics — venturesome thinkers like Thales, Anaximander, Heraclitus, Parminides, Anaxagoras, and Democrites — tried to find the one natural element common to all being and nature. Many of the more daring and courageous scorned the older, more conventional explanations of life and its origins; they scoffed at the gods and their frailties. Some endured expulsion from the city of Athens. The high-minded Socrates, though he stood in reverence before the gods, suffered death as his penalty for being both rational and skeptical.

Eventually and almost inevitably, most of them (notable exceptions; Democritus and Protagoras) arrived at a belief in one God; Aristotle refers to Xenophanes as having been the first one to believe in a unity of everything: "There is one God who is greatest among gods and men and is not like mortals in either form or in thought." Plato and Aristotle influenced religious thought profoundly through the next two and a half thousand years, Plato probably more so than his pupil, Aristotle: Both emphasized the goodness and greatness of God. In spite of the philosophers, however, the popular religions continued with scarcely any change.

The persuasive power of works by such dramatists and poets as Aeschylus and Sophocles, Aristophanes and Pindar in the fifth century B.C. caused a literal, unthinking, uncritical belief in the gods to begin to give way. The effort of poets and philosophers to envisage a universe wherein the supreme problem was the moral struggle had a far-reaching effect. The Greek dramatists, focusing on good and evil, revenge and retribution, guilt and punishment, also upheld the objective of the good life: "Know thyself! Never exceed. The middle way is best."

In the closing years of the fourth century B.C., the Greeks in Asia minor and, later, in Athens were attracted by the teachings of a philosopher named Epicuras. To him philosophy was more than its literal definition ("the love of wisdom"): it was the subordination of metaphysics to ethics so that pleasure might be the highest good. Although intent on making life happy, Epicuras did not counsel a careless indulgence: he advocated serenity and the avoidance of pain, intellectual rather than bodily pleasures, and a prudential society code of strict honesty and justice. A more rigorous, somewhat sterner, but no less attractive school of philosophy was Stoicism. Led by Zeno of Citium and instructed by him in the *stoa poecile* ("the painted porch"), the young men of these same decades adhered to Zeno's interpretations of Socrates' ideals of self-sufficiency and virtue, Heraclitus' explanation of the physical universe, and Aristotle's logic.

After a century, Stoicism was introduced in Rome. In later decades, it includes among its ardent adherents, the scholar-emperor Marcus Aurelius, and the dramatist-philosopher statesmen Seneca. The Stoics' ethical creed, "to live consistently with nature," led them to subdue their passions, curb unjust thoughts, restrain all indulgence, and do their duty. Although mystery religions still attracted the Romans, many of them found Stoicism more in accord with their way of thinking and mode of life. They preferred the Stoic outlook to any other school of Greek philosophy, for this approach to life, imported from Greece, had all the grace, logic, and power a vital religion was expected to give a man.

In their later centuries the religions of Greece and Rome, were similar to each other and appeared to call for the worship of the same gods; but in the earlier period of the religion of Rome was uniquely its own, quite different from that of the Greeks. The Greeks may have thought of their gods as persons, but Roman religious observances were much more animistic and were used to propitiate innumerable spirits for the purpose of safeguarding the worshippers' lives.

Primarily, the Romans concerned themselves with the spirits of their houses and fields, their professions, ambitions and ancestors. Holding these spirits in awe, they placated them with prayers and offerings. To them religion was like the fulfillment of a contract; the gods not only were to be appeased, but could even be controlled by invoking the right words and using the proper rituals. To perpetuate his family the farmer gave offerings to his guardian spirit Genius for virility in men and to the goddess Juno for the power in women to conceive. To maintain his household's safety, the Roman worshipped Vesta, guardian spirit of the hearth fire; the lares, deified spirits of ancestors, who watched over their descendants and guarded the fields; the penates, guardians of the entire household; and Janus, god of the beginnings and the guardian of the door.

Eventually, a hierarchy of priests developed. The priests, looked upon as public officials, practiced divination, borrowing from the Babylonians the art — or the pretense — of determining the will of the gods by studying the constellations, observing flights of birds, and examining entrails of sacrificed animals. Often they were tempted to use their powers for purely political ends; public offenses in Rome were secured as political spoils and civic morality was brought to a low level. These conditions Caesar Augustus tried to remedy without success.

In the western hemisphere arose the religions of the Aztecs in Mexico, the Mayas of the Yucatan and parts of Central America, and the Incas on fertile plateaus high in the Andes Mountains of Bolivia and Peru. Although these religions are more recent (some of the rites developed to their highest forms in the twelfth to sixteenth centuries A.D.), the observances and beliefs have remained vague to us. Our ignorance about them is due partly to our limited ability to decipher their hieroglyphics and interpret their codices, and partly to the Spanish conquistadors of only four centuries ago, who thought they were serving their Christian God by effacing such records as existed and thus obliterated almost all traces of these well developed religions.

Of these religions, that of the Aztecs seems to have been the most advanced. An elaborate priesthood in the temples conducted the rituals with rigor and regularity, performed the sacrifices, led the people in regular classes of instruction, interpreted the life-after-death concepts, held confessionals, and granted absolution. Despite rituals that were bloody and fertility ceremonies that were unrestrained, the Aztecs had a distinctive, highly developed re-

Aztec Temple of Quetzalcoatl,
city of Teotihuacan

ligion of rare beauty and meaning. Its practices paralleled, in some instances, those of the Jewish and Christian religions: the monasteries and convents of the priests and priestesses, and the hymns so akin to the Psalms. Some of their leaders in later centuries held views which bordered on the belief in one God; in one place a temple was built to the "unknown god," not pictured in material or physical fashion and possessing spiritual attributes of a high level.

The Mayas, farther to the south, constructed a complex civilization graced with artistry, a unique development because such culture and beauty seldom flourished in the torrid zones. Many clues about Mayan religion survive, but specific information on names and meanings is lacking. Their gods were many and bizarre; their followers reflected awe before the mysterious, fear before the unpredictable and unknown. Lovely temples, daringly designed and tastefully executed, reflect a high level of aspiration and imagination among these Indians.

The religion of the Incas, parallel in many ways to those of the Aztecs and the Mayas, had elaborate ritual and complex organization, at the heart of which was the worship of *huacas* ("holy places or things"). In this state religion, the sun was the center of veneration; but above Ynti, the sun, was the supreme being, Viracocha. Human sacrifice did not prevail as among the Aztecs, but it did exist. The Incas had no written language but recorded history in quipas (colored strings with knots) and in this way distinguished themselves from the Aztecs and Mayas who used hieroglyphics.

Such were some of the precursors of today's prevailing religions, groping, sometimes feebly but often courageously, toward the light of reason and more creative "revelations." Still others might be mentioned, the religions of the Celts, the Slavs, and the Teutons, the Polynesians, the American Indians, and many another; each reveals faltering, often crude, yet noble and admirable attempts of the ancients to seek clues to seek clues to the mystery of existence. Most of these faiths from long ago are now dead, but each in its era was a striking example of mankind's ceaseless search for any thing.

Nineteen centuries ago Plutarch, Greek essayist and biographer, ascribed to the goddess Athena the saying: "I all that has been, is, and will be and no mortal has yet lifted My veil." These words were inscribed by a priest to his deity Neith (whom the Hellenes identified with their Athena) on the wall of an ancient temple at Sais in the northwest delta of the Nile. Many years later, according to the tradition, a pilgrim of another era visited the sacred site and wrote on the opposite wall: "Veil after veil have we lifted and ever the face is more wonderful."

– Carl Herman Voss
Excerpt from *Living Religions of the World*, Prometheus Books

Zoroastrianism: Blueprint for Christianity and Judaism

Zarathushtra is the Iranian word for Zoroaster, who founded a religion in ancient Persia. It was he who roused in mankind the need for the hatred of unworthy things — thereby discovering the devil and, incidentally, paradise, the last judgment, and the resurrection of the dead. Mithraism is an offshoot, and Christianity stole some of the popular Zoroastrian beliefs.

Ahura Mazda; Detail from Zoroastrian Temple in Iran

Ahura Mazda was the lord of light and wisdom in ancient Iranian mythology. Originally an equal of Mithra, god of light and justice, he was later elevated to the supreme being by the prophet Zoroaster. His name was shortened to Ormazd.

Perhaps the stark contrasts found on the Iranian plateau — steep-sided mountains and flat valleys, bitterly cold winters and boiling hot summers — encouraged this singular rethinking of myth. Certainly, it had an effect on the attitudes of the peoples who came under Iranian domination. It may even be seen to linger on in the outlook of certain Christians and Muslims today.

The Religion Which Might Have Been Ours

In 480 B.C., on a marble throne high above the narrow strait which stretched between the island of Salamis and the southern coast of Attica, the great Xerxes sat waiting to watch his navy defeat the Greek fleet. At his back burned the city of Athens, fired by the torches of his soldiers. At the pass of Thermopylae lay the bodies of 300 Spartans with that of their leader, Leonidas, slain by the Asiatic hosts of the Persian Empire. There remained only the task of destroying the Greek fleet, to wipe out the bitter shame of the Persian failure at Marathon ten years before, and to establish the Persian Empire in Greece, from whence it could sweep throughout Europe.

The Persian ships outnumbered the Greek fleet three to one, and were of heavier construction. But the Greeks, using the same superior strategy at sea that Miltiades had used on land at Marathon, sank 200 of the Persian vessels, captured others, and drove the rest from the strait.

The flight of the terror-stricken Xerxes signaled not only the end of his dream of conquest in Europe, but also a vastly changed religious prospect for the Western World. For, according to no less an authority than the late Max Muller, had it not been for the Persian defeats at the decisive battles of Marathon and Salamis, if, in other words, the western march of the Persian Empire had not been stopped there, Zoroastrianism rather than Judeo-Christianity might have been the prevailing religion of Europe and the Americas.

Yet in spite of these crushing military and naval defeats, with the resulting decline of the Persian Empire, and the eventual near-extinction of Zoroastrianism, so great was this religion's vitality and so appealing to the human heart were many of its conceptions and precepts that much of Zarathushtra's creed lives on in the religions of Christianity and Judaism.

What if this religion, instead of Judeo-Christianity, had become our faith? Would we have a vastly different theology and code of ethical conduct? We would believe in a loving Father-God who is omniscient and concerned with the welfare of his children. We would have, instead of Jesus, Zarathushtra who, while not peculiarly the son of God, was sent to earth by God to spread his doctrine and do his work.

We would look forward to "the Kingdom of God." We would have the ancient statement of a region of darkness and a region of light, of heaven and hell, of the good power in conflict with the evil. We would have Angra Mainyu, instead of Satan — a mere difference in name. We would have angels and archangels. We would have a statement of the final resurrection of the dead very similar to that in the Judeo-Christian Bible.

These things we have now. Did they come to us from the pious and vigorous mind of Zarathushtra by way of the later prophets of Israel and Christ, or were they original conceptions of Judeo-Christianity? How well acquainted the chroniclers of the Jewish Old Testament were with the Persian branch of the Indo-European wanderers is evidenced by their frequent reference to the Medes and the Persians. But there is also definite evidence of borrowing from Zoroastrianism in the religious creeds which Christianity absorbed from later Judaism.

Up to the time of the exile, the source of both good and evil in the religion of the Israelites was thought to be the God Jehovah. But after the exile, which is to say after the influence of Zarathushtra's monotheistic doctrine began to be felt, the Old Testament writers recorded the doctrine that Jehovah was the one God of the universe and a God of pure righteousness, while Satan was charged with all evil creations. It is probable that Satan — or the devil of later Judaism and Christianity — is none other than Angra Mainyu, the arch daeva of Zoroastrianism.

The elaborate angelology and demonology of later Judaism, the idea of a divine judgment and a final resurrection, and a future life in a region which may be definitely described — all seem to have come from the doctrines of Zarathushtra, though there is no definite proof of this. Indeed there are Christian and Hebrew commentators who believe that Zoroastrianism borrowed these conceptions from later Judaism, but they speak with less conviction than do those who hold the opposite view. Almost certainly the Magi who are said to have visited Jesus in the manger were Zoroastrian priests, and Christ's word "paradise" was taken from the Persian pairidaeza.

In the field of human ethics and social behavior we would have in Zoroastrianism a code which, if followed, would produce a state of human welfare that would be difficult to surpass. The chief differences would be in matters of emphasis. While Zoroastrianism and Christianity both state the necessity of faith and works, the emphasis in Christianity is on faith, in Zoroastrianism on works.

When Alexander the Great conquered Persia, and Greek cities were established there, the decline of Zoroastrianism began. Under the Mohammedans the decline continued until today there are scarcely ten thousand followers of Zarathushtra in the land of his birth.

– from The World Bible, edited by Robert O. Ballou

The Power of the Sun

Many peoples have worshipped the powers of the natural world. Resplendent among these is the Sun. To a philosopher such as Plato, the Sun symbolized the ultimate. It gave the power of sight, which symbolized the power of insight. The Sun is light and fire, and many mystics all the world over have spoken of their highest experience in terms of light.

But if the Sun brings light and warmth, it also brings scorching heat and destruction. Its rays are often called arrows. Light and darkness are at war with one another. So religions focusing on the Sun have often tended to militarism. Two examples will suffice.

Zoroastrianism, whose origins are now thought to go back to the second millennium B.C.E., became the creed of the militant Achaemenid dynasty in Persia in the sixth century. It centered on the struggle between the forces of Order and Chaos, Light and Darkness, and the Sun was one of the powers fighting on the side of Order and Light.

A second example comes from the period when, after a century of largely untroubled peace, the Roman Empire experienced a century of wars and disasters. In their distress, they looked for a new divine champion, and went to the Sun, the Unconquered Sun, Sol Invictus.

In 274 C.E., the emperor Aurelian actually adopted the Sun as the Supreme God of the Roman Empire. Moreover, Constantine's family were worshippers of the Unconquered Sun. When he was marching on Rome, he had his famous vision of a Cross superimposed on the Sun. It came from his family god. In the form of a chi-rho in a circle (or, as often, an iota-chi) it presented the initial letters of the name of Christ (or of Jesus Christ) in the form of a sun wheel. Constantine was in fact a syncretist. His statue in Constantinople bore the rayed crown of the Sun god, made, as he believed, from the nails of Christ's Cross. His god was a god of war, not peace.

Yet, the Sun, in its all-embracing power, could speak of peace as well as war. The rulers of Persia were drawn in the direction of universalism and toleration. What is more, the all-seeing eye of the Sun made for justice. The Persians were particularly strong about keeping one's word, about the value and importance of truth, honesty, uprightness. So although peace does not stand high among the values of traditional Zoroastrianism, the religion has much in it which gives positive content to peace. This is why the Parsis, retaining the strong monotheism of Zarathustra, have been a force for peace. They influenced the Moghul Akbar to use good counsel, not the sword, in spreading religion. Ever since they have been in the forefront in developing philanthropy and social responsibility.

– from *The Portable World Bible*, Viking Press

Horus: The Way, the Truth, the Life

It is a Christian belief that life and immortality were brought to light, and death, the last enemy, was destroyed by a personal Jesus only 2,000 years ago. The very same revelation had been accredited to Horus, the anointed, at least 3,000 years before. Horus, as the impersonal and ideal revealer, was the Messiah in the astronomical mythology and the Son of God in the eschatology. The doctrine of immortality is so ancient in Egypt that the "Book of Vivifying the Soul Forever" was not only extant in the time of the First Dynasty but was then so old that the true tradition of interpretation was at that time already lost.

Horus, Egyptian
tomb painting

The Egyptian Horus, as revealer of immortality, was the ideal figure of the ancient spiritualists that the soul of man, or the Manes, persisted beyond death and the dissolution of the present body.

The Origin and Evolution

We find, depicted on stones in many countries where the Stellar Cult people migrated, remains of this old Astronomical religion which proves their perfect knowledge of the revolutions of the Starry Vast and the Laws governing these revolutions, all of which they imaged through iconography or by Signs and Symbols. And where they have not built Pyramids they have recorded the truth in the so-called "Cups and Rings" and "curious carvings" found on boulders, cist-covers, on living rock, and on standing stones throughout the British Isles, Europe, Asia, Africa, and other parts of the world — which hitherto have been deemed to involve insoluble problems and have been to all our learned professors an outstanding puzzle in prehistoric research. But they are easily read, and the secrets are unfolded in the Sign Language of the Astronomical, or Stellar Cult Religion of the Ancient Egyptians.

The mutilation of Osiris in his coffin, the stripping of his corpse and tearing it asunder by Set, whom scattered it piecemeal, has its equivalent by the stripping of the dead body of Jesus whilst it still hung upon the Cross, and parting the garments amongst the spoilers.

In St John's account the crucifixion takes place at the time of the Passover, and the victim of sacrifice in human form is substituted for, and identified with, the Paschal Lamb. But, as this version further shows, the death assigned is in keeping with that of the non-human victim. Not a bone of the sufferer to be broken. This is supposed to be in fulfillment of prophecy. It is said by the Psalmist (34:20): "He keepeth all His bones; not one of them is broken." But this was in strict accordance with the original law of Tabu. No matter what the type, from bear to lamb, no bone of the sacrificial victim was ever permitted to be broken; and the only change was in the substitution of the human type for the animal, which had been made already when human Horus became the type of sacrifice instead of the calf or lamb.

When the Australian natives sacrificed their little bear, not a bone of it was ever broken. When the Iroquois sacrificed the white dog, not a bone was broken. This was a common custom, on account of the resurrection as conceived by the primitive races, and the same is applied to Osiris-Horus. Every bone of the skeleton was to remain intact as a basis for the future building.

It is an utterance of the Truth that is eternal to say that Horus as the Son of God had previously been all the Gospel Jesus is made to say he is, or is to become:

Horus and the Father are one.
Jesus says: "I and My Father are one. He that seeth Me, seeth Him that sent Me."

Horus is the Father seen in the Son.
Jesus claims to be the Son in whom the Father is revealed.

Horus was the light of the world, the light that is represented by the symbolical eye, the sign of salvation.
Jesus is made to declare that He is the light of the world.

Horus was the way, the truth, the life by name and in person.
Jesus is made to assert that he is the way, the truth, and the life.

Horus was the plant, the shoot, the natzar.
Jesus is made to say: "I am the true vine."

Horus says: "It is I who traverse the heaven; I go round the Sekhet-Arm (the Elysian Fields); Eternity has been assigned to me without end. Lo! I am heir of endless time and my attribute is eternity."
Jesus says: "I am come down from Heaven. For this is the will of the Father that everyone who beholdeth the Son and believeth in Him should have eternal life, and I will raise him up at the last day." He, too, claims to be the lord of eternity.

Horus says: "I open the Tuat that I may drive away the darkness." Jesus says: "I am come a light unto the world."

Horus says: "I am equipped with thy words O Ra (the father in heaven) (ch32) and repeat them to those who are deprived of breath. (ch38). These were the words of the father in heaven."

Jesus says: "The Father which sent me, he hath given me a commandment, what I should say and what I should speak. Whatsoever I speak, therefore, even as the Father said unto me, so I speak. The word which ye hear is not mine, but the Father's which sent me."

A comparative list of some pre-existing types to Christianity shows further how these types were brought on in the canonical Gospels and the Book of Revelation:

HORUS	JESUS
Horus baptized with water by Anup	Jesus baptized with water by John
Anup, the Baptizer	John, the Baptist
Aan, the divine scribe	John, the divine scribe
Horus born in Annu, the place of bread	Jesus born in Bethelehem, the house of bread
Horus the Good Shepard with the crook upon his shoulders	Jesus the Good Shepard with the lanb/kid upon his shoulders
Seven onboard the boat with Horus	Seven fishers onboard the boat with Jesus
Horus as the Lamb	Jesus as the Lamb
Horus as the Lion	Jesus as the Lion
Horus identified with the Tat or Cross	Jesus identified with the Cross
Horus of twelve years	Jesus of twelve years
Horus made a man of thirty years in his baptism	Jesus made of a man of thirty years in his baptism
Horus the Krst	Jesus the Christ
Horus, the manifesting Son of God	Jesus, the manifesting Son of God
Trinity of Atum the Father, Horus the Son, and Ra the Holy Spirit	Trinity of the Father, Son, and the Holy Spirit
The first Horus as child of the Virgin, the second as the Son of Ra	Jesus as the Virgin's child, the Christ as Son of the Father
Horus the sower and Set the destroyer in the harvestfield	Jesus the sower of the good seed and Satan the sower of tares
Horus carried off by Set to the summit of Mount Heep	Jesus spirited away by Satan into an exceedingly high mountain
Set and Horus contending on the Mount	Jesus and Satan contending on the Mount
The Star, as announcer of the child Horus	The Star in the East that indicated the birthplace of Jesus
Horus the avenger	Jesus who brings the sword
Horus as Iu-em-Hetep, who comes with peace	Jesus the bringer of peace
Horus the afflicted one	Jesus the afflicted one
Horua as the type of life eternal	Jesus the type of eternal life

Horus as Iu-em-Hetep, the child teacher in the temple	The child Jesus as teacher in the Temple
The mummy bandage that was woven without seam	The vesture of the Christ without a seam
Twelve followers of Horus as Har-Khutti	Twelve followers of Jesus as the twelve disciples
The revelation written down by Aan (Te-huti) the scribe of divine words	The revelation by John the divine
The saluter Aani, who bears witness to the word of Ra and to the testimony of Horus	John who bears witness to the Word of God and the testimony of Jesus Christ
The secret of the Mysteries revealed by Taht-Aan	The secret of the Mysteries made known by John
Horus the Morning Star	Jesus the Morning Star
Horus who gives the Morning Star to his followers	Jesus who give the Morning Star to his followers
The name of Ra on the head of the deceased	The name of the Father written on the forehead
The Paradise of the Pole Star-Am-Khemen	The Holy City lighted by one luminary, that is neither the Sun nor the Moon
The Har-Shesu, or servants of Horus	The servants of Jesus Christ

– Excerpt from Albert Churchward's *Book of Religion*, first published in 1924.

Reprints are available from Health Research, Mokelumne Hills, CA 95245.
Albert Churchward *was a student of the British poet and Egyptologist Gerald Massey.*

" *Mythology is what grown-ups believe, folk-lore is what they tell their children, and religion is both.* "

Cedric Whitman

Astro-Theology

The Christian religion is a parody on the worship of the Sun, in which they put a man whom they call Christ, in the place of the Sun, and pay him the same adoration which was originally paid to the Sun.

– Thomas Paine

In the New Testament, a provocative and most serious challenge is laid on the whole of Christianity. Since it bears directly on our subject, we will quote it: "…if Christ be not risen, then our preaching is in vain, and your faith is also in vain. Yea, and we are found false witnesses of God…And if Christ be not raised, your faith is vain; ye are yet in your sins" G Cor. 15:13-17.

Let's closely examine the original, conceptual foundations of the faith, and then decide. But in order to do that, we must go back not 2000 years to the birth of Christ, but 10 to 15,000 years to the birth of modern man. For when one seeks to establish foundations, one must begin at the beginning.

Many thousands of years ago, in what we refer to as the "primordial world" of the ancients, human life was a far different experience from that which we enjoy today. While it is true that we have less documentation on that prehistoric world than we have on our own age, enough is known from the ancient writings to paint a rather clear picture of our remote ancestry. If we have learned anything at all, it is this: "That the more we change, the more we stay the same." And nowhere is this more clearly demonstrated than in the history of man's quest for "God," and the ancient religion we still keep holy.

According to the best understanding we have gleaned from the available records, life for our ancient forefathers was a mixture of wonder and fear. Each day, just finding food for one's family without becoming a meal oneself was a life-and-death struggle. It was from these meager, distressful conditions of the human race that our long history of the search for God and meaning of life has come.

Any evolution, at its most accelerated rate, is always agonizingly slow. But from the beginning, man's profound questions demanded answers. When no clear answers were forthcoming from the universe, man turned inward and developed his own. The study of this subject is termed "Astro-Theology" or the worship of the heavens. It did not take ancient man very long to decide that in this world the single greatest enemy to be feared was the darkness of night. Simply stated, man's first enemy was darkness.

With this one fact alone, one can readily understand why the greatest and most trustworthy friend the human race would ever have was heaven's greatest gift to the world, the Glorious Rising Orb of Day, THE SUN. With this simple truth understood, we can now begin to unravel an ancient and wonderful story.

Today, as in all of mankind's history, it has once again been told anew. This is the story of Christianity: "The Greatest Story Ever Told." We shall see that the parallels between Christian metaphors and the natural reality of sun and sky are so striking that they constitute — the whole story.

Modern-day Christianity has often belittled our ancient ancestors who are not here to defend themselves. They accuse them of being nothing more than ignorant worshippers of miscellaneous gods. Therefore we can, with assurance, summarily dismiss 14,000 years of human spirituality as ignominious myth believed by well-meaning but gullible primitives. Too much of this kind of spiritual arrogance and religious pride has continued without challenge...until now! The time has come to set matters straight.

The "Greatest Story" went something like this:

The ancient peoples reasoned that no one on Earth could ever lay claim of ownership to the Great Orb of Day. It must belong to the unseen Creator of the universe. It became, figuratively speaking, not man's, but "God's Sun." Truly, "God's Sun" was "The Light of the World."

As stated before, in the dark cold of night man realized his utter vulnerability to the elements. Each night, mankind was forced to wait for the "Rising of the Sun" to chase away the physical and mental insecurity brought on by the darkness. Therefore, the morning Sun focused man's attention on heavenly dependence for his frail, short existence on Earth. Doing so, it became an appropriate symbol of divine benevolence from heaven.

So, just as a small fire brought limited light into man's own little world of darkness, likewise, the "Great Fire of Day" served the whole Earth with its heavenly presence. For this reason, it was said at Deut. 4:24 and Heb. 12:29 that the God of the Bible was a "Consuming Fire" in heaven. And so He was! It was accepted by all that man was bound to a life on Earth, but the sky was the abode of God's Sun. He resides "up there" in "Heaven." Ancient man saw in his male offspring his own image and likeness, and his own existence as a father was proved by the person of his son.

It was assumed that "God's Sun" was but a visible representative of the unseen Creator in heaven. So it was said, "When you have seen the Son, you have seen the Father." Said another way, "The Father is glorified in His Son."

Ancient man had no problem understanding that all life on Earth depended directly on life-giving energy from the Sun. Consequently, all life was lost without the Sun. It followed that "God's Sun" was nothing less than "Our very Savior."

Logically, even if man himself dies, as long as the Sun comes up each day, life on Earth will continue forever. Therefore, it was said in the ancient texts that everlasting life was "the gift" that the Father gives through his Sun. Not for you personally — but for the Earth, everlasting life!

Since evil and harm lurked at every turn in the fearful dark of night, all evil or harmful deeds were naturally the "Works of Darkness."

And of course the evil of night was ruled over by none other than "The Prince of Darkness." Hence, evil is of the Dark or: Devil.

We now have before us two cosmic brothers — one very good, and one very bad. One brings the "truth to light" with the "light of truth." The other is the opposite, or in opposition to the light, "The Opposer," the Prince of the World of Darkness.

At this point we come to Egypt. More than three thousand years before Christianity began, the early morning "Sun/Savior" was pictured in Egypt as the "New Born Babe." The infant savior's name was "Horus."

At daybreak, this wonderful, newborn child is of course "Born Again" (hallelujah). Horus is risen on the Horizon.

And of course "God's Sun" goes to His death wearing a "crown of thorns" or "corona." Remember the Statue of Liberty? To this day, kings still wear a round crown of spikes, symbolizing the rays of the Sun!

Crown of Thorns

Ancient Aztec Priest with Crown of Thorns

The rays of the sun are symbolized by the "Crown of Thorns."

The Sun on the Cross
(These symbols can be seen in churches around the world.)

Statue of Liberty with Crown of Thorns

The Egyptians knew that the Sun was at its highest point in the sky (or high noon) when no shadow was cast by the pyramid. At that point, all Egypt offered prayers to the "Most High" God! As stated before, to the ancients, the sky was the abode, or heavenly temple, of the "Most High." Therefore, "God's Sun" was doing His heavenly Father's work in the temple at 12 noon!

The world of ancient man kept track of times and seasons by the movement of the Sun — daily, monthly, yearly. For this, the sundial was devised. Not only the daily movement of the Sun was tracked on the round dial, but the whole year was charted on a round calendar dial. Examples: Ancient Mexican, Mayan, Inca, Aztec, Sumerian, Babylonian, Assyrian, Egyptian, Celtic, Aryan, etc. With this method, certain new concepts emerged in the mind of ancient man.

Since the Earth experiences four different seasons, all the same and equal (in time) each year, the round calendar was divided into four equal parts. This represented the complete story of the life of "God's Sun." The famous painting of The Last Supper pictures the 12 followers of the Son in four groups (of three), the four seasons of the year!

On the round surface of the yearly calendar, you draw a vertical line directly across the middle, cutting the circle in half — one end being the point of the winter solstice; the other end being the point of the summer solstice. Then draw another straight line (crossing the first one). One end of the new line is the spring equinox; the other end is the autumn equinox.

You now have the starting points for each of the four seasons. This is referred to by all major encyclopedias and reference works, both ancient and modern, as "The Cross of the Zodiac." Thus, the life of God's "Sun" is on "the Cross." This is why we see the round circle of the Sun on the crosses of Christian churches. The next time you pass a Christian church, look for the circle (Sun) on the cross.

On December 21 or 22, the Sun, going south, reaches its lowest point in the sky (our winter solstice). By December 25th, it is clear that the Sun is returning northward. Therefore, on December 25th the sun is "Born Again."

Christians stole December 25 from the Roman celebration of Sol Invictus — the Sun Unconquered. And to this day, His worshippers still celebrate His birthday — Merry Christmas, and Happy New Year.

As noted before, the year was divided into 12 equal parts, or months. And to each month was appointed a heavenly symbol or astrological "Sign." Each of the 12 monthly signs were called "Houses" of the Heavenly Zodiac.

The Pisces of the Zodiac is still prominent on church windows of all denominations.

We are told in Matthew 14:17 & 19 that

God's Son tends to His people's needs with "Two Fishes." The two fishes represent the astrological sign all astrologers know as "Pisces." Thus, we have had for almost 2000 years God's Sun ruling in His "Kingdom" in the sign of Pisces/Two Fishes. As stated before, these signs are called houses. Therefore, Pisces is the "Lord's House" at this time. Truly, The Greatest "Fish" Story Ever Told!

According to astrology, sometime after the year 2000, the Sun will enter His new Sign, or His new Kingdom, as it was called by the ancients. This next coming Sign/Kingdom, soon to be upon us, will be, according to the Zodiac, the House or Sign of Aquarius. So when we read in Luke 22:10, we now understand why God's Son states that He and His followers, at the last Passover, are to go into "the house of the man with the water pitcher." So we see that in the coming millennium, God's Sun will bring us into His new Kingdom or House of Aquarius (the man with the water pitcher).

Once we realize that in Astrology, each month is assigned one of the so-called "Houses" of the Zodiac and in heaven are 12 houses (12 monthly signs), then the words we read of God's Son saying "In my Father's House are many mansions/' makes sense (when translated correctly). The proper translation is as follows: Father's House = Heavenly Abode; Mansions = Houses. So, correctly read in the original text, we read: "In my Father's heavenly abode are many houses." Yes, 12 to be exact.

Anyone familiar with modern-day Christianity must surely know we are said to be living in the "Last Days." This teaching is, in part, based on the idea expressed in Matthew 28:20 of the King James Bible, where God's Son says, "I am with you always, even unto the end of the world." End of the World??!! Yet another simple mistranslation to clarify with a proper understanding of the actual words used. This "end of the world" is translated differently in various Bibles. Some say "End of Time," "End of the Days," and still others say "Conclusion of this system of things." So what does all this talk of the "End Times/Last Days" really mean?

Here is the simple answer: When the scriptures speak of "the end of the world," the actual word used is not, I repeat, not end of the world. The actual word in Greek is "Aeon," which, when correctly translated, means "Age," that's spelled "A-G-E"! Any library will have Bible Concordances. Strong's Bible Concordance is a good reference work to use here. Look up the word "age" in any secular dictionary or Bible Concordance. There you will find the word for "age" is from the Greek "Aeon." Remembering that in astrology each of the 12 houses (or signs) of the Zodiac corresponds to a 2000-year period of time, called an "age," we now know we are nearly 2000 years into the House or Age of Pisces. Now, correctly understood, it can rightly be said that we today, in fact, are living in the "Last Days."

Yes, we are in the last days of the old "Age of Pisces." Soon, God's Sun will come again into His New Kingdom or "New Age" of Aquarius (man with the water pitcher). That's right, "The New Aeon" or "The New Age." This is the theme in the New Testament — God's Sun and his coming Kingdom/Age. "The New Age of Aquarius."

It was well understood by ancient man that our weather was caused and controlled by the Sun. It was a simple fact that God's Sun had the power to control storms at will. The ancient Egyptians taught that He did this as He rested in His heavenly boat while crossing the sky. The story of Jesus calming the storm (Matt. 8:23-27) echoes this.

The next point to be made requires first a little background: Christians have always referred to God as "The Father." But viewing God as a father didn't start here — it goes back far into the ancient world. The reason is: Our planet was always viewed as our "Mother Earth or Mother Nature." And since rain (the life-bringing fluid), falling from heaven, impregnated and brought life to Mother Earth, it was therefore believed that our Father was in Heaven.

As you enter the city, a man carrying a jar of water
will meet you. Follow him into the house that he enters.
Luke 22:10

All this life-bringing intercourse between God the Father and Mother Earth would be after a proper marriage ceremony at a spring wedding. In the area today called Israel, called by the ancients 'The Land of Canaan," the (sexual/fertility) rites of spring were celebrated each year in what was called "The Marriage Feast of Canaan." And so the New Testament story was Mother Earth asked God's Sun to draw water (from the sea) for the grapes to make fine wine for the wedding feast. This marriage feast story is over 5000 years old — 3000 years before the New Testament story.

It is at this point we need to go back to the ancient Egyptians to further understand "The Greatest Story Ever Told." Though all of the essential pieces of the Christian story were long in existence before Egypt, it was with the coming of the Pharaohs that the story was finally codified and became religious dogma. Though the story varied in some details from place to place in Egypt, the essence was always the same: God's Sun was the "Light of the World," who gave His life for us.

In ancient Egypt it was said that if you wanted to follow the life of God's Sun and thereby "live in the light of God's Word," one would first have to leave his old ways of life to "Follow the Sun." But before beginning this new life in "The Word," one must die to the old way of life and be "Born Again." Your first birth was "out of the water" your mother formed you in. Because her water broke and your new life began, rebirth is symbolized by coming out of total immersion in water — baptism — or being born again.

These points here mentioned are a few of hundreds, if not thousands, of direct connections that can be made between the Judaeo-Christian Bible Story and the far more ancient, original Story. My purpose for drawing your attention to this literary plagiarism is best stated by Alfred North Whitehead who said, "No lie can live forever," and Egyptologist Gerald Massey, 'They must find it difficult, those who have taken authority as the truth, rather than truth as the authority."

Now for a few thoughts on the "Old Testament" Word of God. In Mai 4:2, the God of Heaven is described as the "Sun of Righteousness with healing in His wings." The Sun with healing in His wings? Then in the New Testament in Matt. 23:37 and Luke 13:34, we see God's Son wanting to gather all under "His wings." This is most appropriate for, in Egypt, the Sun was always pictured with His wings.

In the ancient Egyptian understanding of things, mankind was called "the sheep of God." And the great Orb of Day, God's Sun, was the overseer or, in the exact words from the ancient Egyptian manuscript, "The Good Shepherd" — and we are His flock.

All ancient kings thought of their people as sheep to be pastured, with themselves as "the shepherd." Sheep are ideal followers, for they do not think for themselves but will blindly follow anyone without question. Truly admirable behavior for animals, but unwise for humans.

With the foregoing in mind, we read again from the Old Testament Book of Psalms: At Psalms 23:4 we read that old, dog-earred, tired, exhausted and equally misunderstood chestnut, used by every "man of the cloth" to put the sheep to sleep, we quote it here: "Yea, though I walk through the valley of the shadow of death, I will fear no evil, for thou art with me. Thy Rod and thy Staff, they comfort me." Thy Rod and thy Staff!!

Here in the Book of Psalms, the Old Testament God is pictured with His Rod and Staff.

The rod here mentioned is the king's "Rod of Discipline" and the staff is the "Shepherd's Staff," or crook. Now for the correct understanding of this old verse: Any good library book on the Egyptian religion will tell you that the ancient Pharaohs were said to be ruling for God's Sun on Earth. The Pharaoh was called "King of the Kingdom" and "The Great Shepherd of His Sheep."

In the hands of the Pharaoh/God (whose arms form the "Sign of the cross" on his chest), were placed the royal symbols of heavenly power, the Rod and Staff.

Incidentally, Jesus is pictured not only with His shepherd's staff but, in Rev. 125 & Rev. 19:15, is also said to "rule with a rod of iron."

– Jordan Maxwell

Jordan Maxwell *is an author, teacher and lecturer on ancient religions and Astromythology,* www.jordanmaxwell.com

Pharaoh with His Rod + Staff

First Pharaoh holds the shepherd's crook as the Good Shepherd; again later, Jesus also carries the same crook.

...though I walk through the valley of the shadow of death, I will fear no evil; for thou art with me – thy rod and thy staff they comfort me.

– Ps. 23:4

Reason and Religion

Religion. Your reason is now mature enough to examine this object. In the first place, divest yourself all bias in favor of novelty and singularity of opinion. Indulge them in any other subject rather than that of religion. It is too important and the consequences of error may be too serious. On the other hand, shake off all the fears and servile prejudices, under which weak minds are servilely crouched. Fix reason firmly in her seat, and call to her tribunal every fact, every opinion. Question with boldness even the existence of God; because, if there be one, he must more approve of the homage of reason, than that of blindfolded fear.

You will naturally examine first, the religion of your own country. Read the Bible, then, as you would read Livy or Tacitus. The facts whish are within the ordinary course of nature, you will believe on the authority of the writer, as you do those of the same kind in Livy and Tacitus. The testimony of the writer weighs in their favor in one scale; and their not being against the laws of nature, does not weigh against them. But those facts in the Bible which contradict the laws of nature, must be examined with more care, and under a variety of faces. Here you must recur to the pretensions of the writer to inspiration from God.

Thomas Jefferson (1743-1826)

"Reason and free inquiry are the only effectual agents against error."

Examine upon what evidence his pretensions are founded, and whether that evidence is so strong, as that its falsehood would be more improbable than a change in the laws of nature, in the case he relates. For example, in the book of Joshua, we are told, the sun stood still several hours. Were we to read that fact in Livy or Tacitus, we should class it with their showers of blood, speaking of statues, beasts, etc. But it is said, that the writer of that book was inspired. Examine, therefore, candidly, what evidence there is of his having been inspired. The pretension is titled to your enquiry, because millions believe it. On the other hand, you are astronomer enough to know how contrary it is to the law of nature that a body revolving on its axis, as the Earth does, should have stopped, should not, by that sudden stoppage, have prostrated animals, trees, buildings, and should after a certain time resumed its revolution, and that without a second general prostration. Is this arrest of the Earth's motion, or the evidence which affirms it, most within the law of probabilities?

You will read next the New Testament. It is the history of a personage called Jesus. Keep in your eye the opposite pretensions: one, of those who say he was begotten by God, born of a virgin, suspended and reversed the laws of nature at will, and ascended bodily into heaven; and two, of those who say he was a man of illegitimate birth, of a benevolent heart, enthusiastic mind, who set out without pretensions to divinity, ended in believing them, and was punished capitally for sedition, by being gibbeted, according to Roman law…

These questions are examined in the books I have mentioned, under the head of Religion. They will assist you in your enquiries; but keep your reason firmly on the watch in reading them all. Do not be frightened by this inquiry by any fear of its consequences. If it ends in a belief that there is no God, you will find incitements to in the virtue or pleasantness you feel in its exercise, and the love of others which it will procure you. If you find reason to believe there is a God, a consciousness that you are acting under his eyes, and that he approves you, will be a vast additional incitement; if that there be a future state, the hope of a happy existence in that increases the appetite to deserve it; if that Jesus was also a God, you will be comforted by a belief of his aid and love.

In fine, I repeat, you must lay aside all prejudices on both sides, and neither believe or reject anything, because any other persons, or descriptions of persons, have rejected or believed it. Your own reason is the only oracle given you by heaven, and you are answerable, not for the rightness, but the uprightness of the decision. I forgot to observe, when speaking of the New Testament, that you should read all the histories of Christ, [including] those which a counsel of ecclesiastics have decided for us, to be pseudo-evangelists…because those pseudo-evangelists pretended to inspiration, as much as the others, you are to judge their pretensions by your own reason, and not by the reason of those ecclesiastics.

– Thomas Jefferson
Letter to Nephew Peter Carr, 1787

Creation Stories

The Creation and Fall of Man

The Old Testament commences with one of its most interesting myths, that of the Creation and Fall of Man. The story is to be found in the first chapters of Genesis, the substance of which is as follows:

> These are the generations of the heavens and the earth when they were created, in the day (not days) that the Lord God made the earth and the heavens.

It then goes on to say that "the Lord God formed man of the dust of the ground," which appears to be the first thing he made. After planting a garden eastward in Eden, the Lord God put the man therein, "and out of the ground made the Lord God to grow every tree that is pleasant to the sight, and good for food; the Tree of Life, also in the midst of the garden, and the Tree of Knowledge of good and evil. And a river went out of Eden to water the garden, and from thence it was parted, and became into four heads."

After the "Lord God" had made the "Tree of Life," and the "Tree of Knowledge," he said unto the man:

> 'Of every tree of the garden thou mayest freely eat, but of the tree of the knowledge of good and evil, thou shalt not eat of it, for in the day that thou eatest thereof thou shalt surely die.' Then the Lord God, thinking that it would not be well for man to live alone, formed — out of the ground — every beast of the field, and every fowl of the air; and brought them unto Adam to see what he would call them, and whatever Adam called every living creature, that was the name thereof.

After Adam had given names to "all cattle, and to the fowls of the air, and to every beast of the field," the Lord God caused a deep sleep to fall upon Adam, and he slept, and he (the Lord God) took one of his (Adam's) ribs, and closed up the flesh instead thereof.

> And of the rib, which the Lord God had taken from man, made he a woman, and brought her unto Adam…And they were both naked, the man and his wife, and they were not ashamed.

After this everything is supposed to have gone harmoniously, until a serpent appeared before the woman — who was afterwards called Eve — and said to her: "Hath God said, Ye shall not eat of every tree of the garden?"

The woman, answering the serpent, said: "We may eat of the fruit of the trees of the garden: but of the fruit of the tree which is in the midst of the garden, God hath said, Ye shall not eat of it, lest ye die."

Whereupon the serpent said to her: "Ye shall not surely die" (which, according to the narrative, was the truth).

He then told her that, upon eating the fruit, their eyes would be opened, and that they would be as gods, knowing good from evil.

The woman then looked upon the tree, and as the fruit was tempting, "she took of the fruit, and did eat, and gave also unto her husband, and he did eat." The result was not death (as the Lord God had told them), but, as the serpent had said, "the eyes of both were opened, and they knew they were naked, and they sewed fig leaves together, and made themselves aprons."

Towards evening (i.e., "in the cool of the day"), Adam and his wife "heard the voice of the Lord God walking in the garden," and being afraid, they hid themselves among the trees of the garden. The Lord God not finding Adam and his wife, said: "Where art thou?" Adam answering, said: "I heard thy voice in the garden, and I was afraid, because I was naked, and I hid myself."

The "Lord God" then told Adam that he had eaten of the tree which he had commanded him not to eat, whereupon Adam said: "The woman whom thou gavest to be with me, she gave me of the tree and I did eat."

When the "Lord God" spoke to the woman concerning her transgression, she blamed the serpent, which she said "beguiled" her. This sealed the serpent's fate, for the "Lord God" cursed him and said: "Upon thy belly shall thou go, and dust shall thou eat all the days of thy life."

Unto the woman the "Lord God" said:

> I will greatly multiply thy sorrow, and thy conception; in sorrow thou shall bring forth children, and thy desire shall be to thy husband, and he shall rule over thee.

Unto Adam he said:

> Because thou hast hearkened unto the voice of thy wife, and hast eaten of the tree, of which I commanded thee, saying, Thou shall not eat of it: cursed is the ground for thy sake; in sorrow shall thou eat of it all the days of thy life. Thorns also, and thistles shall it bring forth to thee; and thou shall eat the herb of the field. In the sweat of thy face shall thou eat bread, till thou return unto the ground, for out of it wast thou taken: for dust thou art, and unto dust shalt thou return.

The "Lord God " then made coats of skin for Adam and his wife, with which he clothed them, after which he said:

> 'Behold, the man is become as one of us, to know good and evil; and now, lest he put forth his hand, and take also of the tree of life, and eat, and live forever;

[he must be sent forth from Eden].' So he [the Lord God] drove out the man [and the woman]; and he placed at the east of the garden of Eden, Cherubim, and a flaming sword which turned every way, to keep the way of the Tree of Life.

Thus ends the narrative.

The Zend-Avesta — the sacred writings of the Parsees (the ancient Persians) — states that the Supreme being Ahuramazda (Ormuzd), created the universe and man in six successive periods of time, in the following order: First, the Heavens; second, the Waters; third, the Earth; fourth, the Trees and Plants; fifth, Animals; and sixth, Man. After the Creator had finished his work, he rested.

The Avesta account of the Creation is limited to this announcement, but we find a more detailed history of the origin of the human species in the book entitled Bundehesh, dedicated to the exposition of a complete cosmogony. This book states that Ahuramazda created the first man and women joined together at the back. After dividing them, he endowed them with motion and activity, placed within them an intelligent soul, and bade them " to be humble of heart; to observe the law; to be pure in their thoughts, pure in their speech, pure in their actions." Thus were born Mashya and Mashyâna, the pair from which all human beings are descended.

To continue the Persian legend; we will now show that according to it, after the Creation man was tempted, and fell. Kalisch[1] and Bishop Colenso[2] tell us of the Persian legend that the first couple lived originally in purity and innocence. Perpetual happiness was promised them by the Creator if they persevered in their virtue. But an evil demon came to them in the form of a serpent, sent by Ahriman, the prince of devils, and gave them fruit of a wonderful tree, which imparted immortality. Evil inclinations then entered their hearts, and all their moral excellence was destroyed. Consequently they fell, and forfeited the eternal happiness for which they were destined. They killed beasts, and clothed themselves in their skins. The evil demon obtained still more perfect power over their minds, and called forth envy, hatred, discord, and rebellion, which raged in the bosom of the families.

Since the above was written, Mr. George Smith, of the British Museum, has discovered cuneiform inscriptions, which show conclusively that the Babylonians had this legend of the Creation and Fall of Man, some 1,500 years or more before the Hebrews heard of it. The cuneiform inscriptions relating to the Babylonian legend of the Creation and Fall of Man, which have been discovered by English archaeologists, are not, however, complete. The portions which relate to the Tree and Serpent have not been found, but Babylonian gem engravings show that these incidents were evidently a part of the original legend. The Tree of Life in the Genesis account appears to correspond with the sacred grove of Anu, which was guarded by a sword turning to all the four points of the compass.

The account of Genesis shows the tree of knowledge, fruit, and the serpent. Mr. Smith says of it:

> One striking and important specimen of early type in the British Museum collection, has two figures sitting one on each side of a tree, holding out their hands to the fruit, while at the back of one (the woman) is scratched a serpent. We know well that in these early sculptures none of these figures were chance devices, but all represented events, or supposed events, and figures in their legends; thus it is evident that a form of the story of the Fall, similar to that of Genesis, was known in early times in Babylonia.

This illustration might be used to illustrate the narrative of Genesis, and as Friedrich Delitzsch[3] has remarked (G. Smith's *Chaldäische Genesis*) is capable of no other explanation.

The idea of the Edenic happiness of the first human beings constitutes one of the universal traditions. Among the Egyptians, the terrestrial reign of the god Râ, who inaugurated the existence of the world and of human life, was a golden age to which they continually looked back with regret and envy. Its "like has never been seen since."

The ancient Greeks boasted of their "Golden Age," when sorrow and trouble were not known. Hesiod, an ancient Grecian poet, describes it thus:

> Men lived like Gods, without vices or passions, vexation or toil. In happy companionship with divine beings, they passed their days in tranquility and joy, living together in perfect equality, united by mutual confidence and love. The earth was more beautiful than now, and spontaneously yielded an abundant variety of fruits. Human beings and animals spoke the same language and conversed with each other. Men were considered mere boys at a hundred years old. They had none of the infirmities of age to trouble them, and when they passed to regions of superior life, it was in a gentle slumber.

In the course of time, however, all the sorrows and troubles came to man. They were caused by inquisitiveness. The story is as follows: Epimetheus received a gift from Zeus (God), in the form of a beautiful woman (Pandora).

She brought with her a vase, the lid of which was (by the command of God), to remain closed. The curiosity of her husband, however, tempted him to open it, and suddenly there escaped from it troubles, weariness and illness from which mankind was never afterwards free. All that remained was hope.

Dr. Kalisch, writing of the Garden of Eden, says:

> The Paradise is no exclusive feature of the early history of the Hebrews. Most of Hie ancient nations have similar narratives about a happy abode, which care does not approach, and which re-echoes with the sounds of the purest bliss.

The Persians supposed that a region of bliss and delight called Heden, more beautiful than all the rest of the world, traversed by a mighty river, was the original abode of the first men, before they were tempted by the evil spirit in the form of a serpent, to partake of the fruit of the forbidden tree Hom.

The ancient Egyptians also had the legend of the "Tree of Life." It is mentioned in their sacred books that Osiris ordered the names of some souls to be written on this "Tree of Life," the fruit of which made those who ate it to become as gods.

The Hindu legend approaches very nearly to that preserved in the Hebrew Scriptures. Thus, it is said that Siva, as the Supreme Being, desired to tempt Brahma (who had taken human form, and was called Swayambhura — son of the self-existent), and for this object he dropped from heaven a blossom of the sacred fig tree.

Swayambhnra, instigated by his wife, Satarupa, endeavors to obtain this blossom, thinking its possession will render him immortal and divine; but when he has succeeded in doing so, he is cursed by Siva, and doomed to misery and degradation. The sacred Indian fig is endowed by the Brahmins and the Buddhists with mysterious significance, as the "Tree of Knowledge" or "Intelligence."

To continue our inquiry regarding the prevalence of the Eden-myth among nations of antiquity:

The Chinese have their Age of Virtue, when nature furnished abundant food, and man lived peacefully, surrounded by all the beasts. In their sacred books there is a story concerning a mysterious garden, where grew a tree bearing "apples of immortality," guarded by a winged serpent, called a Dragon. They describe a primitive age of the world, when the earth yielded abundance of delicious fruits without cultivation, and the seasons were untroubled by wind and storms. There was no calamity, sickness, or death. Men were then good without effort; for the human heart was in harmony with the peacefulness and beauty of nature.

Partly by an undue thirst for knowledge, and partly by increasing sensuality, and the seduction of woman, man fell. Then passion and lust ruled in the human mind, and war with the animals began. In one of the Chinese sacred volumes, called the Chi-King, it is said that:

> All was subject to man at first, but a woman threw us into slavery. The wise husband raised up a bulwark of walls, but the woman, by an ambitious desire of knowledge, demolished them. Our misery did not come from heaven, but from a woman. She lost the human race. Ah, unhappy Poo See! thou kindled the fire that consumes us, and which is every day augmenting. Our misery has lasted many ages. The world is lost. Vice overflows all things like a mortal poison.

Thus we see that the Chinese are no strangers to the doctrine of original sin. It is their invariable belief that man is a fallen being; admitted by them from time immemorial.

The inhabitants of Madagascar had a legend similar to the Eden story, which is related as follows:

> The first man was created of the dust of the earth, and was placed in a garden, where he was subject to none of the ills which now affect mortality; he was also free from all bodily appetites, and though surrounded by delicious fruit and limpid streams yet felt no desire to taste of the fruit or to quaff the water The Creator, had, moreover, strictly forbid him either to eat or to drink. The great enemy, however, came to him, and painted to him, in glowing colors, the sweetness of the apple, and the lusciousness of the date, and the succulence of the orange.

After resisting the temptations for a while, he at last ate of the fruit, and consequently fell.

A legend of the Creation, similar to the Hebrew, was found by Mr. Ellis among the Tahitians, and appeared in his "Polynesian Researches." It is as follows:

> After Taarao had formed the world, he created man out of arsea, red earth, which was also the food of man until bread was made. Taarao one day called for the man by name. "When he came, he caused him to fall asleep, and while he slept, he took out one of his ivi, or bones, and with it made a woman, whom he gave to the man as his wife, and they became the progenitors of mankind. The woman's name was Ivi, which signifies a bone.

That man was originally created a perfect being, and is now only a fallen and broken remnant was, we have seen to be a piece of mythology, not only unfounded in fact, but, beyond intelligent question, proved untrue. What, then, is the significance of the exposure of this myth? What does its loss as a scientific fact, and as a portion of Christian dogma, imply? It implies that with it — although many Christian divines who admit this to be a legend, do not, or do not profess, to see it — must fall the whole Orthodox scheme, for upon this MYTH the theology of Christendom, is built. The doctrine of the inspiration of the Scriptures, the Fall of man, his total depravity, the Incarnation, the Atonement, the devil, hell, in fact, the entire theology of the Christian church, falls to pieces with the historical inaccuracy of this story, for upon it is it built 'tis the foundation of the whole structure.

According to Christian dogma, the Incarnation of Christ Jesus had become necessary, merely because he had to redeem the evil introduced into the world by the Fall of man. These two dogmas cannot be separated from each other. If there was no Fall, there is no need of an atonement, and no Redeemer is required. Those, then, who consent in recognizing in Christ Jesus a God and Redeemer, and who, notwithstanding, cannot resolve upon admitting the story of the Fall of man to be historical, should exculpate themselves from the reproach of inconsistency. There are a great number, however, in this position at the present day.

Cherubs

We have noticed that the "Gardens of Paradise" are said to have been guarded by Dragons, and that, according to the Genesis account, it was Cherubim that protected Eden. This apparent difference in the legends is owing to the fact that we have come in our modern times to speak of Cherub as though it were another name for an Angel. But the Cherub of the writer of Genesis, the Cherub of Assyria, the Cherub of Babylon, the Cherub of the entire Orient, at the time the Eden story was written, was not at all an Angel, but an animal, and a mythological one at that. The Cherub had, in some cases, the body of a lion, with the head of another animal, or a man, and the wings of a bird. In Ezekiel they have the body of a man, whose head, besides a human countenance, has also that of a Lion, an Ox and an Eagle. They are provided with four wings, and the whole body is spangled with innumerable eyes. In Assyria and Babylon they appear as winged bulls with human faces, and are placed at the gateways of palaces and temples as guardian genii who watch over the dwelling, as the Cherubim in Genesis watch the "Tree of Life."

Most Jewish writers and Christian Fathers conceived the Cherubim as Angels. Most theologians also considered them as Angels, until Michaelis[4] showed them to be a mythological animal, a poetical creation.

We see then, that our Cherub is simply a Dragon.

– T.W. Doane
From *Bible Myths and Their Parallels in Other Religions*

FOOTNOTES:
1. Kalisch, *Biblical Commentary Volume I*
2. Bishop Colenso, *The Pentateuch and Book of John Critically Examined*
3. Friedrich Delitzsch, Professor in Theology, *Biblical Commentary on the Old Testament in Three Volumes*
4. Michaelis, *Introduction to the New Testament in Four Volumes*

Goddess Worship

In the beginning, the feminine principle was seen as the fundamental cosmic force. Many ancient peoples believed that the world was created by a female deity, who brought the universe into being either alone or in conjunction with a male consort — usually her son — whom the Goddess created parthenogenetically. Perhaps it was because procreation was not yet understood to be connected with coitus that some thought that women, like the Goddess, brought forth life alone and unaided. Awe of the universal Goddess was expressed as reverence for women, and the female body was repeatedly represented in art as a powerful symbol of birth and rebirth.

Women's generative power was represented by a multitude of female figurines that emphasized breasts, belly, hips, and vulva. These figurines have been discovered among the remains of civilizations all over the world, signifying a time when women were revered, a veneration that translated into social and political authority. Archaeological evidence suggests that these gynecratic agricultural societies — which were egalitarian, democratic, and peaceful — gradually gave way to male-dominated political states in which occupational specialization, commerce, social stratification, and militarism developed.

As men gained control of civilization, the power of the Goddess was diminished or altogether destroyed. For the first time, the idea arose that life originated entirely from a male — rather than a female — source, a dramatic change in thinking that is possible to trace in myths, legends, and images of the Goddess. Her original primacy gave way to gradual subordination to male gods. In some cases, the sex of the female deity was simply altered and her attributes transferred. Then the rituals and temples of the various goddesses were taken over by religions dedicated to male gods. Soon the originally benevolent power of the remaining goddesses began to be viewed as negative, destructive, or evil. Finally the Judeo-Christian tradition absorbed all deities into a single male godhead.

At first the Jews, like many early peoples, worshipped both God and Goddess. It required six centuries for Yahweh to replace Astoreth as the primary Jewish deity, though for a long time their temples stood side by side. After the Jewish patriarchs finally succeeded in destroying Goddess worship, women's former status gradually diminished.

This same story is repeated in culture after culture. As a result of successive Greek invasions, the matriarchal culture of Crete was overthrown and

Cretan deities were incorporated into Greek myths. Although the Greeks were already patriarchal by this time, Goddess worship continued there, as it would in Rome. But Greco-Roman goddesses paled beside their historic antecedents, and the position of Greek women was summed up in this famous remark by the Greek historian Thucydides: "That woman is best who is least spoken of among men, whether for good or evil."

The destruction of the Goddess reflected the gradual erosion of women's political, social, and religious authority. However, women did not accept this loss of power passively, as is evidenced in legends, literature, and images about the Amazons and various warrior queendoms. It is unknown whether women warred among themselves during the thousands of years of gynocracy, but myths suggest that some of these societies engaged in warfare against the emerging male-dominated societies in a vain effort to turn the tide.

While Roman women were in a similar legal position to that of their Greek predecessors, in reality they were far less oppressed. Although women were considered "perpetual minors" and subject to the jurisdiction of their fathers and husbands, public sentiment was at odds with the laws. As a result of protests organized by Roman women, these laws were improved, though the gains were short lived. When Christianity first developed, there were a number of early religious communities in which men and women enjoyed equal rights, partly as a result of their commitment to the idea that "in Christ there is neither male or female." Throughout the early Middle Ages, the Church offered women refuge from the invasions and violence that made them subject to capture, rape, and forcible marriage. Many girls went to convents to be educated, sometimes making religious houses their permanent homes or returning to them in later life. Those who wished to devote themselves to scholarship and the arts gathered in the convents with or without taking vows.

During these years, upper-class women began to lose more and more of their property rights. In an effort to retain their lands, countless noblewomen established and ruled religious houses as abbesses, a process encouraged by the Church. As many abbesses were members of the royal families, they were allowed the rights and privileges of feudal barons and often acted as representatives of the king during his absence. These women frequently administered vast lands, managed convents, abbeys, and monasteries, provided their own troops during wartime, enjoyed the right to coinage, and were consulted in political and religious affairs.

In the later Middle Ages, the family emerged as the most stable social force of the secular world. Because women were generally central to the family, some played major roles in their communities. Wealthy women were able to own and administer property and, when their husbands were away, they often managed the estates, presided over the courts, signed treatises, made laws, and sometimes even commanded troops. In their courts, royal women supported troubadours who traveled around singing songs venerating both women and the Virgin Mary. It was during this period that worship of Mary increased among all classes of women.

As Christianity spread, it absorbed many indigenous religious practices, including the ongoing worship of the Goddess, maintained particularly by peoples far away from the centers of power. In an effort to attract converts, the Church had allowed this worship to be transferred to the figure of Mary, whose image was derived from the ancient Goddess with her son/lover on her lap. Mary worship became so common that it was often said that "in the thirteenth century God changed sex." But by the end of the Middle Ages, the Church was well established and increasingly unwilling to tolerate a female deity.

At this point in history, Church leaders no longer needed help from women in the spreading of Christian doctrine, as they had in earlier centuries. This made them more willing to attack the last vestiges of Goddess worship and to restrict women's remaining power even further. In some cases, Goddess worship was tied to the practice of witchcraft, which the Church had permitted for centuries. But Church leaders — all of whom were men — felt more and more threatened by the prominent position women occupied in the witches' covens. In addition, a number of heretical sects had developed in which women were allowed to preach, a practice that incensed the Church.

The Church joined hands with the emerging nation states of Europe to build the social and political institutions that were to become the foundation of modern society. Using the Inquisition to eliminate all those who resisted their authority, Church leaders targeted witches, heretics, lay healers (who practiced medicine despite the objections of male physicians), political dissenters, and peasant leaders (many of whom were women), as well as anyone who opposed the power of the Church and the consequent destruction of what was left of female authority.

Witch hunts were prevalent between the thirteenth and seventeenth centuries. According to male scholars, no more than three hundred thousand people were murdered, but contemporary feminist scholars speculate that there were many more. Eighty-five percent of those accused and executed as witches were women, and the terror induced by the witch hunts, combined with the decline of feudalism and the steady contraction of women's position, virtually eliminated women's independent power. By the late Renaissance, the economic and political base that had supported women's medieval predecessors had disappeared, and they were barred from the newly formed universities, craft guilds, and developing professions.

Women's property and inheritance rights, slowly eroded over the centuries, were totally eliminated. Marriage became the only acceptable option for women, and when the convents were dissolved by the Reformation, female education — formerly available through the Catholic Church — became increasingly difficult to obtain. To the reformers, for a woman to have any intellectual aspirations was considered not only absurd but also perilous. They never tired of repeating that a woman's learning should be restricted to reading and writing for the purpose of teaching the Bible to her children.

Reformation leaders insisted that a woman's sole duty was silent obedience to her husband, although within the family women were accorded a degree of respect. Because work was centered in the home, women's lives were busy and productive, as the activities of all the family members were crucial to economic survival. The Reformation supported some education for women, though only for purposes related to the family. Having access to at least some form of education gradually contributed to women's advancement, however slow.

– Judy Chicago

Excerpt from The Dinner Party: From Creation to Preservation, *Merrell Publishers of London and New York, 2007. The Dinner Party presents a symbolic history of this obscured yet heroic past, pieced together from small fragments to form a visual image of women's long struggle for liberation throughout the history of Western civilization.*

Isis Mysteries and Christianity

In the days of the early Roman Empire, the cult of Isis was very popular throughout the Mediterranean region. Like Christianity and Mithraism, it emerged in Rome as a mystery religion. Many of the cult's traditions are thought by scholars to parallel some of the Christian myths. Isis, Osiris and Horus were worshipped together in a similar fashion to the Holy Trinity. Stories depicted a virgin birth and the image of Isis with Horus is nearly identical to the later symbol of the Madonna holding Baby Jesus.

Their legends also included a resurrection, which gave adherents hope that they too could cheat death.

The cult of Isis was never favorable to Augustus and the Roman senate. It was too secretive and exotic.

The sexual nature of the Isis Imagery was thought of as pornographic to the emperor. Most notably, Isis worship had come from Egypt. Augustus' enemy, Cleopatra had often dressed herself as Isis and even claimed to be her reincarnated.

Despite its detractors, the cult of Isis was widely practiced among women and the lower classes until the fourth century A.D. when the cult's identity began to be absorbed into Christianity. By the sixth century, it had been completely driven underground.

II

World Religions

" *The Jews say, that their word of God was given by God to Moses, face to face; the Christians say, that their word of God came by divine inspiration: and the Turks say, that their word of God was brought by an angel from Heaven. Each of those churches accuse the other of unbelief; and for my own part, I disbelieve them all.* "

Thomas Paine
The Age of Reason

Islam

Afghanistan, Albania, Algeria, Azerbaijan, Brunei, Chad, Djibouti, Egypt, Gabon, Gambia, Guinea, Gunae-Bissau, Indonesia, Iran, Iraq, Jordan, Kuwait, Kyrgyzstan, Lebanon, Libya, Malaysia, Mali, Mauritania, Morocco, Niger, Nigeria, Oman, Pakistan, Palestine, Qatar, Saudi Arabia, Senegal, Sierra Leone, Somalia, Sudan, Syria, Tajikistan, Tunisia, Turkey, Turkmenistan, United Arab Emirates, Uzbekistan, Yemen.

What do all of these countries have in common?

War, severe neglect of human rights, poverty, torture, widely practiced incest, barbaric punishments, public executions, judicial and police corruption, state censorship of media, poor education, curfews, oppression of women and homosexuals, and a thriving gun culture. Moreover, all of the aforementioned countries are considered to be Islamic — at least in the sense that the majority of the people who live in such countries are Muslims.

Second only to Christianity, Islam is one of the fastest growing monotheistic faiths. Some sources claim it to be the fastest growing religion in the world. Indeed one fifth of all humans are Muslim, mostly under 25 years of age and of the Sunni sect. Bizarrely, although Islam is the religion of Arabia, only 20 percent of the world's Muslims are in fact Arabs. The majority of Muslims are Southeast Asians, Africans and Pakistanis.

A religion which asserts that there is one God, Allah, and that his prophet is Mohammad (570-632 B.C.E.), Islam has overtaken in numbers the approximately 360 million Buddhists and 900 million Hindus in the world and is rapidly catching up with the two thousand million (or billion) Christians.

But what is Islam, and who was the prophet who inspired so many people to believe in his teachings? Although he was a man of no divine parentage, Mohammad was apparently blessed with the ability to perform miracles such as splitting the moon in half and reuniting it again.

Unfortunately, however, a later miracle backfired when he tried to summon a mountain to his side, but failed in the attempt and had to travel to the unmoved mountain instead. Mohammad excused the failure to summon the mountain as an act of God's mercy, being that if the mountain had indeed been transported to his side, it would have flattened and killed the followers who stood beside him.

Mohammad's final miracle before he was taken up to Paradise was to make the stone on which he stood float so he could mount his sacred human-headed horse, al-Borak. The no longer floating stone's current location is apparently under Jerusalem's Dome of the Rock mosque. Despite going to

Paradise, Mohammad is buried in Medina.

In general, Muslims take their religion seriously, too seriously for my liking, and follow the basic guidelines of praying five times every day, fasting, giving money to the poor, declining to eat pork, and going on a pilgrimage (Hajj) to the sacred Haram enclosure in the Saudi Arabian city of Mecca (Makkah) at least once in their lifetime.

Allah, Moon God?

Allah. Islamic name for God. Is derived from Semitic El, and [Allah] originally applied to the Moon; he seems to have been preceded by Ilmaqah, the Moon-god. Allat is the female counterpart of Allah.
– Egerton Sykes, *Everyman's Dictionary of Non-Classical Mythology*

The god Il or Ilah was originally a phase of the Moon God, but early in Arabian history the name became a general term for god, and it was this name that the Hebrews used prominently in their personal names, such as Emanu-el, Israel, etc., rather than the Bapal of the northern semites proper, which was the Sun. Similarly, under Mohammed's tutelage, the relatively anonymous Ilah became Al-Ilah, The God, or Allah, the Supreme Being.
– Carleton S. Coon, *Southern Arabia*

Each state or tribe had had its own moon god under a national or local name. The temples had been centers of religious life, and the priests of the moon gods had normally provided oracle services. Pilgrimage had been performed to certain temples of the moon gods, with rituals similar in many details to those of the pre-Islamic and Islamic pilgrimage to Mecca.
– from *Encyclopedia Britannica*, "History of Arabia"

The Ka'aba was dedicated to al-Ilah, the High God of the pagan Arabs, despite the presiding effigy of Hubal. By the beginning of the seventh century, al-Ilah had become more important than before in the religious life many of the Arabs. Many primitive religions develop a belief in a High God, who is sometimes called the Sky God...But they also carried on worshipping the other gods, who remained deeply important to them.
– Karen Armstrong, *Muhammad*

Inside the mosque, pilgrims walk around the Kaaba ("Black stone"), a cube of rock hidden behind curtains. Although Muslims believe the cube was fashioned by Abraham, its status as a tool of worship was in place centuries before Mohammad was born. Indeed, the Kaaba was formally used by Persians in their worship of Saturn (Kronos), the god of time. For this reason, unknown to most Muslims, the Kabba is itself an un-Islamic idol, and according to the Qur'an, should be destroyed.

Not all Islamic practices are so worthy of being labelled holy as the Hajj.

Similar to Jews, Muslims like to rid baby boys of their foreskins, although not as a religious necessity.

As with Jews, Muslims like to hang kicking and struggling animals upside down and slit their throats, allowing the unfortunate beasts to slowly bleed to death. A disgusting practice designed to produce meat that is free of blood, the liquid dwelling in the place of the animal's impure soul. Not only is this Halal meat required for all meals, every Muslim who undertakes the Hajj pilgrimage must pay to have an animal slaughtered in this manner as a sacrifice to God.

As mentioned, the holy text of Muslims is called the Qur'an ("the recital"), and was written in the name of Allah (God), to be his divine and infallible word on Earth. The book itself contains 114 Suras, or chapters, which deal with morality, proper conduct and how to best serve God.

Having said that, one should examine the following Suras, with regard to the belief that Islam does not preach the hatred of non-Muslims:

> [2:193] Fight them until there is no more Fitnah [non-believers, those who are not Muslims]. But if they cease, let there be no transgression except against Az Zalimun [wrong doers, polytheists, Hindus].

> [3:118] Take not as Bitanah [friends, advisors] those outside your religion, since they will not fail to do their best to corrupt you.

> [5:51] Take not the Jews and the Christians as Auliya [supporters, friends]. Allah guides not those people who are the Zalimun [polytheists, Hindus].

> [60:1] Take not my enemies, and your enemies [non-Muslims] as friends, while they have disbelieved in what has come to you of the truth.

> [60:13] Take not as friends the people who have incurred the wrath of Allah [Jews; punished for the idolatry of the Golden Calf].

Now that we have a small flavor of the Qur'an as a "holy" book, we should also discover the man behind it. Although Mohammad was himself illiterate, he dictated the Qur'an to a succession of personal secretaries who remembered his words and wrote them down, in some cases, generations after the prophet's death.

The fact that Mohammad was illiterate is one of the main reasons why Muslims believe he was God's prophet. For how else could he compose such beautiful poetry than if Allah had not spoken such to him. But if God really wanted to dictate a life-saving message, why would he utter such to a man who could not write it down? Why didn't God choose a literate, educated person to be his conduit and human agent on Earth?

Muslims forget that Mohammad, whilst perhaps illiterate, was certainly not stupid. The prophet of Islam was in fact a successful merchant by the time he was apparently approached by God in 610 B.C.E., and would therefore have had the ability to compose his own poetry.

Aside from the poetic wisdom, the text of the Qur'an reveals some interesting yet basic knowledge of science, cosmology and evolutionary theories such as the notion that the world is not flat, that the expanding universe began in the manner of an original explosion, that human life came from the seas, and even that extra-terrestrial life exists. However, the description of the first stages of human life in the womb as being clay, then a blood clot, a leech and a "chewed thing" are rather naïve. Surely God could have described his own creation in more exact medical terminology.

Islam News

If anyone killed a person not in retaliation for murder or to spread mischief in the land, it would be as if he killed the whole of mankind. And (likewise) if anyone saved a life, it would be as if he saved the whole of mankind.

– Sura Al-Maaida 5:32

June, 2004; Fallujah adopts Taliban theocracy: Women must cover their hair and faces. Those who don't are beaten in the streets. Beauty parlors have been shut down. Men have been ordered to grow beards and barbers have been warned not to shave customers. Several alcohol dealers have been flogged naked in the streets of Fallujah.

– jihadwatch.org

A Pakistani cleric announced Friday a $1 million bounty for killing a cartoonist who drew Prophet Muhammad.

– Riaz Khan, AP

A Pakistani Muslim cleric said Friday that he and supporters were offering rewards of more than $1 million for killing Danish cartoonist who drew a depiction of the prophet, Mohammed.

– www.msnbc.com

"Roses of the Prophet Mohammed." That's how you order a Danish these days in Iran.

– Editor

It was widely reported that Iran's president, Mahmoud Ahmadinejad stated on the record that he hoped for the death of Israel's Prime Minister, Ariel Sharon. He had already received criticism internationally for suggesting Sharon be "wiped off the map."

- Editor

Two hundred lives have been lost since the bombing of the bombing of a Shi'ite shrine set off a wave of retribution against Sunnis and pushed Iraq towards civil war.

– Washington Times

It was widely reported that Iran's president, Mahmoud Ahmadinejad stated on the record that he hoped for the death of Israel's Prime Minister, Ariel Sharon. He had already received criticism

internationally for suggesting Sharon be "wiped off the map." The destruction of a Shi'ite shrine set off a wave of retribution against Sunnis and pushed Iraq towards civil war.
– Robert H. Reid, *Adelphia.net*

The symbolic empty shrine bears the words: Mustafa Mahmoud Mazeh, born Conakry, Guinea. Martyred in London, August 3, 1989. The first martyr to die on a mission to kill Salman Rushdie.
– Anthony Loyd, *New York Times* Online

Controversial Dutch filmmaker and newspaper columnist Theo van Gogh, who made a film about violence against women in Islamic societies, has been murdered in Amsterdam, police said.
– www.cnn.com

The last recorded sounds are the roaring engines and the Arabic prayers of one of the hijackers: "Allah is the greatest. Allah is the greatest. Allah is the greatest. Allah is the greatest."
– Recording from United Airlines, Flight 93, played to the jury at the Zacharias Moussaoui trial

The Muslim Brotherhood was established in Gaza in 1946. Hamas is an offshoot organization which formed officially in 1987. It carried out its first suicide bombing in 1993. It is listed as a terrorist organization by the United States, the European Union and most of the west. This is a result of multiple attacks on civilians in heavily populated places such as restaurants and supermarkets.
– *The Good News Magazine*

Christian mobs rampaged through a southern Nigerian city Tuesday, burning mosques and killing several people in an outbreak of anti- Muslim violence that followed deadly protests against caricatures of the Prophet Muhammad.
– Dulue Mbachu, Associated Press writer, reported on www.breitbart.com

Aslam Abdullah emphatically asserts that for the Taliban, Islam is not an actual religious faith, but a rallying cry for political action by a zealous and dangerous minority.
– ACFnewsource: Abdullah is a spokesperson for the Muslim Public Affairs Council

Sadly, for anyone who has read of the Ancient Greek philosophy and scientific discoveries, there is little in the Qur'an that was not already said by the Greeks. Furthermore, as the Arabs preserved the teachings of Aristotle, we know of their love of such Greek philosophy and were obviously influenced by such. It is a pity then that Muslims have forgotten the words of Aristotle: "Plato is dear to me, but dearer still is truth."

Regardless of whether or not the Qur'an was influenced by the incredible discoveries of Greek philosophers such as Aristotle, it unfortunately joins the Bible in its "wrath of God" mentality, with the almighty creator dealing out rewards and punishments left, right and center — the details of which should leave a skeptical reader in no doubt that Islam is a man-made religion, just the same as any other.

Or is it the same?

After the terrorist attacks of September 11th Islam was the subject of much debate, especially with regard to the moral virtues it promotes.

However, politicians eventually agreed that Islam itself was not to blame for the dreadful attacks, but rather misguided fundamentalists who were using religion to excuse their barbaric acts of violence. Yet, it could be argued that this is just a "politically correct" statement to avoid a bloody crusade between Muslims and Christians, and not a conclusion based on fact. Could Islam promote violent behavior? Many detractors of Islam have concluded that it could.

Of course, to the accusations that Islam promotes violence and the need for revenge, Muslims would reply that what we know of their religion comes mainly from the translations and research undertaken by Western Jewish and Christian "Orientalists," religious academics whom Muslims believe to be rather biased in their negative opinions of Islam.

There is indeed a pre-judgmental attitude taken by Westerners towards Islam. According to the eminent psychiatrist Eric Berne, in a study of the cultural aspects of murder, Muslims are more likely to commit murder in times of stress and depression than Christians.

This is due to the cultural norm of expressing sadness or elation in an overt and external fashion, including tearing out hair and screaming in times of woe, yet dancing in the street in times of happiness. However, I do not completely agree with this theory. Men and women of all religions and cultures have the potential to commit murder and publicly express their feelings.

Yet it should be clear to any observer that there does seem to be a general lack of emotional restraint in Islamic countries, even though it is far from politically correct in the western world to even hint at such. To remind those of the background to September 11th, the Taliban or "Students" of the Qur'an, were the rulers of Afghanistan prior to an allied invasion in 2003 to overthrow them. The Qur'an's students were the gun-wielding maniacs who supported al-Qaeda in killing thousands of people in New York's World Trade Center.

These students were the same people who banned women from education and forced them to wear head-to-toe burquas, lest any tempting flesh be witnessed by men. The Taliban were also the unenlightened student union who destroyed the 2000-year-old statues of Buddha in their own Bamiyan Valley. The Taliban was acting against the worship of idols by destroying historical and culturally important art. To destroy the evidence of civilization thus proving to be as vile as faith in a religion.

The point is this: When religion is one day replaced with rational thought, as opposed to another religion, it would, for example, be a disgusting and unpalatable act to blow up Istanbul's Blue Mosque or the Vatican, or Salt Lake City's Mormon Temple, or any other house of worship. Art and history must neither be destroyed nor hidden nor altered to suit the product of rational evolution.

Just as we have preserved Stonehenge, so must we preserve Mecca, the Dome of the Rock or the Golden Temple in a thousand years' time. Without them we will not be properly able to see just how far we have come from our currently primitive position.

Returning to the concept of Islamic society being violent, here is yet another true and gloomy tale. Shortly after he was appointed, the transport minister for the newly reformed Taliban-free Afghanistan was beaten to death by an angry mob of Muslim pilgrims. This was the minister's punishment for keeping them waiting at an airport. Apparently the group of Hajj pilgrims could not fly to Mecca, as the transport minister intended to use their aircraft for a diplomatic mission.

The religious murderers were not the least bit regretful for their act of barbarity, and laughed and joked with reporters only an hour or so after they had spilled the blood of an innocent man's life. So the question is raised whether the extreme behavior of people in Arab and Islamic countries is directly related to the Qur'an, or simply the product of a backward culture.

In reading the Qur'an one will find that the book gives great advice on self restraint and how wrong it is to make hasty decisions when one is angry. The "holy" text also instructs readers to respect all men, regardless of their religion. However, to respect and tolerate other religions is not the same as believing a member of another religion will be saved from hell fire on Judgment Day.

Despite what politicians say, both the Qur'an and Hadith emphasize that those who know of Islam, and who do not follow or convert to the belief in such, will not be allowed to enter Paradise. Jews (Yahudi) and Christians (Nasara) who have never heard of Islam, and have done what is right on the Earth, will however be let into the heavenly garden with nothing to fear, but I think this is a very unlikely situation, unless one is deaf, dumb and blind.

> Whoever seeks a religion other than Islam, will be one of the losers in the Hereafter. (Qur'an 3:85)

> Those who have disbelieved and died in disbelief, they will have a painful punishment, and they will have no helpers. (Qur'an 3:91)

As with the Bible and Torah, the initial premise of the Qur'an is that it is God's word. In this case, as revealed to the prophet Mohammad over a period of 23 years. Yet the deception of Islam is that the Qur'an alone guides Muslim society. It does not!

Islamic society is guided by the Sunna, or "path to be followed." The Sunna is composed of the teachings of the Qur'an combined with the Hadith, or further teachings and actions of Mohammad. Therefore it is the Sunna which Muslims regard as the path to God, and it is Shari'ah law ("the path"), which shapes Islamic society. Quoting the Qur'an alone is therefore quite inappropriate when Western politicians attempt to evaluate the beliefs of Muslims.

As with Judaism and Christianity, Islam is also a man-made religion of control, completely unconnected to God except to the degree that religion is a product of human imagination, which is itself the creation of God. However, there is certainly a darker side to Islam springing from both the actions and history of Mohammad and the fundamental principles of Islamic law. Indeed, even the old Muslim proverb that describes where God is in relation to humankind reeks of a sinister threat: "God is as close as our jugular vein."

Although the word Islam itself denotes peace or, "entering into a condition of peace through allegiance to God," its history and traditions are anything but peaceful. The alternative definition of Islam is "the surrender of the will to God" implying the threat of punishment for those who do not surrender.

The mythical foundation of the religion in fact confirms a forced surrender by Mohammad, rather than a voluntary decision deriving from reason.

The story goes that in the cave of Hira, during the "Night of Power," the archangel Gabriel crushed the 40-year-old Mohammad and grabbed his throat until he could no longer breathe, only releasing him when Mohammad agreed to accept God into his life, and to spread the poetic verse of Allah's divine word and revelations. However, if Mohammad had wanted to live and breathe again he did not have a choice in the matter, and it was therefore not of his free will that he surrendered!

The violent aspect of Islam is further highlighted by considering that the traditional idea of a spiritual leader does not really sit well with Mohammad, being that he was trained as a combat archer who was versed in the art of war. And although the Qur'an tells us that "to kill is to kill all," the book excuses killing if it is of a person who intends to kill us first.

Furthermore, the concept of killing for the sake of Islam is apparently honourable. Martyrs for the cause ("Shaheed") supposedly go straight to Paradise to be greeted by a wealth of beautiful young women called "houri," poor soulless beings created only to have sex with men. The paradox of Muslims killing to protect Muslim values is further complicated if we consider that one such value is not to kill!

There is also a degree of ambivalence surrounding the position of Muslims not being allowed to kill indiscriminately, taking the lives of women and children. Yet the defense of the Islamic Republic of Pakistan relies on nuclear missiles, an entirely indiscriminate weapon. Not to mention the indiscriminate killing of those who were present at the World Trade Center, by Islamic terrorists.

The notion of Jihad can also be confusing if heralding Islam as a peaceful religion. Jihad, or "Holy War," is supposedly a two-fold struggle. A greater Jihad is a struggle with oneself, an internal war with one's own emotions and aggression. A lesser Jihad is a physical, external war with an enemy, with the latter Jihad being all too common. Indeed, Mohammad himself once called his followers to war with the Byzantine Empire, and punished those who refused to kill enemy soldiers. Punishment, the suppression of freedom of speech and aggressive behavior being paramount to Islam.

Islam is not a religion of peace. In fact, it was Muslims who gave the English language the word "Assassin," corrupted from "Hashshashin," or one who smokes or eats hashish. Essentially the Assassins were a vicious band of killers who murdered rival Muslims and political enemies, circa 1092 B.C.E. These were vile acts which occurred after long sessions of drug taking, and prayers to Allah.

About Those Virgins...

In a study by scholar Christoph Luxenberg, he states clearly that the Koran has been mistranslated.

The word hur is taken to stand for the word houri, which means "virgin." He insists that in both Aramaic and early Arabic, the literal meaning for hur is "white raisin."

This could be quite a disappointment for anyone motivated to lose their life for those seventy greeting virgins.

Luxenberg makes it clear that it is food and drink that is being offered and not unsullied maidens or houris.

– *Guardian Unlimited*

The Islamic Jihad is running a summer school that teaches young Palestinian boys aged 12 through 15, the benefits of becoming suicide bombers.

They are taught that it is good to kill and die. They will be guaranteed a place in heaven as a martyr, and will be greeted there by 70 virgins.

– Jeremy Cooke, BBC News

The reasons for such murders sprung from the hatred of Sunni Muslims, a majority faction that believed that after Mohammad's death his successor should have been he whom was most qualified to lead.

Shiites, on the other hand, thought Mohammad's successor should have been Ali, the husband of Mohammad's daughter Fatima. However, Shiites themselves could not even agree on the lineage of Imams, or holy teachers. For, once Ali had died, his successor became Musa Al-Kazim, a descendant who himself had an older brother, Ismail Al-Kazim. Thus, Assassins were the supporters of Ismail's right of succession and became the first Muslim terrorists.

But it was not the Assassins alone who were overtly violent and hungry for blood. Mohammad himself said that if a Muslim turns his back on his religion, and then acts against fellow Muslims, he should be killed!

Not only is Islamic violence greatly disturbing, the Islamic treatment of women is rather sickening. In the Qur'an, Suras 24:31 and 33:53 state the first case for oppressing women — that they should lower their gaze in the company of men and that they should even be put behind a curtain (Purdah) or barrier.

A Few More Differences between Sunnis and Shi'ites

• They disagree on the Hadith (narrations on the actions of Muhammad) and what determines valid Hadith. In general, Shi'ites reject Bukhari, while Sunnis consider this to be the primary source of Hadith.

• Shi'ites believe that to lead the Muslims you have to be from the direct lineage of Muhammad. Sunnis believe that any qualified person has the right to lead.

• Shi'ites have a belief that twelve religious leaders called imams will rule, the last of whom is currently sleeping in a cave. Sunnis are at odds with this, and feel that these imams are imbued with powers that only God has, which could be considered heresy to Sunnis.

• There are minor differences in their laws. For example, Shi'ites can marry with the intention of a temporary union. Sunnis can only marry for permanence.

• Certain rituals differ slightly. For example, the Shi'ites pray with their arms down at their sides, Sunnis pray with their arms folded at the sternum.

Mohammad himself clarified the Qur'an's position on equality by showing his followers how to modify their wives' behavior by beating them with strips of folded cloth. Symbolic or not, it underlines the contempt for women's rights in Islam. Furthermore, the Qur'an recommends: "To those women you suspect of ill conduct, banish them to their beds, beat them!"

It is disgusting that many Muslim women around the world are treated like virtual slaves by both their own families and the society in which they are forced to live. I say forced because even if a woman did indeed get access to education, and learned of the folly of religion and her dire situation when compared to women in the West, she may still be prevented from leaving her family and country.

In Saudi Arabia, the Wahhabi state religion, being a puritan version of Islam, instructs that women can have no role in society other than nurses and teachers. Women are even prevented from getting driving licenses. If women are victims of crime, they as victims may receive punishment for bringing shame on their families.

If a woman is raped she may even be killed by her own father for allowing herself to be ravaged by someone other than her husband. However, Muslim scholars would suggest that such an "honour killing" is a pre-Islamic tradition. The point is, this treatment has been, at the least, adopted by the Muslim faith.

If the rape in question was deemed to be adultery on the woman's part, she may be stoned to death. This is a punishment which ranks among the most evil in Muslim countries, together with amputating the hands of a thief or public beheadings.

In marriage, women are commanded by Mohammad to be treated fairly by their husbands, aside from the occasional slap (Qur'an 4:34). But women are also encouraged by Shari'ah law to secretly steal money from their husbands if they do not think they are receiving their fair share, and on the event of their husband's death they will only be eligible to receive half of his money, whilst male relations will receiving a full share of such.

Islam, despite claiming to treat women as equal by Allah's command, actually treats women as property, not as human beings. Since women are property they can be replaced when things grow tiresome, and a man can marry up to four women all together. This was a "revelation from God" appearing in the Qur'an conveniently for the sake of Mohammad after he had been married for the thirteenth time.

The portrait of the wives of Mohammad is further sullied when we realize that not only did the prophet marry an older rich woman to fund his religious obsessions, he also married girls as young as nine and twelve to satisfy his lust. Indeed, one such wife was given to him as a present by his own son. Before becoming a present, she had formally been Mohammad's son's wife. Today this would make a good topic for Jerry Springer.

Prior to the "War Against Terror" in Afghanistan, women were not only denied all formal education, they, like in most Islamic states, were required by law to wear a face and body veil — the veil being used to cover women's faces and hair in public, lest they insult God by revealing such. Such an insult is unlikely, however, for if God did not like women's hair he would not have created them with hair in the first place.

The true reason for the veil is to prevent sex-starved men from gazing at other men's wives and children, as they are regarded as property. Indeed, it was forbidden by Mohammad for single girls to be alone in the same room with a male stranger, lest they exchange lustful glances.

So the use of the head veil or Hijab was a "barrier" against sexual temptation. Such a device, aiming to stop the lustful feelings of men, would indicate a lack of male self-control, or the lack of will power.

A lack of will power would suggest that men are not in possession of free will, but are led by their hormones. A lack of free will would also imply that Muslims cannot surrender such to God, as they don't have free will to start with, thus defeating the entire philosophical point of Islam.

Aside from the indignity of forcing women to wear ludicrous sacks over their heads, Muslims are especially fond of punishing those who step out of line. Punishing criminals is of course a necessity in any society, but is rather sinister in countries which have punishment dictated by apparently Holy Scriptures, and have religious police such as the Saudi "Mutawa" to enforce the law.

The problem with religion being obsessed with punishment is quite obvious. God would not be so unmerciful. Moreover, if a father required that his children's hands be cut off with a sword if they were caught stealing, he would be a wicked man. Why then would a god who demanded such punishment be anything less?

Indeed, even with regard to the Islamic understanding of Christ's death, there is a curious belief in God's wicked nature. Unlike Christians who believe God allowed his own son to be crucified, Muslims believe God saved Jesus ("Esa") by putting his face onto another man who was then killed in his place (Qur'an 4:157). Whilst it was correct of God to save his son from crucifixion, it was a cruel act to condemn an innocent man to take his place on the cross.

The notion that God can be cruel is also summed up by some of the 99 names which Muslims know him as: al-Qahhar (the subduer), al-Qabid (the constrictor), al-Khafid (the abaser), al-Muzill (the dishonourer), al-Muntaqim (the avenger), al-Mani' (the preventer) and ad-Darr (the distresser). A collection of rather unusual names for a merciful god, and yet a god who decides who he will make laugh or cry, according to Sura 53:43. Allah's wrongful actions and tendencies, just mentioned, are evident despite the Qur'an telling us in 11 separate Suras that he wills no wrong to mankind.

The conflicting nature of Islam, that it is a holy and peaceful religion, yet favors the philosophy of the sword and the whip, is complicated even more by the cornucopia of textual inconsistencies in the Qur'an.

The first most striking theological anomaly in the Qur'an comes when it states that Jesus sits beside Allah in Paradise ("Jannah"), and then goes on to say that all those who are worshipped other than Allah will burn in hell

("Jahannum") with their followers.

So where exactly is Christ and his Christians? Are they in heaven or frying their skins off in hell? According to Suras 2:62 and 5:69, Christians enter Paradise when they die, and yet Suras 3:85 and 5:72 deny this.

Even if we are assured that Christians were allowed entry to Allah's lofty garden, the Qur'an is rather unsure of exactly what such a Paradise actually entails. Is it the many gardens detailed in Suras 18:31, 22:23, 35:33 and 78:32, or is there only one garden as detailed in Suras 39:73, 41:30, 57:21 and 79:41?

Furthermore, if Christians were indeed allowed to sit in Allah's heaven beside their Muslim brothers, would they celebrate with a drink? Who knows? One minute the Qur'an states that there are rivers of wine in Paradise, in Suras 47:15 and 83:22, and the next minute alcohol is called "Satan's handiwork," care of Suras 5:90 and 2:219.

Speaking of time, the Qur'an also seems to be confused about chronology and the order in which things were created. In Sura 2:29 the Earth was created prior to heaven, yet in Sura 79:27-30 it is the other way around. Surely God would not have forgotten the details of such important events. Maybe the Qur'an is not Allah's infallible dictation after all.

The Qur'an says it took Allah six days to create heaven and Earth, Sura 7:54, and two days in 41:9, despite claims that Allah can create anything in an instant ("Be! and it is"), Sura 2:117. Time is an issue that is shrouded with doubt in the pages of Islam's holy book. One day for Allah is equivalent to 1,000 years on Earth (found in Suras 22:47 and 32:5). Yet in Sura 70:4, one day for God is 50,000 years for humans.

To be confused about the chronological order of creation is bad enough, but for a culture which has mastered and embraced arithmetic and complicated geometry to also confuse the amount of times they are expected to pray each day, well, that's just embarrassing.

Muslims pray five times a day, despite the Qur'an's advice that four times is all that is required: "Wherefore glorify God, when the evening overtaketh you, and when ye rise in the morning, and in the evening, and when ye rest at noon" (Sura 30:16-17).

With regard to the practice of eating Halal meat, the Qur'an actually excuses Muslims for eating anything, Halal or otherwise, if they are forced to do so out of "necessity" or "severe hunger." Suras 2:173, 5:3, 6:145 and 16:115 say that Allah will even forgive Muslims for eating meat sacrificed in the name of another god, if such Muslims will die if they do not eat. I therefore suggest that humans who do not eat anything will die, and that this is enough "necessity" (see context, above) for Muslims to stop butchering meat in the vile fashion of Halal.

Even though the Qur'an often trips itself up as a result of human error, its flaws are dwarfed when compared to the contradictions between Islam's Holy

Scriptures and the documented life of Mohammad, the Hadith. It is here that Muslims will be quick to point out that aside from Orientalists wrongly translating the Qur'an, they have also wrongly translated the Hadith. Moreover, they also state that the word of God was revealed in Arabic and cannot be considered pure in any other form.

However, the Hadith was not God's word, but the observations and anecdotes of Mohammad's followers, and can therefore be translated without concern for purity. Furthermore, Orientalists have usually only translated the Hadith, that has already been scrutinized by Islamic scholars themselves, and not some of the hundreds of thousands of fantastic myths concerning the prophet.

Indeed, the well-respected ninth-century Muslim academic Imam Bukhari only published Hadith which he was certain of being factual. Yet it is these stories which are so comical that they give Monty Python a run for its money.

For example, in the Hadith it is said that Mohammad took a disliking to black dogs and ordered that every one of these unfortunate animals be killed; destroyed for being devils in disguise. The Qur'an, however, says nothing about canine demons.

It seems from the stories of Mohammad's life that he did not get on well with animals, and would often punish them as he would men. Indeed, the Prophet even stoned a monkey to death, accusing it of committing adultery.

Mohammad's punishment and killing of dogs and monkeys is curious considering his statement that when an animal is slaughtered it should be killed in the best way possible. Stoning to death, and for that matter being slowly bled for Halal meat, hardly seems the "best way" to be killed.

If you are a Muslim and you are about to issue a Fatwa ("religious verdict") upon me at this point, let me just remind you of Sura 16:93 before you pray for my death: "If Allah so willed he could make you all one people. But he leaves straying whom he pleases and guides whom he pleases."

I would therefore suggest that Allah has chosen to let me stray as a non-Muslim, and that the situation only concerns Allah and my good self. To interfere with God's will by seeking revenge on me would be to assume the will of God — not something for mortals to assume.

But seriously, can we really believe that Allah is the kind of god who creates men, women and children, in order to abandon them and punish them if they cannot find their way back to his side? Indeed, the Qur'an states that Allah created Jinn ("hidden ones") in order to do his bidding, but which will ultimately be destined for hell.

Why create a demon or a man simply to punish him? God surely cannot be that cruel, or bored! Such tales must only be the product of cruel men. I therefore submit this fact as evidence to prove the Qur'an was not created by divine authorship. Moreover, that God should receive an apology from

Muslims who believe that he is responsible for writing the nonsense in the Qur'an.

I also accuse Muslims of committing "Shirk," or attributing God as the author of books or holy teachings without good grounds to do so. Just as with the Torah and the Bible, the Qur'an was not written or dictated by God or his angels. The authors of such books were human, with human failings, customs, beliefs and cultural baggage. Three monotheistic religions, three gargantuan blunders.

One could also suggest that Sufi Muslims and Marabouts ignore the Islamic warning not to practice magic. Sufis engage in the mystical and philosophical aspect of Islam, the Arabic version of Zen or Yogic belief. Marabouts are wandering Muslim hermits of African origin who claim to have the power to heal and divine the future.

Another Muslim breach of Islamic law, which is labelled in the Qur'an as a prohibited activity, or "Haram," is drinking alcohol. Despite there being alcohol in Paradise, its "harm is greater than the benefit" (Qur'an 2:219). Thinking that the Qur'an did not give a great enough warning against alcohol, Mohammad stated that people who sell, transport, serve, store or buy alcohol were to be cursed by Allah himself. It is then a pity about all the poor Muslims who own corner shops that sell alcohol.

Other practices and activities which are deemed Haram or prohibited in Islam are the taking of drugs, gambling, going into business with non-Muslims and the playing of stringed instruments. So Muslim pop stars and musicians beware!

Aside from the alarming aspects of Islam in relation to punishment and war, the most frightening aspect of political power corrupted by religion in the twentieth century must lie in the bloody hands of Saddam Hussein. A veritable Majnun (madman) if ever there was one. Not only was the mass murdering megalomaniac a threat to the entire world, he made it quite clear that he was a devout Muslim and that Iraq was a paragon of Islamic civilization. Indeed, that he himself was a direct descendant from the prophet Mohammad.

Before we conclude this journey into the world of Islam let us review the case of Salman Rushdie as an example of how the world is still fearful of offending religion. In his book *The Satanic Verses*, Rushdie refers to Muslims as Mahounds (Mahun, Mahoun), a highly derogatory and Satanic term for both Mohammad and Muslims alike.

It was this description of Muslims that of course landed a Fatwa upon the author's head, sending him into hiding, lest he be brought to Iran to receive the punishment of execution. But in terms of freedom of speech Rushdie should be able to say anything he wants without fear of being murdered for it — we all should have that freedom. This is another reason why religion should be destroyed. However, Muslims missed the point of *The Satanic Vers-*

es somewhat.

The original "Satanic verses" are those found in the Qur'an, which pay respect to the pre-Islamic god-forms such as Manat, al-'Uzza and al-Lat, ancient gods mentioned by Mohammad to attract the pagan audience to his new religion. However, their reference is also "Satanic"—for it is believed that Satan put their names on Mohammad's lips, and that the prophet did not utter the names of the pagan gods himself. Therefore, anything which is of the Satanic Verses simply means that the Devil is responsible. Therefore Rushdie's book was a result of the Devil's handiwork, not the poor hunted author in question. A subtle point Rushdie undoubtedly wishes he had made himself.

Finally, although Islam is wrong about God in general, the philosophy of Sufi Muslims may be nearer to the truth than anything else which the religion has to offer. Sufis, "wool wearers," are regarded by both Sunni and Shiite Muslims as being on the very edge of their religion, and even as being blasphemous. This is due to the Sufi belief that if they vanquish their ego entirely they can become closer to God than simply by using prayer to do so.

Moreover, through the practice of Fanna ("annihilation"), or the ridding of one's feelings of "Self" and concern for one's surroundings or material goods from one's consciousness, Sufis can become at one with God. In other words, a Sufi recognizes that he is in fact God himself, and not an entity which exists outside of God. Sufis thus produce the controversial statement: "Praise to me, for my greatest glory," substituting the word "God" for "me" and "my." This is a profane statement to most Muslims.

An examination of the precise theological meaning of the commonly used Islamic statement, "There is no god, but Allah," may amaze most Muslims as to its close proximity to Sufi philosophy. The original Arabic for the aforementioned statement is "la ilaha illa'llah." In Arabic, this statement authors two possibilities. 1) That there is one god called Allah. Or 2) that there is another all-powerful being known as Allah, but whom is not a god.

The conundrum is further complicated by the statement, "Allahu akbar," or "Allah is great." Does this mean that Allah is powerful, but not a god? Or does it mean that Allah is a god, and in fact is everything in the universe, in a pantheistic context?

Therefore, if Muslims believe that there is a being known as Allah who resides in Paradise, they are limiting the spatial dimensions, and therefore power, of this being. However, if, as with Sufis, God is more than simply a being known as Allah, and is indeed everything, we too must be God.

Whilst I myself see the beauty of extreme Sufi philosophy, as it is relatively similar to pure Zen, I also must point out that Sufis are not entirely without flaw. Sufis have taken part in armed and bloody conflict with Russians in Chechnya and the Caucasus. Moreover, Chechnyan Sufis are also known for their brutal and barbaric acts of terrorism and kidnapping. Therefore, whilst the Sufi philosophy may be something to investigate further, the religious aspect is, like most other religions, welded to violence, politics and the concern for national boundaries.

Finally, before we move on to further insanity, we must ask Muslims a question. If the Qur'an is the revealed word of God, given to his prophet Mohammad, what are we expected to think of his previous "words" given to Moses and Christ, amongst others? Moreover, if the Qur'an is indeed the word of God, why did God wait so long to give it to us?

Furthermore, it seems that Muslims are on shaky ground if they believe the Qur'an to be the last of God's revelations. After all, if God changed his mind twice before about how he wanted humans to live, and exactly who would be his most cherished people on Earth, he could certainly change his mind in the future. Mormons would say that he already has!

– Rich Stanit
Excerpt from *Religion Must Die*, The Book Tree,
www.thebooktree.com

" *Theologies have never been gold — they create uneducated multitudes, eliminate a middle class, are historically anti-democratic — as a result make the ruling leaders richer and more unjustly powerful.* "

Tim C. Leedom

Dome of the Rock

The Dome of the Rock is one of the world's most famous and contentious sacred sites in the world. To the Moslems it is their third most sacred shrine. Abdal-Malik built the Dome in Jerusalem between 687 and 691. It is often referred to as the Mosque of Umar; although in actuality it is not a mosque.

The Dome is not just sacred to the Moslems, but also to the Jews and the Christians. Certain actual and mythological events regarding all three religions have been reported there. To Muslims, the Dome sits in the Noble Sanctuary, the same location that Jews and Christians refer to as the Temple Mount. It is sacred to the three faiths and is one of the most sought out places in Jerusalem.

In the legends of Islam, Mohammad ascended to heaven accompanied by the angel Gabriel, where he consulted with Moses and was given the new obligatory Islamic prayers before returning to earth. This story is rejected out of hand by Christian and Jews, much like the crucifixion and resurrection stories are rejected by the Moslems. A verse in the Koran states that Muhammad took a night journey from a sacred mosque to a far away mosque (al-Masjid al-Aqsa) which later in history has been identified with Jerusalem, although the Koran is silent on this detail.

Dome of the Rock, Jerusalem

Other similar stories are associated with the Dome of the Rock, but each religion has its own version. Abraham was supposedly instructed by god to take the life of his son…to the Moslems it was at the dome…to the Jews it was at Mount Moriah (also the site in Christian mythology of Jacob's ladder to heaven). Other ethnocentric stories by the Jews and Christians include the legend the fantasy that the rock of the dome was the site of the laying of the first cornerstone of the world.

Ironically located in Jerusalem, the city of peace, the dome has been the site and focal point of religious hatred and dogma for 2000 years. It was an important site for the crusaders and the Knights Templar who believed it to be near the ruins of King Solomon's Temple. During most of the twelveth century, the Catholic crusaders occupied the former Islamic mosque and used it as their headquarters. They called it the "Templum Domini" and it was from there where they eventually began to call themselves "Templar." Much of the Templar seals and architecture was blended into European Catholicism, which is still evident today.

Unfortunately, these romantic and unrealistic stories have been incorporated into today's political and religious landscape. The twenty-first century finds the Christians wanting to destroy the heretic Moslem's temple and rebuild their temple. This would fulfill their prophecy requirements, enabling Jesus to return to earth and bring eternal peace or Armageddon; depending on which sect of Christendom is weaving the story. The Jews want the temple moved to Mecca in Saudi Arabia, which will never happen without a total religious war that the Jews win outright.

A Seed in the Mind

All origins are obscure, the origins of religions even more so than others. The product of the most spontaneous instincts of human nature, religions do not recall their infancy any more than an adult remembers the history of his childhood and the successive stages of development of his consciousness; mysterious chrysalides, they appear in broad daylight only in the perfect maturity of their forms. It is the same with the origin of religions as with the origin of humanity. Science shows that on one particular day, in virtue of the natural laws that, up to now, had governed the development of things without exception and without external interference, the thinking being emerged, in full possession of all his faculties and complete in his essential elements — and yet, to try to explain how man appeared on earth by laws which govern the phenomena of our globe since nature has ceased to create, would be to open the door to such extravagant fancy, that not a single serious thinker would wish to give it a moment's thought.

– Ernst Renan
Originally published in *Revue des Deux-Mond*e, 1851

Ernest Renan, *a well respected historian, came to the conclusion that the existence of Mohammed is verified, putting to rest the Western doubts. He came to a less confident conclusion regarding the historicity of Jesus Christ.*

"

The problem with 'an eye for an eye' is that you end up with two blind people.

"

Mahatma Gandhi

"

In our research; we have found that most religionists, particularly Christians, are quick to point out that rival religions have their origins in the heavens. Their own is never connected with pagan worship. It springs solely from revelation or holy prophets.

"

Tim C. Leedom

Jewish Humanism

Jewish history is the saga of a vulnerable international family. It is the tale of its struggle to survive. What is worst in Jewish history is the surrender to faith and humility. What is best in Jewish experience is the discovery of reason and dignity.

So many historians of the Jewish people have devoted their attention to what Jews theoretically believe that they have been unable to focus on what they actually do. Monotheism can produce placid peasants just as easily as it can produce nervous intellectuals. Torah study can create rote memorizers just as easily as it can produce analytic thinkers

What is most interesting about the Jews is not a devotion to an invisible deity, who has his rivals in other traditions, and to moral platitudes, which are present in all cultures, but a personality style that deeply distrusts destiny and finds itself more comfortable with change than with eternity.

– Sherwin T. Wine
Excerpt from his essay "Jewish Humanism"

Jews for Jesus

The rivalry and hatred between Reformed, Orthodox, and Secular Jews pales in comparison to the disdain they all have for "Jews for Jesus"/ "Messianic Jews."

Jews for Jesus have enrolled Billy Graham's daughter, Anne Graham. She is proselyting Jews in Israel and the U.S. to come to the alter of Christ and recognize Jesus as the long awaited Messiah.

What is Zionism?

Zionism is the Jewish national movement of rebirth and renewal in the land of Israel — the historical birthplace of the Jewish people. The yearning to return to Zion, the biblical term for both the Land of Israel and Jerusalem, has been the cornerstone of Jewish religious life since the Jewish exile from the land two thousand years ago, and is embedded in Jewish prayer, ritual, literature and cultur

Modern Zionism emerged in the late nineteenth century in response to the violent persecution of Jews in Eastern Europe, anti-Semitism in Western Europe. Modern Zionism fused the ancient Jewish biblical and historical ties to the ancestral homeland with the modern concept of nationalism into a vision of establishing a modern Jewish state in the land of Israel.

The "father" of modern Zionism, Austrian journalist Theodor Herzl, consolidated various strands of Zionist thought into an organized political movement, advocating for international recognition of a "Jewish state" and encouraging Jewish immigration to build the land.

– Excerpt from the U.N. World Conference Against Racism:
Anti-Defamation League; www.adl.org

The Star of David

The Star of David originally appeared approximately 6,000 B.C. in the most ancient history of India as the symbol for the sun. Much later it was borrowed by the Semitic Cult of Saturn of ancient Jerusalem evolving into the Jewish Star of David.

Map of Palestine

History of Palestine
from 70 A.D.

The popular belief perpetuated by many Zionists is that they have a "deed from God" to the Holy City. The facts contradict this: Until 1948, when a guilt-ridden world established the State of Israel — on Arab land, they had had more absence then occupation from 70 A.D. There has not been peace ever since.

66-70 A.D.: A Jewish party called "The Zealots" led a rebellion against the Roman authorities. Jerusalem fell when Titus of Rome laid siege to the city. To seal his victory, Titus ordered the total destruction of the Herodian Temple. The Romans built a new city named Aelia over the ruins of Jerusalem, and erected a temple dedicated to Jupiter.

313: The Roman emperor Constantine I legalized Christianity. His mother, Helena, visited Jerusalem, making "The Holy Land" a focus of Christian pilgrimage. Most of the population became Hellenized and Christianized.

324: Constantine of Byzantium rebuilt the city walls and commissioned the Church of the Holy Sepulchre.

638: Muslim Arab armies invaded Palestine and captured Jerusalem. Al Aqsa mosque was built soon after. The Arab conquest began 1300 years of Muslim presence in what then became known as Filastin. After a century, the majority had converted to Islam. To the Muslims, the Christians and Jews who remained were considered People of the Book. They were allowed autonomous control in their communities and guaranteed security and freedom of worship.

1096: Pope Urban II launched the first crusade.

1099: The crusaders captured Jerusalem and slaughtered all of the Jews and the Muslims. Many of the Christians were also killed.

1187: Saladin took back Jerusalem.

1492: King Ferdinand and Queen Isabella of Spain order all the Jews to be either baptized or expelled. More than 150,000 Jews left and went to

Ottoman Turkey, The Balkans, and North Africa. Thousands remained, and converted to Christianity.

1516: The Ottoman Turks of Asia Minor took over Filastin, and ruled with few interruptions until the winter of 1917-18. The country was divided into several districts, such as that of Jerusalem.

1831-1840: Muhammad Ali, the modernizing viceroy of Egypt, expanded his rule to Palestine.

1840: The Ottoman Empire reasserted its authority, instituting its own reforms.

1862: Moses Hess published Rome and Jerusalem, one of the first Zionist books.

1882: Early Zionist communities were established in Filastin by Russian Jews fleeing pogroms. The first aliya began (a wave of Jewish immigration to the Holy Land).

1896: The Austrian journalist Theodor Herzl published The Jewish State, a pamphlet that argued for a Jewish state in the Holy Land or elsewhere.

1897: Herzl organized the first Zionist Congress in Basel, Switzerland.

1904: The second aliya began.

1914: World War I began.

1916: British and French leaders made the Sykes-Picot agreement, agreeing to carve up the Ottoman Empire after the war. Britain would get Palestine.

November 2, 1917: The British government issued The Balfour Declaration, endorsing a Jewish homeland in Palestine.

December 9, 1917: British General Edmund Allenby's army entered Jerusalem. Soon after, all of Palestine was under British control.

1919: The Versailles Peace Conference ended WWI and solidified The British and French control of the Middle East.

1919-23: The third aliya.

1920-21: Arabs began to riot against Jews in Hebron, Jerusalem and

Jaffa. Zionists organize militias.

1924-32: The fourth aliya.

1933-35: The fifth aliya.

1936-39: The Palestinians revolted. The British Peel Commission responded by recommending the partition of Palestine, with two-for Arabs and one-third for Jews.

1939-45: World War II.

1946: The British Government resisted increased Jewish immigration from Europe to Palestine. Irgun Zvai Leumi (The National Military Organization) responded with a terror campaign.

November 29, 1947: After the British gave up; The United Nations stepped in and voted to partition Palestine into two states. Fighting immediately ensued.

April 10, 1948: Irgun massacred Arab villagers at Deir Yassin. Palestinians fled their homes.

May 14, 1948: Britain's mandate expired. Israel was established. Five Arab armies, coming to the aid of the Palestinians, immediately attacked it. Uncoordinated and outnumbered, they were defeated by Israeli forces. Israel enlarged its territory. Jordan took the West Bank of the Jordan River, and Egypt took the Gaza Strip (Israel occupied these lands after the Six Day War of 1967). The war produced 780,000 Palestinian refugees. About half probably left out of fear and panic, while the rest were forced out to make room for Jewish immigrants from Europe and from the Arab world.

– Sources: *Understanding the Holy Land* by Mitch Frank;
"A Brief History of Palestine" essay by Esam Shashaa

Jews Against Zionism

These people who falsely claim to represent us, "the idol worshippers of the golden calf" of modern history the Zionist organizations of the lands of our exile, and in particular of the Zionist state, have caused a great deal of anguish and pain for Jews the world over.

The power of the media being such, that the voice of the weak and the Just are ignored, and the actions of the wicked and the powerful are widely proclaimed as the Just and Righteous, so we are forced to protect our good name in the eyes of the people's of the World, who have received us with open arms in our hour of the need, and those who have opened their lands to receive us in our exile.

I and my colleagues here today thank you for giving us the opportunity to explain what we as Orthodox Jews feel our duty as a religious people, to publicize this tragic misrepresentation. I hope and pray that with the Almighty's help my words come over loud and clear, to convince you all of our sincerity, in wishing to see a world of Peace and Tranquility for all Nations, and People.

It would perhaps help to try and understand what is Zionism, why do we speak out so strongly against it? Are they not Jews the same way as we, why are Jews fighting Jews?

Let us consider the origins of the Zionist movement. Founded over a 100 years ago, mostly by secular people who had discarded their religion but still could not rid themselves of what they considered the stigma of being Jews in exile. They thought that our state of exile was due to our own subservient attitude — "the exile mentality" — and not a Divine Decree. They wanted to throw off the constraints of exile establishing a new form of Jewish identity. Not religion based but land based. This was a typical, emotion driven, secular nationalistic view, similar to the aspirations of most other stateless nations. Their policy had as its centre pin the aim of setting up a Jewish State (preferably in Palestine), and they were forging a new kind of Jew. In fact not a Jew at all, but a Zionist.

Zionism was a complete abandonment of our religious teachings and faith — in general — and in particular an abandonment of our approach to our state of exile and our attitude to the peoples among whom we live.

The practical outcome of Zionism in the form of the state known as "Israel" is completely alien to Judaism and the Jewish Faith. The very name "Israel" which originally meant the Children of Israel i.e. the Jewish People was usurped by the Zionists. For this reason many orthodox Jews avoid referring to the Zionist State by the name "Israel."

Initially when Zionism reared its ugly head, all the Rabbi's in the lands of their exile spoke out in no uncertain terms, and warned against the dangers of such acts, both in terms of the heavenly punishment that would follow such action, as well as the futility of trying to contravene the heavenly decree.

Unfortunately these people who were devoid of any religious feeling neither cared about lives of their fellow Jews in the lands of their exile, nor have they shown any human feelings to their fellow men, having achieved if we can call it an achievement, their aims in setting up a state, the cost in life and property was not allowed to stands in their way. Be they the Jews from the ghettos of hell, who were used as political ammunition, or be they the Palestinian people in their hundreds of thousands who were forced to flee from their homes and livelihood.

How can any sane person support such an existence?

Neturei Karta was set up to combat this unjust state of affairs, Religious Jews have organized themselves in order to decry the lie that they have some sympathy or God forbid direct support for this anti-God state.

Most Orthodox Jews accept the Neturei Karta view, to the extent that they do not agree in principle to the existence of the Zionist State and would not "shed a tear" if it came to an end.

We have problem in that; the Zionists have made themselves to appear as the representatives and spokespeople of all Jews thus, with their actions, arousing animosity against the Jews. Those who harbor this animosity to Zionism are accused of anti-Semitism. However, what has to be made abundantly clear is that Zionism is not Judaism. Zionists cannot speak in the name of Jews. Zionists may have been born as Jews, but to be a Jew also requires adherence to the Jewish belief and religion. So what becomes abundantly clear is that opposition to Zionism and its crimes does not imply hatred of Jews or "anti-Semitism." On the contrary Zionism itself and its deeds are the biggest threat to Jews and Judaism.

The strife between Arab and Jew in Palestine only began when the first Zionist pioneers came to Palestine with the express aim of forming a State over the heads of the indigenous Arab population. That strife has continued until this very day and has cost and continues to cost thousands upon thousands of lives both of Jews and Muslims. The oppression, abuse and murder, in Palestine is a tragedy not only for the Palestinians but for the Jewish people as well. And is in fact part of the dire consequences of which we are warned if we transgress our religious requirement not to rebel against our exile.

I wish to add that the connection between Muslims and Jews goes right back into ancient history. Mostly the relationship was friendly and mutually beneficial. Historically, the situation frequently was that when Jews were being persecuted in Europe, they found refuge in the various Muslim countries. Our attitude to Muslims and Arabs can only be one of friendliness and respect.

I would like to finish with the following words, to the People of the World, and in particular to our Muslim neighbors, there is no hatred or animosity between Jew and Muslim or indeed any God-fearing people. We wish to live together as friends and neighbors as we have done mostly over hundreds even thousands of years in all the Arab countries. It was only the advent of the Zionists and Zionism which upset this age-old relationship.

> – Excerpts from a speech delivered by Mr. Yakov Konig: a spokesman for Neturei Karta UK; at the meeting on the crisis in the Middle East, March 30, 2004 at the House of Commons, London, England.

> *Neturei-Karta International is an organization of Jews against Zionism, www.nkusa.org*

"
Judaism and the Jewish Cult of Christianity ironically survived and expanded because of the Roman Empire, who suppressed and nearly exterminated them both. During the first 50 years of the cult, only Jews were allowed to be members of this sect.
"

Tim C. Leedom

Genocidal Depopulation:
The Deir Yassin Massacre

The massacre of Palestinians at a village called Deir Yassin (now renamed Givat Shaul Bet) was one of the most significant events in twentieth century history. It stands as one of the starkest and most pivotal initial tragedies in a genocidal depopulation affecting more than 400 Arab villages and cities and the expulsion of over 700,000 native Palestinians to make room for invading Jewish immigrants from all over the world.

On a beautiful spring day, when the skies of the Holy Land are a tender blue and the grass is a verdant green, air-conditioned buses ferry tourists from the City of the Plain to the City in the Mountains. A small distance past the halfway point, just beyond the reconstructed Ottoman inn of Babal-Wad, the Gate of the Valley, the bus drives by the red-painted skeletons of armored vehicles. This is where the tour guides make their routine pitch:

> These vehicles are in memory of the heroic breakthrough of Jews relieving the blockade of Jerusalem imposed by the aggression of nine Arab states.

The number of Arab states varies with the mood of the guide and how they size up their audience. The battle for the road to Jerusalem was a high point of the 1948 civil war in Palestine, and it ended with the Zionist Jews of the Plain capturing the prosperous West End of Jerusalem with its white stone mansions of Arab nobles and German, Greek and Armenian merchants. In the course of these battles they also subdued the neutral, non-Zionist Jewish neighborhoods. Zionists expelled the gentiles in a massive sweep of ethnic cleansing and contained the local Jews in the ghetto. In order to achieve this feat, they razed to the ground the Palestinian villages on their path to the city. The rusted junk is barely an adequate backdrop for the standard Israeli narration, and they would not qualify for a realistic film production. It is a staged scene that lacks the authentic look needed by movie directors. The story of the blockade and aggression is a theater play, not a cinema script. It is an encore performance for the tourist receiving indoctrination on the non-stop trip to the Wailing Wall and the Holocaust Museum.

The war for this road was over in April 1948, weeks before Israel declared independence on May 15, before the hapless ragtag units of Arab neighbors entered Palestine and saved what remained of the native population. As T.S. Eliot observed, April is the cruelest month. And so it was on that fateful April day when the Palestinians were doomed to start a journey to five decades of exile. Its apotheosis was reached near the entrance to Jerusalem, where the Sacharov Gardens lead to a cemetery, to a lunatic asylum, and to Deir Yassin.

Death has many names. For every Palestinian, it is "Deir Yassin." On the night of the ninth of April, 1948, the Jewish terrorist groups Etzel and Lehi attacked the peaceful village and massacred its men, women and children. I do not want to repeat the gory tale of sliced-off ears, gutted bellies, raped women, torched men, bodies dumped in stone quarries or the triumphal parade of the murderers. Existentially, all massacres are similar, from the Ludlow massacre to Deir Yassin.

Yet, the Deir Yassin massacre is special for three reasons. One, it is well documented and was witnessed. Other Jewish fighters from the Hagana and Palmach, Jewish scouts, Red Cross representatives and the British police of Jerusalem left complete records of the event. It was just one of many massacres of Palestinians by the Jews during the war of 1948, but none received as much attention. This is probably due to the fact that Jerusalem, the seat of the British Mandate in Palestine, was just around the corner.

Second, Deir Yassin had dire consequences beyond its own tragic fate. The horror of the massacre facilitated the mass flight from nearby Palestinian villages and gave the Jews full control over the western approaches to Jerusalem. The flight was a prudent and rational choice for the civilian population. As I write this, my TV glares with the image of Macedonian peasants fleeing a war zone. My mother's family escaped from a burning Minsk on June 22, 1941, and survived. My father's family remained and perished. After the war, my parents could return like other war refugees. The Palestinians, however, have not been allowed to come back, even to this very day.

The third reason the Deir Yassin massacre is special is the careers of the murderers. The commanders of the Etzel and Lehi gangs, Menachem Begin and Yitzhak Shamir, eventually became Israeli prime ministers. None of them expressed any remorse, and Begin lived the last days of his life with a panoramic view of Deir Yassin from his house. No Nuremberg judges, no vengeance, no penitence; just a path of roses all the way to a Nobel Peace prize. Begin was proud of the operation, and in his letter to the killers he congratulated them for fulfilling their national duty. "You are creators of Israel's history," he wrote.

Shamir was also pleased that it helped to achieve his dream: to expel the nochrim (non-Jews) from the Jewish state.

The field commander of the operation, Judah Lapidot, also had quite a career. His superior, Begin, appointed him to run the campaign for the right of Russian Jews to immigrate to Israel. He called for compassion and family reunion; he orchestrated the demonstrations in New York and London with that memorable slogan "Let My People Go." If you supported the right of Russian Jews to immigrate to Israel, maybe you came across this man. By then the blood stains of Deir Yassin had presumably washed off. For the political indoctrination of Russian immigrants, he even published a Russian-language version of *Oh Jerusalem*, a best-seller by Lapierre and Collins, expurgating the story of Deir Yassin.

But there is yet another reason why this event was historically significant. Deir Yassin demonstrated the full scope of Zionist tactics. After the mass murder be came known, the Jewish leadership blamed the Arabs. David Ben Gurion, the first prime minister of Israel, announced that the Arab rogue gangs perpetrated it. When this version collapsed, the Jewish leaders began the damage control procedures. They sent an apology to Emir Abdallah.

Ben Gurion publicly distanced himself and his government from the bloody massacre, saying it stained the name of every honest Jew and that it was the work of dissident terrorists. His public relations techniques remain a source of pride for the good-hearted pro-Zionist "liberals" abroad. "What a horrible, dreadful story," a humanist Jew told me when I drove him by the remaining houses of Deir Yassin. Then he added: "But Ben Gurion condemned the terrorists, and they were duly punished." "Yes," I responded, "they were duly punished and promoted to the highest government posts."

Just three days after the murder, the gangs were incorporated into the emerging Israeli army, the commanders received high positions, and a general amnesty forgave their crimes. The same pattern, an initial denial, followed by apologies, and a final act of clemency and promotion, was applied after the first historically verifiable atrocity committed by Prime Minister Sharon. It was at the Palestinian village of Qibya, where Sharon's unit dynamited houses with their inhabitants still in them and massacred some 60 men, women and children. After the murders became public, Prime Minister Ben Gurion, at first, blamed rogue Arab gangs. When that did not wash, he blamed "Arab Jews," who, he said, being Arabs by their mentality, committed the unauthorized wild raid of vengeance and killed the peasants.

For Sharon, it was the usual path of roses all the way to the post of prime minister. It sometimes appears that to become the prime minister of Israel, it helps to have a massacre to your name. The same pattern was repeated after the massacre of Kafr Kasem, where Israeli troops lined up the local peasants and machine-gunned them down. When the denial failed, and a communist MP disclosed the gory details, the perpetrators were court-martialed and sentenced to long prison terms.

They were out before the end of the year, while the commander of the murderers became the head of Israel bonds. If you ever purchased Israeli bonds, maybe you met him. I am certain he washed the blood off his hands by the time he shook yours. Now, with the passing of 50 years, the Jewish establishment has decided to, once again, take a stab at Deir Yassin revisionism. The Zionist Organization of America (ZOA) pioneered the art of denying history and published, at the expense of American taxpayers, a booklet called *Deir Yassin: History of a Lie*. The ZOA revisionists discount the eyewitness accounts of the survivors, the Red Cross, the British police, Jewish scouts and other Jewish observers who were present at the scene of the massacre. They discount even Ben Gurion's apology, since, after all, the commanders of these gangs became in turn prime ministers of the Jewish state.

For ZOA, only the testimony of the murderers has any validity. That is, if the murderers are Jews. Still, there are just people, and probably because of them the Almighty does not wipe us off the face of the earth. There is an organization called Deir Yassin Remembered, which fights all attempts to erase the memory of that massacre. They publish books, organize meetings, and are working on a project to build a memorial at the scene of the massacre, so the innocent victims will have this last comfort—their name and the memory saved forever (Isaiah 56:5). It will have to do, until the surviving sons of Deir Yassin and neighboring villages return from their refugee camps to the land of their fathers.

– Israel Shamir, essay from *The Barnes Review*

From The Press

Cared for, watched over & protected by God, or the U.S.? The main reason the U.S. is hated in the Arab world is its unequivocal support for the State of Israel and its various indefensible behavior – including the violation of at least 65 UN resolutions.

Since 1967, the U.S. has been the primary patron for Israel, and it has been for fear of alienating the United States that Israel has rejected the elimination of the Palestinian threat until now.

– George Friedman, www.foxnews.com

Seeing God behind all events is not necessary to explain what happens; human desire and natural laws do quite well. It is also potentially embarrassing. If Yahweh arranged for the exodus, he also arranged for the holocaust.

– Sherwin T. Wine

If you abandon Israel, God will never forgive you.

– Michael D. Evans, from *The American Prophecies*

Ever since its 1979 Islamic revolution the only fate Iran has had in mind for Israel has been simple: its destruction. Now that Teheran seems to be moving towards acquiring its own nuclear arsenal, its plans for its great enemy threaten to be both fiery and radioactive.

– Tim Butcher, *News Telegraph*

Jerusalem – Four years ago, Brother David moved into an apartment on the Mount of Olives to secure what he believes will be a front row seat for the return of Christ in 2000.

– Karin Laub, AP

Religion has ruined an otherwise peaceful city.

– George Carlin

Far-right activists took credit Thursday for the severe deterioration in Ariel Sharon's health, claiming that a pulsa denura — Aramaic for "lashes of fire" — death curse they instigated against the prime minister in July was the real catalyst behind his current state of health.

– Yaakov Katz, *Jerusalem Post*

A Jewish Defense League activist imprisoned for his role in a plot to bomb a California mosque and the office of a Lebanese-American congressman was killed at a federal prison in Phoenix, an FBI spokesman said Saturday.

– Alex Veiga, AP

Prime Minister of Israel Yitzhak Rabin was shot by Yigal Amir after addressing a peace rally at Tel Aviv's Kings of Israel Square.

Amir said, he acted "alone, but maybe with God."

– Tim C. Leedom

Hinduism

The oldest formal religion is Hinduism (2500 B.C.) which grew out of early paganism and stellar worship in the Indus River Valley, now modern day India. Its rituals, stories, heroes, and mythologies have been the basis for various forms of God worship in all of the major world religions including Taoism.

The first early variant evolved into Buddhism when Siddhartha Gautama, a Hindu in Nepal at the time became the Buddha. His break was brought on by his enlightenment and rejection of Hinduism's non-democratic caste system, which relegated many of the unwashed to a subsistent level for eternity. Buddhism spread throughout the world, but Hinduism for the most part stayed in India, Pakistan and immediate areas.

It is said that India has a million gods, which is most likely true. Organized Hinduism has five main icons. Brahma is the creator god; much like Yahweh of Judaism. Krishna is the eighth incarnation of Vishnu and the deity of the Bhagavad-Gita; the holy book, which is comparable to the new testament of Christianity. Vishnu is god the preserver and the third member of the Trimurti; much the same as the trinity that was forced on early Christianity by the Catholic Church in the fourth and fifth centuries. The other main Gods are Shiva and the Goddess Shakti. Reincarnation is a main tenet of Hinduism, as it is in all religions, particularly the eastern version of religions; Buddhism, Daoism, and Shintoism (the Japanese nationalistic version of Buddhism).

Of the icons of Hinduism, Krishna is probably the closest to an historical person, as the others are mystical, mythological gods much like the Roman, Egyptian and Greek gods of Zeus, Apollo, Hercules and Horus. Krishna's life has been compared with Jesus': a supposed virgin birth, being the savior of "mankind" if not just India, is step-fathered by a carpenter and in some conflicting accounts, even crucified.

Non-violence, idealistically is one of Hinduism's highest teachings, but throughout history has been a victim of nationalism and also self appointed and anointed prophets and leaders. Today the Hindu's main opponent for spiritual control are the Moslems, who they have fought for centuries, with thousands killed in the name of either Krsna or Allah. This different approach to God split India in the 1940s after a united peaceful revolution against the colonist empire of Great Britain. Ironically, the uniting inspirational leader of non-violence, Gandhi, was gunned down by a fellow Hindu in early January 1948 because of Gandhi's insistence that they live in peace as children of God.

Today there are over one billion Hindus, hardly united, with different warring sects taking center stage in different parts of the country. One of the offshoots is Sikhism which has now grown to 18 million; mostly in the Punjab area and has its main temple, Amstar. The sect's last guru, Gobind Singh was an establisher in the late 1600s A.D. He would be comparable to Joseph Smith of the Mormons, or the Bab (the gate) of the Bahai faith founded in the 1800s which is an off shoot of Shiite branch of Islam.

Hinduism is the official religion of the second most populous country in the world, India. The people have been victimized by a theocracy and an imposed religious caste system, no middle class, one of the highest infant mortality rates in the world, and one of the highest poverty rates on earth, all in the shadow of religious temples worth of 100s of billions of dollars. Gandhi's words of peace and his simple commandment, "be peaceful to all and feed thy children, for they are god's gift," have fallen on deaf ears for the most part.

Basic Information on Various Religions

RELIGION	DATE FOUNDED	SACRED TEXTS	MEMBERSHIP	WORLD PERCENTILE
Christianity	30 C.E.	The Bible	2,039 million	32 percent (dropping)
Islam	622 C.E.	Qu'ran, Hadith	1,226 million	19 percent (growing)
Hinduism	1,500 B.C.E. (very ancient roots)	Bhagavad-Gita, Upanishads, Rig Veda	828 million	13 percent (stable)
No religion	none	none	775 million	12 percent (dropping)
Chinese folk religion	270 B.C.E.	none	390 million	6 percent
Buddhism	523 B.C.E.	The Tripitaka, Sutras	364 million	6 percent (stable)
Tribal Religions, Shamanism, Animism	Prehistory	Oral tradition	232 million	4 percent
Aetheists	none	none	150 million	2 percent
New Religions	various	various	103 million	2 percent
Sikhism	1500 C.E.	Guru Granth Sahib	23.8 million	< 1 percent

RELIGION	DATE FOUNDED	SACRED TEXTS	MEMBERSHIP	WORLD PERCENTILE
Judaism	debated	Torah, Tanach, Talmud	14.5 million	< 1 percent
Spiritism	?	?	12.6 million	< 1 percent
Baha'i Faith	1863 C.E.	Alkitab Alaqdas	7.4 million	< 1 percent
Confucianism	520 B.C.E.	Lun Yu	6.3 million	< 1 percent
Jainism	570 B.C.E.	Siddhanta, Pakrit	4.3 million	< 1 percent
Zoroastrianism	600-6000 B.C.E.	Avesta	2.7 million	< 1 percent
Shinto	500 C.E.	Kojiki, Nohon Shoki	2.7 million	< 1 percent
Taoism	550 B.C.E.	Tao-te-Ching	2.7 million	< 1 percent
Other	various	various	1.1 million	< 1 percent
Wicca	800-B.C.E., 1940 C.E.	none	0.5 million?	< 1 percent

III

The Bible

> *The Christian Bible is a drugstore; its contents remain the same, but the medical practice changes.*
>
> Mark Twain

Bible Illiteracy

The Bible is the best-selling, least read and least understood book.

– Reverend Andy Dzurovcik, Faith Lutheran Church in Clark, New Jersey

About 92 percent of Americans own at least one bible and the average household has three. Two-thirds say it holds the answers to the basic questions of life.

Four Americans in five believe the Bible is the inspired word of God, and many of those who do not, still regard it as the basis for moral values and the rule of law.

Four in ten Americans say they would turn to the Bible first to test their own religious beliefs, while a solid one-third believe that "holding the Bible to be God's truth is absolutely essential for someone to truly know God."

Despite the large percentage of Americans who believe the Bible is the word of God, only one-third of Americans read it at least once a week. Another 12 percent read the Bible less than weekly, but at least once a month. More than half of all Americans read the Bible less than once a month, including 24 percent who say they never read it and 6 percent who can't recall the last time they read the Bible.

This lack of Bible-reading explains why Americans know so little about the Bible that is the basis of the faith of most of them. For example, eight in ten Americans say they are Christians, but only four in ten know that Jesus, according to the Bible, delivered the Sermon on the Mount. Many named Billy Graham as the sermon deliverer, not Jesus.

Fewer than half of all adults can name Matthew, Mark, Luke and John as the four Gospels of the New Testament, while many do not know that Jesus had twelve disciples or that he was born in Bethlehem. A large majority of Americans believe that the Ten Commandments are still valid rules for living today, but they have a tough time recalling exactly what those rules are.

Fewer than half of Americans can name the first book of the bible (Genesis).

Twelve percent of Christians think Noah's wife was Joan of Arc, while 80 percent of born-again Christians believe it is the bible that says, "God helps those who help themselves." Actually, Ben Franklin said that.

One-quarter do not know what is celebrated on Easter (The Resurrection, the foundational event of Christianity.) The decline in Bible-reading is due to many factors: the feeling that the Bible is inaccessible; the belief that it has little to say to today's world; a decline in reading in general and less emphasis on religious training.

A large majority (80 percent) say the Bible is confusing. But the most widely read contemporary translation, the New International Version, representing half of all bibles sold today, is written at a seventh-grade reading level. The percentage of people with a college education has more than tripled since 1935, but the level of biblical knowledge appears to have hardly budged.

Despite the publicity given to fundamentalist ministers and Televangelists in recent years, the proportion of Americans who are fundamentalists — that is, who believe that every word in the Bible is literally true — continues to decline. Only 31 percent of Americans believe the Bible is "the actual word of God and is taken literally, word for word," down from 34 percent in 1985. Americans revere the Bible but they don't read it. Because they don't read it, they have become a nation of biblical illiterates.

– Source: *The People's Religion* by George Gallup & Jem Castelli, Macmillan Publishing Co.; Barna Organization poll; and David Gibson, www.beliefnet.com.

Gideon Exposed

 The Gideon Society places Bibles in hotel rooms for your edification. Just who was Gideon? One would assume that he was a person of exemplary character and great worth to have a worldwide society named after him. Here are some of Gideon's accomplishments:

[a] Gideon slaughtered thousands in battle by plotting with the "Lord" to use treachery.
• Gideon murdered thousands more for worshipping "false Gods."
• Gideon tortured and killed still more for daring to taunt him.
• Gideon plundered the bodies of his victims (to fashion a jeweled priestly vestment).
• Gideon fathered an offspring who killed 69 of his stepbrothers.

Read the Bible for yourself. You will find the story of Gideon in Judges, chapters 6-9. The tale of Gideon is just one of many horror stories in the Bible, a book that glorifies behavior you abhor Millions of people have been hoodwinked by what their clergy and leaders have told them of the Bible. Make up your own mine about the Bible — read it for yourself.

The Age of Reason

It has been my intention, for several years past, to publish my thoughts upon Religion. I am well aware of the difficulties that attend the subject; and from that consideration, had reserved it to a more advanced period of life. I intended it to be the last offering I should make to my fellow-citizens of all nations; and that at a time when the purity of the motive that induced me to it could not admit of a question, even by those who might disapprove the work.

The circumstance that has now taken place in France of the total abolition of the whole national order of priesthood, and of everything appertaining to compulsive systems of religion, and compulsive articles of faith, has not only precipitated my intention, but rendered a work of this kind exceedingly necessary; lest, in the general wreck of superstition, of false systems of government and false theology, we lose sight of morality, of humanity and of the theology that is true.

As several of my colleagues, and others of my fellow-citizens of France, have given me the example of making their voluntary and individual profession of faith, I also will make mine; and I do this with all that sincerity and frankness with which the mind of man communicates with itself.

I believe in one God, and no more; and I hope for happiness beyond this life.

I believe in the equality of man, and I believe that religious duties consist in doing justice, loving mercy, and endeavoring to make our fellow creatures happy.

But, lest it should be supposed that I believe many other things in addition to these, I shall, in the progress of this work, declare the things I do not believe, and my reasons for not believing them.

I do not believe in the creed professed by the Jewish Church, by the Roman Church, by the Greek Church, by the Turkish Church, by the Protestant Church, nor by any church that I know of. My own mind is my own church. All national institutions of churches — whether Jewish, Christian or Turkish — appear to me no other than human inventions, set up to terrify and enslave mankind, and monopolize power and profit.

I do not mean to condemn those who believe otherwise. They have the same right to their belief as I have to mine. But it is necessary to the happiness of man that he be mentally faithful to himself. Infidelity does not consist in believing, or in disbelieving; it consists in professing to believe what he does not believe.

It is impossible to calculate the moral mischief, if I may so express it, that mental lying has produced in society. When a man has so far corrupted and prostituted the chastity of his mind as to subscribe his professional belief to things he does not believe, he has prepared himself for the commission of every other crime. He takes up the trade of a priest for the sake of gain, and in order to qualify himself for that trade, he begins with a perjury. Can we conceive any thing more destructive to morality than this?

Soon after I had published the pamphlet "Common Sense," in America, I saw the exceeding probability that a revolution in the system of government would be followed by a revolution in the system of religion. The adulterous connection of church and state, wherever it has taken place — whether Jewish, Christian or Turkish — has so effectually prohibited by pains and penalties every discussion upon established creeds, and upon first principles of religion, that until the system of government should be changed, those subjects could not be brought fairly and openly before the world,

Thomas Paine

but that whenever this should be done, a revolution in the system of religion would follow. Human inventions and priestcraft would be detected, and man would return to the pure, unmixed and unadulterated belief of one God, and no more.

Every national church or religion has established itself by pretending some special mission from God, communicated to certain individuals. The Jews have their Moses; the Christians their Jesus Christ, their apostles and saints; and the Turks their Mahomet — as if the way to God was not open to every man alike.

Each of those churches show certain books, which they call revelation, or the word of God. The Jews say that their word of God was given by God to Moses, face to face; the Christians say that their word of God came by divine inspiration; and the Turks say that their Word of God (the Koran) was brought by an angel from heaven. Each of those churches accuses the other of unbelief; and for my own part, I disbelieve them all.

As it is necessary to affix right ideas to words, I will, before I proceed further into the subject, offer some observations on the word revelation. Revelation, when applied to religion, means something communicated immediately from God to man.

No one will deny or dispute the power of the Almighty to make such a communication, if He pleases. But admitting, for the sake of a case, that something has been revealed to a certain person, and not revealed to any other person, it is revelation to that person only. When he tells it to a second person, a second to a third, a third to a fourth, and so on, it ceases to be a revelation to all those persons. It is revelation to the first person only, and hearsay to every other, and consequently they are not obliged to believe it.

It is a contradiction in terms and ideas, to call anything a revelation that comes to us at second-hand, either verbally or in writing. Revelation is necessarily limited to the first communication — after this it is only an account of something which that person says was a revelation made to him; and though he may find himself obliged to believe it, it cannot be incumbent on me to believe it in the same manner, for it was not a revelation made to me, and I have only his word for it that it was made to him.

When Moses told the children of Israel that he received the two tablets of the commandments from the hand of God, they were not obliged to believe him, because they had no other authority for it than his telling them so; and I have no other authority for it than some historian telling me so. The commandments carry no internal evidence of divinity with them; they contain some good moral precepts, such as any man qualified to be a lawgiver, or a legislator, could produce himself, without having recourse to supernatural intervention.

When I am told that the Koran was written in heaven and brought to Mahomet by an angel, this comes too near the same kind of hearsay evidence and second-hand authority as the former. I did not see the angel myself and, therefore, I have a right not to believe it.

When also I am told that a woman called the Virgin Mary, said, or gave out, that she was with child without any cohabitation with a man, and that her betrothed husband, Joseph, said that an angel told him so, I have a right to believe them or not; such a circumstance required a much stronger evidence than their bare word for it; but we have not even this — for neither Joseph nor Mary wrote any such matter themselves; it is only reported by others that they said so. It is hearsay upon hearsay, and I do not choose to rest my belief upon such evidence.

It is curious to observe how the theory of what is called the Christian Church sprung out of the tail of the heathen mythology. A direct incorporation took place in the first instance, by making the reputed founder to be celestially begotten. The trinity of gods that then followed was no other than a reduction of the former plurality, which was about twenty or thirty thousand — the statue of Mary succeeded the statue of Diana of Ephesus. The deification of heroes changed into the canonization of saints. The mythologists had gods for everything; the Christian mythologists had saints for everything; the Church became as crowded with the one as the Pantheon had been with the other, and Rome was the place of both. The Christian theory is little else than the idolatry of the ancient mythologists, accommodated to the purposes of power and revenue; and it yet remains to reason and philosophy to abolish the amphibious fraud.

Nothing that is here said can apply, even with the most distant disrespect, to the real character of Jesus Christ. He was a virtuous and an amiable man. The morality that he preached and practiced was of the most benevolent kind; and though similar systems of morality had been preached by Confucius, and by some of the Greek philosophers, many years before; by the Quakers since; and by many good men in all ages, it has not been exceeded by any.

Jesus Christ wrote no account of himself, of his birth, parentage, or anything else. Not a line of what is called the New Testament is of his writing. The history of him is altogether the work of other people; and as to the account given of his resurrection and ascension, it was the necessary counterpart to the story of his birth. His historians, having brought him into the world in a supernatural manner, were obliged to take him out again in the same manner, or the first part of the story must have fallen to the ground.

The resurrection and ascension, supposing them to have taken place, admitted of public and ocular demonstration, like that of the ascension of a balloon, or the sun at noon-day, to all Jerusalem at least. A thing which everybody is required to believe, requires that the proof and evidence of it should be equal to all, and universal; and as the public visibility of this last related act was the only evidence that could give sanction to the former part, the whole of it falls to the ground, because that evidence never was given. Instead of this, a small number of persons, not more than eight or nine, are introduced as proxies for the whole world to say they saw it, and all the rest of the world are called upon to believe it. But it appears that Thomas did not believe the resurrection, and, as they say, would not believe without having ocular and manual demonstration himself. So neither will I, and the reason is equally as good for me, and for every other person, as for Thomas.

The best surviving evidence we now have respecting this affair is the Jews. They are regularly descended from the people who lived in the times this resurrection and ascension is said to have happened, and they say, it is not true. It has long appeared to me a strange inconsistency to cite the Jews as a proof of the truth of the story. It is just the same as if a man were to say, I will prove the truth of what I have told you by producing the people who say it is false.

That such a person as Jesus Christ existed, and that he was crucified - which was the mode of execution at that day — are historical relations strictly within the limits of probability. He preached most excellent morality, and the equality of man; but he preached also against the corruptions and avarice of the Jewish priests, and this brought upon him the hatred and vengeance of the whole order of priesthood. The accusation which those priests brought against him was that of sedition and conspiracy against the Roman government, to which the Jews were then subject and tributary; and it is not improbable that the Roman government might have some secret apprehensions of the effects of his doctrine, as well as the Jewish priests. Between the two, this virtuous reformer and revolutionist lost his life.

But if objects for gratitude and admiration are our desire, do they not present themselves every hour to our eyes? Do we not see a fair creation prepared to receive us the instant we are born — a world furnished to our hands, that cost us nothing? Is it we that light up the sun, that pour down the rain, and fill the earth with abundance? Whether we sleep or wake, the vast machinery of the universe still goes on.

I know that this bold investigation will alarm many, but it would be paying too great a compliment to their credulity to forbear it upon that account; the times and the subject demand it to be done. The suspicion that the theory of what is called the Christian Church is fabulous is becoming very extensive in all countries; and it will be a consolation to men staggering under that suspicion, and doubting what to believe and what to disbelieve, to see the object freely investigated.

When the Church mythologists established their system, they collected all the writings they could find and managed them as they pleased. It is a matter altogether of uncertainty to us whether such of the writings as now appear under the name of the Old and New Testaments are in the same state in which those collectors say they found them, or whether they added, altered, abridged or dressed them up.

Be this as it may, they decided by vote which of the books out of the collection they had made should be the Word Of God, and which should not. They rejected several; they voted others to be doubtful, such as the books called the Apocrypha; and those books which had a majority of votes were voted to be the Word of God. Had they voted otherwise, all the people, since calling themselves Christians, had believed otherwise — for the belief of the one comes from the vote of the other. Who the people were that did all this, we know nothing of; they called themselves by the general name of the Church, and this is all we know of the matter.

When Samson ran off with the gate-posts of Gaza, if he ever did so (and whether he did or not is nothing to us), or when he visited his Delilah, or caught his foxes, or did anything else, what has revelation to do with these things? If they were facts, he could tell them himself, or his secretary, if he kept one, could write them, if they were worth either telling or writing; and if they were fictions, revelation could not make them true; and whether true or not, we are neither the better nor the wiser for knowing them. When we contemplate the immensity of that Being who directs and governs the incomprehensible whole, of which the utmost ken of human sight can discover but a part, we ought to feel shame at calling such paltry stories the Word of God.

– Thomas Paine, political writer, statesman and author of *Common Sense*,
The Declaration of Independence, *Rights of Man* and *The Age of Reason*.

" *The Bible was written and put together by human beings doing the best they knew how.* "

A Humanist

A Brief History of the English Bible

The "Englishing" of Scripture has a long and fascinating history involving both religious and governmental politics. The term "Englishing" was coined when so many different English versions of the Bible were appearing in the British Isles culminating with the Authorized Version of Scripture better known in America as the King James Version of 1611. This article is a condensed accounting of the origin of our English Bible versions. It was originally written in response to and based upon questions I was asked about our English Bible versions during my lectures throughout the United States and Canada.

Christianity and Great Britain

The greatest obstacle to an early English translation of the Bible was the mixing and blending of languages on the isles of Britain. Christianity entered Great Britain sometime in the latter half of the second century. However, it did not take root until three or four centuries later. Ireland became the rich, fertile ground for the growth and expansion of the Christian church. Its progress in the Emerald Isle was so steady that by the sixth century Christianity had spread into Scotland and northern England. During this period of history few could read or write. It was the intense preaching of the gospel by the educated monks and their students that brought about the extension of Christianity throughout Britain.

At that particular time the language of the church's worship was Latin and its version of the Scriptures was also in Latin — the Old Latin MSS. (Old Latin was a translation from the Septuagint Greek Scriptures of the Old Testament and not from Hebrew. The New Testament was based on various Greek versions.) Jerome (342–420) had been commissioned by Pope Damasus in 382 to revise the Old Latin version of the gospels. He used a Greek MS as the basis of his revision but did not complete the rest of the New Testament. When Jerome revised the Old Testament he began with the Psalms. Further work on the other books of the Old Testament was based on Hebrew texts and was a direct translation. The work was completed around the latter part of the fourth century. This version, known as the Vulgate, was widely used in the West, and its original intent was to end the great differences of text in the

Old Latin MSS. As the Vulgate superseded the Old Latin version, the latter lost its authority in the church. Remember, it was the educated monks who interpreted the Latin Bible in the tongues and dialects of their listeners.

Early English Manuscripts

In the middle of the seventh century the earliest beginning of an English Bible (if one could call it such) made its appearance. Bede (673–735), the great Anglo-Saxon biblical scholar and "Father of English History," was the first known individual to render certain biblical subjects into the Anglo-Saxon tongue beginning with the creation story.

In South England there was a zealous monk by the name of Aldhelm, Abbot of Malmesbury who was also an outstanding musician. According to English historians, Aldhelm became the first bishop of Sherborne and the first known translator of the Psalms into Anglo-Saxon English. We are told that the people of South England received their religious instruction through popular poetry attuned to the harp of Aldhelm. This shrewd official observed that the usual sermon had little attraction for the ordinary run of Englishmen. Being a skillful musician, he put on the garb of a minstrel and took up a position on a bridge over which many people were obliged to pass. His artistic playing soon attracted a group of listeners. As soon as he had thus collected an audience he gave his music and words a religious turn, and by the strains of his splendid instrument and the persuasive form of his attractive language won many to Christianity (*The Ancestry Of Our English Bible*, Price, p. 226).

Then there appeared Richard Rolle of Hampole (1300–1349) who translated the Psalms into Middle English and wrote commentaries on the same. He was known as a hermit and mystic. About that same time the biblical works of William of Shoreham became popular. "The spread of the Shoreham-Rolle versions of the Psalter was the beginning of the triumph of the English language proper." It was these two translations of the Psalms that initiated a strong craving throughout Great Britain for more translations of the Bible.

Vernacular Translations Forbidden

It should be noted that Pope Innocent III, in 1199, had declared the following,

> The secret mysteries of the faith ought not to be explained to all men in all places, since they cannot be everywhere understood by all men.

Also Pope Gregory VII stated,

Not without reason has it pleased Almighty God that Holy Scripture should be a secret in certain places, lest, it were plainly apparent to all men, perchance it would be little esteemed and be subject to disrespect; or it might be falsely understood by those of mediocre learning and lead to error.

But despite these declarations of Ecclesiastical powers, translation of Scripture could not be stopped. Men desired to drink of the fountains of knowledge that had been hidden from them by those in authority.

The Wycliffe Version

In the fourteenth century, a period of great political and sociological transition and ecclesiastical controversies, John Wycliffe, scholar and lecturer at Oxford, translated the Bible from Latin into English. The New Testament was translated about 1380; and in 1382 the entire Bible was finished. Other scholars under the direction of Wycliffe worked on the translation of the Old Testament. In fact most of the work of the Old Testament was translated by his devoted disciples and co-workers. Wycliffe died two years after the completion of the Bible in 1382. His translation was stilted and mechanical. The language of his work, a Midland dialect, did not represent the central strand of development in English. Wycliffe's version needed revision, and it was undertaken not long after his death.

The Response

What was the reaction of the religious world? What did church authorities have to say? Archbishop Arundel in 1412, when writing the Pope concerning Wycliffe said,

…that wretched and pestilent fellow of damnable memory, the very herald and child of anti-Christ, who crowned his wickedness by translating the Scriptures into the mother tongue.

A provincial council at Oxford early in the fifteenth century stated,

No one shall in the future translate on his own authority any text of Holy Scriptures into the English tongue—nor shall any man read this kind of book, booklet or treatise, now recently composed in the time of the said John Wycliffe or later, or any that shall be composed in the future, in whole or part, publicly or secretly under penalty of the greater Excommunication.

Did this decree put out the flaming desire to see the light of Scripture translated into the common tongue of English? No!

The Renaissance

The fifteenth century, the great epoch of awakening, witnessed the Renaissance. Its first powerful stirrings occurred in Italy under the guidance of certain freethinkers and writers of that country. No one was able to hold back the tide of change and the profound forces at work in the culture of Europe. The church also was impacted by these powerful forces. There was another translator by the name of William Tyndale (1494?–1536) who, because of persecution in England, had to cross over to the Continent to translate the Bible into English.

Tyndale was a Greek scholar and had access to the Greek text of Erasmus and other biblical writings which Wycliffe did not possess. He was martyred before he completed the Old Testament, and there was much blood shed by religious powers in the ensuing days. But, because of the "new birth movement" of that age the Ecclesiastical walls of ignorance and fear could not hold back the rising flood of translations of the Bible into English.

Next came Miles Coverdale (1488–1568), a friend of Tyndale. This version was based on Tyndale's translation of Scripture with some help from the Latin text and other versions. Then the *Matthew's Bible* made its appearance. This version was based on the work of Tyndale and Coverdale, that is, it was a revision of the work of Tyndale, pieced out with Tyndale's unpublished MSS and portions of the Coverdale's Old Testament. The editor of this version was John Rogers (1500–1555). He was the first British Protestant Martyr under Queen Mary. In 1537 under the name of Thomas Matthew, he published the first complete version of the Bible in English.

In 1539, the *Great Bible* made its showing and was based upon the Matthew, Coverdale and Tyndale translations. This Bible won out among all the other translations and was "appointed to the use of the Churches." For nearly 30 years (except in the reign of Queen Mary) it was the only version that could lawfully be used in England. It is very important to remember the name of this Bible because the *King James Version* derived its "translation" not only from the *Great Bible* but, as you will see, from the *Bishops' Bible* as well.

The Counter Reformation

The Counter Reformation began to take hold in England under Queen Mary, and many Protestant scholars took refuge in Geneva. Thus, in 1560, the Geneva version of the Bible came into existence. This translation was a revision of the *Great Bible* and was based on other English reworked versions of Scripture. It is interesting to know that the Geneva Bible was the English translation which the Puritans brought with them to America.

The notes and annotations in the *Geneva Bible* were strongly Protestant and leaned heavily toward Calvinism. (John Calvin, 1509–1564, French reformer and theologian, was also thought of, by certain individuals, as a "theocratic tyrant." Calvinism: the theological system formulated by John Calvin. He strongly advocated the absolute authority of the Bible, that the State must be subject to the Church, and many other biblical doctrinal beliefs.)

Shakespeare quoted the *Geneva Bible* in his works. It was after meditation on the Geneva translation that John Bunyan wrote his famous Pilgrims' Progress. The Geneva version of the Bible became very popular. The Archbishop of Canterbury, along with other bishops during the reign of Queen Elizabeth, decided to make a revision of the *Great Bible* of 1539. The decision was prompted by the popularity of the *Geneva Bible*. This "new" translation or revision was called the *Bishops' Bible* of 1568.

The Authorized Version

James Stuart of Scotland, since 1603 King of England, ordered that a new "revision" be made of the *Bishops' Bible*. Remember, the *Bishops' Bible* is a revision of the *Great Bible* which was based on other English translations and revisions. This work was immediately begun by 47 scholars under the authorization of King James.

In 1611 the new version was published. Although the title page described it as "newly translated out of the original tongues," the statement is not entirely in accord with the facts. The work was actually a revision of the *Bishops' Bible* on the basis of the Hebrew and Greek. It did not win immediate universal acceptance, taking almost 50 years to displace the *Geneva Bible* in popular favor. In other words, the KJV was a revision of the Bible based on the *Bishops' Bible* which was a revision of the *Great Bible*, the *Great Bible* being based on the Matthew, Coverdale and Tyndale Bibles.

The Deluge of English Versions

The nineteenth and twentieth centuries have brought many more translations of Scriptures such as the *Revised Standard* version, the *American Standard* version, the *New English Bible*, TANAKH—The Holy Scriptures, The New JPS translation according to the traditional Hebrew Text, *The New American Bible*, the Amplified, Weymouth, Moffatt, the Wuest expanded version and many others too numerous to mention.

Most of the English versions of Scripture of the twentieth century are translated works from Greek and Hebrew. Old Testament translations into English are usually based on the Hebrew tenth-century Massoretic text. This text was named after the Massoretes, Jewish grammarians who worked on the Hebrew text between the sixth and tenth centuries. (There is a Greek rendering of the Hebrew text known as the Septuagint and it has been translated into English from the Greek text of the fifth century C.E.)

New Testament English translations are usually based on various Greek texts and versions. However, in 1957 there appeared for the first time a translation of Old and New Testaments into English from the Aramaic, Semitic Peshitta Texts (fifth and sixth centuries), also known as the Lamsa translation. The translator, Dr. George M. Lamsa, claimed there are about ten to twelve thousand outstanding differences between these Aramaic Peshitta manuscripts and those of the Hebrew and Greek texts of the Bible.

Our Modern World

In the last sixty years, and especially in the last three decades, significant changes have taken place in the field of biblical scholarship. New methodologies for interpreting and translating Scripture are being employed. These modern and current sociological and historical methods provide us with the necessary tools to carefully analyze the social and historical contexts of biblical narratives. The present research and scholarship draws on biblical and extra-biblical evidence to help us understand the people of the Bible, their world and their faith. There is an ongoing explosion of pertinent information in the fields of religion, philology, sociology, archaeology and ancient history which has uncovered the early world of Mesopotamia and the basic social and religious structure of first-century Palestine.

Our present knowledge of Aramaic and Hebrew usage of words, idioms and special religious and philosophical terminology has clarified many obscure passages of Scripture. Discovery and work on the Dead Sea Scrolls has aided biblical scholarship in its perception and presentation of the overall Jewish background of the times and will continue to yield more information. (The Dead Sea Scrolls were hidden in desert caves by Jews as they fled Roman soldiers in 68 C.E.)

Today, in the Western world, there is a greater comprehensive knowledge of Eastern people culturally and psychologically than in the past. Many native-born Near Eastern authors have helped us realize the unique thought patterns of their people, their customs and mannerisms which are so distinct from ours. As our understanding of the Near Eastern world increases, especially of biblical days, so will our English translations of the Bible reflect our new comprehension.

– Rocco A. Errico, Ph.D.

Rocco Errico is a lecturer, author, ordained minister, and Bible scholar whose approach emphasizes Eastern sources and customs, especially the Aramaic language.

Inspired Words of God

Question: Can a document, tampered with by kings, tyrants, fools and scholars be the "true" inspired words of God?

The Revised Standard Version of the Bible, published in 1952, is an authorized revision of the American Standard Version, published in 1901, which was a revision of the King James Version, published in 1611.

The following are all inspired versions of the New Testament, many with glaring contradictions. These do not include the many versions of the Bible itself.

- The New Testament of Our Lord and Savior Jesus Christ, American Bible Union Version (John A. Broadus et al)
- The New Testament (Henry Alford)
- Good News for Modern Man
- The New Testament in Basic English
- The New Testament in the Language of Today (Wm. F. Beck)
- The Berkeley Version of the New Testament (Gerrit Verkuyl)
- The New Testament: An American Translation (Edgar J. Goodspeed)
- The New Testament in the Translation of Monsignor Ronald Knox
- The New Testament According to the Eastern Texts (George M. Lamsa)
- The New Testament: A New Translation (James Moffatt)
- The Centenary Translation: The New Testament in Modern English (Helen Barrett Montgomery)
- The New American Standard Bible: New Testament
- The New English Bible: New Testament
- The New Testament: A New Translation (Olaf M. Norlie)
- The New Testament in Modern English (J.B. Phillips)
- The Emphasized New Testament: A New Translation (J.B. Rotherham)
- The Twentieth Century New Testament
- The New Testament in Modern Speech (Richard F. Weymouth)
- The New Testament: A Translation in the Language of the People (Charles B. Williams)

Nonexistent Prophecies:
A Problem for Bible Inerrancy

Any challenge to the integrity of the Bible will very likely draw the familiar prophecy-fulfillment response. "If the Bible is not inspired of God," Christian fundamentalists will ask, "how do you explain all of the prophecies that Jesus fulfilled?" The answer to this question is quite simple. The so-called prophecy fulfillments that the New Testament writers claimed in the person and deeds of Jesus of Nazareth were prophecy fulfillments only in the fertile imagination of the writers. The famous virgin-birth prophecy (Isaiah 7:14 and Matt. 1:23), the prophecy of the messiah's birth in Bethlehem (Micah 5:2 and Matt. 2:6), the prophecy of King Herod's slaughter of the children of Bethlehem (Jere. 31:15 and Matt. 2:18) — these and many like them became prophecy fulfillments only through the distortions and misapplications of the original Old Testament statements.

To discuss these in depth would require an entire book, so instead I will concentrate on another aspect of the prophecy-fulfillment argument: New Testament claims of prophecy fulfillment for which no Old Testament sources can be found. An example would be John 7:37-38, where Jesus allegedly said, "If anyone thirsts, let him come to me and drink He who believes in me, as the Scripture has said, Out of his heart will flow rivers of living water." At that time, the only scriptures were the Old Testament, yet try as they have, Bible inerrantists have never found this statement that Jesus said was in the scriptures of his day. The prophecy was nonexistent.

Similar to this is a "prophecy fulfillment" that was referred to in Matthew 2:23. Here it was claimed that when Joseph took his family to Nazareth, he fulfilled that "which was spoken by the prophets, 'He [Jesus] shall be called a Nazarene.'" In all of the Old Testament, however, neither the word Nazareth nor Nazarene is even mentioned, so how could it be true that the prophets (plural) had predicted that the messiah would be called a Nazarene? To avoid admitting that a mistake was made, inerrantists point out that Matthew did not say that this prophecy had been written; he said only that it had been "spoken" by the prophets.

A weakness in this "explanation" is the fact that Matthew routinely introduced alleged prophecy fulfillments by saying that thus-and-so had been "spoken" by the prophets. He claimed, for example, that the preaching of John the Baptist fulfilled what had been "spoken" by Isaiah the prophet: "The voice of one crying in the wilderness, Make ye ready the way of the Lord,

Make his paths straight" (2:3). However, this statement that Matthew said Isaiah had spoken is a quotation of what had been written in Isaiah 40:3.

Other written "prophecies" that Matthew introduced by saying that they had been "spoken" can be found in 4:14-16 (Isaiah 9:1-2), 12:17-21 (Isaiah 42:1-4), 13:35 (Psalm 78:2), and 21:4-5 (Zechariah 9:9). Since all of these alleged prophecy statements can be found written in the Old Testament, we can only assume that Matthew's style was to use the word spoken to introduce statements that had in fact been written. Undoubtedly, he intended the expression to mean the same thing in 2:23 as it did elsewhere when he referred to things that had been "spoken" by the prophets. Hence, he made a mistake in 2:23, because no prophet (much less prophets) had ever written anything about Nazareth or Nazarenes.

In telling the story of Judas's suicide, Matthew erred again in claiming that Jeremiah had prophesied about the purchase of the field where Judas was buried. After casting down in the sanctuary the thirty pieces of silver that he had been paid for betraying Jesus, Judas went away and hanged himself.

The priests then took the money and bought the potter's field to bury Judas in. Matthew claimed that this was a prophecy fulfillment: "Then was fulfilled that which was spoken through Jeremiah the prophet, saying, And they took the thirty pieces of silver, the price of him that was priced, whom certain of the children of Israel did price; and they gave them for the potter's field, as the Lord appointed me" (27:9-10). In reality, however, no statement like this can be found in the book of Jeremiah. Inerrantists will sometimes defend Matthew by referring to Zechariah 11:12-13, which makes mention of thirty pieces of silver but in a context entirely different from the statement that Matthew "quoted." Besides, even if Zechariah had obviously written the statement that Matthew quoted, this would hardly acquit Matthew of error, because he said that Jeremiah, not Zechariah, had made the prophecy.

A more serious nonexistent prophecy concerns the very foundation of Christianity. On the night of his alleged resurrection, Jesus said to his disciples, "Thus it is written, that the Christ should suffer, and rise again from the dead the third day" (Luke 24:46). The Apostle Paul agreed with this claim that the scriptures had referred to a third-day resurrection of the messiah: 'Tor I delivered unto you first of all that which also I received: that Christ died for our sins according to the scriptures; and that he was buried; and that he hath been raised on the third day according to the scriptures" (1 Cor. 15:4-5).

Two New Testament writers, then, claimed that the scriptures had spoken of a resurrection of the messiah on the third day. The problem that this claim poses for the prophecy-fulfillment argument is that no one can cite a single Old Testament scripture that mentions a third-day resurrection. As a matter of fact, no one can even cite an Old Testament scripture that clearly and undeniably refers to a resurrection of the messiah, period, but that is another article for another time.

There are other major weaknesses in the prophecy-fulfillment argument, but the fact that New Testament writers so often referred to prophetic utterances that can't even be found in the Old Testament is enough to cast serious doubt on their many claims of prophecy fulfillment. If they were wrong when they referred to prophetic statements that cannot be found anywhere in the Old Testament, how can we know they were right when they claimed fulfillment of statements that can be found? The truth is that we can't.

– Farrell Till

Farrell Till is the editor of The Skeptical Review, a journal of Bible criticism, and is engaged informal, organized debates, both written and verbal, with Biblical inerrantists.

Prayer

We will pray that God take the lives of these Hitler-like men from the face of the earth.
> – Rev. R.L. Hymers, Pastor, Fundamentalist Baptist Tabernacle of Los Angeles, praying for the deaths of Justice William Brennanand four other Justices, 1986.

We all pray to god...we asked him to tell us who our enemies are...He said the atheists, secular humanists and sinners.
> – Dr. Robert Schuller, relating results of Joint Prayer Session of Churches Uniting for Global Mission Trinity Broadcasting Network, Spring 1992

O Lord our God...thou who art love and compassion...help us to tear their soldiers to bloody shreds...help us to drown the thunder of the guns with the shrieks of their wounded...writhing in pain...O Thou who art love and compassion...help us to wring the heart of the widows with unavailing grief.

O Thou who art love...be with us as we water their way with tears and stain the white snow with the blood of their children. We ask it...in the spirit of love...of Him, who is the source of love...Amen.
> – Mark Twain

Hands that help are better far than lips that pray.
> – Robert Green Ingersoll

And when thou prayest, thou shaft not be as the hypocrites are: for they love to pray standing in the synagogues and in the comers of the streets, that they may be seen of men. Verily I say unto you, they have their reward. But thou, when thou prayest, enter into thy closet, and when thou hast shut thy door, pray to thy Father which is in secret; and thy Father which is in secret shall reward thee openly.
> – Jesus Christ (Matt. 6:5,6)

Noah's Flood as Composite Literature

Before we examine the Noah's ark story, we should locate the real problem and bring it out into the open. The basic problem is not the interpretation of archaeological, geological, or literary evidence, but rather, the interpretation of the Bible. It is the fundamentalist approach to the Bible that is the fundamental problem. As we use the term "fundamentalist," we are not referring to particular sects, but to an ultraconservative point of view in respect to the Bible. What is the fundamentalist approach?

Attitude Toward The Bible

The fundamentalist approach begins with the supposition that God inspired the whole Bible verbatim, so that every word of it is literally "God's word." Therefore, the fundamentalists are obsessed with the faith that "the Bible is true." This belief seems so important that they regard it as a fundamental doctrine that every person should accept A story that the Bible plainly presents as a story, for example, is the parable of the Prodigal Son, recognized as fiction. But any story in a historical framework is stoutly defended by them as literal history. This includes the story of the Hood.

The attitude that the whole Bible must be true leads to the opinion that there can be no factual errors and no contradictions. They who hold this opinion either ignore or oppose the suggestion that the biblical Flood story contains contradictions. Needless to say, they do not like the idea that two Flood stories are interwoven in Genesis.

Method of Interpretation

The fundamentalists' attitude toward the Bible determines their method of interpreting it. One feature of their method is the screening out of evidence they dislike. When contradictions are encountered in the bible, one statement may be accepted and the conflicting statement ignored. An example is the question of how many animals of a kind were taken aboard the ark in the Flood story.

God's instruction to Noah to take two of each kind (Gen. 6:19) is readily accepted, while the contradictory instruction to take seven pairs of birds and seven pairs of clean animals (Gen. 7:2-3) is usually ignored. If someone does call attention to such details, he is liable to be denounced for "picking the

Bible to pieces." Actually, the failure to consider all the evidence is a violation of another basic principle of scholarship. The only way really to understand the Bible is to consider all the evidence, both inside and outside it.

Another feature of the fundamentalists' method is the reinterpretation of biblical passages to make the Bible agree with their beliefs. A related feature is the effort to twist evidence outside the Bible to support their beliefs. A popular form of twisting outside evidence is the misuse of archaeology to force it to support the historical accuracy of the Bible. This practice is engaged in not only by fundamentalists, but also by various writers and occasionally even by archaeologists themselves for the sake of producing something sensational.

Sir Charles Marston, Werner Keller, and others wrote books to defend the traditional view of the Bible, using archaeology as evidence. Even the famous Jewish archaeologist, Nelson Glueck, was too eager to find archaeological support for the Old Testament. On the other hand, books by Frederic Kenyon, Millar Burrows, Andre Parrot, and others represent honest, accurate use of archaeology in the interpretation of the Bible. The truth is that some archaeological evidence supports the Bible, but other archaeological discoveries disagree with it

Effects of Fundamentalism

When belief in the literal truth of the whole Bible becomes essential in a religion, that religion is placed on a very shaky foundation. It is easily demonstrated that the Bible is a human product of its time, containing some history, some fiction, some borrowing from neighboring religions, some truth, some errors, and some contradictions. Many undesirable effects result from making the truth of religion dependent upon the truth of such notions:

- A low standard for religion is set. Religion is forced to continue to contain some of the superstitions and ignorance of the ancient past. A distorted sense of values in religion results when unimportant or erroneous beliefs are regarded as of equal value with religious principles and ethics.

- Much modern knowledge and many ideals are shut out of religion because they are not in the Bible. Intelligent development of religion is blocked.

- Misunderstanding of the Bible itself is a consequence. The nature of the Bible, the religious development within it, and the relation of the Bible to the total history of religion are hidden from view by the fundamentalist approach. For example, within the Old Testament there is a shift from the narrow racism in Ezra and Nehemiah to the broad universalism in Second Isaiah (Isa. 40-55) and Jonah. Treating the whole Bible as literally the word of God prevents its readers from understanding the variety and development within it.

- Often the noblest passages of the Bible are not given a fair chance to speak to us today because they are equated with inferior passages. Belief in the unity of the Bible obscures the fact that sometimes a biblical writer was trying to elevate religion to a higher plane than the level in some other biblical books. Second Isaiah's effort to promote universalism is an example.

• The unreasonable claims and conjectures made to protect the belief in the literal truth of the whole Bible tend to bring religion into disrepute in the sight of the general public. Religion is ill-served by this. The wild claims include those made to support the belief in the Flood and the Ark.

The Story in the Bible

The Flood story in Genesis is more complex than the other Flood accounts. Unlike them, it contains significant contradictions and inconsistencies. One is the number of birds and clean animals taken aboard; another is the term for deity: "the Lord" vs. "God."

Another contradiction is the duration of the Flood. In Gen. 7:12; 8:6, 10a, 12a, the total of 54 days (40 plus 7 plus 7) passed from the time that the Flood began until Noah left the ark. In Gen. 7:11; 8:13a, 14-16a, however, the period was the equivalent of a solar year.

Biblical fundamentalists invariably either ignore these differences or try to interpret the verses to eliminate the difference and to harmonize the passages. Such procedure fails because it distorts the evidence. Either device — ignoring parts of the text or reinterpreting parts of the text — usually leads to misinterpretation of the text.

The Discovery of Sources – Composite Literature

The only way to understand the cause of the inconsistencies is to recognize that we have before us an example of ancient composite literature. Two separate written sources have been interwoven into one account, without rewriting them to make their vocabulary, style, and ideas agree with each other. This produces contradictions and inconsistencies, and sometimes duplications.

Composite literature was very prevalent in the ancient world, and a major contribution of modern biblical scholarship is the recognition that much of both the Old Testament and the New Testament is composite. The same two sources that are used in the Genesis Flood story run through the Pentateuch, where they are combined with other source material.

The presence of several sources for the Creation story in the Bible was first observed when J. B. Witter in 1711 recognized the significance of the different terms for God. Gradually biblical scholars discovered more and more evidence of earlier sources and later editing in the Pentateuch. The famous Graf-Wellhausen Hypothesis assigned letters to the four main sources: J, E, P, and D. The two sources for the Flood story are J and P.

Although the hypothesis has been revised and refined, it is basically sound. Orthodox Jews and Christians attack it because it upsets the traditional view that Moses wrote the Pentateuch, but the evidence for written sources is quite decisive. The contradictions, duplications, and linguistic inconsistencies cannot be sensibly explained as the composition of a single writer.

Parallels with Other Flood Stories

The Flood accounts in both J and P contain these essential features of the Mesopotamian versions:

- A god becomes displeased with mankind.
- Therefore the god decides to destroy all mankind, except one man and his wife or family, by means of a Flood.
- A deity — either the same or a different god — warns the man that the Flood is coming; the god tells him to build a boat, and to put aboard himself, his wife, and some animals.
- Storm or heavy rain is a major — and sometimes only — indicator of the Flood.

The other Flood stories generally have these same features in common. Thus these elements were characteristic of the basic story.

The Mesopotamian Versions

J has additional parallels with one or more of the Sumerian and Babylonian versions of the story. The exact day that the Flood will begin was predetermined; a special period of seven days preceded the Flood; one or more intervals of seven days occurred at the end of the Flood; the hero opened a window or hatch at the end voyage; a covering for the ark is mentioned; a dove and a raven were sent out from the Ark as the Flood neared its end, and the raven did not return. In J, as in the Sumerian and Babylonian accounts, the hero offered a sacrifice after emerging from the Ark. The Lord liked the smell of burnt offering, as did gods in general in the Gilgamesh Epic.

P, too, has parallels with one or more of the Mesopotamian accounts. The size of the Ark is given; the deity specifies its size, shape, and number of decks; pitch is used in its construction, the ark's door is mentioned; the ship lands on a mountain or mountains. After the Flood was over, the god Enlil blessed the hero and his wife in the Gilgamesh Epic, as God blessed Noah and his sons in P.

The large number of parallels demonstrates that both the J and P Flood accounts are derived ultimately from the Mesopotamia versions that preceded them. An interesting discovery is that J's parallels are generally not in P. This fact indicates that J's source was not identical with P's source, which is not surprising, considering that many forms of the story were in circulation, and that P was incorporated in Genesis four or five centuries later than J.

Greek, Roman, and Syrian Versions

The Greek and Roman versions of the Flood story have been changed yet further from the Mesopotamian accounts. This is in harmony with the fact that they were written later than the two Hebrew stories adapted to other cultures. Lucian probably used a Hellenistic source which combined elements from the Hebrew and non-Hebrew accounts.

Story or History?

When the Genesis Flood is traced back to its ultimate sources, which are the Sumerian story and the Babylonian versions of it, those sources very clearly are fictional. The sources are poetry, composed and transmitted for entertainment and to promote various ideas.

The differences between the Hebrew versions and the Mesopotamian versions are not at all an indication that the Hebrew accounts are independent in origin. Josephus, writing in the first century of the Christian era, clearly illustrates for us the ease with which Jews (and others) readily appropriated and reinterpreted foreign material. In his treatise *Against Apion* he comments on Berossus' account:

> This author, following the most ancient records, has, like Moses, described the Flood and the destruction of mankind thereby, and told of the ark in which Noah, the founder of our race, was saved when it landed on the heights of the mountains of Armenia (1. 128-30).

In Berossus' account the name of the man who was saved by a boat he built is Xisuthros; Josephus conveniently ignores this fact and claims that Berossus was writing about Noah.

The prominence of the mythological features demonstrates that the story is indeed a myth, not a report or even a faint "memory" of a historical event. If we are to be fair to it, we must accept it on its own terms, as a story.

– Howard M. Teeple, Excerpt from *The Noah's Ark Nonsense*, published by the Religion and Ethics Institute, Inc., Evanston, Illinois, 1978.

Dr. Teeple, *a Bible scholar and former fundamentalist, has written numerous books and articles, including* The Literary Origin of the Gospel of John.

God

Irreverence is another person's disrespect to your God; there isn't any word that tells what your disrespect to his God is.

– Mark Twain

"If God did not exist, it would be necessary to invent him," suggested Voltaire as if to say God was an invention of man. Even a three-year-old child, when told God created man, the earth, the sea, and all creatures great and small, will ask: "Who created God?"

– "Is God dead?" cover of *Time Magazine*, 1966

I cannot imagine a God who rewards and punishes the objects of his creation, whose purposes are modeled after our own — a God, in short, who is but a reflection of human frailty. Neither can I believe that the individual survives the death of his body, although feeble souls harbor such thoughts through fear or ridiculous egotism.

– Albert Einstein

It may be that our role on this planet is not to worship God...but to create him. If we affirm that God does not exist, perhaps only then can we begin to recognize fully that human beings are autonomous and that we are responsible for our own destinies and those of our fellow human beings. Perhaps only then can we summon the courage and wisdom to develop a rational ethics based on a realistic appraisal of nature and an awareness of the common moral decencies.

– Paul Kurtz, *Forbidden Fruit*

There are many gods which Christians reject. I just believe in one less god than they do. The reasons that you might give for your atheism toward the Roman gods are likely the same reasons I would give for not believing in Jesus.

– Dan Barker

A questioner declared that few churches allow black Africans to pray with the white because the Bible says that is the way it should be, because God created Negroes to serve.

"But suppose God is black. What if we go to Heaven and we all our lives have treated the Negro as an inferior and we look up and he is not white? What then is our response?"

There was no answer, only silence.

– Sen. Robert F. Kennedy, "Suppose God Is Black," *Look Magazine*

Those silly earthlings worshipping the Gods they made up.

– Ming the Merciless of Flash Gordon

...And the people bowed and prayed, to the neon god they'd made...

– Simon and Garfunkel

Bible Morality

The Ten Commandments in the Old Testament and the Sermon on the Mount, including the Golden Rule, in the New, are supposed to comprise the best moral teachings of the Bible. They are declared to be so far superior to all other moral codes as to preclude the idea of human origin.

The Decalogue is a very imperfect moral code; not at all superior to the religious and legislative codes of other ancient peoples. The last six of these commandments, while not above criticism, are in the main just, and were recognized alike by Jew and Gentile. They are a crude attempt to formulate the crystallized experiences of mankind. The first four (first three according to Catholic and Lutheran versions) possess no moral value whatever. They are simply religious emanations from the corrupt and disordered brain of priestcraft. They only serve to obscure the principles of true morality and produce an artificial system which bears the same relation to natural morality that a measure of chaff and grain dogs to a measure of winnowed grain.

As a literary composition and as a partial exposition of the peculiar tenets of a heretical Jewish sect, the Sermon on the Mount is interesting; but as a moral code, it is of little value. Along with some admirable precepts, it contains others, like the following, which are false and pernicious:

- Blessed are the poor in spirit
- Blessed are the meek, for they shall inherit the earth
- If thy right eye offend thee, pluck it out
- If thy right hand offend thee, cut it off
- Whosoever shall marry her that is divorced, committeth adultery
- Resist not evil
- Whosoever shall smite thee on the right cheek turn to him the other also
- If any man will sue thee at the law, and take away thy coat, let him have thy cloak also
- Love your enemies
- Lay not up for yourselves treasures upon earth
- Take no thought for your life, what ye shall eat, or what ye shall drink, nor yet for your body, what ye shall put on
- Take therefore no thought for the morrow

Christians claim that unbelievers have no moral standard, that they alone have such a standard — an infallible standard — the Bible.

If we ask them to name the best precept in this standard they cite the

Golden Rule. And yet the Golden Rule is purely a human rule of conduct. "Whatsoever ye (men, not God) would that men should do to you, do ye even so to them." This rule enjoins what Christians profess to condemn, that every person shall form his own moral standard. In this rule, the so-called divine laws are totally ignored.

The Golden Rule, so far as the Bible is concerned, is a borrowed gem. Chinese, Greek, and Roman sages had preached and practiced it centuries before the Sermon on the Mount was delivered. This rule, one of the best formulated by the ancients, is not, however, a perfect rule of human conduct. It does not demand that our desires shall always be just. But it does recognize and enjoin the principle of reciprocity, and is immeasurably superior to the rule usually practiced by the professed followers of Jesus: Whatsoever we would that you should do unto us, do it; and whatsoever we wish to do unto you, that will we do.

The three Christian virtues, faith, hope, and charity, fairly represent his whole system of so-called Bible morals — two false or useless precepts to one good precept. Charity is a true virtue, but "faith and hope," to quote Volney, "may be called the virtues of dupes for the benefit of knaves." And if the knaves have admitted charity to be the greatest of these virtues, it is because they are the recipients and not the dispensers of it.

Bible Models

The noblest types of manhood, like Bruno, Spinoza, Paine, and Ingersoll, have been slandered, anathematized, and slain by Christians, while the gods, the heroes, the patriarchs, the prophets, and the priests of the Bible have been presented as the highest models of moral excellence. Of these, Jehovah, Abraham, Jacob, Moses, David, Paul, and Christ are represented as the greatest and the best.

Who was Jehovah? "A being of terrific character — cruel, vindictive, capricious, and unjust," said Thomas Jefferson.

Who was Abraham? An insane barbarian patriarch who married his sister, denied his wife, and seduced her handmaid; who drove one child into the desert to starve, and made preparations to butcher the other.

Who was Jacob? Another patriarch, who won God's love by deceiving his father, cheating his uncle, robbing his brother, practicing bigamy with two of his cousins, and committing fornication with two of his housemaids.

Who was Moses? A model of meekness; a man who boasted of his own humility; a man who murdered an Egyptian and hid his body in the sand; a man who exterminated whole nations to secure the spoils of war, a man who butchered in cold blood thousands of captive widows, a man who tore dimpled babes from the breasts of dying mothers and put them to a cruel death;

a man who made orphans of thirty-two thousand innocent girls, and turned sixteen-thousand of them over to the brutal lusts of a savage soldiery

Who was David? "A man after God's own heart." A vulgar braggadocio, using language to a woman the mere quoting of which would send me to prison; a traitor, desiring to lead an enemy's troops against his own countrymen; a thief and robber, plundering the country on every side; a liar, uttering wholesale falsehoods to screen himself from justice; a red-handed butcher, torturing and slaughtering thousands of men, women, and children, making them pass through burning brick-kilns, carving them up with saws and axes, and tearing them in pieces under harrows of iron; a polygamist, with a harem of wives and concubines; a drunken debauchee, dancing half-naked before the maids in his household; a lecherous old libertine, abducting and ravishing the wife of a faithful soldier; a murderer, having this faithful soldier put to death after desolating his home; a hoary-headed fiend, foaming with vengeance on his dying bed, demanding with his latest breath the deaths of two aged men, one of whom had most contributed to make his kingdom what it was, the other a man to whom he had promised protection.

Who was Paul? A religious fanatic; a Jew and a Christian. As a Jew, in the name of Jehovah, he persecuted Christians; as a Christian, in the name of Christ he persecuted Jews; and both as a Jew and a Christian, and in the names of both Jehovah and Christ, he practiced dissimulation and hallowed falsehood.

Who was Christ? He is called the "divine teacher." As Mary Shelley wrote:

> He led
> The crowd, he taught them justice, truth, and peace,
> In semblance; but he lit within their souls
> The quenchless flames of zeal, and blessed the sword
> He brought on earth to satiate with the blood
> Of truth and freedom his malignant soul.

Immoral Teachings of the Bible

In the modern and stricter sense of the term, morality is scarcely taught in the Bible. Neither moral, morals, and morality, nor their equivalents, ethical and ethics, are to be found in the book. T. B. Wakeman, president of the Liberal University of Oregon, a life-long student of sociology and ethics, says:

> The word 'moral' does not occur in the Bible, nor even the idea. Hunting for morals in the Bible is like trying to find human remains in the oldest geologic strata — in the eozoon, for instance. Morals had not then been born.

I refuse to accept the Bible as a moral guide because it sanctions nearly every vice and crime. Here is the long list of wrongs which it authorizes and defends:

- Lying and deception
- Cheating
- Theft and robbery
- Murder
- Wars of conquest
- Human sacrifices
- Cannibalism
- Witchcraft
- Slavery
- Polygamy
- Adultery & prostitution
- Obscenity
- Intemperance
- Vagrancy
- Ignorance
- Injustice to woman
- Unkindness to children
- Cruelty to animals
- Tyranny
- Intolerance & persecution

The Bible is, for the most part, the crude literature of a people who lived 2,000 years, and more, ago. Certain principles of right and wrong they recognized, but the finer principles of morality were unknown to them. They were an ignorant people. An ignorant people is generally a religious people, and a religious people nearly always an immoral people. They believed that they were God's chosen people — God's peculiar favorites — and that because of this they had the right to rob and cheat, to murder and enslave the rest of mankind. From these two causes, chiefly, ignorance and religion, i.e., superstition, emanated the immoral deeds and opinions which found expression in the writings of their priests and prophets.

The passages in the Bible which deal with vice and crime may be divided into three classes:

1. There are passages which condemn vice and crime. These I endorse.
2. There are many passages in which the crimes and vices of the people are narrated merely as historical facts without either sanctioning or condemning them. The book merits no censure because of these.
3. There are numerous passages which sanction vice and crime. These, and these alone, suffice to prove the charges that I make against the Bible as a moral guide.

– John E. Remsburg

John E. Remsburg *was one of the ablest and best-known freethought writers and speakers of the last quarter of the nineteenth century and president of the American Secular Union. This article is from one of his books,* The Bible, *Truth Seeker Company, New York, 1905.*

" *The Bible teaches that woman brought sin and death into the world. She was to play the role of a dependent on man's bounty for all her material wants, and for all the information she might desire . . . Here is the Bible position of woman briefly summed up.* "

Elizabeth Cady Stanton

Inerrancy

Inspiration was completely adequate to accomplish the task of giving God's will to man in written form in all its parts…divine superintendence extended to the verbal expression of the thoughts of the writers…fee Scriptures never deceive nor mislead — the Bible is binding on all people and all people will give an account of how they lived in light of its teaching. "Inerrant" means "wholly true" or "without mistake" and refers to the fact that the biblical writers were absolutely errorless, truthful, and trustworthy in all of their affirmations. The doctrine of inerrancy does not confine itself to moral and religious truth alone. Inerrancy extends to statements of fact, whether scientific, historical, or geographical. The biblical writers were preserved from the errors that appear in all other books.

– Dave Miller who teaches at the Brown Trail
School of Preaching in Bedford, Texas.

I write as a Christian who loves the church. I am not a hostile critic who stands outside religion desiring to make fun of it. I look at die authority of the Scriptures as one who has been both nurtured by and then disillusioned with the literal Bible. My devotion to the Bible was so intense that it led me into a study that finally obliterated any possibility that the Bible could be related to on a literal basis. The Bible is not a scientific textbook. A literal Bible presents me with far more problems than assets. It offers me a God I cannot respect, much less worship. Those who insist on biblical literalism thus become unwitting accomplices in bringing about the death of the Christianity they so deeply love.

– John Shelby Spong

Traditionally, purveyors of the Bible inerrancy doctrine have profited from the ignorance, superstition, and gullibility that characterize societies in which mystical religions thrive, but recent discoveries and developments in biblical archaeology and criticism, coming in an age of increased scientific enlightenment, have cut deep inroads into territory once firmly held by the forces of inerrancy. Early Christian apologists, for example, claimed that not just the original Bible autographs were inspired of God but also all copies and translations that scribes and linguists had transmitted to later generations. Such a position was sustainable in a time when illiteracy was commonplace, Bible manuscripts rare, and textual criticism all but nonexistent, but with the discovery of Bible manuscripts unknown to previous generations of Christians, the invention of the printing press and the ensuing proliferation of vernacular translations, the contributions of archaeology and higher criticism to the field of Bible research, and the advent of public education, the absurdity of this belief became so obvious that it could not survive. Today, not even the staunchest fundamentalist would dare claim that all copies and translations of the Bible have been divinely protected from error.

– Farrell Till

It has been frequently pointed out that if God thought errorless Scripture important enough to inspire its composition, he would surely also have further inspired its copying, so that it might remain error free. Surely a God who can inspire error-free composition could also inspire error-free copying. Since he did not, it would appear he did not think our possession of error-free Scripture very important. But if it is not important for us, why was it important originally? (p. 71-72).

– Paul Achtemeier
Excerpt from *Inspiration of Scripture: Problems and Proposals*, where
Achtemeier competently explains the absurd implications of this last-
ditch effort of Bible Fundamentalists to save their cherished inerrancy.

Whether it is the inerrancy of the Bible, the special creation of human beings, or even the very existence of God, it Is common to find people offering what they believe to be rational, logical arguments. And, as long as they think that their arguments are sound, they continue to use and rely upon them. As soon as flaws and weaknesses in those arguments are pointed out, however, do believers then adopt a more critical, skeptical stance towards their religious doctrines? That's what people would do in most situations, but not when it comes to religion. No, should their rational arguments fail to provide support for the doctrines they wish to defend, reason itself is almost entirely abandoned in favor of faith.

– www.atheism.about.com

Every sect, as far as reason will help them, make use of it gladly; and where it fails them, they cry out, "It is a matter of faith, and above reason."

– John Locke, *An Essay Concerning Human Understanding* (1690)

A Few Contradictions in the Old Testament

(a) (2 Samuel 24: 1) God incited David to count the fighting men of Israel.
(b) (I Chronicles 2 1:1) It was Satan.

(a) (2 Samuel 24:9) Eight hundred thousand fighting men were found in Israel.
(b) (I Chronicles 21:5) There were one million, one hundred thousand.

(a) (2 Samuel 24:9) Five hundred thousand fighting men were found in Judah.
(b) (I Chronicles 21:5) The count was four hundred and seventy thousand.

God sent his prophet to threaten David with how many years of famine?
(a) (2 Samuel 24:13) God sent his prophet to threaten David with seven years of famine.
(b) (I Chronicles 21:12) It was three years.

(a) (2 Kings 8:26) Ahaziah was twenty-two when he began to rule over Jerusalem.
(b) (2 Chronicles 22:2) He was forty-two.

(a) (2 Kings 24:8) Jehoiachin was eighteen when he became king of Jerusalem.
(b) (2 Chronicles 36:9) He was eight.

(a) (2 Kings 24:8) He ruled over Jerusalem for three months.
(b) (2 Chronicles 36:9) He ruled for three months and ten days.

(a) (2 Samuel 23:8) The chief of the mighty men of David lifted up his spear and killed eight hundred men at one time.
(b) (I Chronicles 11: 11) He killed three hundred.

(a) (2 Samuel 5 and 6) David brought the Ark of the Covenant to Jerusalem after defeating the Philistines.
(b) (I Chronicles 13 and 14) It was before.

(a) (Genesis 6:19, 20) God told Noah to take two pairs of clean animals into the Ark.
(b) (Genesis 7:2) The number was seven although only two pairs went into the ark despite this last instruction.

(a) (2 Samuel 8:4) When David defeated the King of Zobah, he captured one thousand and seven hundred horsemen.
(b) (I Chronicles 18:4) He captured seven thousand.

(a) (I Kings 4:26) Solomon had forty thousand stalls for horses.
(b) (2 Chronicles 9:25) He had four thousand stalls.

(a) (I Kings 15:33 - 16:8) In King Asa's reign, Baasha the King of Israel died in the twenty-sixth year.
(b) (2 Chronicles 16:1) He was still alive in the thirty-sixth year.

(a) (2 Chronicles 2:2) Solomon appointed three thousand, six hundred overseers for the work of building the temple.
(b) (I Kings 5:16) He appointed three thousand three hundred.

(a) (1 Kings 7:26) Solomon built a facility containing two thousand baths.
(b) (2 Chronicles 4:5) There were over three thousand.

(a) (Ezra 2:6) Two thousand, eight hundred and twelve of the Israelites who were freed from the Babylonian captivity were the children of Pahrath-Moab.
(b) (Nehemiah 7:11) The number was two thousand, eight hundred and eighteen.

(a) (Ezra 2:8) Nine hundred and forty-five were the children of Zattu.
(b) (Nehemiah 7:13) It was eight hundred and forty-five.

(a) (Ezra 2:12) One thousand, two hundred and twenty-two were the children of Azgad.
(b) (Nehemiah 7:17) There were two thousand, three hundred and twenty-two.

(a) (Ezra 2:15) Four hundred and fifty-four were the children of Adin.
(b) (Nehemiah 7:20) There were six hundred and fifty-five.

(a) (Ezra 2:19) Two hundred and twenty-three were the children of Hashum.
(b) (Nehemiah 7:22) There were three hundred and twenty-eight.

(a) (Ezra 2:28) Two hundred and twenty-three were the children of Bethel and Ai.
(b) (Nehemiah 7:32) It was one hundred and twenty-three.

(a) (2 Chronicles 13:2) The name of King Abijah's mother was Michaiah, daughter of Uriel of Gibeah
(b) (2 Chronicles 11:20) Her name was Maachah, daughter of Absalom
(c) (2 Samuel 14:27) But Absalom had only one daughter whose name was Tamar.

(a) (Joshua 10:23, 40) Joshua and the Israelites captured Jerusalem.
(b) (Joshua 15:63) They did not.

(a) (Numbers 25:1 and 9) When the Israelites dwelt in Shittin they committed adultery with the daughters of Moab. God struck them with a plague. Twenty-four thousand people died in that plague.
(b) (I Corinthians 10:8) Twenty-three thousand Died.

(a) (Genesis 4&27) Seventy souls that were members of the house of Jacob came to Egypt.
(b) (Acts 7:14) Seventy-five souls came.

(a) (I Samuel 17:23, 50) David killed Goliath.
(b) (2 Samuel 21:19) Elhanan did.

(a) (I Samuel 31:4-6) "Saul took his own sword and fell upon it...Thus Saul died...
(b) (2 Samuel 1:1- 16) An Amalekite slew him.

(a) (Genesis 37:28) The Midianites sold Joseph to the Ishmaelites.
(b) (Genesis 37:36) They sold him to Potiphar, an officer of Pharaoh.

(a) (Genesis 37:28) The Ishmaelites bought Joseph and then took Joseph to Egypt.
(b) (Genesis 37:36) The Midianites sold him in Egypt.
(c) (Genesis 45:4) Joseph said to his brothers "I am your brother, Joseph, whom you sold into Egypt."

–Source: Shabir AllyAl-Attique Int'l Islamic Publications

IV

The Dead Sea Scrolls and the Gnostic Gospels

The Calendar of the Zodiac
The basis for most religions in world history

Astrology in the Dead Sea Scrolls

It is truly amazing that any of the Dead Sea Scrolls have survived into the twenty-first century. There is now proof that there is a link between these ancient scrolls, first-century Judaism, the early Christian church, and the ancient practice of astrology. Scholars and churchmen alike are astonished to know of this connection and are still having a problem with reconciling a discredited occult practice like astrology with the edited, revised, and sanitized version of religion that is presented to the public in our modern churches.

The Dead Sea Scrolls were discovered in the Judean desert in 1947 by a Bedouin Arab in the caves near an archeology site near Kirbet Qumran in what is now the State of Israel. Today's readers will be surprised to learn that some of the Bedouin Arabs used some of these priceless scrolls as fuel for their campfires. The clay containers that protected the scrolls for the last two thousand years were reused as water jugs on the Bedouin donkeys. Some of the leather scrolls were recycled by local cobblers by sewing them to the bottom of their sandals. Several of the scrolls found their way into the marketplace where merchants of antiquities would sell them to private collectors and tourists.

The scrolls of the astrological horoscopes were found in Cave 4 near the ruins of the Essene community in Qumran, where the community hid their religious library. At this time the Romans were invading the land of Judea and were destroying everything in their path. Some modern Biblican scholars and archaeologists believe that these scrolls could have been hidden in the caves as late as the Jewish revolt of 132-135 A.D.

The inclusion of horoscopes with the other sectarian writings and the commonly accepted Hebrew Scriptures has three significant implications:

- These horoscopes were chosen to be carefully saved for future generations.
- This "science" of astrology was practiced and believed in by the devotees of the Essene sect.
- It was also practiced by the early church of the New Testament, the Jewish and Roman rulers of first-century Judea, and by all of the Gentile nations that surrounded Judea.

Many modern Biblical scholars believe that the "star prophecy" that was so popular during the time of Jesus was astrological. The three magi of the Christian nativity legend in the New Testament are now believed to have been astrologers and not the fabled "three kings" of an alternative nativity narrative. The Hellenized Jewish historian Josephus mentioned the "star prophecy," as did the Roman historians Suetonius and Tacitus. Even the militant Jewish revolutionary Simon bar Kochba (Simon the "son of a star") used the star reference in his name to show his followers that he was one of the men whom God had destined "to go forth and rule the world."

The authors of the Dead Sea Scrolls were Zealots and believed in the God-ordained destiny of the people of Israel. The Essenes believed that their community was the true and righteous Israel and did not recognize neutrality. They considered as enemies all who did not join them. These would be the followers of the Herodians — the Sudducees in the Temple of Jerusalem and the puppet kings appointed by the Emperor of Rome. Many different shades of Jews Zealous for the Law (of Moses) are associated with the devotees of Qumran.

Modern Biblical scholars and archaeologists are just now learning much that is new and enlightening about the traditional Bible through the Dead Sea Scrolls. These first-century documents are shedding new light on lost meanings of ancient Aramaic and Hebrew terms that have been so clouded and mystified by sectarian misunderstandings of ancient Biblical readings

The connection between the Early Church and Judaism is now believed by many modern scholars to be the Essene Qumran community. The spectacular similarities in ritual practices, teachings, and literary terms are so obvious that only the most stubborn and fundamentalist Christian will continue in believing in the special uniqueness of the so-called Christian message. Christianity is now being seen as a kind of religio-cultural mutation, over the first hundred years of the Christian era, of the Essene community in Jerusalem. It is now believed that Jesus' brother, James the Righteous, is the same Teacher of Righteousness who plays such a central role in the texts of the Dead Sea Scrolls.

The Essenes called themselves the Nozrei ha-Brit, known also as the Nozrim, Nasoreans, Nazarenes, and the Keepers of the Covenant. The early Christians called themselves Nazarenes before they were called Christians in paganized Antioch. By the time that so many Gentles were coming into the Nazarene religious community, the Nazarenes were moving farther and farther away from their Jewish roots. The Qumran community's ritual of washing in a ritual bath for the washing away of sins became the Christian baptism. The Essene common meal of bread and wine became the Christian Mass. The observant Jewish rabbi Jesus the Nazarene became the effeminate Serapis-style Gentile god.

The Hebrew Scriptures were demoted to the Old Testament, as opposed to the Hellenized and paganized New Testament for the Greek world. The separation of Judaism and the new Gentile Christianity was complete.

The literal accuracy of the Bible has had to be reconsidered in the last one hundred years. The new sciences of archaeology and literary criticism have voided many of our presuppositions about the historicity of many of the events in Judea at the time of Jesus. Many modern Biblical archaeologists now believe that the village of Nazareth did not exist at the time of the birth and early life of Jesus. There is simply no evidence for it. There is a village of Nazareth that appears on the Roman Judean maps *after* the death of Jesus. This new archeological discovery would agree with the way that the Essenes referred to themselves in the Dead Sea Scrolls.

As noted above, they called themselves the Keepers of the Covenant, the Nazarenes ha-Brit (the community of the Nazarenes). Jesus was referred to as Jesus the Nazarene (ha-Brit); in other words, there are now many reasons to believe that Jesus was simply an observant Essene Jew of his time, not the Greco-Roman god of the later Roman Empire State Church under Emperor Constantine!

It is now speculated that the Hellenic Greek writers of the Greek New Testament had lost this fine distinction between the late town of Nazareth and the meaning of the term Nazarenes. This could easily have happened after the destruction of the Jewish state in either 70 A.D. or 135 A.D. Much of the New Testament was written as late as seventy years after the death of Jesus the Nazarene.

Another misunderstanding in the traditional teachings of religious orthodoxy is that both the first-century Jews and early church used the same lunar calendar that is used by modern Jews all over the world for determining the true Jewish holidays. The writers of the Dead Sea Scrolls and, very likely, the early observant Hebrew Christians (the early church), carefully placed their solar calendars in the same caves where they stored their scriptures and sectarian writings.

These two sets of calendars mat were in use in Judea at the time of Jesus explain the differences in the gospel stories and the conflicts in the timing of the final days of Jesus. These two calendars also explain why the followers of the Herodian High Priest in Jerusalem could work on days that were forbidden to the Essenes in the Judean desert. Their same holidays and holy days were falling on different days of the week! More of the details of the uses of the solar calendar will be brought to light as soon as these particular scrolls are studied in greater detail by modern Biblical scholars.

Scholars and other interested individuals are fortunate to be living in twenty-first century when religious authorities and other "special interest" experts can no longer edit out the astrological references and other historically hidden information in the Dead Sea Scrolls. This rediscovered way of viewing the first-century world must be accepted and recognized by the entire modern academic Community.

The intellectual elitists of the traditional orthodox religions who kept this information from fellow scholars and the general public had their monopoly broken by the (American) Biblical Archaeology Society in 1991. All of the "unpublished" Dead Sea Scrolls were finally given to the whole world in the unedited, uncensored, and un-revised two-volume set titled: *A Facsimile Edition of the Dead Sea Scrolls*, (Biblical Archaeology Society, November 19, 1991).

– Dr. Alan Albert Snow

Dr. Alan Albert Snow *was a member of the Board of Directors of the Institute for Judeo-Christian Origins Studies, California State University, Long Beach. He was also a charter member of the Institute for Dead Sea Scrolls Studies, Biblical Archaeology Society, and earned his MA. at the School of Theology, Claremont, California.*

In a verdict that could have significant implications for research on the Dead Sea Scrolls, a Jerusalem court ruled that an Israeli professor has the copyright on his reconstruction of one of the most important ancient Jewish manuscripts.

Horoscopes

Two documents of the Dead Sea Scrolls, from Cave 4, one in Hebrew, the other in Aramaic, both dating probably to the end of the first century B.C., contain fragments of "horoscopes," or more precisely, astrological physiognomies claiming a correspondence between a person's features and destiny and the configuration of the stars at the time of his birth.

The Hebrew text, published by J. M. Allegro, is written in a childish cipher. The text runs from left to right instead of the normal right to left and uses, in addition to the current Hebrew "square" alphabet, letters borrowed from the archaic Hebrew (or Phoenician) and Greek scripts.

The spiritual qualities of three individuals described there are reflected in their share of Light and Darkness. The first man is very wicked: eight parts of Darkness to a single part of Light. The second man is largely good: six parts of Light against three parts of Darkness. The last is almost perfect: eight portions of Light and only one of Darkness.

As far as physical characteristics are concerned, shortness, fatness, and irregularity of the features are associated with wickedness, and their opposites reflect virtue.

In the astrological terminology of the document, the "second Column" doubtless means the "second House" and a birthday "in the foot of the Bull" should probably be interpreted as the presence at that time of the sun in the lower part of the constellation Taurus. The Aramaic "horoscope" is, according to its editor J. Starcky, that of the final Prince of the Congregation, or Royal Messiah. It is just as likely, however, that the text alludes to the miraculous birth of Noah.

Whether the sectaries forecast the future by means of astrology, or merely used horoscope-like compositions as literary devices, it is impossible to decide at present, though I am inclined towards the latter alternative. That such texts are found among the Scrolls should not, however, surprise anyone. For if many Jews frowned on astrology, others, such as the Hellenistic Jewish writer Eupolemus, credited its invention to Abraham!

– G. Vermes
Excerpt from *The Dead Sea Scrolls in English*

The Dead Sea Scrolls and Christianity

The Dead Sea Scrolls were discovered in 1947 in caves near the plateau called Qumran, at the northwest corner of the Dead Sea. After it was established beyond doubt that they had come from the general period of the rise of Christianity, scholars were stunned to find that the community which wrote them were so close to the early Christians that there would have to be a historical connection. Some wild claims were made, that they disproved the uniqueness of Christianity. These were soon replaced with greater caution. But the world was alerted that the greatest archaeological discovery ever made had filled in the vacuum in our knowledge about the real Jesus and his times.

Only a small number were in the complete form of scrolls, the majority in fragments of varying size. At a rough estimate, the remains of some 800 documents were found. The greater proportion of these were copies of books of the Old Testament, showing that the writers were Jews. But they were not orthodox Jews. The other

Scrolls for Sale

"The Four Dead Sea Scrolls: Biblical manuscripts dating back to at least 200 B.C. are for sale. This would be an ideal gift to an educational or religious institution by an individual or group. Box F206."

This was actually an advertisement in the *Wall Street Journal* on June 1, 1954.

documents, new works that have attracted the greatest interest, show that the writers belonged to a strongly integrated community which lived in a way that separated them from mainstream Jews.

Each of their differences from the mainstream paralleled a distinctive practice of the earliest Christians. The Qumran community — as they are best called — met every day for a sacred meal of bread and new wine. They put all their property into a common stock. According to the New Testament Book of Acts, this combination was also true of the first generation of Christians. "All who believed were together and had all things in common…Every day…breaking bread in houses, they received food in gladness and simplicity of heart" (Acts 2:44-46).

The Qumran community practiced baptisms, using the deep rectangular cisterns that are the most striking feature of the buildings excavated near the caves. In their separation from the world, they renounced marriage, expressing in their works the belief that sexual intercourse was sinful and defiling. The early Christians also used baptism as a rite of initiation, and they held, in a more moderate form, a belief that celibacy was preferable to the married state.

The two groups even had names in common. The name the New Covenant — the term that gave New Testament — was used for the Qumran community, and also by Christians. Both used the name "The Way," as well as a word that came to mean "church." Both were under the authority of bishops, who had the same particular duties.

Most strikingly of all, both groups had a messianic expectation, laying great emphasis on an ideal age soon to come. But at Qumran there would be two Messiahs, one a priest, one a layman. They were called the Messiah of Aaron and the Messiah of Israel. With them would be another called the Prophet.

In the coming time, for Qumran, there would be a great final battle, between the Sons of Light and the Sons of Darkness. It would result in the destruction of all evil men, so that only the initiates of the community would remain in a purified world. The Christians also used the name Sons of Light, and in their book of Revelation anticipated a coming Armageddon which would have the same effect.

While these were parallels that must necessarily link the two groups in some way, there were also major differences, so that the Qumran group cannot be called Christian. They were extremely legalistic, insisting on an even stricter application of the laws of Moses than mainstream Jews. The Sabbath had to be observed with the utmost rigor. One of the emphases of the gospels is on Jesus' breaking the Sabbath rules, and being attacked by Jews for his disregard of their purification rites.

As soon as it was recognized that there were close parallels, there was a theological crisis. For popular Christianity, Jesus was a founder of something that was new in every way, directly revealed by God through him. This was the reason for the authority of Christian belief. If other people at the same time had been doing the same things, yet were not Christian, how could it be said that Christians had the sole, unique Truth, against which all else had to be measured?

The theological issue soon began to influence historical study. Much greater emphasis was laid on the differences between the two groups than on their similarity. It was accepted that there were points of contact, but this was only because everyone at the time was doing much the same thing. The Scrolls were said to supply merely a general background for the rise of Christianity. The differences between Qumran and mainstream Jews were underplayed, and it was assumed, without closer observation, that all Scrolls must have originated at the same date. Because of indications in them that some belonged in the late second or early first century B.C., it became accepted that all belonged in that time. There was thus a long way between them and the time of Jesus, and it could not be said that his religion came directly from them.

This opinion, that the Scrolls all belonged to the B.C. period, has been called the consensus case. It has been challenged to the point of being no longer held except by a few remaining scholars of the first generation.

There is very strong evidence that the sectarian works — as the previously unknown ones may be called — were composed over a long period of time, the whole period when the Qumran buildings on the plateau near the caves are known to have been occupied, from the second century B.C. up to 70 A.D.

Of the new works discovered in the caves, the complete or nearly complete ones are called the Temple Scroll, the Community Rule, the Damascus Document, the War Scroll, the Hymns of Thanksgiving. Another group, more fragmentary, are called the pesharim. We will be dealing with them closely, as they are the most important for the Christian case. In addition, there are a very great number of fragments, the remains of scrolls that have suffered the ravages of time.

Here is a brief outline of the events of the last two centuries B.C. and the first century A.D.:

A great crisis took place in 168 B.C., when the foreign conqueror Antiochus Epiphanes invaded and defiled the Jerusalem temple. This was the Abomination of Desolation, ever afterwards remembered. The Seleucid successors of Antiochus Epiphanes were opposed, heroically, by the sons of an obscure priest, who succeeded in obtaining the rule of the country for themselves. As rulers they were called the Hasmoneans, and presided over a long period of relative independence.

In 63 B.C. the Roman general Pompey claimed control of Jerusalem and Judea for the rising Roman power. Taxes had to be paid to Rome, but domestic rule was left to their own high priests. At this time there appeared an ambitious Idumean, of Arab descent, called Antipater. He worked his way into Roman confidence, with the result that his son, Herod the Great, was able to claim the title of monarch, with Roman approval. Herod reigned from 37 to 4 B.C., leaving an enduring mark. From his nine wives he produced many progeny.

In his declining years Herod became insanely jealous, putting to death several sons who he thought were plotting against him. After his death only the weak son Archelaus had any claim. Rome refused to allow him the title of monarch, and in 6 A.D. the next major crisis of the history took place. Rome decided to occupy the country and put it under the direct rule of its own governors. The imposition of a census, signaling the end of Jewish independence, provoked the uprising of Judas the Galilean. Throughout the first century A.D. guerilla attacks were made on the occupying Romans, resulting finally in the destruction of Jerusalem by the Romans in 70 A.D.

The gospels of the New Testament narrate the career of Jesus from 29 A.D., for a ministry of only a few years which ended in his crucifixion. He was contemporary with an ascetic preacher, John the Baptist, who is better known from the external history. That history is supplied by the Jewish writer Josephus, in his books the Jewish War and Jewish Antiquities. Jesus, called the Christ, is named by Josephus, but the authenticity of the passages concerning him has been disputed. It is for these reasons, as well as the miraculous content of much of the gospels, that some historians have doubted whether Jesus ever existed. It does not appear, on the face of it, that he interacted with contemporary events, and no convincing reason is given why he was crucified. The absence of a context could be for one of two reasons. Either he lived and taught in social isolation, in contact only with a small group of followers. Or, he did relate to the tumultuous times he lived in, and much about him has been suppressed. It was with the discovery of the Dead Sea Scrolls that it became possible to consider this latter alternative.

– Dr. Barbara Thiering
This essay was first published in the website:
http://www.pesherofchrist.infinitesoulutions.com

An Introduction to Gnosticism and the Nag Hammadi Library

What is Gnosticism?

Gnosis" and "Gnosticism" are still rather arcane terms, though in the last two decades they have been increasingly encountered in the vocabulary of contemporary society. The word Gnosis derives from Greek and connotes "knowledge" or the "act of knowing." On first hearing, it is sometimes confused with another more common term of the same root but opposite sense: agnostic, literally "not knowing." The Greek language differentiates between rational, propositional knowledge, and a distinct form of knowing obtained by experience or perception. It is this latter knowledge gained from interior comprehension and personal experience that constitutes gnosis.

In the first century of the Christian era the term "Gnostic" came to denote a heterodox segment of the diverse new Christian community. Among early followers of Christ it appears there were groups who delineated themselves from the greater household of the Church by claiming not simply a belief in Christ and his message, but a "special witness" or revelatory experience of the divine. It was this experience or gnosis that set the true follower of Christ apart, so they asserted. Stephan Hoeller explains that these Christians held a "conviction that direct, personal and absolute knowledge of the authentic truths of existence is accessible to human beings, and, moreover, that the attainment of such knowledge must always constitute the supreme achievement of human life."

What the "authentic truths of existence" affirmed by the Gnostics were will be briefly reviewed below, but first a historical overview of the early Church might be useful. In the initial century and a half of Christianity — the period when we find first mention of "Gnostic" Christians — no single acceptable format of Christian thought had yet been defined. During this formative period Gnosticism was one of many currents moving within the deep waters of the new religion. The ultimate course Christianity, and Western culture with it, would take was undecided at this early moment. Gnosticism was one of the seminal influences shaping that destiny.

That Gnosticism was, at least briefly, in the mainstream of Christianity is witnessed by the fact that one of its most influential teachers, Valentinus, may have been in consideration during the mid-second century for election as the Bishop of Rome. Born in Alexandria around 100 C.E., Valentinus distinguished himself at an early age as an extraordinary teacher and leader in the highly educated and diverse Alexandrian Christian community. In mid-life he migrated from Alexandria to the Church's evolving capital, Rome, where he played an active role in the public affairs of the Church. A prime characteristic of Gnostics was their claim to be keepers of sacred traditions, gospels, rituals, and successions — esoteric matters for which many Christians were either not properly prepared or simply not inclined. Valentinus, true to this Gnostic predilection, apparently professed to have received a special apostolic sanction through Theudas, a disciple and initiate of the Apostle Paul, and to be a custodian of doctrines and rituals neglected by what would become Christian orthodoxy. Though an influential member of the Roman church in the mid-second century, by the end of his life Valentinus had been forced from the public eye and branded a heretic by the developing orthodoxy Church.

The tide of history can be said to have turned against Gnosticism in the middle of the second century. No Gnostic after Valentinus would ever come so near prominence in the greater Church. Gnosticism's emphasis on personal experience, its continuing revelations and production of new scripture, its asceticism and paradoxically contrasting libertine postures, were all met with increasing suspicion. By 180 C.E. Irenaeus, bishop of Lyon, was publishing his first attacks on Gnosticism as heresy, a labor that would be continued with increasing vehemence by the church Fathers throughout the next century.

Orthodoxy Christianity was deeply and profoundly influenced by its struggles with Gnosticism in the second and third centuries. Formulations of many central traditions in Christian theology came as reflections and shadows of this confrontation with the Gnosis. But by the end of the fourth century the struggle was essentially over: the evolving ecclesia had added the force of political correctness to dogmatic denunciation, and with this sword so-called "heresy" was painfully cut from the Christian body. Gnosticism as a Christian tradition was largely eradicated, its remaining teachers ostracized, and its sacred books destroyed. All that remained for students seeking to understand Gnosticism in later centuries were the denunciations and fragments preserved in the patristic heresiologies. Or at least so it seemed until the mid-twentieth century.

Discovery of the Nag Hammadi Library

It was on a December day in the year of 1945, near the town of Nag Hammadi in Upper Egypt, that the course of Gnostic studies was radically renewed and forever changed. An Arab peasant, digging around a boulder in search of fertilizer for his fields, happened upon an old, rather large red earthenware jar. Hoping to have found a buried treasure, and with due hesitation and apprehension about the jinn who might attend such a hoard, he smashed the jar open. Inside he discovered no treasure and no genie, but instead books: more than a dozen old codices bound in golden brown leather. Little did he realize that he had found an extraordinary collection of ancient texts, manuscripts hidden a millennium and a half before — probably by monks from the nearby monastery of St. Pachomius seeking to preserve them from a destruction ordered by the church as part of its violent expunging of heterodoxy and heresy.

Today, now over fifty years since being unearthed and more than two decades after final translation and publication in English as The Nag Hammadi Library, their importance has become astoundingly clear: These thirteen papyrus codices containing fifty-two sacred texts are representatives of the long lost "Gnostic Gospels," a last extant testament of what orthodox Christianity perceived to be its most dangerous and insidious challenge, the feared opponent that the Church Fathers had reviled under many different names, but most commonly as Gnosticism. The discovery of the Nag Hammadi texts has fundamentally revised our understanding of both Gnosticism and the early Christian church.

– Lance S. Owens, M.D.

Lance S. Owens *is a physician in clinical practice and an ordained priest who serves a parish of the Ecclesia Gnostica. He completed his undergraduate degree in history at Georgetown University and Utah State University, and received his doctorate from Columbia University. Since 1995 he has served as the creator and editor of The Gnosis Archive website.*

A Brief Summary of Gnosticism

Gnosticism is the teaching based on Gnosis, the knowledge of transcendence arrived at by way of interior, intuitive means. Although Gnosticism thus rests on personal religious experience, it is a mistake to assume all such experience results in Gnostic recognitions. It is nearer the truth to say that Gnosticism expresses a specific religious experience, an experience that does not lend itself to the language of theology or philosophy, but which is instead closely affinitized to, and expresses itself through, the medium of myth. Indeed, one finds that most Gnostic scriptures take the forms of myths. The term "myth" should not here be taken to mean "stories that are not true," but rather, that the truths embodied in these myths are of a different order from the dogmas of theology or the statements of philosophy.

In the following summary, we will attempt to encapsulate in prose what the Gnostic myths express in their distinctively poetic and imaginative language.

The Cosmos

All religious traditions acknowledge that the world is imperfect. Where they differ is in the explanations which they offer to account for this imperfection and in what they suggest might be done about it. Gnostics have their own — perhaps quite startling — view of these matters: they hold that the world is flawed because it was created in a flawed manner.

Like Buddhism, Gnosticism begins with the fundamental recognition that earthly life is filled with suffering. In order to nourish themselves, all forms of life consume each other, thereby visiting pain, fear, and death upon one another (even herbivorous animals live by destroying the life of plants). In addition, so-called natural catastrophes (earthquakes, floods, fires, drought, volcanic eruptions) bring further suffering and death in their wake. Human beings, with their complex physiology and psychology, are aware not only of these painful features of earthly existence. They also suffer from the frequent recognition that they are strangers living in a world that is flawed and absurd.

Many religions advocate that humans are to be blamed for the imperfections of the world. Supporting this view, they interpret the Genesis myth as declaring that transgressions committed by the first human pair brought about a "fall" of creation resulting in the present corrupt state of the world. Gnostics respond that this interpretation of the myth is false. The blame for the world's failings lies not with humans, but with the creator. Since — especially in the monotheistic religions — the creator is God, this Gnostic position appears blasphemous, and is often viewed with dismay even by non-believers.

Ways of evading the recognition of the flawed creation and its flawed creator have been devised over and over, but none of these arguments have impressed Gnostics. The ancient Greeks, especially the Platonists, advised people to look to the harmony of the universe, so that by venerating its grandeur they might forget their immediate afflictions. But since this harmony still contains the cruel flaws, forlornness and alienation of existence, this advice is considered of little value by Gnostics. Nor is the Eastern idea of Karma regarded by Gnostics as an adequate explanation of creation's imperfection and suffering. Karma at best can only explain how the chain of suffering and imperfection works. It does not inform us in the first place why such a sorrowful and malign system should exist.

Once the initial shock of the "unusual" or "blasphemous" nature of the Gnostic explanation for suffering and imperfection of the world wears off, one may begin to recognize that it is in fact the most sensible of all explanations. To appreciate it fully, however, a familiarity with the Gnostic conception of the Godhead is required, both in its original essence as the True God and in its debased manifestation as the false or creator God.

Deity

The Gnostic God concept is more subtle than that of most religions. In its way, it unites and reconciles the recognitions of Monotheism and Polytheism, as well as of Theism, Deism and Pantheism.

In the Gnostic view, there is a true, ultimate and transcendent God, who is beyond all created universes and who never created anything in the sense in which the word "create" is ordinarily understood. While this True God did not fashion or create anything, He (or, It) "emanated" or brought forth from within Himself the substance of all there is in all the worlds, visible and invisible. In a certain sense, it may therefore be true to say that all is God, for all consists of the substance of God. By the same token, it must also be recognized that many portions of the original divine essence have been projected so far from their source that they underwent unwholesome changes in the process. To worship the cosmos, nature, or embodied creatures is tantamount to worshipping alienated, corrupt portions of the emanated divine essence.

The basic Gnostic myth has many variations, but all of these refer to Aeons, intermediate deific beings who exist between the ultimate, True God and ourselves. They, together with the True God, comprise the realm of Fullness (Pleroma) wherein the potency of divinity operates fully. The Fullness stands in contrast to our existential state, which in comparison may be called emptiness.

One of the aeonial beings who bears the name Sophia ("Wisdom") is of great importance to the Gnostic world view. In the course of her journeys, Sophia came to emanate from her own being a flawed consciousness, a being who became the creator of the material and psychic cosmos, all of which he created in the image of his own flaw. This being, unaware of his origins, imagined himself to be the ultimate and absolute God. Since he took the already existing divine essence and fashioned it into various forms, he is also called the Demiurgos or "half-maker." There is an authentic half, a true deific component within creation, but it is not recognized by the half-maker and by his cosmic minions, the Archons or "rulers."

The Human Being

Human nature mirrors the duality found in the world: in part it was made by the false creator God and in part it consists of the light of the True God. Humankind contains a perishable physical and psychic component, as well as a spiritual component which is a fragment of the divine essence. This latter part is often symbolically referred to as the "divine spark." The recognition of this dual nature of the world and of the human being has earned the Gnostic tradition the epithet of "dualist."

Humans are generally ignorant of the divine spark resident within them. This ignorance is fostered in human nature by the influence of the false creator and his Archons, who together are intent upon keeping men and women ignorant of their true nature and destiny. Anything that causes us to remain attached to earthly things serves to keep us in enslavement to these lower cosmic rulers. Death releases the divine spark from its lowly prison, but if there has not been a substantial work of Gnosis undertaken by the soul prior to death, it becomes likely that the divine spark will be hurled back into, and then re-embodied within, the pangs and slavery of the physical world.

Not all humans are spiritual (pneumatics) and thus ready for Gnosis and liberation. Some are earthbound and materialistic beings (hyletics), who recognize only the physical reality. Others live largely in their psyche (psychics). Such people usually mistake the Demiurge for the True God and have little or no awareness of the spiritual world beyond matter and mind.

In the course of history, humans progress from materialistic sensate slavery, by way of ethical religiosity, to spiritual freedom and liberating Gnosis. As the scholar G. Quispel wrote: "The world-spirit in exile must go through the Inferno of matter and the Purgatory of morals to arrive at the spiritual Paradise." This kind of evolution of consciousness was envisioned by the Gnostics, long before the concept of evolution was known.

Salvation

Evolutionary forces alone are insufficient, however, to bring about spiritual freedom. Humans are caught in a predicament consisting of physical existence combined with ignorance of their true origins, their essential nature and their ultimate destiny. To be liberated from this predicament, human beings require help, although they must also contribute their own efforts.

From earliest times Messengers of the Light have come forth from the True God in order to assist humans in their quest for Gnosis. Only a few of these salvific figures are mentioned in Gnostic scripture; some of the most important are Seth (the third Son of Adam), Jesus, and the Prophet Mani. The majority of Gnostics always looked to Jesus as the principal savior figure (the Soter).

Gnostics do not look to salvation from sin (original or other), but rather from the ignorance of which sin is a consequence. Ignorance, whereby is meant ignorance of spiritual realities, is dispelled only by Gnosis, and the decisive revelation of Gnosis is brought by the Messengers of Light, especially by Christ, the Logos of the True God. It is not by His suffering and death but by His life of teaching and His establishing of mysteries that Christ has performed His work of salvation.

The Gnostic concept of salvation, like other Gnostic concepts, is a subtle one. On the one hand, Gnostic salvation may easily be mistaken for an unmediated individual experience, a sort of spiritual do-it-yourself project. Gnostics hold that the potential for Gnosis, and thus, of salvation is present in every man and woman, and that salvation is not vicarious but individual. At the same time, they also acknowledge that Gnosis and salvation can be, indeed must be, stimulated and facilitated in order to effectively arise within consciousness. This stimulation is supplied by Messengers of Light who, in addition to their teachings, establish salvific mysteries (sacraments) which can be administered by apostles of the Messengers and their successors.

One needs also remember that knowledge of our true nature — as well as other associated realizations — are withheld from us by our very condition of earthly existence. The True God of transcendence is unknown in this world; in fact He is often called the Unknown Father. It is thus obvious that revelation from on High is needed to bring about salvation. The in-dwelling spark must be awakened from its terrestrial slumber by the saving knowledge that comes "from without."

Conduct

If the words "ethics" or "morality" are taken to mean a system of rules, then Gnosticism is opposed to them both. Such systems usually originate with the Demiurge and are covertly designed to serve his purposes. If, on the other hand, morality is said to consist of an inner integrity arising from the illumination of the indwelling spark, then the Gnostic will embrace this spiritually informed existential ethic as ideal.

To the Gnostic, commandments and rules are not salvific; they are not substantially conducive to salvation. Rules of conduct may serve numerous ends, including the structuring of an ordered and peaceful society, and the maintenance of harmonious relations within social groups. Rules, however, are not relevant to salvation; that is brought about only by Gnosis. Morality therefore needs to be viewed primarily in temporal and secular terms; it is ever subject to changes and modifications in accordance with the spiritual development of the individual.

As noted in the discussion above, "hyletic materialists" usually have little interest in morality, while "psychic disciplinarians" often grant to it a great importance. In contrast, "Pneumatic spiritual" persons are generally more concerned with other, higher matters. Different historical periods also require variant attitudes regarding human conduct. Thus both the Manichaean and Cathar Gnostic movements, which functioned in times where purity of conduct was regarded as an issue of high import, responded in kind. The present period of Western culture perhaps resembles in more ways that of second and third century Alexandria. It seems therefore appropriate that Gnostics in our age adopt the attitudes of classical Alexandrian Gnosticism, wherein matters of conduct were largely left to the insight of the individual.

Gnosticism embraces numerous general attitudes toward life: it encourages non-attachment and non-conformity to the world, a "being in the world, but not of the world"; a lack of egotism; and a respect for the freedom and dignity of other beings. Nonetheless, it appertains to the intuition and wisdom of every individual "Gnostic" to distill from these principles individual guidelines for their personal application.

Destiny

When Confucius was asked about death, he replied: "Why do you ask me about death when you do not know how to live?" This answer might easily have been given by a Gnostic. To a similar question posed in the Gnostic Gospel of Thomas, Jesus answered that human beings must come by Gnosis to know the ineffable, divine reality from whence they have originated, and whither they will return. This transcendental knowledge must come to them while they are still embodied on earth.

Death does not automatically bring about liberation from bondage in the realms of the Demiurge. Those who have not attained to a liberating Gnosis while they were in embodiment may become trapped in existence once more. It is likely that this might occur by way of the cycle of rebirths. Gnosticism does not emphasize the doctrine of reincarnation prominently, but it is implicitly understood in most Gnostic teachings that those who have not made effective contact with their transcendental origins while they were in embodiment would have to return into the sorrowful condition of earthly life.

In regard to salvation, or the fate of the spirit and soul after death, one needs to be aware that help is available. Valentinus, the greatest of Gnostic teachers, taught that Christ and Sophia await the spiritual man — the pneumatic Gnostic — at the entrance of the Pleroma, and help him to enter the bridechamber of final reunion. Ptolemaeus, disciple of Valentinus, taught that even those not of pneumatic status, the psychics, could be redeemed and live in a heavenworld at the entrance of the Pleroma. In the fullness of time, every spiritual being will receive Gnosis and will be united with its higher Self — the angelic Twin — thus becoming qualified to enter the Pleroma. None of this is possible, however, without earnest striving for Gnosis.

Gnosis and Psyche: The Depth Psychological Connection

Throughout the twentieth century the new scientific discipline of depth psychology has gained much prominence. Among the depth psychologists who have shown a pronounced and informed interest in Gnosticism, a place of signal distinction belongs to Carl G. Jung. Jung was instrumental in calling attention to the Nag Hammadi library of Gnostic writings in the 1950s because he perceived the outstanding psychological relevance of Gnostic insights.

The noted scholar of Gnosticism, G. Filoramo, wrote: "Jung's reflections had long been immersed in the thought of the ancient Gnostics to such an extent that he considered them the virtual discoverers of 'depth psychology' …ancient Gnosis, albeit in its form of universal religion, in a certain sense prefigured, and at the same time helped to clarify, the nature of Jungian spiritual therapy." In the light of such recognitions one may ask: "Is Gnosticism a religion or a psychology?" The answer is that it may very-well be both. Most mythologems found in Gnostic scriptures possess psychological relevance and applicability. For instance the blind and arrogant creator-demiurge bears a close resemblance to the alienated human ego that has lost contact with the ontological Self. Also, the myth of Sophia resembles closely the story of the human psyche that loses its connection with the collective unconscious and needs to be rescued by the Self. Analogies of this sort exist in great profusion.

Many esoteric teachings have proclaimed, "As it is above, so it is below." Our psychological nature (the microcosm) mirrors metaphysical nature (the macrocosm), thus Gnosticism may possess both a psychological and a religious authenticity. Gnostic psychology and Gnostic religion need not be exclusive of one another but may complement each other within an implicit order of wholeness. Gnostics have always held that divinity is immanent within the human spirit, although it is not limited to it. The convergence of Gnostic religious teaching with psychological insight is thus quite understandable in terms of time-honored Gnostic principles.

Conclusion

Some writers make a distinction between "Gnosis" and "Gnosticism." Such distinctions are both helpful and misleading. Gnosis is undoubtedly an experience based not in concepts and precepts, but in the sensibility of the heart. Gnosticism, on the other hand, is the world-view based on the experience of Gnosis. For this reason, in languages other than English, the word Gnosis is often used to denote both the experience and the world view ("die Gnosis" in German, "la Gnose" in French).

In a sense, there is no Gnosis without Gnosticism, for the experience of Gnosis inevitably calls forth a world view wherein it finds its place. The Gnostic world view is experiential, it is based on a certain kind of spiritual experience of Gnosis. Therefore, it will not do to omit, or to dilute, various parts of the Gnostic world view, for were one to do this, the world view would no longer conform to experience.

Theology has been called an intellectual wrapping around the spiritual kernel of a religion. If this is true, then it is also true that most religions are being strangled and stifled by their wrappings. Gnosticism does not run this danger, because its world view is stated in myth rather than in theology. Myths, including the Gnostic myths, may be interpreted in diverse ways. Transcendence, numinosity, as well as psychological archetypes along with other elements, play a role in such interpretation. Still, such mythic statements tell of profound truths that will not be denied.

Gnosticism can bring us such truths with a high authority, for it speaks with the voice of the highest part of the human — the spirit. Of this spirit, it has been said, "it bloweth where it listeth." This then is the reason why the Gnostic world view could not be extirpated in spite of many centuries of persecution.

The Gnostic world view has always been timely, for it always responded best to the "knowledge of the heart" that is true Gnosis. Yet today, its timeliness is increasing, for the end of the second millennium has seen the radical deterioration of many ideologies which evaded the great questions and answers addressed by Gnosticism. The clarity, frankness, and authenticity of the Gnostic answer to the questions of the human predicament cannot fail to impress and (in time) to convince. If your reactions to this summary have been of a similarly positive order, then perhaps you are a Gnostic yourself!

– Stephan A. Hoeller (Tau Stephanus, Gnostic Bishop) www.gnosis.org

The Gnostic Gospels are largely ignored because they are odds with fundamentalist dogma.

V

Jesus

Jesus Pantocrator

This sixth-century representation of Jesus is the oldest known hand-painted icon in the world. It is believed to have been inspired by the Holy Shroud of Edessa.

– Santa Caterina Monastery Library, Sinai

The World's Sixteen Crucified Saviors

Rival Claims of the Saviors

It is claimed by the disciples of Jesus Christ that he was of supernatural and divine origin; that he had a human being for a mother, and a God for his father; that, although he was woman-conceived, he was Deity begotten, and molded in the human form, but comprehending in essence a full measure of the infinite Godhead, thus making him half human and half divine in his sublunary origin.

It is claimed that he was full and perfect God, and perfect man; and while he was God, he was also the son of God, and as such was sent down by his father to save a fallen and guilty world; and that thus his mission pertained to the whole human race; and his inspired seers are made to declare that ultimately every nation, tongue, kindred, and people under heaven will acknowledge allegiance to his government, and concede his right to reign and rule the world; that "every knee must bow, and every tongue confess that Jesus is Lord, to the glory of God the Father."

But we do not find that this prophecy has ever been or is likely to be fulfilled. We do not observe that this claim to the infinite deityship of Jesus Christ has been or is likely to be universally conceded. On the contrary, it is found that by a portion, and a large portion of the people of even those nations now called Christian, this claim has been steadily and unswervingly controverted, through the whole line of history, stretching through the nearly two thousand years which have elapsed since his advent to earth.

Even some of those who are represented to have been personally acquainted with him — aye! some of his own brethren in the flesh, children in the same household, children of the same mother — had the temerity to question the tenableness of his claim to a divine emanation. And when we extend our researches to other countries, we find this claim, so far from being conceded, is denied and contested by whole nations upon other grounds. It is met and confronted by rival claims.

Upon this ground hundreds of millions of the established believers in divine revelation — hundreds of millions of believers in the divine character and origin of religion — reject the pretensions set up for Jesus Christ. They admit both a God and a Savior, but do not accept Jesus of Nazareth as being either. They admit a Messiah, but not the Messiah; these nations contend that the title is misplaced which makes "the man Christ Jesus" the Savior of the world. They claim to have been honored with the birth of the true Savior among them, and defend this claim upon the ground of priority of date. They aver that the advents of their Messiahs were long prior to that of the Christians, and that this circumstance adjudicates for them a superiority of claim as to having had the true Messiah born upon their soil.

It is argued that, as the story of the incarnation of the Christians' Savior is of more recent date than those of these oriental and ancient religions (as is conceded by Christians themselves), the origin of the former is thus indicated and foreshadowed as being an outgrowth from, if not a plagiarism upon the latter — a borrowed copy, of which the pagan stories furnish the original. Here, then, we observe a rivalry of claims, as to which of the remarkable personages who have figured in the world as Saviors, Messiahs, and Sons of God, in different ages and different countries, can be considered the true Savior and "sent of God"; or whether all should be, or the claims of all rejected.

For researches into oriental history reveal the remarkable fact that stories of incarnate Gods answering to and resembling the miraculous character of Jesus Christ have been prevalent in most if not all the principal religious heathen nations of antiquity; and the accounts and narrations of some of these deific incarnations bear such a striking resemblance to that of the Christian Savior — not only in their general features, but in some cases in the most minute details, from the legend of the immaculate conception to that of the crucifixion, and subsequent ascension into heaven — that one might almost be mistaken for the other.

More than twenty claims of this kind — claims of beings invested with divine honor (deified) — have come forward and presented themselves at the bar of the world, with their credentials, to contest the verdict of Christendom, in having proclaimed Jesus Christ, "the only son, and sent of God"; twenty Messiahs, Saviors, and Sons of God, according to history or tradition, have, in past times, descended from heaven, and taken upon themselves the form of men, clothing themselves with human flesh, and furnishing incontestable evidence of a divine origin, by various miracles, marvelous works, and superlative virtues; and finally these twenty Jesus Christs (accepting their character for the name) laid the foundation for the salvation of the world, and ascended back to heaven.

1. Krishna of Hindustan
2. Buddha Sakia of India
3. Salivahana of Bermuda
4. Zulis, or Zhule, also Osiris and Orus, of Egypt
5. Odin of the Scandinavians
6. Crite of Chaldea
7. Zoroaster and Mithra of Persia
8. Baal and Taut, "the Only Begotten of God," of Phoenicia

9. Indra of Tibet
10. Bali of Afghanistan
11. Jao of Nepal
12. Wittoba of the Bilingonese
13. Thammuz of Syria
14. Atys of Phrygia
15. Xamolxis of Thrace
16. Zoar of the Bonzes
17. Adad of Assyria
18. Deva Tat, and Sammonocadam of Siam
19. Alcides of Thebes
20. Mikado of the Sintoos
21. Beddru of Japan
22. Hesus or Eros, and Bremrillah of the Druids
23. Thor, son of Odin, of the Gauls
24. Cadmus of Greece
25. Hil and Feta of the Mandaites
26. Gentaut and Quetzacoatl of Mexico
27. Universal Monarch of the Sibyls
28. Ischy of the island of Formosa
29. Divine Teacher of Plato
30. Holy One of Xaca
31. Fohi and Tien of China
32. Adonis, son of the virgin Io of Greece
33. Ixion and Quirinus of Rome
34. Prometheus of Caucasus
35. Mohamed, or Mahomet, of Arabia

These have all received divine honors, have nearly all been worshipped as Gods, or sons of God; were mostly incarnated as Christs, Saviors, Messiahs, or Mediators; not a few of them were reputedly born of virgins; some of them filling a character almost identical with that ascribed by the Christians' bible to Jesus Christ; many of them, like him, are reported to have been crucified; and all of them, taken together, furnish a prototype and parallel for nearly every important incident and wonder-inciting miracle, doctrine and precept recorded in the New Testament, of the Christians' Savior. Surely, with so many Saviors the world cannot, or should not, be lost.

And now, upon the heel of this question, we find another formidable query to be met and answered, viz.: was he (Christ) the only Savior, seeing that a multitude of similar claims are now upon our council-board to be disposed of?

We shall, however, leave the theologians of the various religious schools to adjust and settle this difficulty among themselves. We shall leave them to settle the question as best they can as to whether Jesus Christ was the only son and sent of God — "the only begotten of the Father," as John declares him to be (John 1:14) — in view of the fact that long prior to his time various personages, in different nations, were invested with the title "Son of God," and have left behind them similar proofs and credentials of the justness of their claims to such a title, if being essentially alike — as we shall prove and demonstrate them to be — can make their claims similar.

We shall present an array of facts and historical proofs, drawn from numerous histories and the Holy Scriptures and bibles appertaining to these various Saviors, which include a history of their lives and doctrines, that will go to show that in nearly all their leading features, and mostly even in their details, they are strikingly similar.

A comparison, or parallel view, extended through their sacred histories, so as to include an exhibition presented in parallels of the teachings of their respective bibles, would make it clearly manifest that, with respect to nearly every important thought, deed, word, action, doctrine, principle, precept, tenet, ritual, ordinance or ceremony, and even the various important characters or personages, who figure in their religious dramas as Saviors, prophets, apostles, angels, devils, demons, exalted or fallen genii — in a word, nearly every miraculous or marvelous story, moral precept, or tenet of religious faith, noticed in either the Old or New Testament Scriptures of Christendom — from the Jewish cosmogony, or story of creation in Genesis, to the last legendary tale in St. John's *Arabian Nights* (alias the Apocalypse) — there is to be found an antitype for, or outline of, somewhere in the sacred records or bibles of the oriental heathen nations, making equal if not higher pretension to a divine emanation and divine inspiration.

This is admitted by all historians, even the most orthodox, to be of much more ancient date; for while Christians only claim, for the earthly advent of their Savior and the birth of their religion, a period less than nineteen hundred years in the past, on the contrary, most of the deific or divine incarnations of the heathen and their respective religions are, by the concurrent and united verdict of all history, assigned a date several hundred or several thousand years earlier, thus leaving the inference patent that so far as there has been any borrowing or transfer of materials from one system to another, Christianity has been the borrower.

And as nearly the whole outline and constituent parts of the Christian system are found scattered through these older systems, the query is at once sprung as to whether Christianity did not derive its materials from these sources — that is, from heathenism, instead of from high heaven — as it claims.

As far back as 1200 B.C., sacred records were extant and traditions were current, in the East, which taught that the heathen Savior (Virishna) was:

- Immaculately conceived and born of a spotless virgin, "who had never known man."

- That the author of, or agent in, the conception was a spirit or ghost (of course a Holy Ghost).
- That he was threatened in early infancy with death by the ruling tyrant, Cansa.
- That his parents had, consequently, to flee with him to Gokul for safety.
- That all the young male children under two years of age were slain by an order issued by Cansa, similar to that of Herod in Judea.
- That angels and shepherds attended his birth.
- That it occurred in accordance with previous prophecy.
- That he was presented at birth with frankincense, myrrh, etc.
- That he was saluted and worshipped as "the Savior of men," according to the report of the late Christian Missionary Huc.
- That he led a life of humility and practical moral usefulness.
- That he wrought various astounding miracles, such as healing the sick, restoring sight to the blind, casting out devils, raising the dead to life, etc.
- That he was finally put to death upon the cross (i.e., crucified) between two thieves.
- After which he descended to hell, rose from the dead, and ascended back to heaven "in the sight of all men," as his biblical history declares.

The New York Correspondent, published in 1828, furnishes us the following brief history of an ancient Chinese God, known as Beddou:

> All the Eastern writers agree in placing the birth of Beddou 1027 B.C. The doctrines of this Deity prevailed over Japan, China, and Ceylon. According to the sacred tenets of his religion, 'God is incessantly rendering himself incarnate,' but his greatest and most solemn incarnation was three thousand years ago, in the province of Cashmere, under the name of Fot, or Beddou. He was believed to have sprung from the right intercostal of a virgin of the royal blood, who, when she became a mother, did not the less continue to be a virgin; that the king of the country, uneasy at his birth, was desirous to put him to death, and hence caused all the males that were born at the same period to be put to death, and also that, being saved by shepherds, he lived in the desert to the age of thirty years, at which time he opened his commission, preaching the doctrines of truth, and casting out devils; that he performed a multitude of the most astonishing miracles, spent his life fasting, and in the severest mortifications, and at his death bequeathed to his disciples the volume in which the principles of his religion are contained.

Here, it will be observed, are some very striking counterparts to the miraculous incidents found related in the Gospel history of Jesus Christ. And no less analogous is the no less well-authenticated story of Quetzacoatl of Mexico, which the Rev. Maurice concedes to be, and Lord Kingsborough and Niebuhr (in his history of Rome) prove to be much older than the Gospel account of Jesus Christ. According to Maurice's "Ind. Ant.," Humboldt's "Researches in Mexico," Lord Kingsborough's "Mexican Ant.," and other works, the incarnate God Quetzacoatl was born (about 300 B.C.) of a spotless virgin, by the name Chimalman, and led a life of the deepest humility and piety; retired to a wilderness, fasted forty days, was worshipped as a God, and was finally crucified between two thieves; after which he was buried and descended into hell, but rose again on the third day.

The following is a part of Lord Kingsborough's testimony in the case: "The temptation of Quetzacoatl, the fast of forty days ordained by the Mexican ritual, the cup with which he was presented to drink (on the cross), the reed which was his sign, the 'Morning Star,' which he is designated, the Teoteepall, or Divine Stone, which was laid on his altar, and which was likewise an object of adoration, all these circumstances, connected with many others relating to Quetzacoatl of Mexico, but which are here omitted, are very curious and mysterious."

Again "Quetzacoatl is represented, in the painting of Codex Borgianus, as nailed to the cross." One plate in this work represents him as being crucified in the heavens, one as being crucified between two thieves. Sometimes he is represented as being nailed to the cross, and sometimes as hanging with the cross in his hands. The same work speaks of his burial, descent into hell, and his resurrection; while the account of his immaculate conception and miraculous birth are found in a work called "Codex Vaticanus."

Other parallel incidents could be cited, if we had space for them, appertaining to the history of this Mexican God. And parallels might also be constructed upon the histories of other ancient Gods, as that of Sakia of India, Salivahana of Bermuda, Hesus, or Eros, of the Celtic Druids, Mithra of Persia, and Hil and Feta of the Mandaites.

We will close with the testimony of a French philosopher, Bagin, on the subject of deific incarnations. He says, "The most ancient histories are those of Gods who became incarnate in order to govern mankind. All those fables are the same in spirit, and sprang up everywhere from confused ideas, which have universally prevailed among mankind, that Gods formerly descended upon earth."

Now, we ask the Christian reader: *What does all this mean? How are you going to sustain the declaration that Jesus Christ was the only son and sent of God, in view of these historic facts? Where are the superior credentials of his claim? How will you prove the miraculous portion of his history to be real and the others false?*

We boldly say it cannot be done. Please answer these questions, or relinquish your doctrine of the divinity of Jesus Christ.

– Kersey Graves, *The World's Sixteen Crucified Saviors*
Truth Seeker Co., New York, 1875

The stories of the death of Krishna vary. One of the two most prevalent is his accidental shooting by a deer hunter. Upon being shot, he forgave all and disappeared into the sky. This happened about 310 B.C.

The other story is similar to the death of Jesus — with crucifixion and disappearance. This story became vogue later and gained acceptance in Greek, Roman and Christian times. Both deaths supposedly occurred in northwest India, in the spring. These stories are examples of composite literature.

The Jesus Myth

Knowing that the Jesus story is hollow and is historically unfounded — but assuming there was a Jewish Rabbi from Nazareth during Roman occupation and that this "rebel" Rabbi was crucified — his legs would have been broken, and his body would have been put into a shallow common grave where his remains would have been eaten by wild dogs or if he had survived…he would have been forced into hiding as a wanted man that appeared several times only to his supporters. A practical point of view taken by most non-Christian historians.

Zeus and Jesus

Zeus: Greek form of Sanskrit Dyhaus pitar, "Father Heaven," probably linked with Babylonian myths of Zu the Storm-Bird, a thrower of thunderbolts. The Romans called him Jupiter, or Jove; the European Christians substituted Jesus for Zeus.

Zeus   **Jesus**

Jesus: The Aramaic-Speaking Shemite

In this perspective of Jesus my intent is to bring the reader into the Eastern Mediterranean setting (the Aram-Mesopotamian culture and language) from which the dramatic and impelling life of this famous Galilean Jew appears to us. This will enhance the reader's perception of Jesus in his own Aramaic-Hebrew culture, religion and social atmosphere.

Ethnically speaking, Jesus was a Shemite (in English the letter "h" is dropped and it is spelled and pronounced as "Semite"). The term "Shemite" is derived from one of the sons of Noah whose name was Shem, Gen. 5:32. The expression "Shemite" applies to many Semitic dialects. It also refers to all the descendants of Shem, such as the Akkadians, Arameans, Assyrians, Chaldeans, Hebrews and Arabs.

What kind of temperament does a son of the Near East, especially a Semite, possess? What of his manner of speech, his deep religious feelings and what would be his general outlook on life? When we discover the answers to these Questions we will be able to see, at least in part, the human Jesus beginning to emerge from his own inherited Eastern psychological environment. As we begin to comprehend the rich cultural and religious philosophy of Jesus' time, in its Judaic context, a clearer sense of the man and his teachings may be grasped.

The four Gospels, Matthew, Mark, Luke and John, are the main sources available to help us uncover the Semitic Jesus. In the modern sense these Gospel writings are not biographical material about Jesus. In fact, no contemporary stylized biographies can be found anywhere in Scripture. As a general rule, ancient Easterners had no deep interest in the details of a great man's life from birth to death. Their basic interest in such a man would be in his teachings and the overall impact of those teachings upon their lives. The Gospels were written after Jesus' death. These writings began as recollections of his words and acts as a teacher and healer. The stories of his birth, death and resurrection were added later.

The texts of the Gospels should not be thought of as mythical creations just because the historians of Jesus' day did not mention him in their writings. We need to keep in mind that he was a provincial teacher from a small village in Galilee and was not widely known. The primary characteristics of Jesus' human nature were not different from those of anyone else in his community.

Since the Gospels are the source of our inquiry, how reliable are the Gospels? For the last two and a half centuries, the four Gospels have been and continue to be subjected to many scholarly (and not so scholarly) historical debates, academic research, and fiery discussions. Despite the fact that the writers and editors of the Gospels present us with a partial and theologically colored portrait of Jesus, we can still find the human, Semitic Nazarene teacher within their pages. This vital point must be considered and included in the search for the man Jesus.

For example, consider the viewpoint of the late Lebanese scholar, Dr. Abraham Rihbany, who was a dedicated minister and an adept, prolific writer/author on the Near East. In his book *The Syrian Christ*, he states his poignant view very clearly and succinctly:

> In the Gospel story of Jesus' life there is not a single incident that is not in perfect harmony with the prevailing modes of thought and the current speech of the land of its origin. [Since] I was born not far from where the Master was born, and brought up under almost the identical conditions under which he lived, I have an inside view of the Bible which by the nature of things, a Westerner cannot have. And I know that the conditions of life in Syria today are essentially as they were in the time of Christ, not from the study of the mutilated tablets of the archaeologist and the antiquarian…but from the simple fact that, as a sojourner in this Western world, whenever I open my Bible it reads like a letter from home. Its unrestrained effusiveness of expression; its vivid, almost flashy and fantastic imagery; its naive narrations; the rugged unstudied simplicity of its parables; its unconventional portrayal of certain human relations; as well as its all-permeating spiritual mysticism, might all have been written in my primitive village home, on the western slopes of Mount Lebanon some thirty years ago…

Let us view the Semitic Jesus in the light of his own language, people and times. We will see him from the background of the ancient Aramaic language, Hebrew Scriptures, customs, metaphors and psychology, as well as from the unencumbered Aramaic style of writing behind the teachings and narratives of the Gospels.

To this day the Galilean teacher receives on-going worldwide acclaim and worship through many forms, yet he never sought worshippers. He never attempted to inaugurate a new system of worship, nor to undermine the religion of his forefathers. He discounted honors and notoriety. He came not for humankind to sacrifice to him, but that he might serve humanity.

From a purely historical perspective, it is certain that Jesus never thought of himself as possessing any superhuman nature; nor was he conscious of any supernatural birth. These ideas which we find in the Gospels of Matthew and Luke were theological and christological additions made by church scribes when these two Gospels were compiled.

In his book *How to Understand the Gospels*, Anthony C. Deane, Canon of Windsor, says:

> Saint Mark is not afraid to attribute human limitations to our Lord; he feels grief, anger, surprise, amazement, fatigue; he asks questions for information; at times he is unable to do what he wills.

Though the humanity of Jesus appears in the Gospels, the theology which developed in and among the early communities of believers in the latter half of the first century C.E. began to overlay Jesus' historical sayings and to obscure his essential human nature.

Jesus never claimed that he was God's only son! He felt himself to be fully human and was motivated by his deep faith and personal relationship with God. He taught no abstruse and mysterious doctrines. He did not wait for people to come to him; he went to them. He preached in synagogues, in the marketplaces, at private homes, on hilltops, at the seashore, and anywhere else he could find listeners. Jesus originated no new terms and used only familiar ideas. His comforting and charismatic personality, his plain words and simple parables captivated the harried Galileans who eagerly listened to him.

The Aramaic Language

Before continuing our view of Jesus in his Near Eastern setting, we need to look into a brief history of the Aramaic language. It made its historical appearance toward the end of the second millennium B.C.E., in Mesopotamia — the fertile crescent of the ancient Near East. Gradually, at the onset of the first millennium B.C.E., the written and spoken forms of the Aramaic tongue began making inroads throughout Near Eastern lands. It was the language of the Arameans, Assyrians, Chaldeans, Hebrews and Syrians.

Historians inform us that the term "Aramaic" is derived from Aram. According to Hebrew Scripture, Aram was a grandson of Noah, Gen. 10:22. Aramaic is a Semitic (more precisely — Shemitic) language. The word "Aram" is formed from an Aramaic noun and adjective: "Araa" meaning earth, land, or terrain and "Ramtha" meaning high. The fertile valley, Padan-Aram (Mesopotamia or Beth Nahreen "the land between the rivers") was the territory in which the descendants of Aram dwelt and in which Aramaic developed and remained pure. In time, because of the practicality of its alphabet and simplicity of style in writing and speaking, it attracted all classes of people, government officials, merchants, and writers.

Thus, by the eighth century B.C.E., Aramaic became the common tongue among the majority of Semitic clans and was the major language from Egypt to Asia Minor to Pakistan. It was employed by the great Semitic empires, Assyria and Chaldea (Babylon). It was also the language of the Persian (Iranian) government in its Western provinces. This Semitic tongue continues to be spoken and written in today's world by a variety of Chaldean, Assyrian and other Semitic communities in the Near and Middle East, Australia, the United States and elsewhere. These communities regularly speak the Aramaic language at home, in their social, political, domestic meetings and in their religious worship Liturgy.

Biblical as well as secular history records the various expulsions of the tribes of Israel from their homeland to Assyria and Chaldea. Historically, the two most important exiles are: In 721 B.C.E., the Assyrians took the ten Northern tribes of the House of Israel captive to Nineveh and scattered them throughout Mesopotamia (Northern Iraq, Afghanistan and Pakistan). These waning conquerors repopulated Northern Israel with some of their own people and other Semitic clans who spoke Aramaic in its Assyrian dialect. (Eastern Aramaic was divided into two dialects, the Northern vernacular spoken in Assyria and the Southern vernacular spoken in Chaldea, i.e., Babylon.) These new inhabitants of the northern sector of Palestine intermarried with the remnant of Israelites that were left behind by the invading armies of Assyria. The descendants of these mixed marriages came to be known as Samaritans. The second exile: In 587 B.C.E., Nebuchanessar, the Chaldean King, deported the remaining two tribes of the House of Judah, the southern kingdom of Israel, to Babylon.

Then in 539 B.C.E., Cyrus, the ruler of Persia (Iran) conquered the great city of Babylon and ended the Chaldean empire. The Persian King granted freedom to the exiled Jews who were living in Babylon. They could now return to Palestine under the protection of the Persian power. By this time, the Jewish people who returned to their homeland were speaking the Southern dialect of Aramaic. Therefore, during the first century in Palestine, the people of Judea spoke in the Southern dialect of Aramaic. But in Galilee, Jesus, his disciples, followers and contemporaries spoke in the Eastern, Northern dialect of Aramaic.

It is interesting to note that the manner of speech, the phraseology, the idioms and the orientation in the four Gospels: Matthew, Mark, Luke and John are vividly and distinctively Aramaic. The constant repetitions are characteristic of Eastern speech. Such phrases as "Truly, truly, I say to you," or "In those days," "And it came to pass," "And he said to them," are peculiarly Aramaic. Hebrew was spoken in some areas of the Holy Land, but there is some discussion among present-day scholars as to its widespread use during the first century C.E.

The first-century evidence clearly indicates that Aramaic was the most common language used throughout Palestine. The message of Jesus of Nazareth was proclaimed and taught all over Palestine, Lebanon, Syria, and Mesopotamia in the Eastern Aramaic language. Aramaic remained the common language of the Near East until the seventh century C.E.; then Arabic gradually began to supplant Aramaic. Nonetheless, the Christians of Mesopotamia (Iraq), Iran, Syria, Turkey and Lebanon kept the Aramaic tongue alive domestically, scholastically and liturgically. In spite of the pressure of the ruling Arabs to speak Arabic, Aramaic is still spoken today in its many dialects, especially among the Assyrians and Chaldeans. It is known as Syriac but this is a misnomer. Syriac is the Greek term for Aramaic.

Another important aspect of the Aramaic language was its use as the major tongue for the birth and spread of spiritual and intellectual ideas in and all over the Near East. According to the research and opinion of an outstanding Aramaic and Arabic scholar, Professor Franz Rosenthal, in the *Journal of Near Eastern Studies*:

> In my view, the history of Aramaic represents the purest triumph of the human spirit as embodied in language over the crude display of material power. Great empires were conquered by the Aramaic language, and when they disappeared and were submerged in the flow of history, that language persisted and continued to live a life of its own…the language continued to be powerfully active in the promulgation of spiritual matters. It was the main instrument for the formulation of religious ideas in the Near East, which then spread in all directions all over the world. The monotheistic groups continue to live on today with a religious heritage, much of which found first expression in Aramaic.

The Eastern Temperament and the Common Language

The best way to understand the Eastern temperament and daily language of the Semites is to receive firsthand information from an Easterner himself. Dr. Rihbany says:

> The Oriental [Easterner] I have in mind is the Semite, the dweller of the Near East, who, chiefly through the Bible, has exerted an immense influence on the life and literature of the West. The son of the Near East is more emotional, more intense, and more communicative than his Far-Eastern neighbors. Although very old in point of time, his (the Semite) temperament remains somewhat juvenile and his manner of speech intimate and unreserved.

> From the remote past, even to this day, the Oriental's [Easterner's] manner of speech has been that of a worshipper, and not that of a business man or an industrial worker in the modern Western sense…his daily language is essentially biblical. He has no secular language. The only real break between his scriptures and the vocabulary of his daily life is that which exists between the classical and the vernacular…

> An Easterner's chief purpose in a conversation is to convey an impression by whatever suitable means, and not to deliver his message in scientifically accurate terms. He piles up his metaphors and superlatives, reinforced by a theatrical display of gestures and facial expressions in order to make the hearer feel his meaning. He speaks as it were in pictures. With him the spoken language goes hand in hand with the most ancient gesture language. His profuse gesticulation is that phase of his life which first challenges the attention of Western travelers in the East. He points to almost everything he mentions in his speech

and would portray every feeling and emotion by means of some bodily movement...

> It is also because he loves to speak in pictures and to subordinate literal accuracy to the total impression of an utterance, that he makes such extensive use of figurative language. Instead of saying to the Pharisees; "your pretensions to virtue" and good birth far exceed your actual practice of virtue / John the Baptist cried: 'Oh generation of vipers, etc.' Just as he loves to flavor his food strongly and to dress in bright colors, so is he fond of metaphor, exaggeration, and positiveness in speech. To him mild accuracy is weakness.

The supreme choice of the Oriental [Easterner] has been religion. What has always seemed to him to be his first and almost only duty was and is to form the most direct, most intimate connection between God and the soul. It is from this Eastern psychological background, religious temperament and language that not only the Gospels' portrait of Jesus comes to us, but also the Bible in its entirety.

The following aspects of Jesus are depicted in the Semitic Aramaic setting and emphasize the purely human side of him. Many of the following Aramaic terms attributed to Jesus, or those that he may have used himself, have been misunderstood over the centuries, and some of them no longer carry their original meaning.

Yeshua – The Name of Jesus

Jesus (Yeshu — the northern Galilean Aramaic dialect) was a common Aramaic name in the first century C.E. Our English form of Jesus' name comes from a shortened classical Hebrew/Aramaic form of Yeshua. However, the name Yeshua is, in turn, a shortened form of the name of the great biblical hero Joshua, son of Nun. The Hebrew name in full is Yehoshua. "Joshua" was the name commonly used before the Babylonian exile. Among the Jews after the Chaldean (Babylonian) exile, the short form of the term was adopted — Yeshua.

Despite this change, the name "Joshua" did not die out entirely. "Jesus" was a common name in Palestine and remained popular among the Jews until the beginning of the second century C.E.; The Jews stopped using "Jesus" as a personal name and revived the classical term "Joshua." Thereafter, "Jesus" became a rare name among the second century Jewish people.

Bar-nasha – The Son of Man

In the three major Semitic languages — Aramaic, Hebrew and Arabic — the term "son of man" means a "human being." In everyday language, Jesus referred to himself as a human being. According to the Gospels, he used the term "son of man" approximately twenty-eight times. "Son of man" is a peculiar Aramaic expression of speech to the Western mind and it has caused a great deal of confusion when attempting to interpret the Gospels without the knowledge of the Aramaic language. The word itself in Aramaic is bar-nasha, a compound noun. Bar means "son" and nasha means "man." It is improper to literally translate this Aramaic term bar-nasha as "the son of man." Yet, many biblical translators have and still do render this term literally.

In Aramaic when the word bar "son" is joined to other words, those words change meaning. For example, barabba literally translated means the "son of the father," but properly translated it means "he resembles his father;" bar-agara literally translated means "son of the rooftop," but properly translated it means "a lunatic." Additional examples are bar-zauga, "son of the yoke" — a friend, a companion; bar-hila, son of power — soldier; bar-yolpana, son of learning — disciple. Thus, bar-nasha, son of man — man, human being.

Bar-dalaha – The Son of God

In the Aramaic-Semitic language and culture, the term bar-dalaha, "son of God," "God's son" or "God's child," is used many ways and may refer to an orphan, a meek young man (in contrast, a meek, mature individual is often called a "man of God"), a peacemaker, a good, kind or pious individual. The word "son," as we learned from the term "son of man," is subtly used to infer "likeness," "resemblance" and to be "in the image of." Thus, "son of God" signifies "like God" or "God-likeness." The intended meaning of "son of God" depends on the context in which it is used in the various passages of the Bible.

The few times that Jesus referred to himself as "son of God," as recorded in the Gospels, were always within the religious tenor and meaning of his day. This "special sonship" in Hebrew scripture and in the New Testament never refers to a "physical-divine" sonship, but rather to a spiritual relationship between the God of Israel and the individual designated as "son." Biblically speaking, "sonship" is a spiritual relationship between God and a human being which is based on love, respect and doing the will of God. Often when Easterners call someone "son" or "my son" it is their way of showing affection and referring to that person as a "beloved." In all forms of relationships, everyday verbal expressions remain more intimate and flowery than those of the West. To this day the religious language of Semites, all over the Middle East, bears witness to their poetic intimacy and imagery in their devotion to God.

Ehedaya – The Only Begotten Son

Jesus never claimed he was God's only son. The claim that Jesus was God's "only begotten son" was made by others. This term is found exclusively in the Gospel of John. The term "only begotten," which appears in John's Gospel as a translation of the Greek word "monogenes," cannot be justified. It is an improper English rendering of this Greek word. "Monogenes" is composed of two Greek words. "Monos" means "singular"; "genos" means "kind." When these two words are combined they literally mean "one of a kind."

However, "genos" is distantly related to the verb "gennan" which means "to beget." It is improper to translate "monogenes" as "only begotten." A better rendering would be "unique son." Jerome, in the Latin Vulgate, translated "monogenes" as "only begotten" in answer to the Arian doctrine which taught that Jesus was not begotten, but made.

The Aramaic word is "Ehedaya" and means a "sole heir," the "beloved," hence, "unique, beloved son." Once again we are dealing with Semitic figures of speech. The term "Ehedaya" in the Aramaic language is not to be taken literally. The gospel writer, by using this term, places Jesus in a precious and endearing setting which is typically an Eastern manner.

M'sheeha – The Messiah

The term "M'sheeha," "Messiah," the "Anointed," the "Appointed One" is a title and not a proper name. The Greek term "Christos," "Christ," is a Greek translation of the Aramaic word "M'sheeha" and has the same significance. Years after the death of Jesus the term "Christ" became a proper name, and Jesus of Nazareth became known as "Jesus Christ." A better rendering in English would be "Jesus the Christ," because Jesus had become known as an "Anointed One." According to Hebrew Scripture, kings, priests and sometimes prophets were anointed with consecrated oil into their respective offices.

Anointing with consecrated oil, applied to the crown of the head like an ointment, is a very ancient rite. In Hebrew the word "anoint" is mashach, hence the title "Messiah" (Anointed One). The act of anointing was considered a transfer of divine powers to the person who was being anointed. Hence, he became known as the "Lord's anointed," (a son by adoption). The Kings of Israel were known as "the Lord's Anointed Ones," or "the Lord's Christs." David called King Saul the "Lord's Anointed" (Messiah-Christ). The above interpretation of the word "messiah" was its original meaning.

Prior to the reign of King David the Hebrews had no thought of a Messiah. The pre-exilic prophets had hoped and worked for their nation to cleanse itself morally so that Israel could become a great beacon to guide all the nations of the earth into paths of justice. According to Isaiah's vision, Israel, having cleansed itself, would then be ruled by a king from the family of David. Under the wise and powerful leadership of this prophesied King, justice, peace, compassion and national contentment would reign and abound in Israel, so much so that other nations would also benefit from this national spiritual revival.

However, after the exile and return of the people of Israel to their homeland, known as the Second-Temple Era, the messianic concept gradually changed. From 167 B.C.E. to the time of the birth of Jesus, the messianic idea underwent many modifications. Malachi predicted that Elijah would appear and prepare the way for the Messiah — a human, earthly Messiah endowed by the God of Israel with the necessary power to lead the people in the paths of peace and justice. After this prediction more and more writings began to appear which transformed the earlier messianic concepts. It was predicted that the Messiah would be an aggressive, militant and political leader who would destroy the enemies of God's people.

It should be noted that the messianic hope was not peculiar only to the Jewish-Christian religion. In almost all ancient religions this belief was expressed, especially whenever nations fell prey to hatred, injustice, persecution and the devastation of war. The hearts of the people were filled with the hope that a Power in the form of some great leader would bring national peace and salvation.

During the first century C.E. a myriad of concepts concerning the Messiah were prevalent, such as a Prince-Messiah of the House of David, a Priest-King, a Warrior, a Mediator between God and man, a pre-existent Messiah, and a Messiah endowed with superhuman powers to destroy Satan and his kingdom. Jesus, a Mediterranean peasant from half-heathen Galilee, a simple teacher and preacher with a small discipleship of fisherman and crowds of poor peasants who followed him, could not possibly measure up to the expectations and requirements set down for a great hero — "a Prince-Messiah of the House of David." We can now understand why Jesus forbade his immediate followers to call him "Messiah-Christ."

Before concluding, one other point needs to be mentioned. The apostle Paul, a visionary who had the ability to enter altered states of consciousness (trances), cast Jesus in yet another messianic role. To Paul, Jesus was a mystical Messiah — a mystical Christ, the heavenly man who conquered principalities and powers of the air. He added his messianic revelation to the already prevailing ideas which were adopted and attributed to Jesus by the second generation of believers. No evidence has been found that the members of the Jerusalem church accepted Paul's mystical Christ who transcended all Jewish expectations. Jesus' immediate disciples who walked, talked and sailed with him on the lake of Galilee never for a moment thought they were associating with the Creator of heaven and earth. The bond of union among the Jewish believers in Jesus was more fraternal than creedal. What they had in common was their devotion to their teacher and his teachings.

Conclusion

Jesus, a Semite and a man among men, continues to speak through all the ages. His human personality, his loving nature and his simple teachings will live forever and continue to enrich and embrace the hearts of the human family everywhere. When the unpretentious teachings of Jesus are fully realized, all subtle forms of imperialism which advocate absolutism — such as an infallible church, infallible bible, infallible doctrines or infallible anything — can no longer stand. The desire for infallibility is a lust for undisputed authority, absolute power, and seeks to dominate individual freedom and free thought.

The human Jesus was a simple man. His source was God, and his spiritual insight continues to ignite the hearts and souls of men, women and children the world over.

– Rocco A. Errico, Ph.D.

The need of the Western readers of the Bible is…to have real intellectual, as well as spiritual, fellowship with those Easterners who sought earnestly in their own way to give tangible form to those great spiritual truths.

Dr. Abraham Rihbany

The Last Supper

"The Last Supper" by Leonardo da Vinci is depicted in a Western setting.

" *The Passover (Last Supper) symbolizes the Sun/Son image with the twelve disciples, who depict the twelve months in a year and are arranged in four groups of three, signifying the seasons.* "

Jordan Maxwell

The Last Supper

Most readers of the Bible visualize this momentous scene of the last supper in a totally Western setting, not realizing that they are being influenced by the famous painting of Leonardo Da Vinci. This renowned Italian artist gave the world a beautiful character study in his painting of the last supper. However, we must understand that Da Vinci was not portraying an historical Eastern setting. His entire work — the room, the table, the attire of the apostles and Jesus, and even the seating arrangements — are of his day and time. What we have in this painting is an Italian provincial scene and not one of the Near East.

The following description, then, is based on the typical Eastern customs observed at such a supper. Jesus and his disciples sat on the floor in a circle in one of the small rooms of a "balakhana," an inn for men only. The apostles and Jesus all wore hats during the supper. Spread on the floor in the center of the room was a cloth called in Aramaic "pathora." Placed on the pathora were an earthen cup, a little jar filled with wine, and two or three large dishes. The cup was put in the center within reach of everyone in the circle. The jar was near Jesus.

According to eastern customs, on such occasions each of the few large plates contained a different kind of food. Bread is passed around. Meat is wrapped in thin loaves of bread, (this is called sop) put into pockets, and often carried home. The guests do not hesitate to reach for food on other men's dishes.

The posture of the beloved disciple, John, who was leaning on Jesus' chest, is also a common social custom. To this day, very dose male friends still maintain this attitude while eating together, and it is as natural as shaking hands in the West. However, this show of affection is especially practiced when intimate friends are about to part from one another, as on the eve of a journey or when about to face a perilous assignment.

During this supper Jesus "let himself go," that is, he expressed his feelings freely and openly to his disciples. He let them know of his disappointment in one who was about to betray him, and because these men would never meet in this manner again, he also made other statements which are often spoken at a "farewell supper." The things Jesus said and did at the last supper were not isolated or uncommon events in the Semitic culture. A brotherly atmosphere and intimate, emotional expressions usually characterize a supper of this type among Eastern people, especially in the shadow of approaching danger.

It is the custom of a gracious host to ask for a joyous ending to a visit by having the whole company of men drink from one cup as a sign of their friendship. The phrase, "Do this in remembrance of me," is an affectionate request and means, "I love you; therefore I am always with you." When Jesus had made this request of his disciples they understood his loving statement to mean, "A powerful bond of love is between us, and because of this love we cannot be separated from one another." In other words, he would no longer be with them.

At Eastern feasts, and especially in the region of Galilee, sharing food with those who stand and serve wine and water to the guests is common. However, exchanges of food with friends take on a deeper meaning. Choice portions of food are handed to friends as signs of close intimacy. This is never done with an enemy. Once again, Jesus let his feelings be revealed when he handed Judas, the betrayer, his "sop." "And when he had dipped the sop, he gave it to Judas Iscariot, the son of Simon" (John 13:16). By understanding this Eastern custom, one quickly comprehends the act of love Jesus demonstrated by sharing his sop with Judas, for Jesus truly practiced his own teachings: "Love your enemies." In essence, he was telling Judas, through this sharing, that he did not in fact consider him an enemy. Jesus felt deep compassion and love for Judas, and with this symbolic gesture he was saying, "Here is my bread of friendship, and what you have to do, do it quickly." Shortly after, Jesus was betrayed and sold to his priestly adversaries by Judas.

It was at this supper that Jesus sealed his love and friendship with his disciples. Pointing to the lamb and the bread and then to the wine, he said that his body was to become like the lamb and bread, broken and eaten; his blood was like the wine, drunk by all. He gave his life to reveal a new way of living for all mankind.

– Rocco A. Errico
Excerpt from *Let There Be Light, The Seven Keys*

The Jesus Movements

The Christian Era and the Last Great Revision of Judaism
Approximately 30 C.E. to 73 C.E.

The conflict between the Hellenism and the traditions of ethnic Judaism was nowhere more obvious than in the northern part of Palestine, which had been so often subject to conquest and which, being on the major trade route between Asia Minor and the Transjordan, was constantly subjected to foreign influence. This northern region apparently didn't even consider itself to be Jewish, but rather a separate nation that had been annexed, apparently involuntarily, by the Maccabean kings of Israel. So here you have Hellenized Semitics under the influence and control of Jewish kings, looking elsewhere for philosophical guidance. It was a volatile mix.

Into this little region, called Galilee, was born a stubborn iconoclast. He resented the Roman occupation but accepted its rule. He was an intellect who understood at least the rudiments of the Cynic school of Greek philosophy and the complex theology of the Semitic Jews around him. But he would have none of it. He felt that there had to be a better way to live. He grew up a suburb of the capital of Galilee, in a place called Nazareth. His name was Jesus.

At least, that's the mythology that has grown up around this figure. For all his influence on the world, there's better evidence that he never even existed than that he did. We have absolutely no reliable evidence, from secular sources, that Jesus ever lived, or that any of the events surrounding his life as described in the four Gospels ever happened.

Indeed, when scholars apply the Negative Evidence Principle, it begins to look like the Jesus we know from the New Testament is the result of late first-century mythmaking.

The Negative Evidence Principle is, of course, not foolproof. It is not a proof in itself, but is rather a guideline, a good rule of thumb. How useful and reliable it is, of course, is subject to debate among logicians. Here's how the N.E.P. works — it states that you have good reason for not believing in a proposition if the following three principles are satisfied: First, all of the evidence supporting the proposition has been shown to be unreliable. Second, there is no evidence supporting the proposition when the evidence should be there if the proposition is true. And third, a thorough and exhaustive search has been made for supporting evidence where it should be found.

As for the first point, the only somewhat reliable, secular evidence we have for the life of Jesus comes from two very brief passages in the works of Josephus, a first-century Jewish historian. And Josephus was a prolific writer — he frequently wrote several pages on the trial and execution of individual common thieves, but on Jesus, he is silent except for two paragraphs, one of which is a known interpolation, and the other is highly suspect. Other references to Jesus in secular writings are ambiguous at best, or known to be later interpolations, or both. The earliest references to Jesus in the rabbinical literature come from the second century, even though known historical figures such as John the Baptist merit considerable discussion, even though his impact on Judaism was minimal. There are no references to Jesus in any of the Roman histories during his presumed lifetime. That he should be so thoroughly ignored is unlikely given the impact the gospel writers said he had on the events and politics of the Jewish kingdom.

So we have to turn to Christian literature for help.

At this point, caution is called for in examining first-century Christian literature. This caution is made necessary by the fact that during this era, it was not considered wrong to write your own material and ascribe it to someone else, someone you consider your philosophical mentor, in whose name and style you are writing. Indeed, not only was this a common practice, but it was actually a skill taught in the schools of the day. This practice has made modern scholarship enormously difficult in dealing with who actually wrote the New Testament books and when. The problem, though difficult, is not insoluble, and modern scholarship has developed techniques which have been applied to early Christian writings, to find out who is saying what, when and why. When these techniques are applied to these early Christian writings, the results have been quite surprising.

The writings of Paul accepted as genuinely his (Galatians I and II and Thessalonians I and II, Corinthians, Romans, Philemon, Philippians, and possibly Colossians) are by far the most pristine of any early Christian literature we have. They were probably written beginning in the fifth decade of the first century — well after the events of Jesus' life. When the letters are examined in isolation, it becomes apparent that Paul was ignorant of the doctrine of the virgin birth, that he never spoke in terms of having lived in Jesus' time, nor does he mention that any of his mentors were contemporaries of Jesus, nor that Jesus worked any miracles and he apparently did not associate the death of Jesus with the trial before Pilate. Only in Galatians 1:19 does he make reference to a contemporary Jesus, and then only in terms of James being the "Lord's brother." The use of the term "Lord's" even makes that single reference somewhat questionable to scholars, as the word "Lord's" did not have currency until the late second century. So the Pauline letters, at least the reliably Pauline letters, aren't good witnesses for a Jesus of the first half of the first century. What makes this particularly interesting is that other non-Canonical early Christian pre-Gospel literature make the very same omissions.

Later Christian writings were written well after the events they describe, none earlier than at least the seventh decade at the earliest. And none of them are known to have been written by the authors to which they are ascribed. Most are second- or third- hand accounts. There was plenty of time for mythmaking by the time they were written, so they're clearly not reliable witnesses.

The next stricture of the Negative Evidence Principle is that there isn't any sound evidence where there should be, and here again this stricture is met. First, there are no records whatever of Jesus' life in the Roman records of the era. That's surprising, since he stirred up so much unrest, at least by Biblical accounts. There at least ought to be a record of his arrest and trial, or some of the political notoriety the gospel writers describe. Yet the Roman histories are silent, even though they are quite thorough (Flavius Josephus alone wrote dozens of volumes, many of which survive, and he is far from the only historian of Palestine in this period whose writings have survived in some form). Second, as mentioned, there is no reliable account in Josephus.

Josephus was a historian who was so very thorough he would write a three-page history of the trial and execution of a common thief, and wrote extensively about John the Baptist, but on Jesus, his two small references are seriously doubted by scholars as being genuine. Unfortunately, the writings of Josephus have come down to us only through Christian sources, none earlier than the fourth century, and are known to have been revised by the Christians. There are a number of reasons why the two references in Josephus are doubted: As summarized by Louis Feldman, a prominent Josephus scholar, they are, first, use of the Christian reference to Jesus being the Messiah is unlikely to have come from a Jewish historian, especially from one who treated other Messianic aspirants rather harshly; second, commentators writing about Josephus earlier than Eusebius (fourth century C.E.) do not cite the passage; third, Origen mentions that Josephus did not believe that Jesus was the messiah. There is a full account available on the Internet that describes the whole long list of problems with the "Testimonium Flavium" as scholars call it.

The earliest secular literary evidence for a religion based on the man we call Jesus comes from many decades after Jesus' supposed death (from about 70 C.E.). Why, if he had as much influence, and caused as much a stir as the Bible says he did, do we not know of him at all from reliable, contemporary testimony?

The third stricture of the N.E.P. holds that we must have conducted a thorough and exhaustive sweep for evidence where there should be evidence. Indeed, thousands of scholars, religionists, crusaders, apologists and skeptics alike have searched for such evidence since the earliest days of the Christian era. That they haven't found any reliable evidence that should have been there says that the third stricture has been clearly satisfied.

So based on the Negative Evidence Principle, we have good reason to doubt the historicity of Jesus and that lack of reliable evidence suggests no good reason to accept it.

How is it, then, that the movement began? Why did it grow as it did?

As discussed above, there was considerable intellectual ferment in Palestine at the time of the beginning of the Jesus movements. Many secular scholars and scholars from non-Judeo-Christian traditions have proposed, and I tend to agree, that it is likely that the Jesus myth began as a social movement to 're-Judaify' Judaism. Remember that at this point, the temple was thoroughly corrupt, the high priest was a Roman political appointee, and many Jews felt that their culture and religion were under threat.

The most prominent of the many movements to 're-Judaify' Judaism was the Essene Movement. Founded in the second century B.C.E., the Essenes were either founded by or greatly influenced by a "Teacher of Righteousness," to which the Dead Sea Scrolls make constant reference without ever naming. One individual who fits the scanty evidence is a Yeishu ha Notzri, Jesus or Jesua, or Yeshua or Joshua ben Pantera or Pentera or Pandera or Pandira, who apparently had some influence with this movement, but may have been much more than that; we simply don't know. Indeed, there are even several first-century Christian references to this supposed miracle worker.

If he was the Teacher of Righteousness referred to by the Dead Sea Scrolls, as some have suggested, his impact on the movement towards Jewish reform was considerable. And if he was the Teacher of Righteousness, it would answer a lot of interesting questions, such as the scattered first-century Christian and Talmudic references to a miracle worker named Yeishu ha Notzri, known to first-century Christians as Jesus or Jesua ben Pantera. Among them are a quote from Origen, saying that his arch-rival Celsus had heard from a Jew in Jerusalem that "Jesus Ben Pantera" was born of Mary as the result of a rape by a Roman soldier named Pantera, and had borne the baby in secret (most scholars now regard this claim to be a first-century legend resulting from misinterpretation of the facts).

That the first-century Christians may have feared there was some truth to this rumor is evidenced by the fact of Mark's obvious embarrassment regarding the origins of Jesus; Mark, the first writer of a canonic gospel, never mentions Joseph as the actual husband of Mary. Note also that it was both the Roman custom and the custom of the Jews to include a patrilineal surname as part of a person's full name; yet nowhere in the New Testament does the surname of Jesus, (or Joseph, for that matter) appear. There is at least one Talmudic reference to Jeshu as being the illegitimate son of an adulteress named Mary Magdala. There are several interesting references to a Yeishu ha Notzri (note the resemblance of the name to "Jesus of Nazareth"), who traveled around and practiced magic during the reign of Alexander Janneus, who ruled Palestine from 104 to 78 B.C.E. As these references are Talmudic (from the Baraitas and the Gemara), and therefore presumed by Christian scholars to be anti-Christian; Christian apologeticists have simply dismissed them as referring to someone else or being fabricated propaganda. But if they are genuine, and they really do refer to the Jesus of whom the Christians speak, they add evidence to the claim that the Jesus of Nazareth story is really based on the life of Yeishu ha Notzri, possibly the Essene "Teacher of Righteousness." Evidence points to him as the founder of the Notzri, as the sects were known in first-century Palestine, and as the Jesus Movements are known to modern scholars.

It must be noted here is that the version of the Talmud still used by most modern Christian scholars, is normally the version known to have been heavily edited by Christians by the sixteenth century — presumably to remove the dangerous references to Yeishu ha Notzri and his followers, the Notzrim, the account of which is absent from this version. But the pristine version, still used by Jewish scholars, gives us some rich detail. Yeishu ha Notzri was considered by the temple authorities of the time to be a troublemaking heretic, and when they had finally had enough of him, they put him on trial. He was convicted of heresy, sentenced to wander the city for 40 days, with a crier going before him, shouting that if anyone had reason why he should not be executed, they should come forward. When no did, he was stoned to death, and his body hung from a tree on the eve of Passover, in 88 B.C.E. Note the death on the eve of Passover. Note also the hanging of the body from a tree — at the time, a sign of despicability, with its resemblance to the crucifixion myth.

The Essene movement was one based on a very strict asceticism. Followers were expected to live in monastic isolation, eating a rough diet of hard, primitive foods and living in very simple, rough accommodations, in the harsh climate and isolation of the Judean desert. Since not a lot of people had a taste for that kind of harsh, strict living, it was not exactly a wildly popular movement, yet its social ideals had a great deal of popular appeal. The result was that many people began to adopt the social ideals if not the religious asceticism, and began to associate with each other; much like the modern Hippie movement borrowed heavily from Eastern mysticism and spawned a social movement in our own times. Many organized themselves into small groups for social sharing and discussion. By the first century, these movements, known to the Jews of the time as the Notzri, and its followers the Notzrim, had become widespread, and were found throughout the Eastern Mediterranean region. It is of considerable importance to note here that it is also known from Talmudic sources and elsewhere that the first century Christians also referred to themselves as Notzrim — lending strong support to the Yeishu ha Notzri theory as the source of the Jesus myth.

The Notzrim, or Jesus Movements, as modern scholars refer to these groups, appeared as isolated groups in widely separated towns and villages throughout the region. What they had in common was that they were a social reform movement, and often referred to a "Jesus" or "Jeshua" or "Yeishu" or "Yeshua" as their inspiration, but we know from contemporary descriptions that they were clearly not a religion, even though they incorporated many religious values.

Each of these Jesus Movement groups had its own ideas, often network-ing with others of a like mind, often disputing with others of conflicting ideas. While we have no writings from them directly, we have many references to them by contemporary historians, so we have some awareness of what they believed and practiced, if only filtered by others. By the time of Paul, the Jesus Movements had become extraordinarily diverse and widespread. Some were bands of itinerant preachers, others were guilds of settled craftspeople. Some were simple study groups, others were formal schools of scholastic research. As mentioned, there was philosophical ferment in first century Palestine, and the Jesus movements were not immune. Rather, they were very much a part of it. While none of what they wrote has survived intact, scholars are rea-sonably certain of a "Sayings Gospel Q" (subsequently revised at least three times), which is lost to us except where Mark quoted from it much later in "his" gospel, and one of the gospels of "Thomas," which has survived to the modern era in at least two versions, contain if not the pristine writings of Jesus Movements, at least quotations from them.

What is interesting about the Jesus Movements as the source of Christi-anity and the Jesus myth is that they were the source of Gnosticism, which for many decades, was considered by scholars to be a Christian heresy from the second century. Scholars had presumed this mostly as a result of the com-ments made in the screeds of Iraeneus, who railed against this widespread and threatening "heresy" endlessly. But it is now widely accepted that Gnos-ticism was widespread by the time Jesus is supposed to have lived, and now, having the Nag Hammadi library as a treasure trove of new information, we now know that its mythology was Jewish, not Christian, its metaphysics was Neo-Platonic and Neo-Stoic, and it shared ideas from Egyptian, Greek, Jewish and "Hermetic" mystery religions, and was an outgrowth of the Jesus Movements. Yet, when one reads the Nag Hammadi gospels we have today, we also read constant references to Jesus, including such stories as the Last Supper and the Crucifixion — evidence that the Gnostic gospels themselves borrowed from later Christian sources. But the Jesus myth's widespread pop-ularity among the Gnostics by the first third of the first century leads to the suggestion that, unless a wholesale and dramatic conversion took place (for which there is no evidence whatever), the Jesus myth was already widespread among the Gnostics by the time Jesus was supposed to have lived and died, and he died a long time ago. He wasn't a contemporary divine Messiah-fig-ure. At least not yet.

The destruction of the Second Temple which occurred during the Roman-Jewish war of 66–73 C.E. and the diaspora that followed also greatly impacted Judaism. The destruction of the Temple-based priesthood made central authority for doctrine and ritual impossible, along with the ability to perform temple-based ritual. So now every local rabbi was on his own. Each had his own response to the rise of Christianity and the contemporaneous diaspora into which Judaism was forced. In certain places at certain times, various rabbinates established local schools and influenced local movements, but as a whole, Judaism split into local factions, each struggling to maintain the tradition as best it could. In the main, the maintenance of a Jewish identity and the basic cultural traditions was possible, but the rigid adherence to a single doctrinal viewpoint was not, since there was no central authority against which to measure local ideas against a common doctrinal standard. So it's not surprising that nearly as many schools of thought arose in the Judaism part of the diaspora as occurred in Protestantism, a millennium and a half later.

The impact of the destruction of the temple on the Jesus Movements was to galvanize them into activism, trying to reform Judaism in order to save it from forced Romanization and the enveloping diaspora. For most of the Jesus Movements, there was no effort to reform the religion as much as the culture, but as we will see, for one Jesus Movement, things were to be quite different. Gnosticism, an outgrowth of the Jesus Movements, was by now and remained an inwardly focused quasi-religion, based as much on personal reform as the basis of the social reform of the Jesus Movements from which it sprang, but which intended to contribute to the salvation of Jewish tradition by making Jewish religion more personal and inwardly focused, and not dependent on outside authority.

The Road to Damascus and the Origins of Christianity
Approximately 50 C.E. to 140 C.E.

In about 50 C.E., a remarkable event occurred, which ultimately changed the course of human history. In Antioch, the local Jesus Movement suddenly and quickly transformed itself from a social and political reform movement into a full-blown religion. As this occurred, a remarkable conversion happened — or maybe the transformation occurred because Saul of Tarsus was "converted" to a new religious vision of his own and evangelized the group as Paul the Apostle. Whichever way it happened, we will probably never know. But secular scholars are pretty much agreed that this group included the first true Christians and that Paul, a Gnostic, was one of the first if not the first convert. And the Antioch Jesus Movement became the first of what modern scholars now refer to as the Christ Cults, the variety of Pauline-inspired cults prior to their consolidation under a single authority centuries later into the Catholic Church.

That Paul was greatly influenced by Gnosticism, there is little doubt, in that many writers quote Gnostic sources as writing favorably of Paul and considering Paul to be their ally. There is also little doubt that Paul, among his contemporary Christian writers (Clement of Rome, Barnabas, and the author of Hebrews), and among the Gnostics and members of the Jesus Movements, all considered Jesus to be a long dead figure, their highly revered founder. None of these writers directly quote people who claimed to have seen Jesus in mortal flesh. Instead, what had changed was that with the advent of Paul, Jesus had now become available for visionary appearances, and, having been shown on the right-hand of God in Paul's visions, was clearly a divine being, not just a great teacher and prophet, as the Gnostics had heretofore held.

By accepting Paul's vision and taking the relatively small step of transforming Jesus from a great teacher of righteousness and great prophet into an actual divine being, Gnosticism became a form of Christianity, albeit one with a very different theology from the catholicized Christianity of later centuries. The form of divinity they eventually accepted, however, was that Jesus was a wholly spiritual being who only "seemingly" appeared to his followers as a man, and exposed himself to persecution and death on the cross. This lack of mortality became known to the catholic Christians as the "docetic" heresy of the Gnostics. It would survive into the sixth century, in spite of repeated attempts by the church and the Empire to stamp it out.

Paul's writings are among the earliest Christian writings that have survived intact, and quite probably because they were the first Christian writings in the sense that we know Christianity. They date to within two decades of the presumed date of the crucifixion. Of the books in the New Testament that are attributed to Paul, there are only a few that are generally agreed by scholars to be the product of his pen. Among these are Galatians I and II and Thessalonians I and II, Corinthians, Romans, Philemon, Philippians, and possibly Colossians. The rest of the New Testament books attributed to him were written by later authors seeking to ride on his credibility and authority. What's remarkable about these writings is that when considered apart from the rest of the New Testament, they paint an interesting and very different picture of Paul himself and of very early Christianity than that accepted by most Christians. Among the possibilities that have been presented to account for this are that Paul was ignorant of many of the important details of the life of Jesus or, more likely, those details are simply myths that were incorporated into Christianity after Paul wrote his letters.

– Scott Bidstrup
Excerpt from essay "The Bible and Christianity – The Historical Origins"

The Evemerists

Evemerism," named after Evemeras, a fouth-century B.C.E. Greek philosopher who developed the idea that, rather than being mythological
creatures as was accepted by the reigning intellectuals, the gods of old were
in fact historical characters, kings, emperors and heroes whose exploits were
then deified. Evemerists have put forth a great deal of literature attempting to prove that Jesus was a great Jewish reformer and revolutionary who
threatened the status quo and thus had to be put to death. Unfortunately for
historicizers, no historian of his purported time even noticed this "great reformer." In Ancient History of the God Jesus, Dujardin states, "This doctrine
[Evemerism] is nowadays discredited except in the case of Jesus. No scholar
believes that Osiris or Jupiter or Dionysus was an historical person promoted
to the rank of a god, but exception is made only in favour of Jesus…It is impossible to rest the colossal work of Christianity on Jesus, if he was a man."
The standard Christian response to the Evemerists has been that no such
Jesus, stripped of his miracles and other supernatural attributes, could ever
"have been adored as a god or even been saluted as the Messiah of Israel"
(Dujardin). This response is quite accurate: No man could have caused such
a hullabaloo and hellish fanaticism, the product of which has been the un-
ending spilling of blood. The crazed "inspiration" that has kept the Church
afloat merely confirms the mythological origins of this tale. "The general assumption concerning the canonical gospels is that the historic element was
the kernel of the whole, and that the fables accreted round it; whereas the
mythos, being pre-extant, proves the core of the matter was mythical, and it
follows that the history is incremental…It was the human history that accreted round the divinity, and not a human being who became divine" (Massey,
The Historical Jesus and the Mythical Christ). The bottom line is that when
one removes all the elements of those preceding deities and myths that contributed to the formation of this Jewish god-man — which is what Evemerists insist on doing — there is nothing historical left to point to. As Massey
says, "…a composite likeness of twenty different persons merged in one…is
not anybody" (*The Historical Jesus and the Mythical Christ*).

– Acharya S
www.truthbeknown.com

Messiahs

Whatever view one takes concerning Jesus of Nazareth, the notion that all the prophetic figures in the Hebrew Bible refer to the same individual simply cannot be supported by a careful investigation of the Bible. Many such prophecies are simply not referring to The Messiah. In addition, there are multiple messiahs spoken of in the Prophets. Every king and priest in ancient Israel was a messiah. The Hebrew word moschiach, from which we transliterate our word messiah, means simply the anointed one, from the practice of anointing one who is chosen with oil.

– Wayne Simpson, "Ten False Messiahs" www.jasher.com

Messiah Criteria:

A. He must build the 3rd Temple (Ezekiel 37:26-28)
B. He must bring all the Jews back to Israel (Isaiah 43:5-6)
C. He must bring world Peace (Isaiah 2:4)
D. He must have universal Knowledge of God (the God of Israel) (Isaiah 11:9, Jer. 31:33)

– Source: www.messiahpage.com

The Christ

"We must get rid of that Christ, we must get rid of that Christ!" So spoke one of the wisest, one of the most lovable of men, Ralph Waldo Emerson. "If I had my way," said Thomas Carlyle, "the world would hear a pretty stern command — Exit Christ."

Since Emerson and Carlyle spoke, a revolution has taken place in the thoughts of men. The more enlightened of them are now rid of Christ. From their minds he has made his exit. Or to quote the words of Prof. Goldwin Smith, "The mighty and supreme Jesus, who was to transfigure all humanity by his divine wit and grace — this Jesus has flown." The supernatural Christ of the New Testament, the god of orthodox Christianity, is dead. But priestcraft lives and conjures up the ghost of this dead god to frighten and enslave the masses of mankind. The name of Christ has caused more persecutions, wars, and miseries than any other name has caused. The darkest wrongs are still inspired by it.

Two notable works controverting the divinity of Christ appeared in the last century, the *Leben Jesu* of Strauss, and the *Vie de Jesus* of Renan. Strauss, in one of the masterpieces of Freethought literature, endeavors to prove, and proves to the satisfaction of a majority of his readers, that Jesus Christ is a historical myth. This work possesses permanent value, but it was written for the scholar and not for the general reader. In the German and Latin versions, and in the admirable English translation of Marian Evans (George Eliot), the citations from the Gospels — and they are many — are in Greek.

Renan's *Life of Jesus*, written in Palestine, has had, especially in its abridged form, an immense circulation, and has been a potent factor in the dethronement of Christ. It is a charming book and displays great learning. But it is a romance, not a biography. The Jesus of Renan, like the Satan of Milton, while suggested by the Bible, is a modern creation. The warp is to be found in the Four Gospels, but the wool was spun in the brain of the brilliant Frenchman.

Renan himself repudiated to a considerable extent his earlier views regarding Jesus. When he wrote his work he accepted as authentic the Gospel of John, and to this Gospel he was indebted largely for the more admirable traits of his hero. John he subsequently rejected. Mark he accepted as the oldest and most authentic of the Gospels. Alluding to Mark he says:

> It cannot be denied that Jesus is portrayed in this gospel not as a meek moralist worthy of our affection, but as a dreadful magician.

This chapter on The Christ was written by one who recognizes in the Jesus of Strauss and Renan a transitional step, but not the ultimate step, between orthodox Christianity and radical Freethought. By the Christ is understood the Jesus of the New Testament. The Jesus of the New Testament is the Christ of Christianity. The Jesus of the New Testament is a supernatural being. He is, like the Christ, a myth. He is the Christ myth. Originally the word "Christ," the Greek for the Jewish "Messiah" (the anointed), meant the office of title of a person, while Jesus was the name of the person on whom his followers had bestowed this title. Gradually the title took the place of the name, so that "Jesus," "Jesus Christ," and "Christ" became interchangeable terms — synonyms. Such they are to the Christian world, and such, by the law of common usage, they are to the secular world.

It may be conceded as possible, and even probable, that a religious enthusiast of Galilee, named Jesus, was the germ of this mythical Jesus Christ. But this is an assumption rather than a demonstrated fact. Certain it is, this person, if he existed, was not a realization of the Perfect Man, as his admirers claim.

Silence of Contemporary Writers

Another proof that the Christ of Christianity is a fabulous and not a historical character is the silence of the writers who lived during and immediately following the time he is said to have existed.

That a man named Jesus, an obscure, religious teacher, the basis of this fabulous Christ, lived in Palestine about 2,000 years ago, may be true. But of this man we know nothing. His biography has not been written. A. Renan and others have attempted to write it, but have failed — have failed because no materials for such a work exist. Contemporary writers of his times have not one word concerning him. For generations afterward, outside of a few theological epistles, we find no mention of him.

The following is a list of writers who lived and wrote during the time, or within a century after the time, that Christ is said to have lived and performed his wonderful works:

Lucanus	Phaedrus	Epictetus	Damis
Silicus Italicus	Aulus Gellius	Statius	Columella
Ptolemy	Djo Chrysostom	Hermogones	Lysias
Valerius Maximus	Josephus	Arrian	Philo-Judaeus
Petronius	Seneca	Dion Pruseus	Pliny the Elder
Paterculus	Suetonius	Appian	Juvenal
Theon of Smyran	Martial	Persius	Pompon Mela
Plutarch	Quintius Curtius	Justus of Tiberius	Lucian
Apollonius	Pausanias	Pliny the Younger	Valerius Flaccus
Tacitus	Horus Lucius	Quintilian	Favorinus
Phlegon			

Enough of the writings of the authors named in the foregoing list remains to form a library. Yet in this mass of Jewish and Pagan literature, aside from two forged passages in the works of a Jewish author, and two disputed passages in the works of Roman writers, there is to be found no mention of Jesus Christ.

Philo was born before the beginning of the Christian era, and lived until long after the reputed death of Christ. He wrote an account of the Jews covering the entire time that Christ is said to have existed on earth. He was living in or near Jerusalem when Christ's miraculous birth and the Herodian massacre occurred. He was there when Christ made his triumphal entry into Jerusalem. He was there when the crucifixion with its attendant earthquake, supernatural darkness, and resurrection of the dead took place — when Christ himself rose from the dead, and in the presence of many witnesses ascended into heaven.

These marvelous events which must have filled the world with amazement, had they really occurred, were unknown to him. It was Philo who developed the doctrine of the Logos, or Word, and although this Word incarnate dwelt in that very land and in the presence of multitudes revealed himself and demonstrated his divine powers, Philo saw it not.

Josephus, the renowned Jewish historian, was a native of Judea. He was born in 37 A.D., and was a contemporary of the Apostles. He was, for a time, Governor of Galilee, the province in which Christ lived and taught. He traversed every part of this province and visited the places where but a generation before Christ had performed his prodigies. He resided in Cana, the very city in which Christ is said to have wrought his first miracle. He mentions every important event which occurred there during the first seventy years of the Christian era. But Christ was of too little consequence and his deeds too trivial to merit a line from this historian's pen.

Justus of Tiberius was a native of Christ's own country, Galilee. He wrote a history covering the time of Christ's reputed existence. This work has perished, but Photius, a Christian scholar and critic of the ninth century, who was acquainted with it, says: "He (Justus) makes not the least mention of the appearances of Christ, of what things happened to him, or of the wonderful works that he did" (Photius' Bibliotheca, code 33).

Judea, where occurred the miraculous beginning and marvelous ending of Christ's earthly career, was a Roman province, and all of Palestine is intimately associated with Roman history. But the Roman records of that age contain no mention of Christ and his works. Greek writers of Greece and Alexandria who lived not far from Palestine and who were familiar with its events, are silent also.

Josephus: Late in the first century, Josephus wrote his celebrated work, *The Antiquities of the Jews*, giving a history of his race from the earliest ages down to his own time. Modern versions of this work contain the following passage:

> Now, there was about this time, Jesus, a wise man, if it be lawful to call him a man, for he was a doer of wonderful works; a teacher of such men as receive the truth with pleasure. He drew over to him both many of the Jews, and many of the Gentiles. He was (the) Christ; and when Pilate, at the suggestion of the principal men amongst us, had condemned him to the cross, those that loved him at the first did not forsake him; for he appeared to them alive again the third day, as the divine prophets had foretold these and ten thousand other wonderful things concerning him; and the tribe of Christians, so named from him, are not extinct at this day (Book XVIII, Chap, iii, sec. 3).

For nearly sixteen hundred years Christians have been citing this passage as a testimonial, not merely to the historical existence, but to the divine character of Jesus Christ. And yet a ranker forgery was never penned.

Its language is Christian. Every line proclaims it the work of a Christian writer. "If it be lawful to call him a man." "He was the Christ." "He appeared to them alive again the third day, as the divine prophets had foretold these and ten thousand other wonderful things concerning him."

These are the words of a Christian, a believer in the divinity of Christ. Josephus was a Jew, a devout believer in the Jewish faith — the last man in the world to acknowledge the divinity of Christ. The inconsistency of this evidence was early recognized, and Ambrose, writing in the generation succeeding its first appearance (360 A.D.) offers the following explanation, which only a theologian could frame:

> If the Jews do not believe us, let them, at least, believe their own writers. Josephus, whom they esteem a great man, hath said this, and yet hath he spoken truth after such a manner; and so far was his mind wandered from the right way, that even he was not a believer as to what he himself said; but thus he spake, in order to deliver historical truth, because he thought it not lawful for him to deceive, while yet he was no believer, because of the hardness of his heart, and his perfidious intention.

Its brevity disproves its authenticity. Josephus' work is voluminous and exhaustive. It comprises twenty books. Whole pages are devoted to petty robbers and obscure seditious leaders. Nearly forty chapters are devoted to the life of a single king. Yet this remarkable being, the greatest product of his race, a being of whom the prophets foretold ten thousand wonderful things, a being greater than any earthly king, is dismissed with a dozen lines.

The Four Gospels were unknown to the early Christian Fathers, Justin Martyr, the most eminent of the early Fathers, wrote about the middle of the second century. His writings in proof of the divinity of Christ demanded the use of these Gospels had they existed in his time. He makes more than 300 quotations from the books of the Old Testament, and nearly one hundred from the Apocryphal books of the New Testament; but none from the four

Gospels. Rev. Giles says:

> The very names of the Evangelists, Matthew, Mark, Luke, and John, are never mentioned by him (Justin) — do not occur once in all his writings.

Papias, another noted Father, was a contemporary of Justin. He refers to writings of Matthew and Mark, but his allusions to them clearly indicate that they were not the Gospels of Matthew and Mark. Dr. Davidson, an English authority on the canon, says; "He (Papias) neither felt the want nor knew the existence of inspired Gospels."

– John E. Remsburg
Excerpts from *The Christ*
The Truth Seeker, 1909

The cross, the pagan image of Jesus and circle of heaven have been institutionalized again and again. Here the image is found on the Church of Saint-Pierre in Moissac, France.

Mary / Mary Magdalene

Mary

One of the first casualties of the Catholic Church was the feminine; "Mother Earth" or "Womb of Creation." The tradition of the goddess, which had developed before organized religion, had started its demise with the early Hindus; they demoted women and even demonized them. This attitude became institutionalized with the rise of the male dominated Catholic Church. In 1998, Father Leo stated, "The Holy Bible has done more to harm women than any other book in the history of the human race."

Did the Word "Virgin" Mean the Same Thing 2000 Years Ago?

Although Matthew and Luke both go to great lengths to make Mary's virginal status clear, the whole question of the Virgin Birth is one more case of mistranslation. Way back in the prophecies of Isaiah, there were many references to a coming Savior. The author of Matthew would have used the Greek translation of the Hebrew prophet Isaiah in which the coming of the Messiah is prophesied. Once Isaiah talked about a son being born to a young woman. But the Greek translation for Isaiah's Hebrew "young woman" was a word that can also mean either "virgin" or "young woman." In other words, Isaiah never prophesied a virgin birth, and he wasn't even talking about the Messiah when he prophesied the birth of a child to King Ahaz of Judah. But to fulfill the mistranslated prophecy, the author of Matthew believed that Jesus must be born of a virgin. Since neither John, Mark, or Paul in his writings discuss the Virgin Birth, some theologians have suggested that this aspect of Jesus' birth was a later invention, as with the relocation of the birth to Bethlehem, to fit the Nativity events into a prophetic scheme. Once again, the entire episode of Jesus' birth reminds readers that the Bible is a work of faith, not history or biology.

– Kenneth C. Davis
Excerpt from *Don't Know Much About the Bible*

What Christianity denied was the possibility of divine femininity that force worshipped in ancient Europe as Epona, Freya, Hertha, Mokosh, and under countless other names. More than just a nominal change was entailed when the utterly non-feminine Christian theology was introduced to these goddesses' devotees. Christianity provided no image of the mother goddess to substitute for the ones they revered so highly.

It was not long, however, before the people located within Christian mythology a female figure that could serve quite adequately. The Virgin Mary, daughter of the grandmotherly Anna, lost and regained her divine son. Once elevated to queen of heaven, she had all the necessary qualifications. Try as the church might, it could not stop the spread of Mariolatry, an extreme reverence toward the power of the Mother of God.

Many scholars have traced the spread of the Marian devotions; some contend that from the first, Christianity contained female-oriented rituals which, like the all-women feasts of the Roman Bona Dea, honored the mother above the son. Whether or not that was so, the excesses of Mary's devoted followers brought warning after warning from church officials that she was not a goddess — despite bearing all the tides and attributes of one.

– Patricia Monaghan
Excerpt from *The New Book of Goddesses and Heroines*

Mary Magdalene

Mary Magdalene is proving to be a prototype feminine character in the Bible. She is presently a star in the eyes of feminists, mythologists, and non-establishment type biblical scholars. To traditionalists, she has become a thorn in their side embodying nagging questions and charges of cover-ups.

She is mentioned only a few times in the gospels. She is never referred to as a prostitute, although this misconception gained much credibility. This is because it was constantly repeated by early church fathers who were fearful of equality in the church.

Another extreme has been brought on by Dan Brown's book, *The Da Vinci Code*. His proposition is that Mary Magdalene had a child fathered by Jesus and moved to France. The bloodline can be traced through royalty and wealth.

Through history, the feminine has been excluded and martyred. We are left searching for the truth in institutionalized fiction.

Virgin Mary

The oldest story in the world is the virgin mother and the newborn baby.

Fathers of the Christian church strongly opposed the worship of Mary because they were well aware that she was only a composite of Mariaune, the Semitic God-Mother and Queen of Heaven, Aphrodite-Mari, the Syrian version of Ishtar, Juno the Blessed Virgin, the Moerae or trinity of Fates, and many other versions of the Great Goddess.

Even Diana Lucifera, the Morning Star Goddess, was assimilated into the Christian myth as Mary's mother, Anna or Dinah, Churchmen knew the same titles were applied to Mary as to her pagan forerunners: queen of heaven, empress of hell, and lady of the world.

– Women in Mythology

The Line of David

The mounting evidence now available from biblical scholars shows that a descendant from the Line of David at the time of Jesus Christ was an impossibility. The last Jewish King from the Line of David was dethroned in 586 B.C. when the Babylonians over through Jerusalem and took the Jewish people as captives. When they were liberated by the Persian king, Cyrus the Great, and returned to Jerusalem, the Jewish Monarchy was not restored. There simply was no one living to be the King of Judea from the Line of David.

Jesus' Family Tree (according to Matthew):

David	Jeconiah
Solomon	Shealtiel
Rehoboam	Zerubbabel
Abijah	Abiud
Asa	Eliakim
Jehoshaphat	Azor
Joram	Zadok
Uzziah	Achim
Jotham	Eliud
Ahaz	Eleazar
Hezekiah	Matthan
Manasseh	Jacob
Amon	Joseph
Josiah	Jesus

Devaki and Krishna

For thousands of years in India, Devaki, Mother of Krishna, has been worshipped as a virgin. She is typically represented with the infant savior in her arms or her womb.

Christmas Surprise

Each year, during the winter solstice, American communities are transformed into gigantic merchandising centers relating to the Christian interpretation of this period. Evergreen trees, both natural and fabricated, are sold together with decorative ornaments, tinsel, and colored lights. Gift giving in gaudy wrappings is promoted. Stores and often streets are transformed. Robust, red-suited Santa Clauses ho-ho everywhere, and wide-eyed children, led by parents, are presented to Santa to express desires for certain gifts and to assure Santa of their merits while minimizing their shortcomings. Christmas carols and hymns are piped into the shopping areas in the hoped-for effect of softening buyer resistance and encouraging the purchase of items that would never be bought under ordinary circumstances. It is a time marked by greed on the parts of merchants and gift-receivers and by pressures of duty, obligation, and guilt for gift-givers.

One can understand the attitudes of merchants who take advantage of any occasion to sell their wares. After all, they are in business, and business operates for profit. Whatever encourages shoppers to buy is to be utilized.

Threaded throughout this gigantic merchandising effort are references to the supernatural birth of Jesus of Nazareth, to a unique star that guided wise men to the birthplace, to choirs of angels who announced the birth to shepherds, and to the insistence by the Christian church that in some mystical, wondrous way the divine intruded into the realm of the human and the supernatural impinged upon the natural. And the Christian church also engages in merchandising its product. Choirs sing Christmas hymns over radio and television. Tinsel and trees, creches and stars adorn the exteriors and interiors of church buildings. Children re-enact the gospel birth stories, and, in Christian homes across the land, the effectiveness of the union of religion and business can be seen in decorated fireplaces, rooms, and trees and in mounds of gaudily wrapped gifts.

There can be no doubt that kind and generous statements and acts abound during this period. Outcasts on skid rows are fed Christmas dinners, food and clothing are distributed to the destitute, and, even in prisons, turkey with all the trimmings is served to inmates.

Humanists can only approve of gestures of goodwill and kindliness — no matter what the motivating occasion. We can understand the efforts of merchants and appreciate the wonderment of little children at the transformation of their visual world. What Humanists do not accept is the presentation of the gospel birth stories as historically real or accurate. Humanists can believe that a child Jesus was born. But, like modern biblical scholars, they can doubt that the birthplace was Bethlehem; they can interpret the ideas of virgin birth, wondrous stars, angelic choirs, the visits of the magi and shepherds, the attempted murder of the infant by Herod as two-thousand-year-old Christian folklore to be placed in the same category as hero stories and myths emanating from other ancient cultures — but not to be believed. There is absolutely no reason to accept the birth narratives as having any foundation in historical reality.

– Gerald A. Lame, *Humanism and Christmas*

Jesus Christ can be calculated only approximately. It says regarding the date attributed to Christ's birth: "The date of December 25 does not correspond to Christ's birth but to the feast of the Natalis Solis Invicti, the Roman sun festival at the solstice.

– *The Watchtower*

The first Christmas manger scene was assembled 767 years ago, using live animals and people…Exchanging gifts was once a pagan practice associated with New Year's…and the earliest carols were not sung — they were danced!

St. Francis of Assisi is credited with creating the first Nativity scene. In the year 1223, the revered saint, then known as Brother Francis, was teaching the villages of Greccio in central Italy the true meaning of Christmas.

To illustrate the story of the birth of Christ, he brought together the local people and their livestock, and created a living manger scene. The idea caught on, and soon manger scenes using carved figures became popular throughout Italy at Christmas time.

Originally, giving gifts had nothing to do with Christmas. Ancient Romans used to exchange presents on the first day of the new year. Early Christian Church leaders frowned upon the pagan custom, but ordinary people refused to give it up.

As time passed, the church linked the exchange of gifts with the story of the Three Kings bringing presents to the Christ Child. And for 700 years, we've been giving each other Christmas presents.

– Larry Haley

Virgin Birth: "Holy Virgin" was the title of harlot-priestesses of Ishtar, Asherah, or Aphrodite. The title didn't mean physical virginity; it simply meant "unmarried." The function of such "holy virgins" was to dispense the Mother's grace through sexual worship; to heal; to prophesy; to perform sacred dances, to sail for the dead; and to become Brides of God…

– *Women's Dictionary of Myth*

Catholic writer Maria Teresa Petrozzi comments on Bethlehem: "Starting from the sixteenth century, [Bethlehem] suffered from the bitter and bloody struggles between Latins [Roman Catholics] and Greeks [Greek Orthodox believers] for the hegemony in the Nativity Church." These recurrent "bloody struggles" for control often centered on the silver star in the Grotto of the Nativity, which is located underground, beneath the Church of the Nativity. This star is said to mark the actual site of Christ's birth.

R.W. Hamilton reports in his book, *The Church of the Nativity, Bethlehem*, "It is well known that two of the questions in the dispute between France and Russia which led up to the Crimean war were concerned with the rival claims to possession of the keys of the main doors of the basilica and of the crypt (Grotto of the Nativity), and with the mysterious theft one night in 1847 of the silver star with a Latin inscription which was let into a slab of marble beneath the Altar of the Nativity."

As a result of the continuous interdenominational conflicts throughout the centuries over rights in these places, "the rights of each denomination are now carefully prescribed. Of the 53 lamps in the grotto, for example, the Franciscans are allowed 19. The Altar of the Nativity is owned by the Greeks, and the Latins are not allowed to hold services there."

– Historical Sites in Israel

It is also noteworthy that during the month of December, Bethlehem and its surroundings are subject to wintry cold weather, chilling rains, and sometimes snow. One does not find shepherds with their flocks outside at night during that time. This is not a recent weather phenomenon. The Scriptures report that Judean King Jehoiakim was "sitting in the winter house, in the ninth month (Chislev, corresponding to November-December), with a brazier burning before him (Jeremiah 36:22). He needed the extra heat to keep warm. Further, at Ezra 10:9,13, we find clear evidence that the month of Chislev was the "season of showers of rain." All of this indicates that weather conditions in Bethlehem in December do not fit the Bible's description of the events connected with the birth of Jesus Christ (Luke 2:8-11).

In a footnote Hamilton writes: "An account of the Nativity which occurs in the apocryphal 'Book of James' or 'Protevangelium,' written about the same period, also introduces a cave, but describes it as lying half-way to Bethlehem. So far as it has any historical value the story suggests that the tradition was not yet linked with any single spot, certainly not with the Cave of the Nativity."

Third-century religious writers Origen and Eusebius tie the tradition as then known to a particular site. Hamilton reasons: "Once the story had become attached to a particular cave it was not likely to wander; and it is safe to infer that the cave shown to visitors soon after 200 A.D. was identical with the present Cave of the Nativity."

What can we conclude from the historical evidence at hand and, more important, from the Scriptural fact that neither Jesus nor his disciples assigned any importance to his birthplace? It is evident that when Queen Helena, the mother of Constantine the Great, fixed the site of the Church of the Nativity in the year 326 C.E., it was not on the basis of history or Biblical proof.

Krishna   *Christ*

- Both are held to be really god incarnate.
- Both were incarnated and born of a woman.
- The mother in each case was a holy virgin.
- The father of each was a carpenter.
- Both were of royal descent.
- Each had the divine title of "Savior."
- Both were "without sin."
- Both were crucified.
- Both were each crucified between two thieves.
- Each taught of a great and final day of judgment.

Probing the Mystery
of Jesus' Second Coming

The events recorded in the New Testament following the death of Jesus would suggest that the disciples did not expect anything more from their master. He had been nailed to a cross and with him were killed all the messianic hopes. Luke makes this very clear and in Chapter 24 of his Gospel, we read the account of two of his disciples returning in disappointment to their home in Emmaus (Luke 24:13).

The reason for the disciples' feeling of disappointment was that they had believed Jesus to be the long-awaited Jewish Messiah as seen in Luke 24:21, But they could see that Jesus had died without accomplishing what a Messiah was predicted to do. In the story, Jesus enlightens them and in Luke 24:27 it says, "And beginning at Moses and all the prophets, he expounded unto them in all the scriptures the things concerning himself."

Today when we ask Christians, how is it possible for Jesus to be the Messiah when he clearly did not do the things a Messiah must do, we are given the answer that he will accomplish all things at his second coming. Jesus was given another chance. His death was only temporary. He arose from the dead and will one day return and do all the things he did not do when he was alive.

Therefore any person, who, at some future date, establishes a Messianic era will be seen to be the true Messiah, but presumably Christians will argue that such a person could only be Jesus who has returned. However, if Messianic expectations are only to be fulfilled by a second coming, what was the point of a first coming? Both John's Gospel and Paul's epistles present Jesus as a pagan deity, who as Matthew and Luke enlighten us, was born of a virgin, just as were Adonis, son of the virgin Myrha, and Hermes, son of the virgin Maia. He was a member of a holy trinity as were Mithra and Osiris, Hermes Tris-Megistus (the thrice-mighty Hermes). He performed miracles like the god Dionysus, who turned water into wine, and he was put to death as were sixteen crucified pagan saviors before him. According to this, Jesus was just another sinbearer, another of the god-men of pagan mythology.

But according to the Messiah of Israel, prophecies such as Isaiah 2 and Ezekiel 38 should have been fulfilled. Because such prophecies were not, and never have been fulfilled by anyone to this day, Jesus, we are told, will come back again and accomplish all things. But why does this future task only have to be fulfilled by Jesus? It is merely because he has been for so long the established Messiah in the mind of the Christian world.

Yet if we are to follow the subject of the second coming as it is written in the New Testament, we will find that the disciples understood that it would be in their own lifetime. Jesus himself spoke about his second coming, but nowhere in the Gospels did he tell his disciples about a return from heaven some thousands of years later.

Let us examine the New Testament references to the second coming. In Matt. 10:23, Jesus addressed his twelve disciples, and told them that they will "not have gone over all the cities of Israel, till the Son of man be come."

Almost two thousand years have gone by since this statement was made and whether or not the twelve disciples managed to travel to all the cities of Israel, one thing is certain, the Son of Man did not come.

Matt. 16:28 explicitly states that "there are some of those who are standing here who will not taste death until they see the Son of man coming in his Kingdom." It is plain to all that none of those to whom Jesus spoke these words is still alive today. Matt. 16:24, especially, indicates that he was speaking to his disciples.

Another whole chapter, that of Matt. 24:1-51, is considered to be a prophecy made by Jesus. Fundamentalists believe that this prophecy will be fulfilled in the "last days," by which they mean prior to Jesus' second coming. However, modern scholars claim that this chapter records events which had already taken place (since Matthew was written in approximately 80–90 A.D.).

A point which has been overlooked by fundamentalists is the fact that Jesus was addressing his disciples in private (Matt. 24:3): "And they came unto him privately, saying, tell us, when shall these things be? And what shall be the sign of thy coming, and of the end of the world?" Jesus then gave a list of happenings, adding to it, "Then shall they deliver you up to be afflicted, and shall kill you: and you shall be hated of all nations for my name's sake" (Verse 9). Thus it appears from those words that the twelve disciples would be around to witness the second coming and the end of time.

Jesus continues, "And then shall appear the sign of the Son of man in heaven: and then shall all the tribes of the earth mourn, and they shall see the Son of man coming in the clouds of heaven with power and great glory." In Verse 33 he was even more explicit: "So likewise ye, when ye shall see all these things, know that it is near, even at the doors."

And in Verse 34 he went on to elaborate, stating, "Verily I say unto you, this generation shall not pass, till all these things be fulfilled."

Yet as the whole world knows, that generation did pass away without Jesus returning. A few of those events did happen during the lifetime of the disciples. For example, the temple was destroyed, false Christs sprang up as mentioned by Paul, and some of the disciples were persecuted by the Romans. It is probable that John lived to a very old age, but he never saw any sign of the Son of man coming from heaven, and with John's death that generation passed away.

Some fundamentalists are of the opinion that "that generation" means the generation alive when this prophecy comes to pass, which they believe has yet to happen. But we need only point out that Jesus was definitely not speaking to some future generation; he was speaking to his disciples and directed this prophecy to them personally. This was not an original prophecy but was based upon Daniel and rehashed to fit the events of the day.

In Mark 14:62, Jesus told the chief priests, "Ye shall see the Son of man sitting on the right hand of power and coming in the clouds of heaven." Yet history shows this to be a false prophecy, because the chief priests have been dead for 1900 years or more. They never lived to see Jesus coming in the clouds of heaven, for, as the world knows, Jesus never returned.

There is a parable in Luke 18:1-5 about a judge who feared neither man nor God. He was described as being unjust. Yet when a certain widow woman implored him daily for his help, he avenged her lest by her continual coming she should weary him. Now we see what is stated in Luke 18:7-8, "and shall not God avenge his own elect, which cry day and night unto him, though he bear long with them? I tell you that he will avenge them speedily. Nevertheless when the Son of man cometh, shall he find faith of the earth?"

If Christians see themselves as God's elect, in this context, it would appear that Jesus was more unjust than the unjust judge of the parable. For 2000 years Christendom has prayed to Jesus day and night: He made a promise to avenge them speedily on his return to earth, but this can no longer be considered speedy by anyone with the least intelligence. The unjust judge did not keep this poor woman waiting 2000 years as Jesus kept his elect waiting, yet this, it would seem, is the whole point of the parable.

Jesus ought to have returned during the lifetime of one of his disciples, because Jesus said, "If I will that he tarry till I come, what is that to thee?" (John 21:22). It was thus believed by the disciples that John, the beloved disciple, would never die. John lived for many years after the death of Jesus, and like the high priest who was also expected to see Jesus' return, he died without it happening.

It is evident throughout the epistles that Paul was not accepted by the apostolic group. He met with opposition and contention throughout his ministry. After establishing churches in Asia Minor he found that all those in Asia had left him. He wrote an epistle to the Romans, yet on his arrival in Rome, only three believers were there to comfort him in his bonds. In Corinth also, Paul was judged by fellow believers and so he said in Cor. I: 4:3, "But with me it is a very small thing that I should be judged of you, or of man's judgment: yea, I judge not mine own self."

He then told those who were contending with him, "...judge nothing before the time." In other words, Paul told them to wait "until the Lord come who both will bring to light the hidden things of darkness and will manifest the counsels of the hearts: and then shall every man have praise of God." It is obvious from these words that Paul believed Jesus would return in his lifetime to vindicate him in this controversy. But Jesus didn't arrive, and the controversy continues to this day as modern scholars expose Paul as a fraud and accuse him of establishing a religion different from the one which Jesus and the apostles followed.

Again, Paul when writing to Timothy expressed, "That thou keep this commandment without spot, unrebukeable until the appearing of our Lord Jesus Christ" (Tim. I: 6:14). Paul must have expected Jesus to return during Timothy's lifetime. The promise of Jesus' coming was to be soon, very quickly, in certain people's lifetime, yet they are long since dead. Almost two thousand years have passed since the promise of a soon return, and fundamentalists of today still echo this age-old promise.

The writer of Hebrews states, "Nor yet that he should offer himself often, as the high priest entereth into the holy place every year with blood of others; for then must he often have suffered since the foundation of the world: but now once in the end of the world hath he appeared to put away sin by the sacrifice of himself" (Heb. 9:25-26). But what about today, 2000 years later? If the time of Jesus was considered to be the "end of the world" as the writer of Hebrews suggests, then we must be living in a new world, so this new world must by now be in need of a new sacrifice. It is obvious to any intelligent reader that Jesus did not come at the "end of the world," for the world is still going on as it has been for millions of years.

And again in Heb. 9:28: "...and unto them that look for him shall he appear the second time..." According to these words Jesus' second coming will only be seen by those who look for him. Therefore the second coming is something secret that will only be known to those who believe in it, requiring no visible appearance to the rest of mankind.

Jesus was expected to return during the lifetime of certain children to whom John addressed his epistle. "And now, little children, abide in him; that, when he shall appear, we may have confidence and not be ashamed before him at his coming" (John I: 2:28). They all died without Jesus ever returning.

– Shmuel Golding

Shmuel Golding *is a contributing editor of* Biblical Problemics *in Jerusalem, Israel.*

" *A dead Messiah could not be victorious. The Messiah must come into the presence of God on high, there to have bestowed upon him the crown he had earned, and there to await the signal for his second advent in triumph. "Hereafter shall ye see the Son of Man sitting at the right hand of Power, and coming in the clouds of heaven.* "

Hugh J. Schonfield

The Cross

Herbert Cutner, in *Jesus: God, Man, or Myth* (The Truth Seeker, 1950) says,

> A *stauros* was a mere stake, and horrible to contemplate; it was used in the crudest fashion to execute criminals and other persons…It was sometimes pointed and thrust through the victim's body to pin him to earth; or he was placed on top of the stake with its point upwards so that it gradually pierced his body; or he was tied upon it and left exposed till death intervened; and there were other methods too. There is not a scrap of evidence that a stauros was ever in the form of a cross or even of a T shape.

If Jesus had been executed, mythically or historically, it would not have been with outstretched arms on a cruciform structure.

Cutner reports that scholars have been aware of the error but have been unable to resist the traditional mistranslation. In the eighteenth century some Anglican bishops recommended eliminating the cross symbol altogether, but they were ignored.

There is no cross in early Christian art before the middle of the fifth century, where it (probably) appears on a coin in a painting. The first clear crucifix appears in the late seventh century. Before then Jesus was almost always depicted as a fish or a shepherd, never on a cross.

Constantine's supposed fourth-century vision of a cross in the sky was not of the instrument of execution: it was the Greek letter "X" (chi) with a "P" (rho) through it, the well-known "monogram" of Christ, from the first two letters of Xpicrtoa.

Any bible that contains the word "cross" or "crucify" is dishonest. Christians who flaunt the cross are unwittingly advertising a pagan religion.

VI

The Doctrine

Triune God

   As far back as we can go into the ancient world, we find that all known cultures had a "three-in-one" *triune* god. The very first trinity was simply the three stages of life of the Sun.

   1)   New Born, at dawn
   2)   Mature, full-grown at 12 noon
   3)   Old and Dying, at the end of the day (going back to The Father)

   At first, Christianity did not hold to the Trinity doctrine. That doctrine. That doctrine developed slowly and did not become officially a creedal fact until C.E. 325.

– Adrian C. Swindler
From *The Trinity: An Absurdity Borrowed From Paganism*

The Trinity

God found out about the Trinity in 325 A.D.

– Dr. Rocco Errico

Christ, according to the faith, is the second person in the Trinity, the Father being the first and the Holy Ghost the third. Each of these three persons is God. Christ is his own father and his own son. The Holy Ghost is neither father nor son, but both. The son was begotten by the father, but existed before he was begotten — just the same before as after. Christ is just as old as his father, and the father is just as young as his son. The Holy Ghost proceeded from the Father and Son, but was equal to the Father and Son before he proceeded, that is to say, before he existed, but he is of the same age of the other two.

So, it is declared that the Father is God, and the Son God and the Holy Ghost God, and that these three Gods make one God.

According to the celestial multiplication table, once one is three, and three times one is one, and according to heavenly subtraction if we take two from three, three are left. The addition is equally peculiar, if we add two to one we have but one. Each one is equal to himself and the other two. Nothing ever was, nothing ever can be more perfectly idiotic and absurd than the dogma of the Trinity.

Is it possible for a human being, who has been born but once, to comprehend, or to imagine the existence of three beings, each of whom is equal to the three?

Think of one of these beings as the father of one, and think of that one as half human and all God, and think of the third as having proceeded from the other two, and then think of all three as one. Think that after the father begot the son, the father was still alone, and after the Holy Ghost proceeded from the father and the son; the father was still alone — because there never was and never will be but one God.

At this point, absurdity having reached its limit, nothing more can be said except: "Let us pray."

– Robert Green Ingersoll
Excerpt from *The Foundations of Faith*, 1895

"
Paul recalled his vision on the Damascus road as; a light from heaven, brighter than the sun shining round me and those who had journeyed with me. And when we had all fallen to the ground, I heard a voice.
"

Acts 26:13-14

Paul: First Christian Heretic

During these first three-and-a-half centuries of the common era, the most powerful rival of Christianity was the religion known as Mithraism. It had been introduced to Rome by Cilician seamen about 70 B.C.E., and later spread throughout the Roman world. Prior to the triumph of Christianity, it was the most powerful pagan faith in the Empire. It was suppressed by the Christians in 376–77 C.E., but its actual collapse seems to have been due rather to the fact that by that time, many of the doctrines and ceremonies of Mithraism had been adopted by the church. Without the need of any mental somersaults, Jesus Christ had supplanted Mithra in man's worship. This fusion of one God with another is called theocrasia, and nowhere did it go on more vigorously than in the Roman Empire.

"After Jesus The Triumph of Christianity" ©1992 The Reader's Digest, Inc., Illustrator Chris Majadini.

Tarsus, the chief city of the Cilicians, and the home of Paul, was one of the chief centers of Mithra worship. H.G. Wells considered it highly probable that Paul had been influenced by Mithraism, because he used phrases very much like Mithraistic ones. What becomes amply clear to anyone who reads Paul's various epistles side by side with the Gospels, is that Paul's mind was saturated by an idea which does not appear prominent in the reported sayings and teachings of Jesus: the figure of a sacrificial person who is offered as an atonement for sin. What Jesus had preached was a new birth of the human soul. What Paul preached was the ancient religion of priest, altar and bloodshed. Jesus to Paul was the Easter lamb, the traditional human victim without spot or blemish who haunts all the pagan religions.

Mithra was sometimes termed "the god out of the rock," and services were conducted in caves. Jesus' origin in a cave is a clear instance of the taking over of a Mithraic idea. Paul says, "They drank from that spiritual rock and that rock was Christ" (I Cor. 10:4). These are identical words to those found in the Mithraic scriptures, except that the name Mithra is used instead of Christ. The Vatican hill in Rome that is regarded as sacred to Peter, the Christian rock, was already sacred to Mithra. Many Mithraic remains have been found there. The merging of the worship of Attis into that of Mithra, then later into that of Jesus, was effected almost without interruption.

Aided by research into the texts of the New Testament and quoting from modern scholars, the fact emerges that the beliefs set forth by Paul were altogether different from those expounded by Jesus and his disciples. What is more, we see from the New Testament itself that Paul was not accepted by the other believers and that his message was rejected by the early church.

Paul claimed to have come to Jerusalem, and to have learned his Judaism there "at the feet of rabbi Gamaliel" (Acts 22:3). He stated that at one point in his life he was a strict Pharisaic Jew (Acts 26:5). What changed him? What event turned a "reportedly observant Jew into a heretic?

We will let Paul speak for himself. There are in fact three passages in Acts, describing Paul's "conversion." In the first account (Acts 9:7) it is stated that the men who were with him "also heard the voice of Jesus." Later, when testifying before a Jewish audience, Paul changed his story. This time he spoke of a great light and said that they "saw the light but did not hear the voice..." (Acts 22:9). The third time when Paul spun his yarn was to King (Herodes-) Agrippas. This time he left the man Ananias out of his story and instead Jesus himself gives him instructions for his future mission (Acts 26:13ff). To us it is highly suspicious that Paul's story should have three versions.

He also claimed to be an apostle (I Cor. 15:9), to have been instructed by the risen Christ, to have seen Christ and to have received his authority from him (I Cor. 12). Yet, for all Paul's claims, they were doubted and disputed by the original apostles and Jewish believers. They did not accept him as a true believer, but considered him preaching falsehood.

Paul, if he knew anything of the life and teaching of Jesus as described in the Gospels, chose to ignore it. Instead he presented to the Gentile world a mystery religion in which he transformed Jesus into a divine spirit who existed before the world began and who had gone away to prepare the kingdom of God, not on this earth but in the world of the hereafter.

– Shmuel Golding

Hell

Christianity has made Hell progressively worse over the centuries. To early Christians such as Plutarch (46–125 C.E.), Hell was only symbolic, not a burning, gaseous fire pit. But it became more literalistic and has remained so. The Jews and Pagans had no Hell. As Christianity was incorporated into the warlike Roman Empire, it found fear and punishment to be a great motivator. Hell now had an overlord, and if the masses who were taken over by the Romans didn't behave, they had an eternal home with Satan.

The Hell that "Jesus" spoke of was an actual place. The Greek word he used was Gehenna, which is a reference to the valley of Hinnom, located just south of the old city of Jerusalem. At one time it was used for ritual human sacrifice by Jews and Pagans. Children were killed by "passing them through the fire to Molech.

**"The Inscription Over Hell's Gate"
by William Blake**

The way to hell, as pictured by the medieval church, began at the mouth of a terrifying pit where damned souls arrived by the cartload. Here fiends stripped them naked and pitched them into two gaping tunnels. Their bloody remains were carried off for further torture by a monk-like assistant, after their bodies had been boiled in oil or partially devoured by a bat-like monster.

Yahweh: Cruelty Against Man

Yahweh, in the Old Testament, operates in much the same way as nature — with punishments and cruelty, with virtually no compassion or forgiveness. Yahweh is said to be the god of this world. He is the alleged creator of this physical world and his actions found in the Bible are truly consistent with nature's way.

Yahweh claims responsibility for evil. In fact, during the time of the Old Testament there was no such thing as the devil. The early Jewish people did not believe in Satan; there was no need for him. Their own God took care of all the nasty deeds and evil things, thank you very much. The "evil one" was their own God.

Remember, friends, God loves you. He really does, you know. But I'm referring to the real God. Not this bogus impostor with severe psychological problems and a streak of cruelty a mile long. There is a God above him whom you are closely connected to in a spiritual way. This major difference is something to keep in mind when discussing God and the Bible with anyone.

– Paul Tice
Excerpt from *Triumph of the Human Spirit* www.thebooktree.com

Good and Evil

When Brahmins were perplexed by evil, they went to the Buddha and asked him whether God was good or evil. The Buddha thought for a moment, then responded, "If God cannot prevent evil, he is not God; and if, being able to prevent evil, he does not, he is not good." It seems, when you think about it, that the absolute divinity of God is impossible in a world of evil.

Regarding evil, theologian Frederick Buechner brings forth three propositions of importance that should be carefully studied. They are:

1) God is all powerful.
2) God is all good.
3) Terrible things happen.

Any two of them, when put them together, will work. Try adding the third one and it creates a problem. This is the enigma of evil, the curse of mankind, which no religion seems to have an adequate answer for.

– Paul Tice
Excerpt from *Triumph of the Human Spirit*

"Satan hasn't a single salaried helper; the Opposition employs a million."

– Mark Twain

"We have a community of devils, and Satan is their commander in chief. Jesus is the commander in chief of the angels. They are very powerful — not all-powerful — and do God's bidding. I believe we have guardian angels. I expect I would have been dead long ago without a guardian angel."

– Billy Graham on *Devils and Angels* from *Time Magazine*

Beelzebub

In Matthew 10:25, Matthew 12:24, Mark 3:22, and openly in Luke 11:18-19, there is an implied connection between Satan and Beelzebub (originally a Semitic deity called Hadad, and referred to as Baal-zebul, meaning lord of princes) Beelzebub (lit. Lord of the Flies) has now come to be analogous to Satan.

– Wikipedia.org

Satan, Lucifer, Beelzebub, the Devil

Christianity has created its own version of evil, with its own persona and image, while rejecting prototypes and forerunners as creatures of mythology and superstition.

> *But of the tree of the knowledge of good and evil, thou shalt not eat of it: for in the day that thou eatest thereof thou shalt surely die.*

Genesis 2:17

Original Sin

[The Doctrine of Original Sin] declares that [man] ate the fruit of the tree of knowledge — he acquired a mind and became a rational being. It was the knowledge of good and evil — he became a moral being. He was sentenced to earn his bread by his labor — he became a productive being. He was sentenced to experience desire — he acquired the capacity of sexual enjoyment. The evils for which (the preachers) damn him are reason, morality, creativeness, joy — all the cardinal values of his existence.

– Ayn Rand

Christians believe in guilty babies; Catholics believe in guilty embryos (Psalm 51:5).

– William B. Lindley

During the early part of 1990, a book titled *The Agony of Deceit* was released. This work, put together by Michael Horton, an Episcopal priest, purported to lay on the table the theological, doctrinal, and scriptural errors of the televangelists. Coming from the perspective of a prominent clergyman, this book initially aroused my intellectual curiosity. That is, until I *read* it and discovered that the greatest *deceit* is the book itself.

What the Rev. Michael Horton would do to us would be far more dangerous and damaging to our mental health than the antics of the TV preachers. Passing off the preaching of the televangelists as unsound, Rev. Horton points us to the way of *true* Christianity. He first spells out the significance of "original sin."

For those who are not familiar with this story from the Bible, it started with the very first couple to walk the earth. God created Adam and Eve "in his own image," declared that what He had made "was very good," then got so enraged with them that He cursed the entire human race with an uncontrollable fury that continues to this very day. Unable to resolve the dilemma of homo sapiens using the free will that He had given them, God in exasperation came down to earth and had Himself nailed to a cross to appease his own wrath. Even this drastic action had little effect.

On page 135, Rev. Horton tackles this sacred subject and explains how original sin still applies to those of us who are struggling in the twentieth century, especially the little babies, the worst offenders of all:

> The idea meant by the expression 'original sin' is that all humans are born sinners. There is no such thing as an innocent little baby. From conception, each of us merits the wrath and judgment of God (Psalm 51:5)...Due to original sin, I am bent toward myself and I am charged with Adam's guilt. I can be sent to

hell whether I have personally committed a sin or not…But original guilt, after all, is the whole point of this biblical teaching (p. 135-137).

The Catholic Church in particular, steeped in the theology of sinful babies, convinces the devout that any child not baptized will be plunged into hell with the rest of the damned, even if the child dies at birth.

Guilt is the cornerstone of the church and fear is its steeple. In Rev. Horton's effort to strip us down completely, he tells us on pages 139 and 140:

> He (God) does not help those who help themselves, but saves those who are entirely helpless to lift a finger.

> But the issue is not a matter of getting the sinner to like God, but of getting God to like the sinner. Over and over in the Bible we read that God 'maintains his wrath against his enemies,' (Nahum 1:2) and that 'God's wrath remains on' the unbeliever every day of his life (John 3:36). Paul says to unbelievers, 'YOU are storing up wrath' (Romans 2:5).

> The Bible speaks vividly of 'the fury of the wrath of God Almighty' (Rev. 19:15) and of the 'wrath of the Lamb' (Rev. 6:16)…God cannot accept us the way we are. He is perfect and we are wicked, self-centered to the very core of our being. In order for His wrath to be propitiated, His justice must be satisfied…

Rev. Horton continues with this advice for the televangelists:

> Need we burden the viewer with such theological details? Indeed we must. We must burden the viewer with his rightful sense of guilt.

This fate of eternal wrath and guilt is apparently reserved for those who are not necessarily evil-doers, such as the little babies. The transgressors, on the other hand/ are blessed, and receive special favors and status from God. This strange sense of justice is clarified on page 142:

> …of course that means that even though the believer will sin many times. God has nevertheless declared that person to be a perfectly law-abiding citizen. The basis for our relationship with God is Christ's track record, not our own.

So, the actual sinner can go right on sinning, no matter whom he offends, and still be, in God's eye, a law-abiding citizen. He is freed from guilt, and God bestows His mercy and grace upon him, that is, as long as he is a "believer" and under control of the church.

It is the innocent upon whom excessive guilt should be heaped. For these hapless creatures, God demands an extraordinary performance of mental and physical endurance. While bogged down under the crushing weight of preacher-inflicted guilt, these individuals are expected to "run the race for the crown" swiftly and victoriously. These spiritual Olympics almost always end up with hell as a reward. The practicing sinners in the meantime are being ushered directly into heaven. As the Bible says, "God's ways are not our ways."

What is particularly astonishing about the ramblings of The Rev. Michael Horton is that what he is saying is absolutely, positively, scripturally correct! It is all there in the Bible that has been handed down to us generation after generation. The "Words of God" that Rev. Horton quoted are not taken out of context; and this is exactly what the Christians are preaching and using to hold people in obedience to them.

The Bible, which was written by man (I have discovered 17 versions of the original King James Bible) is the ultimate tool for the orchestrated, professional manipulation of the human race by playing upon man's deepest fears and superstitions.

A contributing writer to *The Agony of Deceit*, Dr. W. Robert Godfrey, explains another mind-deluder springing from "original sin" that will assist the Christian in his own entrapment. His views are significant, since Dr. Godfrey is Professor of Church History at Westminster Theological Seminary, Escondido, California. This means that the following doctrine is drilled into seminary students:

> Elders are appointed for our sakes, and we need to submit ourselves to their authority in the local church if we are to be obedient to the Lord and His vision of the Christian life...Elders are necessary to teach and admonish and discipline us. But how can elders carry out that work unless we submit to them? What is church membership but joining our local congregation and submitting to the authority of the elders? To be sure, elders are not infallible. Sometimes they can deviate; indeed, they have, from time to time, been known to leave the faith entirely. But the fact that some elders are unreliable does not eliminate our responsibility to find godly elders and submit to them.

Perpetual submission is the goal. This keeps people in bondage to one another, which at the same time makes the pastor's quest to control his flock through guilt easier. The pastor is under submission to the hierarchy. The hierarchy is under submission to no one, and that includes God.

Dr. Godfrey preaches that even when these elders betray us through misconduct, we are given the responsibility to go and submit to another elder who may do the same thing to us.

The need to be punished is paramount in Christian theology. Dr. Godfrey advises on page 157:

> Many people do not like the idea of a disciplined church. They believe they should be able to do whatever is right in their own eyes. Such an attitude reflects the militant individualism of our society. But it does not reflect Christ's teaching about the life of His church. Proper discipline by the officers of the church is necessary for the well-being of individual Christians as well as for

the church as a whole. Such discipline can take place only in the context of membership in a local church.

Dr. W. Robert Godfrey has served as chairman of the Consultation on Conversion in Hong Kong, for the Lausanne Committee on World Evangelism, and is a senior editor of *Eternity* magazine.

With a heap offering of guilt, fear, the wrath of God and sinful babies, Rev. Michael Horton says:

> I, for one, have been deeply impressed with the reverence and comfort of these truths…We need to rediscover for ourselves the richness of biblical, historic Christian truths, and then integrate those truths into our daily practice and share them with our neighbors.

Only a sick mind could ever take comfort in the so-called truths as described. And to suggest that Christians attempt to pollute the minds of their neighbors with this madness is enough to demand that all of them be put into strait-jackets. As chemical waste dumped into rivers fouls the water, the spiritual sludge of Christianity poisons our minds.

In his closing statements on page 150, Rev. Horton does give a tidbit of excellent advice:

> It is time we — all of us — give serious thought to what the content of the gospel really is.

I will give a big "Amen" to that.

When I Was A Christian...

When I was a Christian and deeply involved with the church, I read the Bible, yet I really did not read it. The preachers skillfully guided me over the majority of its passages, which I later found to be horrifying. Cloaked in the beauty of its poetic language, and having temporarily taken leave of my capacity to think or reason, I missed the real blood-and-guts issue of this classic literature.

One of the first things that I read in the Bible as an adult while in the state of non-thinking, was that God rested from his work on the seventh day. The All-Powerful, Omnipotent, Omnipresent, Omniscient God got tired? And He had to rest!?

This fatigue overtook the Almighty after He had created all living things "after their kind." After what kind? If this was THE creation of the world and its creatures, where did God get his models from which to pattern his creatures if nothing had existed before that? Moreover, how did I miss this? Perhaps I was preoccupied with my original sin of being born.

Why didn't I question how and where Cain found a wife when, according to the Bible we are supposed to believe, there were only four people in existence: his father, mother, and brother, along with himself? But then again, it was considered taboo in those days, indeed in bad taste, to challenge the Bible. Having been indoctrinated from an early age, I just blindly accepted what inquiring minds would have found to be absurd.

If God can do anything, if He is the master architect of the universe who can control any and all things, then why did he viciously cause to drown the entire human race, with the exception of Noah and his family, because he got irritated with a few? Then Noah, the man who found such favor with God, went out and got drunk as soon as the waters subsided.

In the meantime, countless innocents, including little babies, lived out their last moments of life in terror as the relentless, mountainous waters swelled around them and without mercy, angrily swallowed them up. This would seem to be a logical heavenly action. God's wrath is especially severe on little babies. They are filled with sin.

God once (according to the words attributed to Him), became so outraged over attempted census-taking in Israel that He killed seventy thousand men! (1 Chronicles 21:2,7,14) Now I personally rebelled over giving information to the 1990 census-takers, but I wouldn't even think of carrying my displeasure to that extreme.

The God that the born-again Christians demand that we love, instructed Moses to order three million people to stone to death one man who had upset Him (Numbers 15:35,36). Talk about overkill! In a strange case of holy retribution, a ranting God struck an entire city of men down with hemorrhoids! (1 Samuel 5:8,9).

With His short-fused temper, why doesn't God justifiably strike down these preachers who use His name to steal, instead of allowing them to continue swindling people? This would make more sense than the repeated wholesale slaughter at the hand of God over something trivial.

To reassure us, the Bible proclaims that "God is not the author of confusion." Yet, we read in that same Bible that God Himself purposely caused the greatest confusion known to man, when He confounded their language at the construction site of the Tower of Babel so that the people He had created could not communicate with one another and complete the project.

These self-contradictions, found throughout the Bible, are so numerous, that not only can they often be found on the same pages, but in at least one case, within a few lines of each other. Galatians 6:2 instructs us to "Bear ye one another's burdens," and then down eight lines to Galatians 6:5 we are informed: "For every man shall bear his own burden." Small wonder the Christians walk around in a daze.

I first became suspicious of the authenticity of the Bible by observing the conduct of those who practice its precepts. When I finally broke free of the church and Christianity, I switched the button of my brain back to "on," and then re-read the Bible. It is an overwhelming experience to actually read that book in its entirety while in a thinking, analytical state, and to concentrate on what the words unquestionably say. Anyone who does this could never again say that they want to "live according to the Bible."

The Bible, as we know it, is not the authentic word of God. It cannot stand up under examination. I will now offer you shocking proof that man not only tampered with the Bible in order to control his fellow man through guilt and fear, but also made king-size blunders in the process.

One day while randomly reading my Bible, I made a startling discovery. After reading 2 Kings 19, I flipped a number of pages and read some more. To my astonishment, I found myself reading the same words. Now, class, open your Bibles to 2 Kings 19 — and also to Isaiah 37. These books are word for word identical! No Bible scholar has been able to give me a satisfactory explanation for this.

Perhaps there is an "original sin," man's innate determination and ability to pervert everything, even the concept of God. To attribute the deeds and thoughts described in the Bible to a benevolent, Almighty God would indeed be blasphemy.

– Austin Miles

Austin Miles *is a minister and author of many articles and books. He is the author of* Don't Call Me Brother *and* Setting the Captives Free, *Prometheus Books, Buffalo, New York.*

" *To view human life as depraved or as victimized by original sin is to literalize a pre-modern anthropology and a pre-modern psychology…To traffic in guilt as the church has done…is simply no longer defensible, if it ever was.* "

Bishop John Shelby Spong, *Rescuing the Bible from Fundamentalism*

The Resurrection: What is the Evidence?

Since the claim of the resurrection is the foundation of the Christian faith, we should certainly examine the credibility of this story. What is the evidence for the belief that Jesus rose from the grave? The entire claim hangs exclusively on the New Testament texts. Is this testimony reliable? As a seeker of truth, you are the judge.

Obviously, a judge must be impartial, and objectively weigh all of the evidence. Realize that this is not a routine case; your relationship with God is at stake. As an individual examining the case for the resurrection, you should not be swayed by conjecture or hearsay, but demand clear proof.

If you were the judge presiding over a murder case, you would want to be absolutely certain before convicting the defendant. If the prosecutor calls his key witnesses, but each tells a different story, his case would be very shaky. The defense attorney will argue for the acquittal of his client by demonstrating the weakness of the prosecutor's case. He will impeach the state's witnesses by showing how their accounts are contradictory.

– Rabbi Tovia Singer

The "Impaled" Savior

Facts, fiction, history, plagiarism and myth are interchangeable in the Crucifixion and Resurrection story – "The Greatest Story Ever Told." Several glaring inconsistencies are the "Christian eyewitness" accounts of what was said on the cross, what Jesus' final words were and whether Jesus was crucified as in the religious story or more probably impaled, not on a cross, but a stake.

Resurrection Contradictions

Who carried the cross?
Matthew, Mark, Luke: Simon of Cyrene.
John: Only Jesus himself carried the cross.

On which day of the month was Jesus crucified?
Matthew, Mark, Luke: On the first day of Passover, the 15th day of Nissa.n
John: On the day before Passover, the 14th day of Nissan.

Did either one of the two thieves on the cross believe in Jesus?
Matthew, Mark: Neither one of the thieves believed in Jesus.
Luke: One thief does not believe, but the other thief does.
John: Not mentioned in John.

What were Jesus' last dying words on the cross?
Matthew, Mark: "My God, my God, why hast thou forsaken me?"
Luke: "Father, into thy hands I commend my spirit."
John: "It is finished."

How many days and how many nights was Jesus in the tomb?
Matthew, Mark, Luke: Three days and two nights.
John: Two days and two nights.

Who were the women who came to the tomb?
Matthew: Mary Magdalene and the other Mary.
Mark: Mary Magdalene, Mary the mother of James and Salome.
Luke: Mary Magdalene, Mary mother of James, Joanna, and other women.
John: Only Mary Magdalene came to the tomb.

What was the angel(s) doing at the tomb and where was he (they)?
Matthew: He was sitting on the stone that he had rolled away from the tomb.
Mark: He was sitting on the right side, inside the tomb.
Luke: They were standing by the women, inside the tomb.
John: In the Book of John, there are no angels when Mary comes to the tomb. When Mary arrives at the tomb a second time, however, she finds two angels sitting inside the tomb. One is at the head and the other is at the feet.

After seeing the angels, whom does Mary meet first, Jesus or the disciples?
Matthew, Mark, John: Jesus.
Luke: The disciples.

To whom does Jesus make his first post- resurrection appearance?
Matthew: The two Marys.
Mark: Only Mary Magdalene.
Luke: Cleopas and another.
John: Only Mary Magdalene.

How many times does Jesus appear after the resurrection?
Matthew, Luke: Two times.
Mark: Three times.
John: Four times.

– Source: Rabbi Tovia Singer's
Resurrection Evidence Chart

Easter Celebration Primer

§ Easter gets its name from the ancient Babylonian fertility goddess; Ishtar.

§ Easter has been celebrated as a fertility rite in many cultures; centuries before it was a commemoration to honor the resurrection of Christ.

§ Pagans celebrated the resurrection of their gods during Spring Solstice for several centuries before Christians did.

§ Rabbits and eggs are fertility symbols. They have nothing to do with Jesus.

§ Neither the apostles nor the early Christian Church ever celebrated Easter.

§ Easter, and like celebrations, are condemned in the bible. In the King James Bible, Easter is only mentioned once and it is considered to be a mistranslation of "Passover."

No Stone Unturned

I have an Easter challenge for Christians. My challenge is simply this: tell me what happened on Easter.

I am not asking for proof. My straightforward request is merely that Christians tell me exactly what happened on the day that their most important doctrine was born.

Believers should eagerly take up this challenge, since without the resurrection, there is no Christianity. Paul wrote, "And if Christ be not risen, then is our preaching vain, and your faith is also vain. Yea, and we are found false witnesses of God; because we have testified of God that he raised up Christ: whom he raised not up, if so be that the dead rise not" (I Cor. 15:14-15).

The conditions of the challenge are simple and reasonable. In each of the four gospels, begin at Easter morning and read to the end of the book: Matt. 28, Mark 16, Luke 24, and John 20-21. Also read Acts 1:3-12 and Paul's tiny version of the story in I Corinthians 15:3-8.

These 165 verses can be read in a few moments. Then, without omitting a single detail from these separate accounts, write a simple, chronological narrative of the events between the resurrection and the ascension: what happened first, second, and so on; who said what, when; and where these things happened.

Since the gospels do not always give precise times of day, it is permissible to make educated guesses. The narrative does not have to pretend to present a perfect picture — it only needs to give at least one plausible account of all of the facts. Additional explanation of the narrative may be set apart in parentheses. *The important condition to the challenge, however, is that not one single biblical detail be omitted.* Fair enough?

I should admit that I have tried this challenge myself. I failed. An Assembly of God minister whom I was debating a couple of years ago on a Florida radio show loudly proclaimed over the air that he would send me the narrative in a few days. I am still waiting. After my debate at the University of Wisconsin, "Jesus of Nazareth: Messiah or Myth," a Lutheran graduate student told me he accepted the challenge and would be contacting me in about a week. I have never heard from him. Both of these people, and others, agreed that the request was reasonable and crucial. Maybe they are slow readers.

Many bible stories are given only once or twice, and are therefore hard to confirm. The author of Matthew, for example, was the only one to mention that at the crucifixion dead people emerged from the graves of Jerusalem, walking around showing themselves to everyone — an amazing event that could hardly escape the notice of the other gospel writers, or any other historians of the period. But though the silence of others might weaken the likelihood of a story, it does not disprove it. Discontinuation arises with contradictions.

Thomas Paine tackled this matter 200 years ago in *The Age of Reason*, stumbling across dozens of New Testament discrepancies:

> I lay it down as a position which cannot be controverted, first, that the agreement of all the parts of a story does not prove that story to be true, because the parts may agree and the whole may be false; secondly, that the disagreement of the parts of a story proves the whole cannot be true.

Since Easter is told by five different writers, it gives us one of the best chances to confirm or disconfirm the account. Christians should welcome the opportunity.

One of the first problems I found is in Matt. 28:2, after two women arrived at the tomb: "And, behold, there was a great earthquake: for the angel of the Lord descended from heaven, and came and rolled back the stone from the door, and sat upon it." (Let's ignore the fact that no other writer mentioned this "great earthquake.") This story says that the stone was rolled away after the women arrived.

Yet Mark's gospel says it happened *before* the (three) women arrived: "And they said among themselves, who shall roll away the stone from the door of the sepulchre? And when they looked, they saw that the stone was rolled away: for it was very great."

Luke writes: "And they found the stone rolled away from the sepulchre." John agrees. No earthquake, no rolling stone. It is a three-to-one vote: Matthew loses. (Or else the other three are wrong.) The event cannot have happened both before and after they arrived.

Some bible defenders assert that Matthew 28:2 was intended to be understood in the past perfect, showing what had happened before the women arrived. But the entire passage is in the aorist (past) tense, and it reads, in context, like a simple chronological account. Matt. 28:2 begins, "And behold," not "For, behold." If this verse can be so easily shuffled around, then what is to keep us from putting the flood before the ark, or the crucifixion before the nativity?

Another glaring problem is the fact that in Matthew the first post-resurrection appearance of Jesus to the disciples happened on a mountain in Galileo, as predicted by the angel sitting on the rock; "And go quickly, and tell his disciples that he is risen from the dead; and behold, he goeth before you into Galileo; there shall ye see him." (This must have been of supreme importance, since this was *the* message of God via the angel (s) at the tomb. Jesus had even predicted this himself during the Last Supper, Matt. 26:32.)

Matt. 28:16-17 says, 'Then the eleven disciples went away into Galilee, into a mountain where Jesus had appointed them. And when they saw him, they worshipped him: but some doubted."

Reading this at face value, and in context, it is clear that Matthew intends this to be the *first* appearance. Otherwise, if Jesus had been seen before this time, why did some doubt? Mark agrees with Matthew's account of the angel's Galilee message, but gives a different story about the first appearance.

Luke and John give different angel messages and then radically contradict Matthew. Luke shows the first appearance on the road to Emmaus and then in a room in Jerusalem. John says it happened later that evening in a room, minus Thomas. These angel messages, locations, and travels during the day are difficult to reconcile.

Believers sometimes use the analogy of the five blind men examining an elephant, all coming away with a different definition: tree trunk (leg), rope (tail), hose (trunk), wall (side), and fabric (ear). People who use this argument forget that each of the blind men was *wrong*. An elephant is not a rope or a tree. And you can put the five parts together to arrive at a non-contradictory aggregate of the entire animal. This hasn't been done with the resurrection.

Another analogy sometimes used by apologists is comparing the resurrection contradictions to differing accounts given by witnesses of an auto accident. If one witness said the vehicle was green and the other said it was blue; that could be accounted for by different angles, lighting, perception, or definitions of words.

I am not a fundamentalist inerrantist: I'm not demanding that the evangelists must have been expert, infallible witnesses. (None of them claimed to have been at the tomb itself, anyway.) But what if one witness said the auto accident happened in Chicago and the other said it happened in Milwaukee? At least one of these witnesses has serious problems with the truth. Luke says the post-resurrection appearance happened in Jerusalem, but Matthew says it happened in Galilee, *60 to 100 miles away*! Something is very wrong here.

This is just the tip of the iceberg. Of course, none of these contradictions prove that the resurrection did *not* happen, but they do throw considerable doubt on the reliability of the supposed witnesses. Some of them were wrong. Maybe they were all wrong.

Protestants and Catholics seem to have no trouble applying healthy skepticism to the miracles of Islam, or to the "historical" visit between Joseph Smith and the angel Moroni. Why should Christians treat their own outrageous claims any differently? Why should someone who was not there be any more eager to believe than doubting Thomas, who lived during that time, or the other disciples who said that the women's news "seemed to them as idle tales, and they believed them not" (Luke 24:11)?

Thomas Paine points out that everything in the bible is hearsay. For example, the message at the tomb (if it happened at all) took this path, at minimum, before it got to our eyes: God, angel(s), Mary, disciples, gospel writers, copyists, translators. (The gospels are all anonymous and we have no original versions.)

But first things first: Christians, either tell me exactly what happened on Easter Sunday, or let's leave the Jesus myth buried next to Eastre (Ishtar, Astarte), the pagan Goddess of Spring after whom your holiday was named.

– Dan Barker

Dan Barker *is the public relations director for the Freedom from Religion Foundation, Madison, Wisconsin. This article was copied and distributed around the country in many different forms. A lot of readers sent it to their area ministers and priests. Only two attempts at accepting the challenge were made and neither one of them kept to the terms, preferring to pick and choose particular contradictions to explain.*

What's in a Name?

The bible has been virtually silent regarding the biographies of the authors of the four main gospels.

One of the biggest challenges for biblical scholars is the time period between the date of the crucifixion and the date the gospels were written. The consensus is at least forty years. The lectures and literature from "The Jesus Seminar" has reduced their research to four thumbnails:

Mark

The Gospel of Mark is attributed to John Mark, a companion of Paul (Acts 12:12, 25; 13:5; 15:36-41; Phlm 24; Col 4:10, 2 Tim 4:11), a cousin of Barnabas (Col 4:10), and perhaps an associate of Peter (1 Pet 5:13). The suggestion was first made by Papias (ca. 130 C.E.), as reported by Eusebius (d. 325), both ancient Christian authors. In this, as in the other matters, Papias is unreliable, because he is interested in the guarantees of an eyewitness rather than in the oral process that produced Mark.

Matthew

It is Papias again, as reported by Eusebius, who names Matthew (Matt 10:3) as the author of the first gospel. Matthew may have another name, Levi, which is the name given to the tax collector in Mark 2:14 and Luke 5:27, but who is called Matthew in the parallel passage, Matt 9:9. We cannot account for the differences in name. Papias' assertion that canonical Matthew was composed in Hebrew is patently false; Matthew was composed in Greek in dependence on Q and Mark, also written in Greek by unknown authors.

Luke

The tradition that Luke the physician and companion of Paul was the author of Luke-Acts goes back to the second century C.E. The Luke in question is referred to in Col 4:14; Phlm 24; 2 Tim 4:11, where he is identified as a physician. It is improbable that the author of Luke-Acts was a physician; it is doubtful that he was a companion of Paul. Like the other attributions, this one, too, is fanciful.

Thomas

The Gospel of Thomas is attributed to Didymus Judas Thomas, who was revered in the Syrian church as an apostle (Matt 10:3; Mark 3:18; Luke 6:15; Acts 1:13; cf. John 11:16; 20:24; 21:2) and as the twin brother of Jesus (so claimed by the Acts of Thomas, a third-century C.E. work). The attribution to Thomas may indicate where this gospel was written, but it tells us nothing about the author.

John

The Fourth Gospel was composed by an anonymous author in the last decade of the first century. About 180 C.E. Irenaeus reports the tradition that ascribes the book to John, son of Zebedee, while others ascribed it to John the elder who lived at Ephesus, and still others to the beloved disciple (John 13:23-25; 19:25-27; 20:2-10; 21:7, 20-23). The Fourth Gospel was opposed as heretical in the early church, and it knows none of the stories associated with John, son of Zebedee. In the judgment of many scholars, it was produced by a "school" of disciples, probably in Syria.

– Robert W. Funk, Roy W. Hoover, and the Jesus Seminar
Excerpt from *The Five Gospels: The Search for the Authentic Words of Jesus New Translation and Commentary*

All the gospels originally circulated anonymously. Authoritative names were later assigned to them by unknown figures in the early church. In most cases, the names are guesses or perhaps the result of pious wishes.

The High Priest

No one religion in the ancient Near East can be studied in isolation. All stem from man's first questioning about the origin of life and how to ensure his own survival. Out of this sense of dependency and frustration, religion was born.

Our present concern is to show that Judaism and Christianity are such cultic expressions of this endless pursuit by man to discover instant power and knowledge. Granted the first proposition that the vital forces of nature are controlled by an extra-terrestrial intelligence, these religions are logical developments from the older, cruder fertility cults. With the advance of technical proficiency the aims of religious ritual became less to influence the weather and the crops than to attain wisdom and the knowledge of the future. The Word that seeped through the labia of the earth's womb became to the mystic of less importance than the Logos which he believed his religion enabled him to apprehend and enthuse him with divine omniscience. But the source was the same vital power of the universe and the cultic practice differed little.

To raise the crops the farmer copulated with his wife in the fields. To seek the drug that would send his soul winging to the seventh heaven and back, the initiates into the religious mysteries had their priestesses seduce the god and draw him into their grasp as a woman fascinates her partner's penis to erection.

For the way to god and the fleeting view of heaven was through plants more plentifully endured with the sperm of God than any other. These were the drug-herbs, the science of whose cultivation and use had been accumulated over centuries of observation and dangerous experiment. Those who had this secret wisdom of the plants were the chosen of their god; to them alone had he vouchsafed the privilege of access to the heavenly throne. And if he was jealous of his power, no less were those who served him in the cultic mysteries. Theirs was no gospel to be shouted from the rooftops: Paradise was for none but the favored few. The incantations and rites, by which they conjured forth their drug plants, and the details of the bodily and mental preparations undergone before they could ingest their god, were the secrets of the cult to which none but the initiate bound by fearful oaths, had access.

Very rarely, and then only for urgent practical purposes, were those secrets ever committed to writing. Normally they would be passed from the priest to the initiate by word of mouth; dependent for their accurate transmission on the trained memories of men dedicated to the learning and recitation of their "scriptures." But if, for some drastic reason like the disruption of their cultic centres by war or persecution, it became necessary to write down the precious names of the herbs and the manner of their use and accompanying incantations, it would be in some esoteric form comprehensibly only to those within their dispersed communities.

Such an occasion, we believe, was the Jewish Revolt of A.D. 66. Instigated probably by members of the cult, swayed by their drug-induced madness to believe God had called them to master the world in his name, they provoked the mighty power of Rome to swift and terrible action. Jerusalem was ravaged, her temple destroyed. Judaism was disrupted, and her people driven to seek refuge with communities already established around the Mediterranean coast-lands. They mystery cults found themselves without their central fount of authority, with many of their priests killed in the abortive rebellion or driven into the desert. The secrets, if they were not to be lost for ever, had to be committed to Writing, and yet, if found, the documents must give nothing away or betray those who still dared defy the Roman authorities and continue their religious practices.

The means of conveying the information were at hand, and had been for thousands of years. The folk-tales of the ancients had from the earliest times contained myths based upon the personification of plants and trees. They were invested with human faculties and qualities and their names and physical characteristics were applied to the heroes and heroines of the stories. Some of these were just tales spun for entertainment; others were political parables like Jotham's fable about the trees in the Old Testament, while others were means of remembering and transmitting therapeutic folk-lore. The names of the plants were spun out to make the basis of the stories, whereby the creatures of fantasy were identified, dressed, and made to enact their parts. Here, then, was the literary device to spread occult knowledge to the faithful.

In order to tell the story of a rabbi called Jesus and invest him with the power and names of the magic drug. To have him live before the terrible events that had disrupted their lives, to preach a love between men, extending even to the hated Romans. Thus, reading such a tale, should it fall into Roman hands, even their mortal enemies might be deceived and not probe farther into the activities of the cells of the mystery cults within their territories.

The ruse failed. Christians, hated and despised, were hauled forth and slain in their thousands. The cult well night perished. What eventually took its place was a travesty of the real thing, a mockery of the power that could raise men to heaven and give them the glimpse of God for which they gladly died. The story of the rabbi crucified at the instigation of the Jews became an historical peg upon which the new cult's authority was founded. What began as a hoax, became a trap even to those who believed themselves to the spiritual heirs of the mystery religion and took to themselves the name of "Christian." Above all, they forgot, or purged from the cult and their memories, the one supreme secret on which their whole religious and ecstatic experience depended: the names and identity of the source of the drug, the key to heaven — the sacred mushroom.

Jewish High Priest

Full sacerdotal robes and mushroom cap. – Garg, (Robes + Cap), ceremonies (greeting of rising sun), sacraments + rituals (gathering of God's manna) are all practiced today. The worship of the Sun dates back to Shemitic/Hebrew cults.

The early "Psilocybe Cubensis" mushroom was referred to in the Bible (see Exodus 16;14, 15) manna literally meant "what is this?" Later it was interpreted as "food from God." The High Priest and his soon to be "high" followers would gather to celebrate the rising of the sun each morning.

The fungus recognized today as the *Amanita Muscaria,* or Fly-Agaric, had been known from the beginning of history. Beneath the skin of its characteristic red-and-white-spotted cap, there is concealed a powerful hallucinatory poison. Its religious use among certain Siberian peoples and others has been the subject of study in recent years, and its exhilarating and depressive effects have been clinically examined. Theses include the stimulation of the perceptive faculties so that the subject sees objects much greater or much smaller than they really are, colors and sounds are much enhanced, and there is a general sense of power, both physical and mental quite outside the normal range of human experience.

The mushroom has always been a thing of mystery. The ancients were puzzled by its manner of growth without seed, the speed with which it made its appearance after rain, and it's as rapid disappearance. Born from a volva or "egg" it appears like a small penis, raising itself like the human organ sexually aroused, and when it spread wide its canopy the old botanists saw it as a phallus bearing the "burden" of a woman's groin. Every aspect of the mushroom's existence was fraught with sexual allusions, and in its phallic form the ancients saw a replica of the fertility god himself. It was the "son of God," its drug was a purer form of the god's own spermatozoa than that discoverable in any other form of living matter. It was, in fact, God himself, manifest on earth. To the mystic it was the divinely given means of entering heaven; God had come down in the flesh to show the way to himself, by himself.

To pluck such a precious herb was attended at every point with peril. The time -before sunrise, the words to be uttered — the name of the guardian angel, were vital to the operation, but more was needed. Some form of substitution was necessary, to make an atonement to the earth robbed of her offspring. Yet such was the divine nature of the Holy Plant, as it was called, only the god could make the necessary sacrifice. To redeem the Son, the Father had to supply even the "price of redemption." These are all phrases used of the sacred mushroom, as they are of the Jesus of Christian theology.

Our present study has much to do with names and titles. Only when we can discover the nomenclature of the sacred fungus within and without the cult, can we begin to understand its function and theology. The main factor that has made these new discoveries possible has been the realization that many of the most secret names of the mushroom go back to ancient Sumerian, the oldest written language known to us, witnessed by cuneiform text dating form the fourth millennium B.C. Furthermore, it now appears that this ancient tongue provides a bridge between the Indo-European languages (which include Greek, Latin, and our own tongue) and the Semitic group, which includes the languages of the Old Testament, Hebrew and Aramaic. For the first time, it becomes possible to decipher the names of gods, mythological characters, classical and biblical, and plant names. Thus their place in the cultic systems and their functions in the old fertility religions can be determined.

The great barriers that have hitherto seemed to divide the ancient world, classical and biblical, have at last been crossed and at a more significant level than has previously been possible by merely comparing their respective mythologies. Stories and characters which seem quite different in the way they are presented in various locations and at widely separated points in history can now be shown often to have the same central theme. Even gods as different as Zeus and Yahweh embody the same fundamental conception of the fertility deity, for their names in origin are precisely the same. A common tongue overrides physical and racial boundaries. Even languages so apparently different as Greek and Hebrew, when they can be shown to derive from a common fount, point to a commonality of culture at some early stage. Comparisons can therefore be made on a scientific, philological level which might have appeared unthinkable before now. Suddenly, almost overnight, the ancient world has shrunk. All roads in the Near East lead back to the Mesopotamian basin, to ancient Sumer. Similarly, the most important of the religions and mythologies of that area, and probably far beyond, are reaching back to the mushroom cult of Sumer and her successors.

– John Allegro
Excerpt from *Sacred Mushrooms and the Cross*

John Allegro *worked on the Dead Sea Scrolls and is a renowned and well-respected author.*

" *And when the dew that lay was gone up, behold, upon the face of the wilderness there lay a small round thing, as small as the hoar frost on the ground.*

And when the children of Israel saw it, they said one to another, It is manna: for they wist not what it was. And Moses said unto them, This is the bread which the Lord hath given you to eat. "

Exodus 16; 14 & 15

Baptism

In 418 A.D., a Catholic Church council decided that every human child is born demonic as a result of its sexual conception, thus automatically damned unless baptized.

During a Catholic baptismal ceremony, the priest still addresses the baby,

> I exorcise thee, thou unclean spirit…Hear thy doom, 0 Devil accursed, Satan accursed.

This exorcism is euphemistically described as "a means to remove impediments to grace resulting from the effects of original sin and the power of Satan over nature…"

Thus, paganism was kinder to infants and their mothers than Christianity, so that theologians often felt called upon to explain God's apparent cruelty in allowing infants to die unbaptized, so condemning them before they had a chance for salvation.

In the sixteenth and seventeenth centuries, churchmen insisted that God's cruelty was perfectly just. Said Martin Del Rio, S.J.,

> If, as is not uncommon. God permits children to be killed before they have been baptized; it is to prevent their committing in later life those sins which would make their damnation more severe. In this, God is neither cruel nor unjust, since, by the mere fact of original sin, the children have already merited death…

– Barbara G. Walker, Editor
Women's Encyclopedia of Myth

What is the Last of the Ten Commandments?
(Answer: C)

A. Don't steal.

B. Don't covet your neighbor's wife and property. This is the final commandment as listed in Exodus 20:2-17, the version often used by Protestants and Catholics. However, these are not the "ten commandments." (See below.) Notice the biblical sexism: women are the property of men.

C. Don't boil a young goat in the milk of its mother. Believe it or not, this prohibition in Exodus 34:26 is the official tenth commandment, from the only set of stone tablets that were called "the ten commandments." There were three sets of commandments:

1) The first time Moses came down from Mount Sinai with commandments, he merely recited a list (Exodus 20:2-17), which is the version most churches today erroneously call the "Ten Commandments," although they were not engraved on stone tablets and not called "the ten commandments."

2) The first set of stone tablets was given to Moses at a subsequent trip up the mountain (Exodus 31:18). In this farcical story, Moses petulantly destroyed those tablets when he saw the people worshipping the golden calf (Exodus 32:19).

3) So he went back for a replacement. God told Moses: "Hew thee two tables of stone like unto the first: and I will write upon these tables the words that were in the first tables, which thou brakest" (Exodus 34:1). Here is what was on the replacement tablets (from Exodus 34:14-26):

1) Thou shalt worship no other God. 2) Thou shalt make thee no molten gods. 3) The feast of unleavened bread shalt thou keep. 4) Six days thou shalt work, but on the seventh day thou shalt rest. 5) Thou shalt observe the feast of weeks. 6) Thrice in the year shall all your menchildren appear before the Lord God. 7) Thou shalt not offer the blood of my sacrifice with leaven. 8) Neither shall the sacrifice of the feast of the passover be left until the morning. 9) The first of the firstfruits of thy land shalt thou bring unto the house of the Lord thy God. 10) Thou shalt not seethe a kid in his mother's milk.

Keep this in mind next time you are tempted to boil a goat. This list differs, obviously, from the one in Exodus 20 (was God's memory faulty?), but it is only this list that is called the "Ten Commandments": "And he wrote upon the tables the words of the covenant, the Ten Commandments" (Exodus 34:28).

D. Love your neighbor as yourself. Even Jesus was unclear about the exact set of commandments. In Matthew 19:18-19 he listed them as:

1) Thou shalt do no murder 2) Thou shalt not commit adultery 3) Thou shalt not steal 4) Thou shalt not bear false witness 5) Honour thy father and thy mother 6) Thou shalt love thy neighbour as thyself. For the Jews, loving your "neighbor" meant loving your Jewish neighbors: it did not mean loving the neighboring tribes or other outsiders, as the intolerant and bloody Old Testament (and Christian) history proves.

– Dan Barker, excerpt from "What do you Really Know about the Bible?" www.fff.org

Rehabilitating Judas Iscariot

"Trial Balloons" to rehabilitate "Judas Iscariot" (evidently emanating from Vatican "sources") are presently in the news with predictable outcries from both "the Right" and "the Left." While this kind of proposal is all to the good — regardless of the impact it might have on one's "Faith" — and, in view of all the unfortunate and cruel effects that have come from taking the picture of "Judas" in Scripture seriously, very much to be desired (especially after the Holocaust); one must first look at the issue of whether there was ever a "Judas" — to say nothing of all the insidious stories encapsulated under his name.

Nor is this to say anything about the historicity of 'Jesus' in the first place or another, largely fictional character, very much now (in view of women's issues) in vogue — his alleged consort and mother of his only child, the so-called "Mary Magdalene."

But while this latter kind of storytelling does no one any specific harm historically speaking or, at least not one, one can readily identify; the case of "Judas" is very different both in kind and in effect. It has had a more horrific and, in fact, totally unjustifiable historical effect and, even if it ever had happened the way Gospel and parallel tradition describe it, effects of this kind are wholly unjustified and reprehensible.

But in the case of "Judas" there are only a few references to him and they are all clearly tendentious — for instance when he is made to complain about Mary's (another of these ubiquitous Marys) anointing Jesus' feet with precious spikenard ointment in terms of why was not this "sold for 300 dinars and given to the Poor" (John 12:5 and pars.) — a variation on the "30 Pieces of Silver" he supposedly took for "betraying" the Master in the Synoptics. But anyone familiar with this field would immediately recognize this allusion as but a thinly-veiled attack on "the Ebionites" or that group of followers of "Jesus" (or his brother 'James') in Palestine — and probably "the aboriginal Christians" — who did not follow the doctrine of "the Supernatural Christ" and saw Jesus as simply a "man" or a "prophet," engendered by natural generation only and exceeding other men in the practice of Righteousness.

In fact, the Lukan version of his death and the Mattathean version do not agree with each other, a normal state of affairs where Gospel recounting is concerned, and the other two gospels do not mention either his death or how he died at all. The point, however, is that the whole character of "Judas Iscariot" is generated out of whole cloth and it is meant to be. Moreover it is done in a totally malevolent way. The creators of this character and the traditions related to him knew what it was they were seeking to do and in this they have succeeded in a manner far beyond and that would have astonished even their hate-besotted brains.

Judas Iscariot is meant to be both hateful and hated — a diabolical character despised by all mankind and a byword for treachery and the opposite of all-perfection and the perfect, Gnosticizing Mystery figure embodied in the person of the "Salvation" figure "Jesus" — the name of whom even translates out into "Saviour." But in creating this character, the authors of these traditions and these "Gospels" (often, it is difficult to decide which came first, either "the Gospels" themselves or the traditions either inspired by or giving inspiration to them) had a dual purpose in mind and in this, as just signaled, he done his job admirably well.

His name very "Judas" in that time and place was meant (as it is today) both to parody and heap abuse on two favorite characters of the Jews of the age, "Judas Maccabee," the hero of Hanukkah festivities to this day, and "Judas the Galilean," the legendary founder (described by Josephus) of what one might either wish to call "the Zealot" or "the Galilean Movement" (even, as we shall see below, "the Sicarii") — and possibly even a third character, called in New Testament tradition "Judas the Zealot" and very probably the third 'brother' of "Jesus" known variously as "Judas of James," "Jude the brother of James," or "Judas Thomas." In fact, if he is "Judas of James," then he is also "Thaddaeus" or "Theudas."

Furthermore, the name "Jew" in all languages actually comes from this biblical name "Judas" or "Judah" ("Yehudah"), a fact not missed by the people at that time and not too misunderstood even today. So therefore the pejorative on "Judas" or "Judah" and the symbolic value of all that it signified in the first century C.E. was not missed either by those who created this particular "blood libel" or by all other future peoples even down to today. It is this the Vatican "trial balloons" are obviously becoming sensitive of and, despite the theological risk involved and a predictable and largely negative outpouring of criticism which has followed, clearly want to try to rectify just as John XXIII did like-minded, similar "blood libels" forty years ago; and it certainly is hard to imagine that such childish but diabolical storytelling could have had such a perverse and enduring effect for so long.

But there is another dimension to this particular "blood libel" which has also not failed to leave its mark, historically speaking, on the peoples of the world and that is "Judas" second name or cognomen "Iscariot." No one has ever found the linguistic prototype or origin of this curious denominative in a manner that would satisfy everyone, but it is also not unremarkable that in the Gospel of John he is also called "Judas the son" or "brother of Simon Iscariot" and at one point even "Judas the Iscariot" (John 6:71, 14:22, etc.). Of course, the closest cognate to any of these re-phrasings is the well-known term used to designate (also pejoratively) "the Sicarii" — the "iota" and the "sigma" of the Greek simply having been reversed, a common mistake in the transliteration of Semitic orthography into unrelated languages further afield like English, the "iota" likewise too generating out of the "ios" of the Greek singular "Sicarios."

There is no other tenable approximation that this term could realistically allude to. Plus the attachment to it of the definite article "the," whether mistakenly or by design, just strengthens the conclusion. Furthermore Judas' association in these episodes with the concept both of "the Poor" (the name of the group led by James, Jesus' brother, in first-century Jerusalem) as well as that of a suicide of some kind in Matthew and in Acts (suicide being one of the tenets of the group, the Jewish first-century historian, Josephus is identifying as carrying out such a procedure at the climax of well-known siege of the Fortress of Masada — to say nothing of the echo of the cognomen of the founder of this Party or "Orientation," the equally famous "Judas the Galilean" or "Judas the Zealot" also mentioned above) just strengthens this conclusion.

I have covered many of these matters in my book: *James the Brother of Jesus: The Key to Unlocking the Secrets of Early Christianity and the Dead Sea Scrolls* (Viking, 1997; Penguin, 1998) and will cover them further — along with other subjects — in the sequel: *The New Testament Code: The Cup of the Lord, the Damascus Covenant, and the Blood of Christ*, due to be published in May.

Equally germane is the fact that another "Apostle" of "Jesus" is supposed to have been called — at least according to Lukan Apostle lists — "Simon the Zealot"/"Simon Zelotes" which, of course, also translates out in the jargon of the Gospel of John as "Simon Iscariot." Moreover, he was more than likely a 'brother' of the curious Disciple, already mentioned above, in the same lists known as "Judas of James," that is, "Judas the brother of James" (the title by which he is designated in the New Testament Letter of Jude/Judas). In a variant manuscript of an early Syriac document, The Apostolic Constitutions, this individual is also designated "Judas the Zealot," thereby completing the circle of all these inter-related and overlapping terminologies which seem to have been coursing through so many of these early documents.

Of course, all these matters are fraught with difficulty, but once they are all weighed together there is hardly any escaping the fact that "Judas Iscariot"/ "the Iscariot"/"the brother" or "son of Simon Iscariot" in the Gospels and the Book of Acts is a polemical pejorative for many of these other characters meant to defame and polemically demonize a number of individuals seen as opposing the new "Pauline" or more Greco-Roman esotericizing doctrine of the "Supernatural Christ." The presentation of this "Judas," polemicizing as it was, was probably never meant to take on the historical and theological dimensions it has, coursing through the last two thousand years and leading up to the present but with a stubborn toughness it has endured.

Nevertheless, its success as a demonizing pejorative has been monumental, a whole people having suffered the consequences of not only of seeing its own beloved heroes turned into demoniacs but of being hunted down mercilessly to some extent the frightening result of its efficacy. If anything were a proof of the aphorism "Poetry is truer than history'" than this was As already remarked, I believe its original artificers would have been astonished by its incredible success. Even beyond this, not only is there no historical substance to the presentation or its after-effects, but if Jesus were alive today — whoever he was, historical or supernatural — he himself would be shocked at such vindictiveness and diabolically inspired hatred and he above all others would have expected his partisans to divest themselves of this single historical shibboleth anyhow.

Not only is a rehabilitation greatly in order in the light of the incredible atrocities committed over the last century (some as a consequence of this particular libel), but the process engendered by this historical polemic and reversal shows no sign of receding, the outcries over proposals to rehabilitate Judas themselves being evidence of this. It is yet another deleterious case of literature, cartoon, or lampoon being taken as history. In the light shed on these matters by the almost miraculous discovery of the Dead Sea Scrolls in our own time, it is time people really started to come to terms with the almost completely literary and a historical character of a large number of figures of the kind of this "Judas" and, in the process, admit the historical error of malevolent-intentioned caricature and move forward into the amelioration of rehabilitation.

– Dr. Robert H. Eisenman

Dr. Robert H. Eisenman *is a Professor of Middle East Religions and Archaeology and Director of the Institute for the Study of Judeo-Christian Origins at California State University, Long Beach; and Visiting Senior Member of Linacre College, Oxford University. The consultant to the Huntington Library in its decision to free the Dead Sea scrolls, he was the leading figure in the worldwide campaign to gain access to the scrolls. A National Endowment for the Humanities Fellow at the Albright Institute of Archaeological Research in Jerusalem, he was a Senior Fellow at the Oxford Centre for Postgraduate Hebrew Studies.*

VII

Catholicism:

2000 Years of Oppression

Catholicism:
The Stamp for All Christianity

Between 325 A.D. and the seventeenth century, Christianity was solely Catholicism.

The Mother Church formed and founded by King Constantine at the Council of Nicea exterminated many of the peaceful mystic sects.

Constantine forced a vote of the gathered bishops and then Jesus, "The King of the Jews" suddenly became "Christ, The Savior of Mankind." The prince of peace was used as a justification for war and cultural domination.

Not since the early days of Christianity dating to 100 years after Jesus' death, has there been such division and turmoil in Christiandom. For many years, Christianity was an exclusive Jewish cult which fought the Romans. Jesus was labeled at one time or another during this struggle as the "Warrior King," "Messiah," or "The Teacher of Righteousness."

This confusion and misidentification is evident even today with well over 2500 different sects, churches and denominations who each claim to be the exclusive disciples of Jesus.

Christian History 101

When Alfred North Whitehead was the Chair of Philosophy at Harvard University, he made this observation: "Christian theology has been the greatest disaster in the history of the human race." Was he correct?

A brief review:

391 A.D. Christians burn down one of the world's greatest libraries in Alexandria that housed over 700,000 scrolls.

1099 A.D. Christian crusaders take Jerusalem and massacre Jews and Muslims. In the streets were piles of heads, hands and feet Millions were killed as a result of the Crusades.

1208 A.D. Pope Innocent orders a Crusade against the French Cathars. Over 100,000 were killed by Arnaud's men at Beziers.

1231 A.D. Pope Gregory IX establishes the Inquisition. Inquisitors were given license to explore every means of horror and cruelty. Victims were rubbed with lard or grease and slowly roasted alive. Ovens built to kill people, made famous by Nazi Germany, were first used in the Christian Inquisition of Eastern Europe. The gruesome tortures used on hundreds of thousands of non-Christians were so repugnant and horrible that I cannot even describe them to you.

1377 A.D. The Pope's army descended on the Italian town of Cessna. For three days and nights beginning on February 3, the slaughter continued. The squares were filled with blood. Women were raped, ransom was placed on children, and priceless works of art destroyed. Over 3000 were butchered.

1497 A.D. The Church began an enormous burning in Florence. The works of Latin and Italian poets, illuminated manuscripts, women's ornaments, musical instruments, and paintings were all burned.

1500s A.D. The witch hunts are going full speed ahead. Members of the clergy proudly report how many they have killed. The Lutheran prelate Benedict Carpzov bragged that he had killed over 20,000 of the horrible "devil worshippers." Historians estimate that more than nine million (NINE MILLION) persons were executed after 1484, mostly women. This was as brutal as anything that happened in the Nazi's twentieth century holocaust.

1572 A.D. On St. Bartholomew's Day, over 10,000 Protestants are s laughtered in France. "We rejoice that you have relieved the world of these wretched heretics." wrote Pope Gregory XIII.

– William Edelen

Constantine

Diocletian: Son of a Slave Makes Good

Diocletian was the product of merit and of the social mobility which was possible in the late third century.

Diocletian ruled the Roman world for over twenty years. Neither mad nor debauched, he (uniquely) retired from power and famously boasted of growing cabbages "with his own hand" in retirement.

**Boys From the Hood:
The Meritocracy of Diocletian**

Diocletian (son of a freed slave) supported by Maximian (son of a shopkeeper) – a successful partnership that lasted over twenty years.

Diocletian and Maximian now supported by two deputy caesars Galerius and Constantius. It was the son of the least of them – Constantine – who set his sights on restoring absolute and undivided power.

Diocletian had recognized that the empire was too vast for one man's autocratic rule and had sensibly divided absolute power between four monarchs. At the same time he put in place a mechanism for orderly succession, with the junior Caesars stepping up to the rank of Augustus and appointing deputy Caesars in turn. Moreover, Diocletian had had the wisdom to choose colleagues and successors on the basis of ability and loyalty, not blood-ties. The tetrarchy provided orderly succession for a generation. The provinces themselves were grouped into a dozen Dioceses, each ruled by a Vicar.

Constantine: Pampered Prince Enters the Ring

As caesar of Britain and Gaul, Constantine's father — Constantius — had been chosen for the most junior post in the tetrarchy. Constantine himself had been obliged to spend his youth at Nicomedia — as "hostage" in the court of Diocletian.

When the ailing Diocletian stepped down as Augustus after twenty years in 305, Constantine was dismayed that he had been passed over for the position of Caesar. Galerius became senior Augustus in the east. Frustrated, and fearful for his life, Constantine fled to Gaul to join his father, and together they campaigned in northern Britain.

Constantius — nicknamed "Chlorus" because of his pale and sickly complexion — died at Eburacum (York) the following year and Constantine was "proclaimed" Augustus by his troops in what was the most marginal of frontier provinces. Constantine immediately moved to establish a court in the northern capital of Trier, but this ambitious prince had his sights on a far bigger prize. An unhappy Galerius reluctantly acknowledged Constantine as a caesar but appointed his own nominee — Severus — as supreme ruler for the west.

In the meantime the usurper Maxentius (son of Diocletian's original colleague Maximian) had been proclaimed Augustus in Rome by the praetorian guard. Severus lost his life in an unsuccessful attempt to remove the usurper.

Conversion? My Enemy's Enemy is My Friend

In Constantine's day, the eastern provinces were by far the richest and most populous of the Roman world. Some of its cities — Pergamon, Symrna, Antioch and so on — had existed for almost a millennium and had accumulated vast wealth from international trade and venerated cult centres. Through its numerous cities passed Roman gold going east in exchange for imports from Persia, India and Arabia. Flowing west with those exotic imports came exotic "mystery religions" to titillate and enthrall Roman appetites.

In contrast, the western provinces now ruled by Constantine were more recently colonized and less developed. Its cities were small "new towns," its hinterland still barbarian. During the crisis decades of the third century many provincial Romans in the west had been carried off into slavery by Germanic raiders and their cities burned. The province of Britain and part of northern Gaul had actually seceded from the empire in the late third century — and had been ruled by its own "emperors" (Carausius, Allectus) with the help of Frankish mercenaries (p. 286-297).

Constantine had no power base in the east from which to mount a bid for the throne — but he had been at Nicomedia in 303 when Diocletian had decided to purge the Roman state of the disloyal Christian element. He had also served under Galerius on the Danube and witnessed at first-hand how the favoured Galerius — designated heir and rival — in particular despised the cult of Christ.

The ambitious and ruthless prince, from his base in Trier, immediately proclaimed himself "protector of the Christians." But it was not the handful of Jesus worshippers in the west that Constantine had in mind — there had not, after all, been any persecution in the west — but the far more numerous congregation in the east. They constituted a tiny minority within the total population (perhaps as few as two percent) but the eastern Christians were an organized force of fanatics, in many cities holding important positions in state administration. Some held posts even within the imperial entourage. By championing the cause of the Christians Constantine put himself at the head of a "fifth column" in the east, of a state within a state.

That Fabulous Fable

At first, Constantine honored the tetrarchy which had stabilized the empire for a generation but Galerius himself died in 311 and Constantine saw his opportunity. In the spring of 312, in the first of his civil wars, Constantine moved against the ill-fated Maxentius to seize control of Italy and Africa, in the process almost annihilating a Roman army near Turin, and another outside of Rome.

A nonsense repeated ad nauseam is the fable of the "writing above the sun" which advised Constantine of his divine destiny. In its worst form, the legend has it that the words "In this sign, you shall conquer" and the sign of the cross were visible to Constantine and his entire army. The words would have been, perhaps, Latin "In Hoc Signo Victor Seris," a bizarre cloud formation unique in the annuls of meteorological observation.

On the other hand, more than one author (e.g. S. Angus, *The Mystery Religions*, p. 236) says that the words were in Greek ("En Touto Nika"), which would have left them unintelligible to the bulk of the army. Then, again, perhaps they were in both Latin and Greek, a complete occluded front of cumulus cloud!

Digging below the legend however we discover that the vision was in fact a dream reported some years later by Constantine to his secretary Lactantius (*On the Death of the Persecutors*, chapter xliv; ANF. vii, 318). The fable was later embellished by the emperor's "minister of propaganda," Bishop Eusebius, in his *Life of Constantine* (1.xxvi-xxxi). The "sign of the cross" was an even later interpolation (the cross was not a Christian symbol at the time of the battle — nor would be until the sixth century). Any "good luck emblem" at this date would have been the chi-rho — ambiguously the first two letters of the word Christos, the Greek word for "auspicious" and also Chronos, god of time and a popular embodiment of Mithras!

What is perhaps most significant about this "origins" fantasy is that "lucky charms" had entered the parlance of Christianity. Constantine did not need to be a Christian; invoking its symbols was sufficient to win divine patronage. But did he invoke its symbols? Coins issued at the time celebrating his victory showed only Sol Invictus: his triumphant arch, still standing, refers only to "the gods." In truth, Constantine was not a particularly pious man. Famously, he delayed his baptism until he was close to death for fear of further sinning — with good reason: among his many murders was that of his first wife Fausta (boiled alive) and eldest son Crispus (strangled).

The Fate of Rome

In the embattled years of the late third century the fortunes of the city of Rome began a down-spin, even as Christianity's star was rising.

By Constantine's day there were about two dozen Christian meeting houses in the city but the imperial court and its bureaucracy had moved north, first to Milan and Trier, and later, to Ravenna and Arles.

Affected both by civil conflict and the recurring epidemics which came in its wake, the city's population began to fall. Worse yet, at the very moment of Christian triumph — the consecration of the Lateran Basilica by the "first Christian Emperor" — the great general was already well ahead with plans for a new capital, eight hundred miles to the east. The Christians had plundered and assimilated much of pagan religious thought and ritual; their conquering hero now sequestered the statuary and fabric of the eastern empire to aggrandize his new city on the Bosphorus.

After 326, Constantine never again stepped foot in Rome; he personally "never liked the city" (J. Norwich, *Byzantium*, p. 61).

In consequence the Bishops of Rome picked up the mantle of falling grandeur and set the city on a new Christian path to power.

Strengthening the Centre, Dividing the Periphery

The wily Diocletian had begun a process (adapted from the Oriental theocracies) which the vainglorious Constantine refined and set as a model for all future monarchs: he surrounded the imperial dignity with a "halo" of sacredness and ceremonial.

A large court-retinue, elaborate court-ceremonials, and ostentatious court-costume made access to the emperor almost impossible. When he eventually reached "God's agent on Earth," a "suppliant" prostrated himself before the emperor as if before a divinity (Augustus had always stood to greet a senator)!

Henceforth, emperors allowed themselves to be venerated as divines, and everything connected with them was called "sacred." Instead of imperial, the word "sacred" had now always to be used.

The egotistical Constantine, not content with concentrating absolute (and "divine") power into his own hands, went on to reduce the authority of provincial governors and generals. Some of this authority fell into the hands of the nouveau riche bishops, at whose head stood Constantine himself. Constantine hoped thus to prevent any rebellion arising in the provinces — but he did so at the cost of weakening the ability of provincials to resist invasion.

State Church: Christianity Goes Royal

Constantine's desire to impose upon the Empire a religion that would identify obsequiousness to the deity with loyalty to the emperor found its perfect partner in Christianity — or at least in the Christianity he was to patronize.

In the century before the ignoble alliance of one particular faction with the imperium many christianities had contended. Before Constantine, Christ had, for most Christians, been the "good shepherd," just like Mithras and Apollo, not a celestial monarch or an imperial judge. Nor did the Christian sects dwell on the crucifixion scene:

> They shrink from the recollection of the servile and degrading death inflicted on their lord, and conceive salvation in the gentle terms of the friendship of Christ, not in the panoply of imperial triumphs (*Oxford History*, p. 14).

But with Constantine's absolute monarchy, Christianity acquired its "panoply of imperial triumphs." The leading Churchman and propagandist Eusibius hailed the autocrat as a new Moses, a new Abraham. Constantine saw himself, more modestly, as the thirteenth apostle, a saint-in-waiting. At the time, perhaps five percent of the empire's population was nominally "Christian." With imperial encouragement, support, funds and force the Universal Church set about the task of gathering in its flock.

In a number of provinces a serious breach had opened within the Christian churches between those who had "apostatised" during Diocletian's brief persecution and those who had suffered penalties for their fanaticism. Some churches already had a "nationalistic" bent, serving as a focus for opposition to the emperor.

Constantine, vexed by all such discord, called for an inclusive "universal" or catholic faith. Of course all factions regarded themselves as that universal "orthodox" faith and maneuvered for preferment. It was inevitable that an autocrat like Constantine would identify with and adopt a church which modeled its organization not merely upon the Roman State but upon its most authoritarian aspect: the imperial army.

In the Constantinian Church, bishops would rule districts corresponding with military dioceses, would control appointments and impose discipline. Lesser clerics would report through a chain of command up to the local pontiff. "Staff officers," in the guise of deacons and presbyters, would control funds and allocations.

Just as well that in Christian morality there was no place for democracy, only for absolute monarchs, chosen by God. In Christianity there were no human rights (for example, of a slave to his freedom), only obligations (thus a slave should be honest and faithful to his master, because, of course, all would be judged on the day of reckoning).

Spoils of Victory: Pillaging the Pagans

The alliance of Roman autocracy and Christian intolerance was a marriage made in hell. The Universal Church eyed with envy the pagan temples and shrines which, through centuries, had amassed their own riches. As propagandists for Constantine, the Christians had the ear of the emperor and successfully urged him to confiscate temple treasures throughout the Empire, much of it redirected to the "One True Faith."

The assault upon the values that had sustained the Empire for a thousand years was merciless and relentless. It began with Constantine's denial of state funds to the ancient pagan shrines which had always depended on state sponsorship. Never having had full-time fund raisers like the Christian churches the pagan cults immediately went into decline.

But having given the Christians the world, what Constantine could not anticipate was the ferocity of Christian discord, which was to dog his reign and the reign of all who were to follow him.

The Christian "community" itself had changed as a consequence of the Constantinian revolution. Official recognition of Christianity, the tax exemptions it gave devotees and state patronage made the Christian faith considerably more appealing to opportunistic pagans. Episcopal posts became highly sought after when, in 319, the clergy were exempted from public obligations and, in 321, priests were exempted from imperial and local taxation. Clerics were even placed outside the jurisdiction of normal courts ("Privilegia Ecclesiastica").

A flood of new converts, many with little or no religious motivation, swamped the church. Fierce rivalries within the Church multiplied, weakened its power and exposed vulnerabilities in both its doctrine and organization.

Constantine successfully established the dynastic principle, but it had bitter fruit. His feeble sons, "born to rule," murdered each other (the survivor died falling from his horse). Worse yet, Constantine's nephew, Julian, though raised as a Christian, detested the doctrine and, on assuming the throne, reversed many of Constantine's policies.

To the alarm of the new Christian "establishment," the pagan world was not yet ready to die quietly.

Post-Constantine: Lurch into Religious Tyranny

Within three years, Emperor Julian had been assassinated on the Persian front (probably by a disaffected Christian soldier) — but it left the Christians fearful of losing the prize that had fallen so unexpectedly into their laps.

Thereafter, the Christians embraced a ruthlessness hitherto unknown in the world, an intolerance which, in the centuries ahead, would wreak unimaginable horror.

In the closing years of the fourth century, draconian laws prohibiting non-Christian beliefs were enacted by the new hero of the Christians, Emperor Theodosius. Heresy was now equated with treason and thus became a capital offence.

Theodosius "the Great" presided over the destruction of temples and icons, the burning of books and libraries, and a rampage of murder of pagan priests, scholars and philosophers. The wisdom and finesse of an entire civilization was sacrificed on the altar of the Christian god-man and delivered Europe into a dark age of barbarism and crass superstition.

Only the very brave, the very foolish or the very hidden would now deny their Christianity. The prologue to the Dark Age had been written.

– Kenneth Humphreys
Excerpt from *Jesus Never Existed*, Iconoclast Press
www.jesusneverexisted.com

The Council of Nicea

Rather than the advent and death a "historical" Christ, the single most important events in the history of Christianity were the "conversion" of the Pagan Emperor Constantine and the convening of the raucous Council of Nicea in 325, which in fact marked the true birth of Jesus Christ. Constantine, of course, "converted" to Christianity because it offered a "quick fix" to all of his heinous crimes, including the murder of several family members, removed simply by confession and "believing unto the Lord," absolutions he could not procure from other religions such as Mithraism, which did not cater to murderers.

At the Council of Nicea were not only Christian leaders from Alexandria, Antioch, Athens, Jerusalem and Rome but also the leaders of the many other cults, sects and religions, including those of Apollo, Demeter/Ceres, Dionysus/Bacchus/Iasios, Janus, Jupiter/Zeus, Oannes/Dagon, Osiris and Isis, and "Sol Invictus," the Invincible Sun, the object of Constantine's devotion. The purpose of this council was to unify the various competing cults under one universal or "catholic" church, which, of course, would be controlled by Constantine and Rome. As noted, Rome claimed the ultimate authority because it purported to be founded upon the "rock of Peter." Thus, the statue of Jupiter in Rome was converted into "St. Peter," whose phony bones were subsequently installed in the Vatican. In a typical religion-making move, the gods of these other cults were subjugated under the new god and changed into "apostles" and "saints."

As stated, it is maintained that during the Nicene Council the names Jesus and Christ were put together for the first time in the phrase "Jesus Christ" or "Christ Jesus," uniting two of the major factions, with Jesus representing the Hesus of the Druids, Joshua/Jesus of the Israelites, Horus/Iusa of the Egyptians and IES/ Iesios of the Dionysians/ Samothracians, and Christ representing the Krishna/Christos of India, the Anointed of the Jews and KRST of Egypt, among others. It is thus alleged that the phrase "Jesus Christ," which had never been a name, does not appear in Greek or Latin authors prior to the first Council of Nicea. Hence, just as the name "Hermes Trismegistus" "represents a tradition rather than a single man," so does "Jesus Christ." It is also purported that one Bishop Eunomius charged fraud and blew the whistle on the Council of Nicea, the record of which was never published, even though it was supposedly made and may be in the Vatican vault to this day.

– Acharya S
Excerpt from *The Christ Conspiracy*, Adventures Unlimited Press

The Crusades

In 1095 Pope Urban II called for the knights of Europe to unite and march to Jerusalem to save the holy land from the Islamic infidel. The crusades provided an opportunity to vastly increase the influence of the Catholic Church. They also served a political purpose much closer to home. When the Pope initiated the first crusade in 1095, many of the imperial powers were outside the Church: the King of France, the King of England, and the German Emperor. The crusades were a means of uniting much of Europe in the name of Christianity.

Joan of Arc

Joan of Arc is classic example of Revisionism by the mother church. The fifth century martyr was once vilified and deserted by the Catholic church. She became a saint in 1920 upon further review. Given to the enemies of the church to burn at the stake, Joan of Arc is now a saint in Heaven.

Crusaders, caught up in their sense of righteousness, brutally attacked the Church's enemies. Pope Gregory VII had declared, "Cursed be the man who holds back his sword from shedding blood."

Later in 1204 Pope Innocent III sent a group of crusaders to Constantinople. The soldiers of Christ fell upon Constantinople with a vengeance, raping, pillaging and burning the city. According to the chronicler Geoffrey Villehardouin, never since the creation of the world had so much booty been taken from a city. The Pope's response to the Greek Emperor:

> ...We believe that the Greeks have been punished through [the Crusades] by the just judgement of God: these Greeks who have striven to rend the Seamless Robe of Jesus Christ...Those who would not join Noah in his ark perished justly in the deluge; and these have justly suffered famine and hunger who would not receive as their shepherd the blessed Peter, Prince of the Apostles...

To the Pope, the rape of Constantinople was just punishment for not submitting to the Roman Catholic Church. Biblical passages supported his stance: "But those mine enemies, which would not that I should reign over them, bring hither, and slay them before me." Following the attack, a Latin patriarch subject to the Pope ruled the domain until 1261. Constantinople, however, was left severely weakened and in 1453 fell to Turkish conquest. In the roughly 200 years of crusades, thousands, if not millions, were killed.

– Helen Ellerbe
Excerpt from *The Dark Side of Christian History*, Morningstar Books, 1995

Books Burned

One of the most notorious book burnings in history was the Catholic lead destruction of the world's greatest library in Alexandria in 391 C.E. Historians estimate that nearly 700,000 documents were burned. The writings were labeled "heresy" and "Satanic," since they did not support the church's view of the world. Porphyry's 36 volumes, all of the books of the Gnostic Basilides, and over 270,000 ancient documents gathered by Ptolemy Philadelphus were all destroyed. Non-Christian academies for learning were ordered closed. Obtaining education was prohibited for anyone other than clergy.

Inquisition, Persecution

The Catholic Church's Inquisition ranks in history as one of the most diabolical means of coercion ever conceived by man. Making the period even worse, was that it was "God's Work" carried out by the Vicar of Christ. Victims were imprisoned and tortured mercilessly until they were forced to confess their crimes. They had to admit atrocities such as worshipping the devil or sexual orgies with demons to make it stop. Once the inquisitors had what they wanted, they were turned over to authorities who either burned them at the stake or hung them to death. Their property and other belongings were usually confiscated by the church, leaving their already grieving families poverty stricken.

* * * *

This obscene institution was the creation of that most saintly Christian king, "Saint" Louis. In 1229, when he was only fifteen, Louis organized the first Inquisition to eliminate the heresy of Catharism in the south of France. The military Crusade of Simon of Montfort had not proved as effective as had been hoped and the heresy continued to flourish, so Louis instructed the Dominicans, who had originally been created to preach peacefully to the heretics, to persecute them instead by inquisitorial methods. The Inquisition continued to operate in the south until 1247 when Louis and his army massacred the last remaining Catharists in cold blood at Montségur. But once Catharism had been wiped out, there were many other heresies to extinguish and the Inquisition continued, as we have seen. It was not surprising that this noxious offspring of the Crusades was eventually used to persecute Muslims and Jews living in Christian territory, who had been forced to convert to Christianity.

– Karen Armstrong
Excerpt from *Holy War*, Anchor; 2nd edition, 2001

European Jews were often the first victims of a crusade. But Christian persecution of Jews continued long after the crusades ended. Jews became the scapegoats for many problems that the Church could not fix. When, for example, the black death, the bubonic plague, struck in the fourteenth century, the Church explained that Jews were to blame and prompted attacks upon them. A whole folklore developed claiming that Jews kidnapped and ate Christian children in Jewish rituals of cannibalism, and that Jews stole and profaned the blessed Christian sacraments. These were the same tales that Romans once told of the hated Christians, the same tales that Christians would tell of witches, and the same tales Protestants would tell of Catholics. Pogroms, the raiding and destroying of Jewish synagogues and ghettos, became a common demonstration of Christian righteousness.

Jews were easy targets for they had never been embraced by Christian society. Under the feudal system, a ceremony of investiture involving a Christian oath excluded Jews from working the land and sent them into commerce and crafts in the towns. However, with the rapid population expansion of the eleventh and twelfth centuries and the consequent influx of people to the cities, artisan guilds were established, each with its own patron saint. Jews were again driven from the crafts into what fields remained: banking, money-changing and money-lending. Persecuting Jews, therefore, also became a convenient means of getting rid of one's creditors. Religious arguments were taken up by indebted kings to justify their confiscation of Jewish property and their expulsion of Jews from their domains.

Anyone who held power became a likely target for the Church. The Knights Templar, a group originally formed to protect crusaders, gained political influence and became known as trustworthy moneylenders. As with the Jews, incredible stories began to circulate about the Templars, including accounts of an initiation ritual which involved denying Christ, God, and the Virgin, and spitting, trampling and urinating upon the cross. Accused of homosexuality, of killing illegitimate children, and of witchcraft, the Templars were murdered and their property confiscated.

– Helen Ellerbe
Excerpt from *The Dark Side of Christian History*, Morningstar Books, 1995

Giordano Bruno

Giordano Bruno (1548–February 17, 1600) was an Italian philosopher during the Dark Ages. He was also a priest, astronomer, and occultist. Best known for his system of mnemonics and as an early proponent of the idea that the Earth rotated around the sun, Bruno was often at odds with the Catholic Church. Eventually, they condemned him to death as a heretic for his theological ideas. He was burned at the stake.

Two other scientists, quickly labeled as "heretics" for their revolutionary scientific discoveries were astronomer, Nicolaus Copernicus, and later philosopher/astronomer Galileo Galilei. Although they avoided death by burning, they were threatened continually. Why? Their theory was that the sun (not the earth) was the center of our universe. This shook the Catholic church, because their doctrine stated "God made the earth the center of the universe because Jesus His son is here." Oops – the church was wrong – but tried to silence all "science." Galileo was finally forgiven in 1993 by the Pope. Copernicus is still in limbo.

The position of the Church at that time:
- The earth was flat;
- Germs were punishment for sin;
- Witches were Satan's brides;
- Dinosaur bones found in France were dragons;
- The age of the earth was 6000 years;
- Archeologists were accused by the church Fathers of contaminating the faith with false facts.

The Cathars

Catharism thrived in southern France, an area then known as Langedoc. Politically and culturally distinct from the north, Langedoc was tolerant of difference. Many races lived together harmoniously — Greeks, Phoenicians, Jews and Muslims.

In 1139 the Church began calling councils to condemn the Cathars and all who supported them. By 1179 Alexander III proclaimed a crusade against these enemies of the Church promising two years' indulgence, or freedom from punishment for sins, to all who would take up arms, and eternal salvation for any who should die. While this set a precedent for providing the Church with a warlike militia to fight the Church's private quarrels, it failed to rally force against the popular Cathars. Then in 1204 Pope Innocent III destroyed what remained of the independence of local churches when he armed his legates with the authority "to destroy, throw down, or pluck up whatever is to be destroyed, thrown down, or plucked up and to plant and build whatever is to be built or planted." In 1208 when Innocent III offered, in addition to indulgences and eternal salvation, the lands and property of the heretics and their supporters to any who would take up arms, the Albigensian Crusade to slaughter the Cathars began.

The savagery of the thirty-year-long attack decimated Langedoc. At the Cathedral of St. Nazair alone 12,000 people were killed. Bishop Folque of Toulouse put to death 10,000. When the crusaders fell upon the town of Beziers and the commanding legate, Arnaud, was asked how to distinguish Catholic from Cathar, he replied, "Kill them all, for God knows his own!" Not a child was spared. One historian wrote that "even the dead were not safe from dishonor, and the worst humiliations were heaped upon women." The total slain at Beziers as reported by papal legates was 20,000, by other chroniclers the numbers killed were between 60,000 and 100,000. The Albigensian crusade killed an estimated one million people, not only Cathars but much of the population of southern France. Afterwards, with its population nearly annihilated, its buildings left in rubble, and its economy destroyed, the lands of southern France were annexed to the north.

– Helen Ellerbe
Excerpt from *The Dark Side of Christian History*, Morningstar Books, 1995

Europe Decays and the Popes Thrive

During the fourth century, along with the lowering of character in the Roman Church there was a singular transformation of its originally simple offices. The Pagans were accustomed to highly-colored and picturesque ceremonies, and the new Church indulgently met their wishes. Hymns, altars, and statues; incense, holy water, and burning candles; silk vestments and bits of ritual — these things were borrowed freely from the suppressed temples.

There must have been a remarkable resemblance between the services in the suppressed temple of Mithra on the Vatican Hill and the services in the new temple dedicated to St. Peter on, or near, the same spot. Other religions contributed their share. The Pagans had been accustomed to variety, and so the worship of the saints and the Virgin Mother, which was unknown in the Church for three centuries, was encouraged.

Then relics had to be invented for the saints, just as saints were sometimes invented for relics. We hear every few years of bishops being directed "in a vision" to discover the body of some martyr or saint. Palestine also began to do a magnificent trade in relics with Italy; beginning with the "discovery of the true cross," at which no historian even glances today.

The events I have described bring us to the close of the fourth century, when Pope Innocent I, a strong man, undertook to enforce the Papal claim in the West. In the Eastern Church there was still nothing but contempt for that claim. In the year 381, the Greek bishops met at Constantinople, and in the third canon of the Council they expressly laid it down that the Bishop of "new Rome" (Constantinople) was equal in rank to the Bishop of "old Rome."

The great figure of the African Church — indeed, of the whole Church — at the time was St. Augustine. Catholic Truth is very concerned to show that this great leader recognized the Papal claim, and it repeatedly puts into his mouth the famous phrase: "Rome has spoken; the case is settled." The heretic Pelagius was then active, and the implication is that St. Augustine recognized the condemnation of this man by Rome as the authoritative settlement of the dispute.

Now, not only did neither Augustine nor any other bishop use those words, but they are an entirely false summary of what he did say. His words, in his 131st sermon, are: "Already the decisions of two (African) councils have been sent to the Apostolic See, and a rescript has reached us. The case is settled." The settlement lies plainly in the joint condemnation of Pelagius by Africa and Rome. Nor did the matter end here. Pope Zosimus at first pronounced in favor of Pelagius, and the African bishops forced him to recant.

In order to justify his further interference, the Pope then quoted two canons of the Council of Nicea which astonished the Africans.

After inquiry in the East, it was proven that these canons were Roman forgeries, and the African bishops, maliciously informing the Pope of their discovery, trusted that they would hear "no more of his pompousness." They did hear more of it, and a few years later they sent the Pope a letter (happily preserved) in which they scornfully reject his claim to interfere, and advise him not to "introduce the empty pride of the world into the Church of Christ, which offers the light of simplicity and lowliness to those who seek God." And Catholic Truth has the audacity to tell the faithful that these African bishops admitted the supremacy of the Pope!

Rome fell in the year 410, but the charm of the great city laid its thrall upon the barbarians, and the Roman See suffered comparatively little. The Spanish Church was next overrun, and the Vandals, crossing the Straits of Gibraltar, trod underfoot the African colony and, as they were Aryans, ruined its Church.

The provincial bishoprics no longer produced prelates of any strength or learning, and the weak new men, quarrelling incessantly amid the ruins of the Empire, began to appeal more frequently to Rome. Dense ignorance succeeded the culture of the great Empire. The Popes did not rise, but the other bishops fell. "In a land of blind men," says an old French proverb, "the one-eyed man is king."

That the Roman bishopric did not change for the better in that age of general corruption is shown by its official records. At the death of Zosimus, it became again the bloody prize of contending factions. Two Popes, Eulalius and Boniface, were elected, and on Easter morn, when each strove desperately for the prestige of conducting the great ceremony, a mighty struggle reddened once more the streets and squares of the city.

A few years later, however, Rome again obtained a strong and zealous Pope, Leo I, and the claim of supremacy advanced a few steps farther. The Church still resisted the Papal claim. When Leo attempted to overrule Bishop Hilary of Gaul, one of the few strong men remaining in the provinces, Hilary used "language which no layman even should dare to use."

In the East, Leo was not innocent of trickery. His Legates attempted to impose upon the Greeks the spurious canons which Pope Zosimus had attempted to use in Africa, and they were mercilessly exposed. In the fifteenth session of the Council of Chalcedon, the Greek bishops renewed the famous canon which declared the Bishop of Constantinople equal to the Bishop of Rome. In an ironical letter, they informed Leo of this, yet we find the Papal clerks sending to Gaul, in Leo's name, shortly afterwards, an alleged (and spurious) copy of the proceedings at Chalcedon, in which the Greek bishops are represented as calling Leo "head of the universal Church"! We shall see that there is hardly one of even the "great" Popes who did not resort to trickery of this kind.

The Greek Church has retained to this day its defiance of Rome. Western Christendom, on the other hand, has submitted to the Papacy, and we have next to see how this submission was secured. This is explained in part by the enfeeblement of the provincial bishoprics, but especially by the dense ignorance which now settled upon Europe. The products of the church's pious forgery industry included documents less innocent than the pretty stories about St. Agnes and St. Cecilia. Some of these — certain spurious or falsified canons of Greek council — we have already met. The forgers grew bolder as the shades of the medieval night fell upon Europe, and some romances of very practical value to the Papacy were fabricated.

The chief of these, *The Acts of St. Silvester*, is believed by many scholars to have been composed in the East, about the year 430. However that may be, it soon passed to Europe, and it became one of the main foundations of the Papal claim of temporal supremacy. After giving a gloriously fantastic account of the conversion and baptism of the Emperor Constantine, it makes that monarch, when he leaves Rome for the East (after murdering his wife and son), hand over to the Papacy the secular rule of all Europe to the west of Greece! It is a notorious and extravagant forgery, but it was generally accepted, and was used by the Popes.

A similar document, *The Constitution of St. Silvester*, is believed by modern historians to have been fabricated in Rome itself, in the year 498. Two Popes were elected once more, and on this occasion the customary deadly feud existed for three years. The document is supposed to have been invented, in the course of this struggle, by the supporters of the anti-Pope.

Rome and Italy were now so densely ignorant that forgers — of relics, legends, canons, pills, or anything else — enjoyed a golden age. The one force on the side of enlightenment was the heretical and anti-clerical King of Italy, Theodoric the Ostrogoth; and the Roman clergy intrigued so busily against his rule that he had to imprison Pope John I.

Rome split into Roman and Gothic factions, and terrible fights and bribery assisted "the light of the Holy Ghost" in deciding the Papal elections. Early in the sixth century there were six Popes in fifteen years, and there is grave suspicion that some were murdered.

At last Pope Silverius opened the gates of Rome to the troops of the Greek Emperor, but the change of sovereign only led the Papacy to a deeper depth of ignominy. The Greek Empress Theodora, the unscrupulous and very pious lady who had begun life in a brothel and ended it on the Byzantine throne, had a little heresy of her own; and a very courtly Roman deacon, named Vigilius, had promised to favor it if she made him Pope. "Trump up a charge against Silverius (the Pope), and send him here," she wrote to the Greek commander at Rome; and the Pope was promptly deposed for treason and replaced by Vigilius. But Pope Vigilius found it too dangerous to fulfill his bargain; and, amid the jeers and stones of the Romans, he was shipped to Constantinople to incur the fiendish vengeance of the pious Theodora. The Romans, who openly accused him of murder, heard with joy of his adventures and death, and they vented their wrath upon his friend and successor, Pope Pelagius.

Such had already become the Papacy which Catholic historians describe as distinguished for holiness and orthodoxy, under special protection of the Holy Spirit, from its foundation. But this is merely a mild foretaste of its medieval qualities. For a time Gregory the Great (590-604) raised its prestige once more; but even the pontificate of that deeply religious man has grave defects. His fulsome praise of the vicious and murderous Queen Brunichildis and of the brutal Eastern Emperor Phocas, and his wild rejoicing at the murder of the Emperor Maurice (who had called him "a fool") are revolting.

His ignorance and credulity were unlimited. His largest works, *The Magna Moralia* and *The Dialogues*, are incredible hotchpotches of stories about devils and miracles. He sternly rebuked bishops who tried to educate their people, and he did not perceive that the appalling vices and crimes which he deplores almost in every letter — the general drunkenness and simony and immorality of the priests, and the horrible prevalence of violence — were mainly due to ignorance. He was one of the makers of the Middle Ages.

After Gregory, the Papacy sinks slowly into the fetid morass of the Middle Ages. The picture of the morals of the Roman Church by Jerome in the fourth century, of the whole Western Church by the priest Salvianus in the fifth century, and by Bishop Gregory of Tours in the sixth century, are almost without parallel in literature.

It would, however, be dreary work to follow the fortunes of the Papacy, as well as we can trace them in the barbarous writings of the time, through that age of steady degeneration. Contested elections, bloody riots, bribes, brawls with the Eastern bishops punctuate the calendar. Twenty obscure Popes cross the darkening stage in the course of a hundred years. I resume the story at the point where the Popes begin to win temporal power.

In the eighth century, the Greek emperors were again in the toils of heresy, and the ruling people in the north of Italy, the Lombards, were still Aryans. The Popes began to look beyond the Alps for an orthodox protector, and their gaze was attracted to the Franks. Rome found it convenient to regard the Franks as an enlightened and pious race, though we know from the reports of St. Boniface to the Popes that the Frank clergy and princes were among the worst in Europe.

Clerics, we read, had four or five concubines in their beds. Drunkenness, brawling, simony, and corruption tainted nearly the whole of the clergy and the monks. These things were overlooked; nor did the Lateran (at that time the palace of the Popes) rebuke Charles Martel for his own corruption in despoiling the Church.

Charles Martel paid no attention to the flattering offer of the Popes, but his son Pippin found occasion to use it. He was "Mayor of the Palace," and he desired to oust the king and occupy his throne. He sent envoys to Pope Zachary to ask if he might conscientiously do so. Not only might he, Zachary replied, but he must; and from that time onward, Rome was able to claim that Pippin and his famous son, Charlemagne, owed their throne to the Papacy.

It was not long before Pope Stephen, being hard pressed by the Lombards, appealed to the gratitude of the ignorant Frank, and a very remarkable bargain was struck. Pippin accepted the title of "Tatricius" (vaguely, Prince) of Rome, and in return he promised to wrest from the Lombard heretics the whole territory which belonged to the Popes.

It is true that very considerable estates had previously been given to the Papacy. Gregory the Great, who believed that the end of the world was at hand, had induced large numbers of nobles to leave their estates to the Church, since their sons would have no use for them, and he farmed and ruled immense territories. He became the richest man and largest slave-holder in Europe. Gregory had been as shrewd in material matters as he had been credulous in religion. But historians suspect, with good reason, that the Papal envoys showed Pippin *The Acts of St. Silvester*, and in virtue of it, claimed nearly the whole of Italy.

The gruff and superstitious Pippin swore a mighty oath that he would win back for "the Blessed Peter" the lands which these hoggish heretics had appropriated, and he went to Italy and secured them. What precise amount of Italy he handed over to the Papacy we do not know. The Papacy has not preserved the authentic text of a single one of these "donations" on which it bases its claims of temporal power.

There is a document, known as the "Fantuzzian Fragment," which professes to give the terms of "the Donation of Pippin," but scholars are agreed that this is a shameless Roman forgery. It is, however, certain that Pippin gave the Papacy, probably on the strength of the older forgery, a very considerable part of north and central Italy, including the entire Governorship of Ravenna, and returned to France.

To this territory, the Papacy had no just title whatever, and the King of the Lombards at once reoccupied it. Pope Stephen stormed the French monarch with passionate and piteous appeals to recover it for him, but Pippin refused to move again. Then the Pope took a remarkable step. Among his surviving letters there is one addressed to Pippin which is written in the name of St. Peter. The Pope had forged it in the name of Peter, and passed it off on the ignorant Frank as a miraculous appeal from the Apostle himself. By that pious stratagem and the earlier forgery, the Papacy obtained twenty-three Italian cities with the surrounding country.

Those who affect to doubt whether the Pope really intended to deceive the King seem to forget that the Papacy of the time was deeply stained with crime and forgery. In 768, a noble of the Roman district named "Toto" got together a rabble of priests and laity, and elected his own brother. 'Tope" Constantine was a layman, but he was hastily put through the various degrees of ordination and consecration by obliging bishops.

No doubt these bishops then claimed their reward and disturbed the older officials. At all events, we read that the chief official of the Papal court, Christopher, and his son Sergius fled to the Lombards, borrowed an army, and marched back upon Rome. A fierce and deadly battle, in which the Lombards won, was followed by the first of a series of horrible acts of vengeance, which will henceforward, from time to time, disgrace the Papacy.

The wretched Constantine, duly consecrated by three bishops, was put upon a horse, in a woman's saddle, with heavy weights to his feet, and conducted ignominiously through the streets of Rome. He was then confined in a monastery, to await trial; but Christopher and Sergius broke into the monastery and cut out the man's eyes. In this condition, his blind face still ghastly from the mutilation, Constantine was brought before a synod in the Pope's palace and tried. The infuriated priests thrashed the wretch with their own hands, and "threw him out."

The end of Constantine is, in the chronicles, left to the imagination. His brother also lost his eyes. One of the consecrating bishops lost his eyes and his tongue. In short, the supporters of the premature Pope were punished with a savagery that tells us plainly enough the character of the Papacy at that time.

Catholic Truth — which, however, generously admits that there were "some bad Popes," though this does not affect its claim of the special interest of the Holy Ghost in the Papacy — imagines the Pope serenely aloof from these horrors. Listen to the sequel. Christopher and Sergius presumed too much upon their services to Pope Stephen, and he grew tired of them and plotted with the Lombard King. They discovered or suspected the plot, and sought to kill the Pope; and it is enough to say that before many days they themselves had their eyes cut from the sockets.

Christopher was mutilated so brutally that he died. There are some Catholic writers who make a show of liberality, and admit that the Pope was "implicated" in this. But the sordid truth is known to us and to these writers on the most absolute authority of the time. In the *Liber Pontificate* itself, we have the explicit testimony of Pope Hadrian I, the greatest Pope of the time, that Pope Stephen ordered the eyes of Christopher and Sergius to be cut out, and for the sordid reason that King Didier promised to restore the disputed lands if he did so. Stephen, Hadrian says, admitted this to him.

To such depths had "the Vicars of Christ" sunk now, that the greed of temporal sovereignty and wealth was added to the ambition for religious supremacy. And they had, naturally, allowed all Europe to sink to the same level. As the letters of St. Boniface and other contemporary documents affirm, the moral condition of England, France, and Germany — Spain had now passed to the Arabs — was unspeakable. Monasteries and nunneries were houses of open debauch — Boniface describes the English nuns as murdering their babies — and the clergy very corrupt. But here I must confine myself to the Vicars of Christ.

– Joseph McCabe (1867-1955)

Joseph McCabe *was an ex-priest and author of many books. This article is from* Popes and Their Church *and is available at most public libraries. Published in London, by Watts 1953.*

Pope Paul VI pressured President John F. Kennedy in 1963 to recognize the Vatican. Kennedy, an avowed Catholic and State/Church Separationist, resisted. In 1984, President Ronald Reagan recognized the Vatican and appointed William Wilson as ambassador.

" *The Church of Rome has made it an article of fact that no man can be saved out of their church, and other religious sects approach this dreadful opinion in proportion to their ignorance, and the influence of ignorant or wicked priests.* "

John Adams, Second President of the United States

> " *If all records told the same tale — then the lie passed into history and became truth. 'Who controls the past,' rants the Party slogan, 'controls the future. Who controls the present controls the past.'* "

George Orwell, *1984*

The Church, now enormously wealthy, interested itself more in collecting money than in relating to its members. The medieval Church's preoccupation with riches was such that its ten commandments were said to have been reduced to one: "Bring hither the money." Priests were selected more on the basis of their money than upon any other virtue. A huge disparity developed not only between the clergy and the laity but also between ranks of the clergy. The income of a wealthy bishop, for example, could range from 300 times to as much as 1000 times that of a vicar. In the twelfth century the Church forbade clergy to marry in order to prevent property from passing out of the Church to the families of clergy. The incongruity of an extravagantly wealthy organization representing the ideals of Jesus Christ prompted the papal bull or edict Cum inter nonnullos in 1326 which proclaimed it heresy to say that Jesus and his Apostles owned no property.

– Helen Ellerbe; excerpt from *The Dark Side of Christian History*,
San Rafael: Morningstar Books, 1995

Missionaries

Throughout the late sixteenth and the seventeenth and eighteenth centuries, Spanish disease and Spanish cruelty took a large but mostly uncalculated toll. Few detailed records of what happened during that time exist, but a wealth of research in other locales has shown the early decades following Western contact to be almost invariably the worst for native people, because that is when the fires of epidemic disease burn most freely. Whatever the population of California was before the Spanish came, however, and whatever happened during the first few centuries following Spanish entry into the region, by 1845 the Indian population of California had been slashed to 150,000 (down from many times that number prior to European contact) by swarming epidemics of influenza, diphtheria, measles, pneumonia, whooping cough, smallpox, malaria, typhoid, cholera, tuberculosis, dysentery, syphilis, and gonorrhea — along with everyday settler and explorer violence."

Using armed Spanish troops to capture Indians and herd them into the mission stockades, the Spanish padres did their best to convert the natives before they killed them. And kill they did. First there were the Jesuit missions, founded early in the eighteenth century, and from which few vital statistics are available. Then the Franciscans took the Jesuits' place...[Most people just assume that the 'missions' were about 'doing the Lord's work' for the benefit of God and the Indians. The recorded history of this time and place, however, do not bear this out.]

And what was done was that they brought more natives in, under military force of arms. Although the number of Indians within the Franciscan missions increased steadily from the close of those first three disastrous years [when the number of deaths caused the Indian population living in the missions to decline] until the opening decade of the nineteenth century, this increase was entirely attributable to the masses of native people who were being captured and force-marched into the mission compounds. Once thus confined, the Indians' annual death rate regularly exceeded the birth rate by more than two to one. This is an overall death-to-birth ratio that, in less than half a century, would completely exterminate a population of any size that was not being replenished by new conscripts. The death rate for children in the missions was even worse. Commonly, the child death rate in these institutions of mandatory conversion ranged from…one of every six to every three…

In short, the missions were furnaces of death that sustained the Indian population levels for as long as they did only by driving more and more natives into their confines to compensate for the huge number were being killed once they got there. This was a pattern that held throughout California and on out across the southwest. Thus, for example, one survey of life and death in an early Arizona mission has turned up statistics showing that at one time an astonishing 93 percent of children born within its walls died before reaching the age of ten…

There were various ways in which the mission Indians died. The common causes were the European-introduced diseases — which spread like wildfire in such cramped quarters — and malnutrition. The personal space for Indians in the missions averaged about seven feet by two feet per person for unmarried captives, who were locked at night into sex-segregated common rooms that contained a single open pit for a toilet. It was perhaps a bit more space than was allotted a captive African in the hold of a slave ship sailing the Middle Passage. Married Indians and their children, on the other hand, were permitted to sleep together — in what Russian visitor V.M. Golovnin described in 1818 as "specially constructed 'cattlepens.'" He explained:

> I cannot think of a better term for these dwellings that consist of a long row of structures not more than 7 feet high and 10 to 14 feet wide, without floor or ceiling, each divided into sections by partitions, also not longer than 14 feet, with a correspondingly small door and a tiny window in each — can one possibly call it anything but a barnyard for domestic cattle and fowl? Each of these small sections is occupied by an entire family; cleanliness and tidiness are out of the question: a thrifty peasant usually has a better-kept cattle-pen.

Under such conditions Spanish-introduced diseases ran wild: measles, smallpox, typhoid, and influenza epidemics occurred and re--occurred, while syphilis and tuberculosis became, as Sherburne F. Cook once said, "totalitarian" diseases: virtually all the Indians were afflicted by them. As for malnutrition, despite agricultural crop yields on the Indian-tended mission plantations that Golovnin termed "extraordinary" and "unheard of in Europe," along with large herds of cattle and the easily accessible bounty of seafood, the food given the Indians, according to him, was "a kind of gruel made from barley meal, boiled in water with maize, beans, and peas; occasionally they are given some beef, while some of the more diligent [Indians] catch fish for themselves." On average, according to Cook's analyses of the data, the caloric intake of a field-laboring mission Indian was about 1400 calories per day, falling as low as 715 or 865 calories per day in such missions as San Antonio and San Miguel. To put this in context, the best estimate of the caloric intake of nineteenth-century African American slaves is in excess of 4000 calories per day, and almost 5400 calories per day for adult male field hands. This seems high by modern Western standards, but is not excessive in terms of the caloric expenditure required of agricultural laborers. As the author of the estimate puts it: "A diet with 4206 calories per slave per day, while an upper limit [is] neither excessive nor generous, but merely adequate to provide sufficient energy to enable one to work like a slave." Of course, the mission Indians also worked like slaves in the padres' agricultural fields, but they did so with far less than half the caloric intake, on average, commonly provided a black slave in Mississippi, Alabama, or Georgia. Even the military commanders at the missions acknowledged that the food provided the Indians was grossly insufficient, especially, said on given "the arduous strain of the labors in which they are employed"; labors, said another, which last "from morning to night"; and labors, note a third, which are added to the other "hardships to which they are subjected." The resulting severe malnutrition, of course, made the natives all the more susceptible to the bacterial and viral infections that festered in the filthy and cramped living conditions they were force to endure — just as it made them more likely to behave lethargically, something that would bring more corporal punishment down upon them...

When not working directly under the mission fathers' charge, the captive natives were subject to forced labor through hiring-out arrangements the missions had with Spanish military encampments. The only compensation the natives received for this, as for all their heavy daily labors, was the usual inadequate allotment of food. As one French visitor commented in the early nineteenth century, after inspecting life in the missions, the relationship between the priest and his flock would "be different only in name, if a slaveholder kept them for labor and rented them out at will; he too would feed them." But, we now know, he would have fed them better.

In short, the Franciscans simultaneously starved and worked their would be converts to death, while the diseases they and others had imported killed off thousands more. The similarity of this outcome to what had obtained in the slave labor camps of Central and South America should not I surprising, since California's Spanish missions, established by Father Junipero Sera aptly dubbed "the last conquistador" by one admiring biographer, and currently a candidate for Catholic sainthood), were direct modeled on the genocidal encomienda system that had driven many millions of native peoples in Central and South America to early and agonizing deaths. Others died even more quickly, not only from disease, but from grotesque forms of punishment. To be certain that the Indians were spiritually prepared to die, when their appointed and rapidly approaching time came they were required to attend mass in chapels where, according to one mission visitor, they were guarded by men "with whips and goads to enforce order and silence" and were surrounded by "soldiers with fixed bayonets" who were on hand in case any unruliness broke out. These were the same soldiers, complained the officially celibate priests, who routinely raped young Indian women. If any neophytes (as the Spanish called Indians who had been baptized) were late for mass, they would have "a large leathern thong, at the end of a heavy whip-staff, applied to their naked backs." More such infractions brought more serious torture.

And if ever some natives dared attempt an escape from the padres — as to lead them to salvation — as, according to the Franciscans' own accounts, the Indians constantly did — there would be little mercy shown. From the time of the missions' founding days, Junipero Serra traveled from it to pulpit preaching fire and brimstone, scourging himself before his incarcerated flock, pounding his chest with heavy rocks until it was feared he would fall down dead, burning his breast with candles and live coals in imitation of San Juan Capistrano. After this sort of self-flagellating exertion, Father Serra had no patience for Indians who still preferred not to obey his holy demands of them. Thus, on at least one occasion when of his Indian captives not only escaped, but stole some mission supplies to support them on their journey home, "his Lordship was so angry," recalled Father Paulo, "that it was necessary for the fathers who there to restrain him in order to prevent him from hanging some of them. He shouted that such a race of people deserved to be put to knife."

– David E. Stannard
Excerpt from *The American Holocaust*, Oxford University Press

Father Serra and the Skeletons of Genocide

Junipero Serra was the first Father-President of the Alta California Missions, and has been beatified, which is the next-to-last step of canonization. Born Miguel Jose Serra, November 24, 1713 of a farming family on the Spanish island of Mallorca, Father Serra was raised in the village of Petra (Fogel 1988:41). Father Serra had a distinguished career as an academic in Europe. Upon arriving in the New World, Father Serra grabbed his chance to fulfill a life-long dream of becoming a spiritual conquistador and leading a nation of pagans to the fold of the church. Being one of the first priests in Alta California, and Father-President of the Alta California missions, Father Serra was instrumental in the formation of the missions' policies, attitudes, and treatment toward the Native Californians. It is this mission legacy that forms one of the bases of Father Serra's candidacy for sainthood, which is still pending.

Through a selective and myopic interpretation of historical events, individuals who wish to perpetuate the popular romantic days of Spanish California myth have created a pristine picture of Father Serra. In defense of Father Serra, Bishop Thaddeus Shubsda of Monterey Diocese commissioned the Serra Report, which is a compilation of eight interviews. The mythic image created within the Serra Report is one of Father Serra possessing a totally forgiving nature for any and all transgressions committed by Native Californians, completely innocent of and separated from any association of forced residency or punishment, such as floggings.

"Making Father Serra a Saint by the Catholic church would be the same as the modern German Republic making Henrich Himmler a patron saint of German democracy."
– B. Burkart, German Historian

This almost antiseptic image of Father Serra is reinforced by Dr. Nunis in the Serra Report, with statements like "There's no evidence that Serra ever instituted physical punishment or any kind of unusual punishment" (Costo 1987: 218). "Unusual punishment" by whose standards, the zealous missionaries who ordered it, or the Indios who received it? Unfortunately, the Indigenous perspective is lacking, or is superficially addressed by the supporters of canonization.

What seems to be occurring is a conflict of perspectives, definitions, and interpretations between the canonization supporters, a group some would identify as "apologists," and the "detractors" who challenge the historical accuracy of Father Serra's case. The apologists have found it necessary to degrade the Indigenous People of California to elevate Serra's reputation.

This paper will address the apologists' myths with historical documentation, especially the letters written by Father Serra connecting him to floggings and forced residency. The apologists are guilty of the same academic sins they accuse the detractors of, and should have conducted a more diligent literature search. A rigorous analysis of the anthropological data should have also been conducted before perpetuating outdated ethnocentric myths about Native Californians.

Pro-Serrans Denigrate Detractors

The ultimate question of whether Father Serra merits sainthood or not rests with the Catholic Church itself, since sainthood is an internal honored position, requiring a lengthy evaluation process based upon established criteria.

Questions have been raised to challenge the myths and the aura of quaint pastoral romanticism shrouding colonial California. The three main points used in the Serra Report to defend canonization are firstly, that Father Serra's detractors are coming from an emotional point of view, rather than using a scholarly approach, and are making historically unsound, unfounded allegations that reflect a lack of research and that neglect the facts. Secondly, Father Serra is being blamed for abuses that occurred long after his death in 1784, and thirdly, no one has yet produced any documentation that Father Serra mistreated anyone.

Most of the Serra Report interviewees exhibited an eighteenth-century European perspective, through a parochial interpretation of historical events, and accepted that period's highly ethnocentric assessment of the Indigenous people at face value. According to this eighteenth-century European perspective, Native California was comprised of wandering bands of neo-Neanderthals with limited intelligence, possessing only a rudimentary culture and technology. Dr. Nunis in the Serra Report reinforces the ethnocentric image by stating that the padres gave the Indians…

> …warm blankets so you [the Indians] wouldn't freeze to death. Now the Indian didn't have to bury himself in (the) sand to keep warm…the California Indians had, at best, a modest level of civilization. I'm being kind…Life was very hard, very hard. They simply had to really grub for a living. And that living meant just eating and staying alive…They had no idea of a social compact, in the strongest sense of the word…They had no sense of morality (Costo 1987:219).

Significant literature was either overlooked or discounted, and the scholars who disagreed with canonization were trivialized. Dr. Engstrand in the Serra Report said the detractors are "some amateur anthropologists and archaeologists, people from the 60s who want a cause, or who want to promote general Indian welfare, and receive a lot of publicity, they think it is a good one to beat the drums about" (Costo 1987:195). Even the clergy who have published in defense of Father Serra concede several points of what the Indigenous community considers to be human rights abuses.

The apologists justified the human rights abuses because such acts were an accepted form of punishment in Europe. The Indigenous perspective was ignored, dismissed, or erroneously interpreted by the apologists. Prominent members of the Native Californian community pointed out that the contributors to the Serra Report who are attempting to interpret an Indigenous perspective are not observed in, much less participating with, the native community.

The Serra Report puts forth a blanket condemnation of all detractors, overlooking that many are Native Americans who were raised in the Catholic tradition. There are many distinguished and respected scholars who are critical of the historical interpretations used to support canonization. Dr. Gloria Miranda describes the authors of historical accounts that were critical of the mission system and contemporary detractors as those who "were very blatant in their anti-Spanish and anti-Catholic attitudes…[with] a deep-rooted and irrational dislike for Catholicism…[and because of] that point it is not sound criticism, based on a valid argument. It's based on an emotional and a religious perspective" (Costo 1987:213-214). Interestingly enough, Bancroft noted the courage of Padre Antonio de la Conception Horra, for complaining to his colleagues of the many abuses suffered by the neophytes within the California mission system. Padre Horra was beaten, declared insane, and exiled from California for his "disloyalty" (Bancroft, 1886:593). No doubt Hubert Bancroft was one of the historians the apologist was referring to.

Punishment Saves

The methods Father Serra instituted in the mission system, and the personal philosophy that guided his motives, should be examined. Father Serra felt that pain and penance were necessary for the purification of the flesh. The painful subject of self-flagellation is often dismissed by the apologists, but it is an important point when dealing with Father Serra's personal philosophy of conversion, punishment, and the purification of the flesh to save the soul. In Father Maynard Geiger's work, "Palou's Life of Fray Junipero Serra" (1955), published by the Academy of American Franciscan History, there is an interesting letter. Father Palou in his letter said:

St. Prosper includes the virtue of penance among the effects of temperance: Vitiosa castigat [it punishes vices]. In such a manner did Fray Junipero exercise this virtue, that for the mortification of his body he was not content with the ordinary exercises of the college in regard to acts of discipline, vigils and fasts, but he privately scourged his flesh with rough hair shirts, made either of bristles or with points of metal wire, with which he covered his body. He also took the discipline unto blood during the most silent part of the night, when he would betake himself to one of the tribunes of the choir. Although the place was so remote and the hour so quiet, there were friars who heard the cruel strokes...Not content to mortify his body for his own imperfection and sins, he also did penance for the sins of others. By strong censures he would move his listeners to sorrow and penance for their sins; he struck his breast with the stone, in imitation of St. Jerome; in imitation of his St. Francis Solanus, to whom he was devoted, he used [a] chain to scourge himself; he used the burning torch, applying it to his uncovered chest, burning his flesh in imitation of St. John Capistran and various other saints. All this he did with the purpose not only of punishing himself, but also of moving his hearers to penance for their own sins (Geiger 1955: 279,280).

The most damaging blows to the apologists come from Father Serra's own pen. Father Antoine Tibesar in his four-volume *Writings of Junipero Serra* (1956), published by the Academy of American Franciscan History as well, is a rich source that allows one an insight into Father Serra's thinking through his pen. Serra in 1752 requested the Tribunal of the Inquisition to look into local witchcraft, and was appointed Head Inquisitor of Sierra Gorda, Mexico.

– Jose Ignacio Rivera

The Vatican Bank Scandal

The French Riviera town of Cannes is known throughout the world for its international film festival, as well as being a magnet for the cosmopolitan jet set. But a different sort of attention fell on the resort last Thursday as Italian and French police swept into Cannes to arrest a man named Licio Gelli, a fugitive since May, and dubbed "the Puppet Master" for his role in some of the most bizarre events of recent decades. Gelli's arrest touches on scandals and secret deals going back to the Second World War; many of these events involve the Vatican, especially the role played by the Holy See in operating a "rat line" expatriation movement for Nazis and other war criminals, and a financial deal linking the papacy with illegal, dirty money flowing through its bank, the IOR or Institute for Religious Works.

Start with a body found on the morning of June 17, 1982 beneath London's Blackfriars bridge. The corpse was dangling from a rope, weighed down with 14 pounds of brick and stone; the victim's hands had been tied behind his back, a fact which seemed to be ignored by the coroner who pronounced the affair a simple suicide. But there was much more. The body was that of Roberto Calvi, head of the elite Banco Ambrosiano, at the time the largest privately owned financial institution in Italy. A second inquest, demanded by Calvi's family, began to blow open a financial and political scandal that has reverberated throughout the continent, and beyond.

When investigators began digging into the Calvi affair, they discovered a shortfall of nearly $1.3 billion at Banco Ambrosiano. Later, the money was traced to accounts owned by the Vatican. Calvi and his bank were also involved with a shadowy figure named Licio Gelli, head of a renegade secret Masonic lodge named P-2 or "Propaganda Due."

The Vatican connection to the Gelli-Calvi affair dates back to rise of Benito Mussolini, who in 1921, organized the Italian fascists of the old Fascio di Combattimento as a political movement. After becoming Prime Minister, Mussolini negotiated a series of agreements with the Vatican and finally settled "the Roman Question" which had arisen in 1870 when the newly formed Italian kingdom annexed the Papal States. Since then, the Italian government had guaranteed the Roman Catholic Church only limited sovereignty, and a subsidy of 3,250,000 lire per year. By published accounts, the popes considered themselves "prisoners" of the state.

The Lateran Treaty, also known as the Vatican Concordant, resolved that dilemma by creating a Catholic state and guaranteed political autonomy to the papacy. A series of financial "compensations" were arranged as well, including seed money for what became the Vatican Bank. It was not until 1984, though, when a revised treaty was signed that ended the Roman Catholic Church's status as the official, government-funded church of Italy.

The Vatican used its resources to provide passports, money and other support for church-run "rat-lines" that transported former Nazis and supporters out of Europe to safer havens in the Middle East, Britain, Canada, Australia, New Zealand, the United States and South America. Organizations like ODESSA (Organization of Former Officers of the S.S.) and "The Spider" took advantage of this service, and by some accounts the Vatican Ratline provided support to as many as 30,000 Nazis. Among the beneficiaries of the Holy See's largesse were former Gestapo operative Klaus Barbie, Adolph Eichman, Dr. Joseph Mengele (the "White Angel" or "Angel of Death of the Auschwitz death camp), Gustav Wagner, Commandant of the Soirbibor camp, and Franz Stangl of the Treblinka extermination facility. Members of the Waffen S.S. "Galician Division" were resettled as well.

– Conrad Goeringer

Pope John Paul II: A Moral, Abject Failure When It Mattered

Let's cut the beatitudes: Pope John Paul II was a moral, abject failure when it mattered. Screw his ecumenical efforts. Never mind his opposition to Communism. Forget his apologies for the horrors that the Roman Catholic Church inflicted upon so many of the world's innocent throughout two millennia. All those "breakthroughs" were inevitable, none of them particularly revolutionary...

Pay attention to the times when the pope had the opportunity to right the Catholic Church in the here and now. Pay attention to the Americas. In two of the more profound matters to affect Roman Catholicism during his 25-year reign — the struggle of liberation theology in Latin America during the 1980s and the sex-abuse scandal in the United States — the man born Karol Wojtyla did worse than nothing: he comforted the comfortable and afflicted the afflicted.

This supposed champion of the oppressed, this Vicar of Christ, consistently supported the church where it aligned itself with the despots of the Americas. Last year he allowed American bishops to publicly declare Democratic presidential nominee and Catholic John Kerry unfit to receive Communion — a blatantly political stance to sway numerous Catholics toward the Republican Party. In Mexico, John Paul II canonized 26 people associated with the Cristeros revolt, the 1920s movement in which the Catholic Church, infuriated by the Mexican government's call to surrender extensive land holdings, organized parishioners against the government.

But John Paul II's most egregious sin was committed in Latin America. There during the 1960s, Catholics married Marx' paean to the working class with Jesus' radical notion that "the meek shall inherit the earth." With the advent of this liberation theology, the Latin American faithful sighed in relief: the Roman Catholic hierarchy, which had aligned itself with the ruling class in the New World since the time of Columbus, would finally fuse the light of heaven with the struggle on earth. Now the Church would join the oppressed rather than merely bathe their wounds with the promise of salvation in the afterlife.

The Latin American gentry, understandably, became furious and called upon the United States for funds and troops — the infamous contras and death squads. Soon came the murder of priests, nuns, brothers, parishioners, even bishops — any Catholic who dared question social inequity. But rather than reprimand these right-wing governments and their henchmen, John Paul II choked the life out of liberation theology. He removed priests and bishops who bravely stood against the marauding forces. In one famous incident, he reprimanded Nicaraguan priest Ernesto Cardenal on national television for his support of the Sandinistas over the Reagan-backed contras and scolded into silence a crowd of parishioners who shouted "We want peace!"

John Paul II's defenders will claim that his opposition to liberation theology wasn't because it loved the poor too much but rather because of its relationship to Marxism, which Wojtyla suffered through as a young priest in Poland. They'll even point out that John Paul II would visit the tomb of Salvadoran Bishop Oscar Romero, the most prominent practitioner of liberation theology, who was shot through the heart by a government sniper's bullet while saying Mass in 1980. At Romero's shrine in 1983, the pontiff remarked the bishop was "a zealous and venerated pastor who tried to stop violence. I ask that his memory be respected and let no ideological interest try to distort his sacrifice as a pastor given over to his flock."

But that was all flapping lips. While Romero lived, John Paul II reprimanded him thrice in private, once even asking him to align himself with the Salvadoran dictatorship. Romero refused, calling the request "unjust." Shortly after Romero's assassination, a Washington Post columnist gasped that "the pope's outrage was so muted that it was taken as a political statement of its own." And while John Paul II rewarded other lesser Catholics with sainthood, Romero isn't so much as beatified, even though his shrine in San Salvador includes crutches, photographs, testimonies — the witness of thousands.

When the opportunity was there, John Paul II spat on the graves of martyrs. Consider Fernando Saenz Lacalle, a member of the ultra conservative Catholic lay organization Opus Dei. In 1996, John Paul II appointed Lacalle as the archbishop of San Salvador, the very position Romero once held. Shortly after assuming the bishopric, Lacalle accepted the post of honorary brigadier general in the Salvadoran military — the very military that covered up the rape and murder of four American nuns in 1980. When the pope visited the country in 1996 for Lacalle's installation, both refused to visit the tomb of six Jesuits murdered by the Salvadoran military in one gruesome night in 1989. Most outrageously, Lacalle asked for and received a two million dollar donation for a brand new cathedral from the Republican Nationalist Alliance (known by its Spanish acronym ARENA), the coalition whose founder, Roberto D'Aubuisson, allegedly ordered Romero's assassination personally and routinely declared his admiration for Hitler.

"While the Church seeks the political, social and economic liberation of the downtrodden, its primary goal is the spiritual one of liberation from evil," the Vatican declared in a 1986 statement, By then its inaction had already led to the murders of hundreds of thousands of Central Americans and the forced migrations of millions. More tellingly, the withdrawal of the Roman Catholic Church from an active role in the Latin American struggles of the 1980s led to a region-wide exodus into Protestantism that continues to this day.

Shortly after the pope's 1996 visit, one Salvadoran Jesuit summed up John Paul II's influence over Latin America in an open letter to one of his slain fellow Jesuits: "Our church has changed, Ellacu. I don't know if you would recognize in her the church of Monsignor Romero, the church that gave voice to the voiceless and the one that reminded us of Jesus of Nazareth…She doesn't cause many stirs anymore. The powerful don't feel she is a threat, and I don't know if the poor find in her help and refuge. I think our church is seen more often than necessary standing beside the powerful of this world."

Closer to home, Catholics should remember John Paul II's ignorance of what's shaping up to be his Church's spiritual genocide: the priestly sex-abuse scandal. His defenders will mention that what the pope told the twelve American cardinals who visited the Vatican in 2002: "There is no place in the priesthood and religious life for those who would harm the young," was penance enough.

That was too little, too late. By then the pope already knew. He knew as early as 1985, when Tom Doyle, a priest and canonist with the Vatican Embassy in Washington, D.C., helped author a confidential report alerting American Catholic officials about the pederast storm gathering on the horizon. He knew as early as 1990 that bishops were advising one another to send potentially incriminating documents to the Apostolic Delegate (the papal representative to the Catholic Church in the United States) because that office has diplomatic immunity. He knew in 1993 when he first addressed the American sex-abuse scandal by accusing the media of treating his prelates; cover-up as an "occasion for sensationalism." He knew!

Last year he propped up former Boston Cardinal Bernard Law with a cushy job in St. Peter's Square, the same Law who was forced to resign in 2o02 lest the feds make him sing about his role in the rape of children! John Paul II opposed the zero-tolerance policies that American bishops installed in 2002 to insure that child rapists would never officiate at Mass again. John Paul II never removed Los Angeles Cardinal Roger Mahoney and Orange Bishop Tod D. Brown from their posts despite their active shielding of child-molesting priests from the law.

In my cubicle, I have a silver medallion of Pope John Paul II. But I place it in a specific spot, away from my rosary, away from my Virgin of Guadalupe Christmas display, away from my statue of the Santo Nino de Atocha, away from my Baptism photo. I keep the medallion directly above an excerpt from the Book of Gomorrah, the landmark study by Saint Damian in which he warned Pope Leo IX of the sex-abuse scandal in the eleventh century! One passage of that study stands out in particular: "For truth says, 'Whoever scandalizes one of these little ones, it were better for him to have a great millstone hung around his neck and be drowned in the depths of the sea.' Unless the strength of the Apostolic See intervenes as soon as possible, there is no doubt that this unbridled wickedness...will be unable to stop its headlong course."

And on this note, Pope John Paul II meets Jesus Christ!

– Gustavo Arellano, *OC Weekly*

Pope Benedict XVI

The Catholic Church finds itself with a former German Nazi as the Vicar of Christ. Viewing the sordid history of the church with its severe record of extermination of Protestants, Jews, Muslims, Native Americans and other "heretics" — even outdistancing butchers and psychopaths such as Stalin, Hitler and Mao, it is actually not that surprising that the church as such a Pope.

Opus Dei:
Select Questions and Answers
from the Unofficial Opus Dei FAQ

Q: What is Opus Dei?
A: Opus Dei a fundamentalistic sect which operates in a Catholic environment. Officially it is part of the Catholic Church and so they claim that they are not a sect. Well, it all depends on how you define the word "sect." It would be best for you to derive your own opinion by reading this FAQ.

Q: What are the negative things in Opus Dei?
A: In short:
- The Fascist ideology in Escriva's teachings.
- The fundamentalism.
- Intolerance towards other religions.
- The dishonesty.
- The danger inherent in the undemocratic structure of blindly following orders.
- The danger inherent in the psychological control they have of their members due to the "weekly chat" where they have to tell the innermost details of their souls to their spiritual leaders.
- The aggressive and manipulative way in which they try to catch new members.
- The evil character of the founder.
- The fact that they do not reveal their true goals and keep a lot of material secret from the public.
- The smug thinking of belonging to an elite.

Q: What is dangerous in the structure of Opus Dei?
A: The inherent danger lies in the undemocratic structure of the Opus which totally reflects the Fascistic ideology in Escriva's teachings. People have to follow the orders given to them by their leaders without doubting them. Leaders have total control over the people subordinated to them through the weekly talk where they learn everything they need to manipulate followers. So, if the topmost leader decides to do something it will happen. They justify this structure with the excuse that it is all in God's name. But the people in the Opus are all humans and there is always a chance that they might make mistakes. In the dictatorship-like structure of the Opus a mistake or an evil decision by just one person on top of the organization can have fatal consequences. Their response is something like: "Oh well we have built a dictatorship, but do not be worried: we have such a nice dictator on top who is such a kind person with a good heart…" Besides: Escriva was not a person with a very good character. And a person who does not admit that he has made a mistake by putting this Fascistic ideology into his work, even after 1945, when the evil of the Fascistic

ideology should have become obvious to everyone is definitely not a saint. Well at least, I think that God is NOT a skin head in camouflage and army boots, who likes Fascism.

Q: Do they abuse the information they get from their members in the weekly talk to manipulate them?
A: Yes. According to Carmen Tapia they do. When she was in the position of a spiritual leader she had to write reports about all the people under her and she sometimes received orders from above on what to tell them.

Q: What is the role of women in the Opus Dei ideology?
A: Let us see how they think about women:
Women are so sinful and are responsible that we have been dislodged from the Garden of Eden. And the only possibility for them to lessen their guilt is by subordinating themselves: "you should be like a carpet where people can step onto," he explained. (Heard by a lot of people at an information evening of the Opus Dei in Dornbirn Austria. Easter, 1994, from the book *Gottes Rechte Kirche* by T.M. Hofer.)

Q: What kind of person was Josemaria Escriva?
A: He was a priest who founded Opus Dei in the year 1928. He was born into a time of war, so perhaps his idea was to found a kind of "army" for God. (Many aspects of the organization of the Opus show similarities to the structure of an army: replaceability of every member; uncritical submission to orders.) According to Carmen Tapia, he was a person with very bad manners. She writes that he could be nice and kindly at time but also very angry. He spoke derogatorily about women. He often shouted. (The most extreme example is in her book. Carmen Tapia writes: when he was angry at a woman (G.) who secretly brought her (Tapia) mail he shouted: "And she there (G.) has to be spanked throughout. Draw up her skirts, tear down her panties and give it to her in the ass!! In the ass! Until she talks. Make her talk!" (translated from the German edition of her book to English).

I think this quote fits well with the sexual obsessions that shine through a lot of statements in his book. Escriva did not live the ascetic live of a saint but always liked delicious dining in his palace-like headquarters in Rome (A building with 24 chapels!). To me he seems to have been a person of medium intelligence who always wanted to be a philosopher. Perhaps he got hurt in discussions with intellectual people and than he tried to compensate for his lack of intelligence with concentration on his religious beliefs, which allowed him to polish up his self esteem again in such a way that he could look down on the people who did not share those beliefs. I am not a psychologist, but this would explain some of his teachings (e.g. the one with: 2+2 = 4; 2 + 2 + God = ?). From what Carmen Tapia tells he was very proud. Cite: "I have met a lot of bishops and different Popes but I am the only founder." Also the value intelligence had for him can be seen in what he told them once: "Do not become so stupid as those nuns (and he was trying to making a dumb face)."

Given all the Fascist ideology in *The Way*, it will not come as a surprise to you to hear that he even had sympathy for Hitler: Wladimir Felzmann, an ex-Opus Dei member tells about a talk with Escriva after he (Escriva) insisted that with Hitler's help the Franco Government has saved Christianity from Communism, he added: "Hitler against the Jews, Hitler against the Slavs, this means Hitler against communism."

To be fair, when judging Senior Escriva we have to consider that he was a child of his time. And a lot of people at the time held that kind of ideology and those ideas; for a lot of people they might have been quite normal. However, this does not make his ideology any better and does not give any justification for mixing it with his religious teachings.

What an unbelievable arrogance of this man that he named his own work "The Work of God."

Q: They claim to be faithful to the Pope and the Catholic Church. Does that mean they cannot be dangerous?
A: There are two points to keep in mind here:

1) Maybe they follow the church. At least they claim to. But what if they manage to further increase their already great influence on the Church and the Pope and can infiltrate the whole Church with their evil ideology? What if they drive it towards more intolerance? What if a person like Mr. McCloskey makes the policy then? People are already afraid that their influence is already so great that the next Pope could be an Opus Dei member.

2) I doubt that they would take "following the Church" all too seriously if we get a liberal Pope. Furthermore Carmen Tapia writes in her book that when she worked at the printing office of Opus Dei they had to change the printing plates with the text of the statutes of Opus Dei that had been signed by the Pope after they had been signed...and she also tells how mister Escriva often had angry words for the Pope. I am not sure if they would still falsify documents today. But a bit of misrepresentation of text as Mr. McCloskey does it with the Vatican II texts also helps them a lot.

– Franz Schaefer, schaefer@mond.at

The Sub-Culture of Fatima

The Catholic Church has tried to look the other way, but the expulsion of the femme keeps coming back to haunt them.

Virgin Visions

On February 11, 1858, a 14-year-old shepherdess named Bernadette Soubirous saw what she believed was a shining female figure in front of a grotto, near Lourdes in the south of France. Bernadette saw this vision 18 times during which the figure finally revealed herself as the "Immaculate Conception." A local priest said this identified her as the Blessed Virgin Mary. During her ninth encounter the vision instructed Bernadette to dig into the ground in the grotto. On doing so, she duly discovered an underground spring. The waters from the spring have since been claimed to possess healing powers.

After her death in 1879, Bernadette was later canonized and Lourdes has since become a place of pilgrimage for sick people all over the globe.

On May 13, 1917, three children from Fatima in Portugal experienced the first of six visions, while they were herding sheep in a nearby pasture. The vision featured a brilliant figure of a lady above a tree. This lady said that she was from heaven and would appear before the three children, Francisco Marto, Jacinto Marto and Lucia dos Santos every 13th day of every month until October. Although news of the childrens' visions quickly spread, the adults who gathered to witness the visions only ever saw a small cloud above a tree. The children continued to claim that they could see the lady but they were soon doubted and arrested. However on August 19th they encountered another vision in which the lady told them that she would make her final appearance on 13th of October.

Over 70,000 observers braved the rain that day to come and witness the sight, but only the three children saw the lady, who described herself as "Our Lady of the Rosary."

"Dances of the Sun" were frequently reported by children in Medjugorje in Bosnia-Herzegovina over a five year period spanning 1981-85. The children claimed that they saw the Virgin Mary each day which led to a count of over 2000 visions in total. Until a completely objective study of this phenomenon takes place, the topic will remain an enigma.

– Karyn Easton www.paranormality.com

Female Victims of Clergy Abuse

Our hearts ache for the thousands of girls and women who have been sexually assaulted by clergy but who continue to suffer in shame, silence, and self-blame. The recent Vatican effort to shift blame for the horrific and on-going Catholic hierarchy's sex abuse crisis will only rub salt into the already deep and often still fresh wounds of girls and women who have been raped, sodomized and fondled by Catholic clerics.

It's very difficult for the victim of any sex crime to come forward. It's even harder when the perpetrator is a revered religious authority figure.

And it's especially hard when others claim or pretend that few people like you are victimized.

Catholic Church officials insist on mischaracterizing and misdiagnosing this scandal, which makes the mishandling of vulnerable youngsters and wounded victims likely to continue. If one can't accurately describe a problem, one certainly can't solve it or prevent its recurrence.

We take issue with the bishops' claim that 80 percent of the victims of abusive clergy are male. First, this figure is based on a very flawed self-survey of bishops themselves. Second, we believe a disproportionate percentage of male victims report the crimes and are believed. Third, fully half of our 6,000+ members across the country are female. And finally, even if this 80 percent figure is correct, it may well reflect greater access to boys by priests rather than greater homosexuality among predators. (Many parents allowed their boys to go to the movies or on overnight trips with priests; few parents allowed their girls to do so.)

There are many reasons for why male victims are more apt to report, be believed, be taken seriously, and get more attention. Among them:

1) Girls and women often wisely fear being blamed for their abuse. (Few male victims are ever asked "Well, what were you wearing at the time?" or "Were you physically well-developed for your age?")

2) Some parents are more outraged and motivated to action when their son is raped rather than their daughter.

3) Girls and women are often subtly urged to deal with their pain privately. Boys and men are often urged to deal with their pain by taking some form of action.

4) To some in our society and the media, male-on-male sex (consen-

sual or non-consensual, legal or illegal) is seen as inherently more sala-cious and "newsworthy."

Innocent children and vulnerable adults are safe only when predators are exposed. Predators are exposed only when we create a supportive climate that encourages victims to speak up. That climate, however, doesn't happen when church officials keep blame-shifting and finger-pointing, and minimizing the risk and harm to half of the members of the church.

– Barbara Blaine, SNAP Founder and President

Exorcism

The Catholic Church revised and renewed the Rite of Exorcism in January 2000 under Pope John Paul II, who reinforced its necessity (and some sources claimed performed three himself during his pontificate).

– about.com Encyclopedia

Today, the Roman Catholic Church still believes in diabolic possession and its priests still practice what is called "real exorcism," a 27-page ritual to drive out evil spirits. The ritual involves the use of holy water, incantations, various prayers, incense, relics, and Christian symbols such as the cross. The Catholic Church has at least ten official exorcists in America today (Cuneo). The Archbishop of Calcutta, Henry Sebastian D'Souza, says he ordered a priest to perform an exorcism on Mother Teresa shortly before she died in 1997 because he thought she was being attacked by the devil.

Many people fear possession by demons, but the exorcists themselves can cause great damage.

Exorcism has caused a number of real-world tragedies over the years, including several deaths.
• Pentecostal ministers in San Francisco pummeled a woman to death in 1995, as they tried to drive out her demons.
• In 1997, a Korean Christian woman was stomped to death in Glendale, Calif., and in the Bronx section of New York City, a 5-year-old girl died after being forced to swallow a mixture containing ammonia and vinegar and having her mouth taped shut.
• In 1998, a 17-year-old girl in Sayville, N.Y., was suffocated by her mother with a plastic bag, in an effort to destroy a demon inside her.
• In 2001, a 37-year-old woman, Joanna Lee, was strangled to death in an exorcism by a Korean church minister working in New Zealand. The minister, Luke Lee, was found guilty of manslaughter.

– Robert Todd Carroll, *The Skeptic's Dictionary*, published by Wiley

The Vatican's chief exorcist has warned that reading Harry Potter could lead young people towards Satanism.

– Jano Gibson, *The Sydney Morning Herald*

Sexual Abuse by Clerics:
Historical Awareness of the Problem

It is often alleged by Catholic Church authorities that the problem of sexual abuse of young boys and girls by the clergy is a new problem, so new that they (the authorities) are only now beginning to realize how serious it is and only know beginning to figure out how to deal with it.

Sexual abuse of minors and other sexual misconduct by Catholic clerics is not a new problem. Evidence for this is found in historical sources. The church has not published historical studies on the problem of sexual abuse of minors by the clergy for obvious reasons. It is a crime that has been held as odious by societies throughout the ages. Because of its odious nature and the negative impact that admission of its existence would have on the church's reputation, instances of sexual abuse of minors by the clergy are generally hidden. Nevertheless, the historical sources reveal a constant concern throughout the ages of Christian history.

The Christian Penitential Books of the sixth to eleventh centuries contain occasional mention of punishments inflicted on clerics for homosexual crimes. The gravity of the punishments, which escalated with the rank of the cleric (less for minor clerics, more for priests and bishops) indicate that the crime itself was deemed particularly hideous by the church at the time.

Gratian the monk composed the most important single historical source for western Canon law, the Decretum, published in 1140. It is a systematic compilation of Canon law sources including the writings of the early church fathers, scripture, regulations, norms, canons from previous church councils, synods and popes. It also contains numerous references to the civil legislation of the Christian Roman emperors. In one section Gratian tends to side with the Roman law which inflicted the punishment of death on men who had sex with boys. In another he advocates the imposition of excommunication upon clerics who so sinned. Gratian referred to the evil of stuprum pueri or the impurities with boys, in several canons, including several which reference clerics.

One of the most important single works is the *Book of Gomorrah of St. Peter Damien*. Written in the mid-ninth century (possibly in 1048), this book is a carefully planned discussion of the problem of homosexuality among the clergy. The story of Peter Damien's exposition, the response of the pope at the time and the subsequent attempts at minimalizing Damien's writings is a stark reminder that history repeats itself.

Sexual abuse of a minor is a specific crime mentioned in the 1917 Code and in the 1983. It has been mentioned over the centuries in the law of the church for a reason: it exists, is a serious problem and has been acknowledged by church to be such. It is not something new that only cropped up with the publicity of the 1984-85 situation in Lafayette, Louisiana. Because of the nature of sexual abuse of minors, the institutional church has attempted to keep the matter under wraps. It has consistently failed to provide adequate pastoral care and concern for the victims of such abuse and it has consistently failed to take responsible steps in dealing with individual priest-abusers.

The history of this problem would strongly suggest that the primary value for the institutional church has been its public image, its public security and the avoidance of any public knowledge of the extent of the problem.

The Susceptibility of the Victims of Sexual Abuse by Priests

A recurring question: how could the victims and their families have allowed such abuse to both begin and continue? This question is asked with regard to the plaintiffs in these cases and in nearly all cases. The answer lies in the concept of "religious duress." In the cases at hand, the victims all came from devout Catholic families close to the church, in that they were practicing Catholics and involved in the day to day life of their church through involvement in their parishes. These families believed that the priest held an exalted position in their lives. They had been taught that the priest occupied a position between them and salvation, between them and the spiritual security offered by the church to those who remain loyal and obedient to its way of life. Such people are taught not to question the wisdom and decisions of a priest, not to question his lifestyle and to presume only the purest motives of his actions. In many cases, such Catholics also believed it a serious sin to question the authority of a priest or to speak ill or gossip about a priest.

It was a common hope of devout and dedicated Catholics families that one or more of their children enter religious life and/or the priesthood. For this reason the attentions of a priest toward a child were often believed to be honest and pure and that such attentions might lead to the great honor for the child himself or herself choosing to follow a religious vocation. For this reason, among others, parents often allowed their children to be alone with priests, to accompany them on trips, to stay with them in their quarters. The bottom line is that parents had been taught to place unquestioning trust in their priests. The idea of a priest sexually abusing or otherwise harming a child would have been, and in the cases of these families herein concerned, was, totally alien.

The victims themselves (this case included) were bound by the power of the priest. It was beyond the imagination of a young boy or girl that a priest, who was a friend, confidant, mentor and spiritual father, would do or attempt something evil or wrong. On the one hand the church taught the virtues of purity and surrounded expressions of sexuality with sin. Young boys and girls at the beginnings of puberty received these messages from their church through the priests and often reacted to their awakening sexuality with fear, shame, wonder and often guilt. To many, when a priest made advances, these were often totally disbelieved by the victim. Once the situation developed, many priest perpetrators continued to use their power by gradually inducing into the victims the believe that no one would believe them if they disclosed what was happening. In fact, prior to the widespread media attention to such abuse in the eighties, rarely would parents, church authorities or others believe a young person who mentioned the fact that a priest was doing strange things to them. The victims, in a very real sense, were caught between a "rock and a hard place."

The result of sexual abuse by members of the clergy has had a variety of effects on the victims. The psychological and emotional impact is the subject for medical experts. There is also however, a severe spiritual impact. The event or events of abuse have caused numerous victims to not only abandon the institutional church but to look upon it with disdain, fear and even hatred. Many are or were unable to make an emotional and intellectual distinction between the priest, the institutional authorities, and the church itself. The persons of the priests, bishops etc. were the church. The church was the source of spiritual security. Faith in God was intimately bound up with faith in and loyalty to the church. It was the church, through the priests, who forgave sins. Now it was the forgiver who was causing the sins. Many victims felt and feel that they have been robbed of their faith and of their spiritual security. They cannot go to the church for relief because the focal point of their trust, the priest, has betrayed them. He has led them into what was and often is still perceived to be the worst kind of sins, sins of the flesh.

In short, the spiritual impact of sexual abuse is profound. In all possibility this impact is related to the psychological and emotional impact and to the patterns of self destructive behavior often found in many victims of clergy sexual abuse.

The concept of religious duress is also directly related to the manipulation of the victims and their families. This manipulation occurs at the hands of church officials whose ultimate aim is to convince them not to press charges, not to go public etc., in order to avoid causing scandal or harm to the church. The same dynamic which was active in the seduction is also active in trying to downplay the events. This manipulation almost always includes the victims and their families but can and does extend to law enforcement officials and others whose intervention could either cause problems for the institution or not.

– Excerpt from *The Thomas Doyle Memo – Part 3; #22*

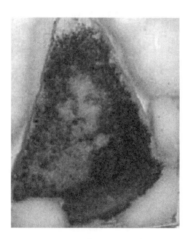

Virgin Mary-embellished Grilled Cheese Sandwich sold for $28,000 on eBay.

Old Myths, New Myths

Some myths about the bishops' sex abuse crisis should now, finally, be put to rest. At the same time, we must be careful to avoid replacing the old myths with new ones.

Here are just a few of the old myths:

Myth One: "It's just a tiny percentage of priests who commit these crimes."
For more than a decade, numerous church leaders in America and in Rome emphatically claimed one percent or even less than one percent of priests molested children. By American bishops own self-survey, the "bare minimum" true figure is at least four percent.

Myth Two: "A lot of the abuse was minor."
According to today's *New York Times*, those tabulating the surveys "were surprised at the high rate of serious offenses." Bishops and their PR staff have consistently used and still use vague and mild terms like "inappropriate conduct" and "boundary violations" to describe what most everyone else would call oral sex or sodomy.

Myth Three: NIMDY: "Not In MY Diocese"
The document apparently indicates that abuse allegations surfaced in more than 95 percent of America's 194 Catholic dioceses.

And here are a few of the potential new or recently-revived myths that may emerge from the reports issued today.

New (Revived) Myth One: "It's gay priests who are responsible."
There's just too little evidence to make this conclusion. Some argue many boys were victimized because abusive priests had greater access to them. Others point out that half of SNAP's membership is female.

New (Revived) Myth Two: "It really IS the fault of the church-paid shrinks."
The Review Board mentioned this excuse. But we must remember that bishops could have afforded top-notch, independent professionals. Instead, they repeatedly relied on (and continue to rely on) trusted Catholic professionals, often without relevant psychological backgrounds or expertise in treating child molesters. (Fr. John Geoghan's "therapists" were a close family

friend who happened to be an MD and a psychologist who was twice accused of sexually abusing patients.)

New Myth Three: "Canon law prevented some bishops from getting rid of abusers."

Where there's a will, there's a way. We in SNAP have seen virtually no evidence to suggest that bishops WANTED to remove abusers but couldn't. We know of only one bishop who was taken to internal church proceedings for removing an abuser. That bishop prevailed.

New Myth Four: "At least bishops are starting to 'come clean' now."

Several bishops fought against launching this anonymous survey in the first place. Several others refused to comply with their own self-survey. Fourteen percent of diocese and religious orders "provided none of the financial information requested." From coast to coast, bishops are still in courtrooms fighting tooth and nail to keep damaging church records from ever seeing the light of day. The examples of continued secrecy are legion.

New Myth Five: "Very few victims came forward until very recently."

This we must take with not a grain but a mountain of salt. Today's *New York Times* reports that "two-thirds of the accusations were reported since 1993." And anecdotally, we in SNAP know that many who spoke up in the last few years had tried in the past, often repeatedly, to be heard by church officials to no avail. It's foolish to assume that since there was no document found in a chancery office file that no one had reported an abusive cleric in the past.

New Myth Six: "There was something strange/aberrant about the priests ordained in the late '60s and early '70s."

Again, there's no solid evidence to suggest this. Our strong hunch is that if these men seem to have abused more, it's simply because their victims have reached the ages where they begin to see troubling behavior patterns in their lives, are getting into therapy, are being more introspective and analyzing their actions, and are finding the strength and courage to report their victimization.

– Barbara Blaine, Chicago Founder and President of SNAP

Is Any Neighborhood Safe?

Molesting priests are not always in far off corners of the world, or in poorer less educated neighborhoods where they can hoodwink and intimidate their flock. A classic example is Balboa Island, California, an exclusive area in an educated Republican stronghold of American ideals. During the last three decades, two of this community's Catholic churches have been way-stations for three troubled monsignors. Two of them were moved there under a program called "The Geographic Solution." It is simply the Church's way of moving problem priests into new neighborhoods where their dark past is not revealed to virtually anyone. Their alleged crimes have been denied by them, and put out of the minds of their parishers, who in many cases have no idea of the past transgressions. But the facts are cold and still undeniable.

Much has been covered up and is still be hidden. Behind the denials, neither one of the living monsignors was available for comment for this article. Various inquiries were met with no returned calls/emails or "No information can be released at this time" Click. It is unfortunate, for they, as accused or guilty may be able to prevent these ugly situations from happening again at their church or in a nearby neighborhood. According to S.N.A.P. [Survivors Network Against Molesting Priests], there still are 1000's of Priests in the Catholic system who are dangerously sick. The need for them to be identified and rooted out for the good of our children is more urgent than ever. The questions I wanted to pose to the accused are simple: "Why can't priests face up to their crimes and why do the sheep rally around the guilty priests more often than not?"

The demand for a church cleansing is usually from a dedicated group of activists, while many of the sheep just wander back to church as though nothing had happened. Pope John never met a molested child, although he was asked many times. Pope Benedict XVI is hoping the crimes will be forgotten (much like his attitude toward World War II crimes), thus he done little or nothing for full disclosure and banishment of those who have preyed on God's children or covered up the crimes. (See S.N.A.P.'s website or call 800 364-3064 for the Orange County Diocese to report a Cleric crime. For a full accounting of criminal Bishops, Priests and Monsignors; Google in "bishop's accountability.")

Orange County, California's settlement was larger than Boston's, and like Boston's, the money payout was reluctant, and it has done little to change policy or attitudes. Expediency and morality have proven to be two different mindsets for the Catholic Church. We suggest you look in the paper every month and see the growing list of crimes, cover-ups, Catholic Church public relations firms spin and the amount of attorney fees paid out by the Mother Church. Then make up your own mind. Is this a cleansing or a whitewash?

A public records look at the Monsignors entrusted with God's Children in Balboa, California over the last 3 decades: Monsignor Lawrence Baird; current head of St. John Vianney Catholic Church, Balboa Island, CA, and head of Our Lady of Mt. Carmel on the Balboa Peninsula, took over for dismissed Monsignor Dennis J. Murray after he settled one of his molestation charges. Monsignor Baird was the media director for the O.C. Diocese during a period in the 1990's in which the Catholic Church was in complete denial and a cover-up mode was fully operational.

St. Vianney Catholic Church

Eventually the diocese for whom Monsignor Baird was media director and Daniel Murray was the Vocations Director, was forced to settle for $100 million to the victims of the Diocese's abuse. During this period O.C. was a way station for convicted, admitted and accused priests. It has been established that the Diocese knew about the crimes, but didn't tell anyone. Baird has denied knowing of the backgrounds of the molesting priests. Following the death of another accused Priest, Joseph E. Sharpe, Baird took over at St. Vianney. Sharpe had been dismissed several years ago from a Catholic Church in Los Angeles County. Monsignor Baird was himself accused of molesting a woman who came to him after being molested and raped by Priest John Lenihan, who Baird served with in the O.C. Diocese for a number of years. Baird denied having ever met the woman, much less molesting her. The victim of the denied molestation took a lie detector test and passed with a 15 plus rating after Baird filed a slander case against her. The Priest refused to take the same test, claiming through his attorney that the evidence was not admissible in court, and the evidence would be manipulated. The case was thrown out of court shortly later in November of 2002.

Baird recently became embroiled in another controversy where he was living in a two-million-dollar home owned by the Diocese when rector facilities were readily available. During this period the Diocese was pleading poverty, after a $100 pedophile settlement. The church at the same time released 11 diocese workers in an economy move.

Monsignor Dennis J. Murray's allegations of abuse of a youth from 1973-1979: The $513,000 settlement [public settlement $1,013,400] was kept secret by him and illegally kept secret by the O.C. Diocese. Adding to outrage, Murray was kept on as the Monsignor for nearly another year. Murray was placed on leave in 2003 by Our Lady of Mt. Carmel, Balboa, CA and now is currently ruled as 'dismissed'. Other sources say he is simply "on leave." During this period of accusations in the '90s, Monsignor Murray was still the Director of Vocations of the Orange County Diocese before being sent to Balboa's Our Lady of Mt. Carmel in 2000. He was also accused of sexual misconduct in 1991 but the Church could not substantiate the charges, thus the investigation ended. The Church would not comment on his whereabouts. He was named in a civil lawsuit and in the Archdiocesan Report Addendum 11.15.05. Records indicate he was on church payroll at least to September 4, 2004. Murray is of the most reassigned priests in Orange County history, and he once housed in Anaheim with two other accused/admitted pedophiles in 1994. At last report, Monsignor Murray still denies any wrong doing.

Monsignor Joseph E. Sharpe landed on Balboa Island in September 1978. According to the Archdiocesan Report, he was named in the O.C. case BC307934 due to a case of alleged molestation from 1958 to 1964 in the Los Angeles area. He was sued and it is still in litigation. In May of 1971 the Los Angeles Archbishop reported improper relations by Sharpe with two sisters. Since the sisters requested privacy, no further action was taken by law enforcement authorities or church officials at Santa Clara Church, Oxnard, CA. In 1973 Sharpe resigned under pressure for various reasons, not all sexual in nature. In January, 1974 he was removed from the pastorate for other issues. He was excardinated from the Los Angeles dioceses in 1976. He was placed on the list of molesting priests officially and died in 1999. He had retired from St. Vianney in 1997.

– Source: S.N.A.P.

" *The thing that I would like to ask of Monsignor Baird who was right in the middle of the unfolding disgrace to our community and church is this: "What did you know, when did you know it, and why didn't to tell anyone…after all you knew these molesters personally as the Media Director for the Orange County Diocese? And if you didn't know, why didn't you?* "

Virginia Snow, Catholic, Balboa Island in 2003

'Functional Atheist' Directs Theology at Catholic Boston College?

Central to the concerns of traditionalists at the school is how the appointment of Vanderhooft to the position of Director of Undergraduate Studies may violate America's Catholic Bishops' overwhelming decision last year to enforce the papal directive Ex Corde Ecclesiae. The encyclical implores Catholic institutions of higher learning to stay true to their roots and calls for, among other things, local Bishops to have input into who teaches Catholic theology. There is no evidence that the local archdiocese was consulted on this matter, though Boston College officials deny that the post they say serves only in an "advisory" capacity comes under the encyclical's umbrella. "Ex Corde Ecclesiae never said anything about non-Catholic professors," asserted Boston College official spokesman John Dunn.

Contrary to both the Reformed and Catholic creeds, Unitarian-Universalists are not Trinitarians (i.e. they deny the divinity of Jesus Christ and the Holy Spirit), they deny the divine and infallible inspiration of the Holy Scriptures, and they hold to universal salvation, that is, that anybody can go to heaven and that there are "many valid paths to spirituality." Many same-sex "marriages" have been performed at Follen Community Church since Vanderhooft has been a part of the congregation. Members of the sect don't necessarily believe in God.

Vanderhooft has allegedly trashed the Trinity at his first tenure review and characterized the Bible as a human document that had nothing to do with the Holy Spirit.

– Eric Langborgh, *Accuracy in Academia's Campus Report*

VIII

Fundamentalism

The Christian Right and the Rise
of American Fascism

D r. James Luther Adams, my ethics professor at Harvard Divinity School, told us that when we were his age, he was then close to 80, we would all be fighting the "Christian fascists."

The warning, given to me 25 years ago, came at the moment Pat Robertson and other radio and televangelists began speaking about a new political religion that would direct its efforts at taking control of all institutions, including mainstream denominations and the government. Its stated goal was to use the United States to create a global, Christian empire. It was hard, at the time, to take such fantastic rhetoric seriously, especially given the buffoonish quality of those who expounded it. But Adams warned us against the blindness caused by intellectual snobbery. The Nazis, he said, were not going to return with swastikas and brown shirts. Their ideological inheritors had found a mask for fascism in the pages of the Bible.

He was not a man to use the word fascist lightly. He was in Germany in 1935 and 1936 and worked with the underground anti-Nazi church, known as The Confessing Church, led by Dietrich Bonhoeffer. Adams was eventually detained and interrogated by the Gestapo, who suggested he might want to consider returning to the United States. It was a suggestion he followed. He left on a night train with framed portraits of Adolph Hitler placed over the contents inside his suitcase to hide the rolls of home movie film he took of the so-called German Christian Church, which was pro-Nazi, and the few individuals who defied them, including the theologians Karl Barth and Albert Schweitzer. The ruse worked when the border police lifted the top of the suitcases, saw the portraits of the Fuhrer and closed them up again. I watched hours of the grainy black-and-white films as he narrated in his apartment in Cambridge.

He saw in the Christian Right, long before we did, disturbing similarities with the German Christian Church and the Nazi Party, similarities that he said would, in the event of prolonged social instability or a national crisis, see American fascists, under the guise of religion, rise to dismantle the open society. He despaired of liberals, who he said, as in Nazi Germany, mouthed silly platitudes about dialogue and inclusiveness that made them ineffectual and impotent. Liberals, he said, did not understand the power and allure of evil nor the cold reality of how the world worked. The current hand wringing by Democrats in the wake of the election, with many asking how they can reach out to a movement whose leaders brand them "demonic" and "satanic," would not have surprised Adams. Like Bonhoeffer, he did not believe that those who would fight effectively in coming times of turmoil, a fight that for him was an integral part of the Biblical message, would come from the church or the liberal, secular elite.

His critique of the prominent research universities, along with the media, was no less withering. These institutions, self-absorbed, compromised by their close relationship with government and corporations, given enough of the pie to be complacent, were unwilling to deal with the fundamental moral questions and inequities of the age. They had no stomach for a battle that might cost them their prestige and comfort. He told me that if the Nazis took over America "60 percent of the Harvard faculty would begin their lectures with the Nazi salute." This too was not an abstraction. He had watched academics at the University of Heidelberg, including the philosopher Martin Heidegger, raise their arms stiffly to students before class.

Two decades later, even in the face of the growing reach of the Christian Right, his prediction seems apocalyptic. And yet the powerbrokers in the Christian Right have moved from the fringes of society to the floor of the House of Representatives and the Senate. Christian fundamentalists now hold a majority of seats in 36 percent of all Republican Party state committees, or 18 of 50 states, along with large minorities in 81 percent of the rest of the states. Forty-five Senators and 186 members of the House of Representatives earned between an 80 to 100 percent approval ratings from the three most influential Christian Right advocacy groups — The Christian Coalition, Eagle Forum, and Family Resource Council. Tom Coburn, the new senator from Oklahoma, has included in his campaign to end abortion: a call to impose the death penalty on doctors that carry out abortions once the ban goes into place. Another new senator, John Thune, believes in Creationism. Jim DeMint, the new senator elected from South Carolina, wants to ban single mothers from teaching in schools. The Election Day exit polls found that 22 percent of voters identified themselves as evangelical Christians and Bush won 77 percent of their vote. The polls found that a plurality of voters said that the most important issue in the campaign had been "moral values."

President Bush must further these important objectives, including the march to turn education and social welfare over to the churches with his faith-based initiative, as well as chip away at the wall between church and state with his judicial appointments, if he does not want to face a revolt within his core constituency.

Jim Dobson, the head of Focus on the Family, who held weekly telephone conversations with Karl Rove during the campaign, has put the President on notice. He told ABC's "This Week" that "this president has two years, or more broadly the Republican Party has two years, to implement these policies, or certainly four, or I believe they'll pay a price in the next election."

Bush may turn out to be a transition figure, our version of Otto von Bismarck. Bismarck used "values" to energize his base at the end of the nineteenth century and launched "Kulturkampf," the word from which we get "culture wars," against Catholics and Jews. Bismarck's attacks split the country, made the discrediting of whole segments of the society an acceptable part of the civil discourse and paved the way for the more virulent racism of the Nazis. This, I suspect, will be George Bush's contribution to our democracy.

Sam Brownback

Each week the Christian right holds a war council on Capitol Hill. Their goal is to turn America into a theocracy. And their leader is Sam Brownback, the Kansas senator evangelicals want to see in the White House.
– Jeff Sharlet, *Rolling Stone*

Brownback belongs to a secret "cell," one of the under-the-radar organizations that shapes public policy to suit the Christian right's ideals. Small but influential, these cells are used as building blocks to impose their agenda on the majority of the unknowing population.

An evangelist named Abraham Vereide established a network of "God-led" cells with like-minded senators and generals, industry leaders and preachers in 1935. It was then called the National Council for Christian Leadership. They met outside of a church setting to pray together and read the Bible.

Now they refer to themselves as The Family (also known as The Fellowship, The Fellowship Foundation, and The International Foundation). Their goal is to construct Christ's Kingdom on Earth, one cell at a time, where Washington will be its capital. They strive to be invisible and to influence political leaders behind the scenes. Prayer groups have met in the Pentagon and at the Department of Defense.

Dominionists and Reconstructionists

The Reconstructionist movement, founded in 1973 by Rousas Rushdooney, is the intellectual foundation for the most politically active element within the Christian Right. Rushdooney's 1,600 page three-volume work, *Institutes of Biblical Law*, argued that American society should be governed according to the Biblical precepts in the Ten Commandments. He wrote that the elect, like Adam and Noah, were given dominion over the earth by God and must subdue the earth, along with all non-believers, so the Messiah could return. This was a radically new interpretation for many in the evangelical movement. The Messiah, it was traditionally taught, would return in an event called "the Rapture" where there would be wars and chaos. The non-believers would be tormented and killed and the elect would be lifted to heaven. The Rapture was not something that could be manipulated or influenced, although believers often interpreted catastrophes and wars as portents of the imminent Second Coming.

Rushdooney promoted an ideology that advocated violence to create the Christian state. His ideology was the mirror image of Liberation Theology, which came into vogue at about the same time. While the Liberation Theologians crammed the Bible into the box of Marxism, Rushdooney crammed it into the equally distorting box of classical fascism. This clash was first played out in Latin America when I was there as a reporter two decades ago. In El Salvador leftist priests endorsed and even traveled with the rebel movements in Nicaragua and El Salvador, while Pat Robertson and Jerry Falwell, along with conservative Latin American clerics, backed the Contras fighting against the Sandinistas in Nicaragua and the murderous military regimes in El Salvador, Guatemala, Chile and Argentina.

Fundamentalism Defined

Fundamentalism is variously described by various authors, but to me it really boils down to a rather simple test: In my view, a fundamentalist religion is a religion, any religion, that when confronted with a conflict between love, compassion and caring, and conformity to doctrine, will almost invariably choose the latter regardless of the effect it has on its followers or on the society of which it is a part.

Fundamentalist religions make this choice because they uniformly place a high priority on doctrinal conformity, with such force that it takes higher priority than love, compassion and service.

Indeed, many fundamentalists are so caught up in doctrinal seriousness, that love, service and compassion seem scarcely to even be a part of their thinking. As one correspondent said to me regarding a certain Christian sect's converts, "It's like they go in and surgically remove any sense of love or any sense of humor."

– Scott Bidstrup

The Institutes of Biblical Law called for a Christian society that was harsh, unforgiving and violent. Offenses such as adultery, witchcraft, blasphemy and homosexuality, merited the death penalty. The world was to be subdued and ruled by a Christian United States. Rushdooney dismissed the number of 6 million Jews killed in the Holocaust as an inflated figure and his theories on race echoed Nazi Eugenics.

"The white man has behind him centuries of Christian culture and the discipline and selective breeding this faith requires..." he wrote. "The Negro is a product of a radically different past, and his heredity has been governed by radically different considerations."

"The background of Negro culture is African and magic, and the purposes of the magic are control and power over God, man, nature, and society. Voodoo, or magic, was the religion and life of American Negroes. Voodoo songs underlie jazz, and old voodoo, with its power goal, has been merely replaced with revolutionary voodoo, a modernized power drive" (see *The Religious Right*, a publication of the ADL, p. 124).

Rushdoony was deeply antagonistic to the federal government. He believed the federal government should concern itself with little more than national defense. Education and social welfare should be handed over to the churches. Biblical law must replace the secular legal code. This ideology remains at the heart of the movement. It is being enacted through school vouchers, with federal dollars now going into Christian schools, and the assault against the federal agencies that deal with poverty and human services. The Office of Faith-Based and Community Initiatives is currently channeling millions in federal funds to groups such Pat Robertson's Operation Blessing, and National Right to Life, as well as to fundamentalist religious charity organizations and programs promoting sexual abstinence.

Rushdoony laid the groundwork for a new way of thinking about political involvement. The Christian state would come about not only through signs and wonders, as those who believed in the rapture believed, but also through the establishment of the Christian nation. But he remained, even within the Christian Right, a deeply controversial figure.

Dr. Tony Evans, the minister of a Dallas church and the founder of Promise Keepers, articulated Rushdoony's extremism in a more palatable form. He called on believers, often during emotional gatherings at football stadiums, to commit to Christ and exercise power within the society as agents of Christ. He also called for a Christian state. But he did not advocate the return of slavery, as Rushdoony did, nor list a string of offenses such as adultery punishable by death, nor did he espouse the Nazi-like race theories. It was through Evans, who was a spiritual mentor to George Bush that Dominionism came to dominate the politically active wing of the Christian Right. The religious utterances from political leaders such as George Bush, Tom Delay, Pat Robertson and Zell Miller are only understandable in light of Rushdoony and Dominionism. These leaders believe that God has selected them to battle the forces of evil, embodied in "secular humanism," to create a Christian nation. Pat Robertson frequently tells believers "our aim is to gain dominion over society." Delay has told supporters, such as at a gathering two years ago at the First Baptist Church in Pearland, Texas, "He [God] is using me, all the time, everywhere, to stand up for biblical worldview in everything I do and everywhere I am. He is training me, He is working with me." Delay went on to tell followers "If we stay inside the church, the culture won't change."

Pat Robertson, who changed the name of his university to Regent University, says he is training his students to rule when the Christian regents take power, part of the reign leading to the return of Christ. Robertson resigned as the head of the Christian Coalition when Bush took office, a sign many took to signal the ascendancy of the first regent. This battle is not rhetorical but one that followers are told will ultimately involve violence. And the enemy is clearly defined and marked for destruction.

"Secular Humanists," the popular Christian Right theologian Francis Schaeffer wrote in one of numerous diatribes, "are the greatest threat to Christianity the world has ever known."

One of the most enlightening books that exposes the ultimate goals of the movement is *America's Providential History*, the standard textbook used in many Christian schools and a staple of the Christian home schooling movement. It sites Genesis 26, which calls for mankind to "have dominion over the fish of the sea, over the birds of the air, over the cattle and over all the earth and over every creeping thing that creeps on the earth" as evidence that the Bible calls for "Bible-believing Christians" to take dominion of America.

"When God brings Noah through the flood to a new earth, He reestablished the Dominion Mandate but now delegates to man the responsibility for governing other men" (p. 19). The authors write that God has called the United States to become "the first truly Christian nation" and "make disciples of all nations (p. 184). The book denounces income tax as "idolatry," property tax as "theft" and calls for an abolish of inheritance taxes in the chapter entitled "Christian Economics." The loss of such tax revenues will bring about the withering away of the federal government and the empowerment of the authoritarian church, although this is not explicit in the text.

Rushdooney's son-in-law, Gary North, a popular writer and founder of the Institute for Christian Economics, laid out the aims of the Christian Right:

"So let's be blunt about it: We must use the doctrine of religious liberty to gain independence for Christian schools until we train up a generation of people who know that there is no religious neutrality, no neutral law, no neutral education, and no neutral civil government. Then they will get busy in constructing a Bible-based social, political and religious order which finally denies the religious liberty of the enemies of God" (*Christianity and Civilization*, Spring, 1982).

Dominionists have to operate, for now, in the contaminated environment of the secular, liberal state. They have learned, therefore, to speak in code. The code they use is the key to understanding the dichotomy of the movement, one that has a public and a private face. In this they are no different from the vanguard, as described by Lenin, or the Islamic terrorists who shave off their beards, adopt western dress and watch pay-per-view pornographic movies in their hotel rooms the night before hijacking a plane for a suicide attack.

Joan Bokaer, the Director of Theocracy Watch, a project of the Center for

Religion, Ethics and Social Policy at Cornell University , who runs the ency-
clopedic web site theocracywatch.org, was on a speaking tour a few years ago
in Iowa. She obtained a copy of a memo Pat Robertson handed out to followers at the Iowa Republican County Caucus. It was titled, "How to Participate
in a Political Party" and read:

> Rule the world for God. Give the impression that you are there to work for the
> party, not push an ideology. Hide your strength. Don't flaunt your Christian-
> ity. Christians need to take leadership positions. Party officers control political
> parties and so it is very important that mature Christians have a majority of
> leadership whenever possible, God willing.

President Bush sends frequent coded messages to the faithful. In his address to the nation on the night of September 11, for example, he lifted a line
directly from the Gospel of John when he said "And the light shines in the
darkness, and the darkness will not overcome it." He often uses the sentence
"when every child is welcomed in life and protected in law," words taken
directly from a pro-life manifesto entitled "A Statement of Pro-Life Principle
and Concern." He quotes from hymns, prayers, tracts and Biblical passages
without attribution. These phrases reassure the elect. They are lost on the
uninitiated.

Christian Identity Movement

This is a number of small, extremely conservative Fundamentalist Christian-based
faith groups who promote racist, sexist, anti-communist, anti-semetic and homo-
phobic teachings.

Their political agenda includes; opposition to gun control, opposition to equal rights
for gays and lesbians and supporting militia movements.

The Ku Klux Klan is traditionally the most well known organization who follows
Christian Identity beliefs. Some of the others are: American Nazi Party; Aryan Nations, Aryan Nations, Confederate Hammerskins, Jubilee, National Association
for the Advancement of White People, White Aryan Resistance (WAR) and White
Separatist Banner.

Quote from the FBI's Megiddo Report on domestic terrorism:
"Christian Identity also believes in the inevitability of the end of the world and
the Second Coming of Christ. It is believed that these events are part of a cleansing
process that is needed before Christ's kingdom can be established on earth. During this time, Jews and their allies will attempt to destroy the white race using any
means available. The result will be a violent and bloody struggle — a war, in effect
— between God's forces, the white race, and the forces of evil, the Jews and non-
whites. Significantly, many adherents believe that this will be tied into the coming
of the new millennium."

Christ the Avenger

The Christian Right finds its ideological justification in a narrow segment of the Gospel, in particular the letters of the Apostle Paul, especially the story of Paul's conversion on the road to Damascus in the Book of Acts. It draws heavily from the Book of Revelation and the Gospel of John. These books share an apocalyptic theology. The Book of Revelation is the only time in the Gospels where Jesus sanctions violence, offering up a vision of Christ as the head of a great and murderous army of heavenly avengers. Martin Luther found the God portrayed in Revelation so hateful and cruel he put the book in the appendix of his German translation of the Bible.

These books rarely speak about Christ's message of love, forgiveness and compassion. They focus on the doom and destruction that will befall unbelievers and the urgent need for personal salvation. The world is divided between good and evil, between those who act as agents of God and those who act as agents of Satan. The Jesus of the other three Gospels, the Jesus who turned the other cheek and embraced his enemies, an idea that was radical and startling in the ancient Roman world, is purged in the narrative selected by the Christian Right.

The cult of masculinity pervades the ideology. Feminism and homosexuality are social forces, believers are told, that have rendered the American male physically and spiritually impotent. Jesus is portrayed as a man of action, casting out demons, battling the Anti-Christ, attacking hypocrites and castigating the corrupt. This cult of masculinity brings with it the glorification of strength, violence and vengeance. It turns Christ into a Rambo-like figure; indeed depictions of Jesus within the movement often show a powerfully built man wielding a huge sword.

This image of Christ as warrior is appealing to many within the movement. The loss of manufacturing jobs, lack of affordable health care, negligible opportunities for education and poor job security has left many millions of Americans locked out. This ideology is attractive because it offers them the hope of power and revenge. It sanctifies their rage. It stokes the paranoia about the outside world maintained through bizarre conspiracy theories, many on display in Pat Robertson's book *The New World Order*. The book is a xenophobic rant that includes vicious attacks against the United Nations and numerous other international organizations. The abandonment of the working class has been crucial to the success of the movement. Only by reintegrating the working class into society through job creation, access to good education and health care can the Christian Right be effectively blunted. Revolutionary movements are built on the backs of an angry, disenfranchised laboring class. This one is no exception. what

The depictions of violence that will befall non-believers are detailed, gruesome and brutal. It speaks to the rage many believers harbor and the thirst for revenge. This, in large part, accounts for the huge sales of the apocalyptic series by Tim LaHaye and Jerry B. Jenkins. In their novel, *Glorious Appearing*, based on LaHaye's interpretation of Biblical Prophecies about the Second Coming, Christ eviscerates the flesh of millions of non-believers with the mere sound of his voice. There are long descriptions of horror, of how "the very words of the Lord had superheated their blood, causing it to burst through their veins and skin." Eyes disintegrate. Tongues melt. Flesh dissolves. The novel, part of *The Left Behind* series, are the best selling adult novels in the country. They preach holy war.

"Any teaching of peace prior to [Christ's] return is heresy," said televangelist James Robison.

Natural disasters, terrorist attacks, instability in Israel and even the fighting of Iraq are seen as signposts. The war in Iraq was predicted according to believers in the ninth chapter of the Book of Revelation where four angels "which are bound in the great river Euphrates will be released to slay the third part of men." The march towards global war, even nuclear war, is not to be feared but welcomed as the harbinger of the Second Coming. And leading the avenging armies is an angry, violent Messiah who dooms millions of non-believers to a horrible and painful death.

The Corruption of Science and Law

The movement seeks the imprint of law and science. It must discredit the rational disciplines that are the pillars of the Enlightenment to abolish the liberal polity of the Enlightenment. This corruption of science and law is vital in promoting the doctrine. Creationism, or "intelligent design," like Eugenics for the Nazis, must be introduced into the mainstream as a valid scientific discipline to destroy the discipline of science itself. This is why the Christian Right is working to bring test cases to ensure that school textbooks include "intelligent design" and condemn gay marriage.

The drive by the Christian Right to include crackpot theories in scientific or legal debate is part of the campaign to destroy dispassionate and honest intellectual inquiry. Facts become interchangeable with opinions. An understanding of reality is not to be based on the elaborate gathering of facts and evidence. The ideology alone is true. Facts that get in the way of the ideology can be altered. Lies, in this worldview, become true. Hannah Arendt called this effort "nihilistic relativism" although a better phrase might be collective insanity.

The Christian Right has fought successfully to have Creationist books sold in national park bookstores in the Grand Canyon, taught as a theory in public schools in states like Alabama and Arkansas. "Intelligent design" is promoted in Christian textbooks. All animal species, or at least their progenitors, students read, fit on Noah's ark. The Grand Canyon was created a few thousand years ago by the flood that lifted up Noah's ark, not one billion years ago, as geologists have determined. The earth is only a few thousand years old in line with the literal reading of Genesis. This is not some quaint, homespun view of the world. It is an insidious attempt to undermine rational scientific research and intellectual inquiry. Tom Delay, following the Columbine shootings, gave voice to this assault when he said that the killings had taken place "because our school systems teach children that they are nothing but glorified apes who have evolutionized out of some primordial mud" (from a speech Delay gave in the House on June 16, 1999).

"What convinces masses are not facts," Hannah Arendt wrote in *Origins of Totalitarianism*, "and not even invented facts, but only the consistency of the system which they are presumably part. Repetition, somewhat overrated in importance because of the common belief in the "masses" inferior capacity to grasp and remember, is important because it convinces them of consistency in time" (p. 351).

There are more than 6 million elementary and secondary school students attending private schools and 11.5 percent of these students attend schools run by the Christian Right. These "Christian" schools saw an increase of 46 percent in enrollment in the last decade. The 245,000 additional students accounted for 75 percent of the total rise in private school enrollment.

The Launching of the War

Adams told us to watch closely what the Christian Right did to homosexuals. He has seen how the Nazis had used "values" to launch state repression of opponents. Hitler, days after he took power in 1933, imposed a ban on all homosexual and lesbian organizations. He ordered raids on places where homosexuals gathered culminating with the ransacking of the Institute for Sexual Science in Berlin. Thousands of volumes from the institute's library were tossed into a bonfire. Adams said that homosexuals would also be the first "deviants" singled out by the Christian Right. We would be the next.

The ban on same sex marriages, passed by eleven states in the election, was part of this march towards our door. A 1996 federal law already defines marriage as between a man and a woman. All of the states with ballot measures, with the exception of Oregon, had outlawed same sex marriages, as do 27 other states. The bans, however, had to be passed, believers were told, to thwart "activist judges" who wanted to overturn them. The Christian family, even the nation, was under threat. The bans served to widen the splits tearing apart the country. The attacks on homosexuals handed to the foot soldiers of the Christian Right an easy target. It gave them a taste of victory. It made them feel empowered. But it is ominous for gays and for us.

All debates with the Christian Right are useless. We cannot reach this movement. It does not want a dialogue. It cares nothing for rational thought and discussion. It is not mollified because John Kerry prays or Jimmy Carter teaches Sunday School. These naive attempts to reach out to a movement bent on our destruction, to prove to them that we too have "values," would be humorous if the stakes were not so deadly. They hate us. They hate the liberal, enlightened world formed by the Constitution. Our opinions do not count.

This movement will not stop until we are ruled by Biblical Law, an authoritarian church intrudes in every aspect of our life, women stay at home and rear children, gays agree to be cured, abortion is considered murder, the press and the schools promote "positive" Christian values, the federal government is gutted, war becomes our primary form of communication with the rest of the world and recalcitrant non-believers see their flesh eviscerated at the sound of the Messiah's voice.

The spark that could set it ablaze may be lying in the hands of an Islamic terrorist cell, in the hands of the ideological twins of the Christian Right. Another catastrophic terrorist attack could be our Reichstag fire, the excuse used to begin the accelerated dismantling of our open society. The ideology of the Christian Right is not one of love and compassion, the central theme of Christ's message, but of violence and hatred. It has a strong appeal to many in our society, but it is also aided by our complacency. Let us not stand at the open city gates waiting passively and meekly for the barbarians. They are coming. They are slouching rudely towards Bethlehem. Let us, if nothing else, begin to call them by their name.

– Chris Hedges

Chris Hedges *is a reporter for* New York Times *and the author of* War Is a Force That Gives Us Meaning and Losing Moses on the Freeway: America's Broken Covenant with the Ten Commandments, *published by The Free Press. He holds a Master of Divinity from Harvard Divinity School.*

Note from Joan Bokaer: Chris refers to a memo I received in Iowa from Pat Robertson's organization. The year was 1986 – two years before his presidential bid, and three years before the Christian Coalition was formed.

The Good Book Taught Wrong

In recent years, in Florida and across the country, there has been increasing controversy over religion in public schools, including whether and how students may be taught about the Bible. Most authorities agree that teaching students about religion is part of a good education. On the other hand, teaching religion, in the sense of proselytizing or attempting to inculcate students in the beliefs of a particular faith, or teaching religious subjects from a sectarian viewpoint, is unsound public education. Such instruction also violates the constitutional requirement that public schools must remain neutral toward religion and cannot endorse religion generally or any particular faith specifically.

People for the American Way Foundation strongly supports teaching students about religion, including the role that religion has played in history. Such instruction can and does take place in any number of classes, such as courses in comparative religion, the history of religion, world history, and American history. As the courts have made clear, however, there is a right way, and a wrong way, for public schools  to present the subject of religion and related topics. When it comes to the Bible, the United States Supreme Court has held that public schools may teach students about the Bible, as long as such teaching is presented "objectively as part of a secular program of education" (*School District of Abington Township v. Schempp*, 374 U.S. 203, 225, 1963).

However, as revealed by cases in which the courts have found legal problems with "Bible" courses in public schools, a number of school districts around the country have ignored the Court's admonition. They have taught the Bible to their students not from an objective perspective as part of a truly academic and secular course, but from a religious perspective, generally from a particular sectarian perspective of Christianity. In such courses, the Bible is typically presented as factually true and students are required to engage in exercises more appropriate for a Sunday school than a public school, including exercises that emphasize rote memorization rather than critical thinking or analysis skills.

Unfortunately, as this report discusses, a significant number of Florida school districts teach such unconstitutional classes. The state of Florida permits its public high schools to offer two semester-long "Social Studies" courses entitled "Bible History: Old Testament" and "Bible History: New Testament." The Florida Department of Education has adopted a short "course description" for each, leaving it up to local school districts to develop their own curricula. In practice, this has turned out to be a recipe for disaster. As this report documents, the school districts teaching the "Bible History" courses are, with minor exceptions, doing so in a manner that violates the Constitution and the rights of their citizens. This conduct also deprives their students of sound academic instruction about the Bible, including instruction that would expose them to more than one particular sectarian view.

– From People for the American Way
www.pfaw.org

Founding Presidents Not Christian

One of my favorite times of the year is the Presidents' month of February. Why? Because it gives me an annual opportunity to make a dent in the historical and religious ignorance of the political and Christian knee jerk right-wingers. They spend almost full time in perverting American history claiming that the bible and Christianity were at the foundation of this nation. What total hogwash. Once a year I get to bring a few undisputed facts to their attention.

THE ENCYCLOPEDIA BRITANNICA, 1968, vol. 2, p. 420, quote: "One of the embarrassing problems for the nineteenth-century champions of the Christian faith was the fact that NOT ONE of the first six presidents of the United States was a Christian. They were Deists."

In Deism there is no personal God, only an impersonal "force" or "energy" or "nature's God" or "providence." In Deism, the bible is nothing but literature, and bad literature at that. Jefferson and Paine both called it "a dunghill" Others of our founders used the same language. In Deism, Jesus was nothing more than a nomadic teacher. I will now let these men speak for themselves.

GEORGE WASHINGTON: "Being no bigot, I am disposed to humor Christian ministers and the church" Looking for servants, he said: "I will be happy to have atheists, Jews, Christians or Mohammedans." In 1831, Episcopalian minister Bird Wilson said in a sermon: "Washington is no more than a Unitarian, if anything." Washington refused to take communion, looking upon it as superstition. He refused to ever kneel in church according to his wife and minister, James Abercrombie. The Treaty of Tripoli, under Washington, Article 11 begins: "As the government of the United States is not in any sense founded on the Christian religion." This Treaty was ratified by the senate in 1797 under Adams, without a single objection.

THOMAS JEFFERSON: Author of the Declaration of Independence. "I have examined all the known superstitions of the world, and I do not find in our particular superstition of Christianity one redeeming feature. They are all alike founded on fables and mythology. Millions of innocent men, women and children since the introduction of Christianity have been burnt, tortured, fined and imprisoned. What has been the effect of this coercion? To make one half the world fools, and the other half hypocrites. And to support roguery and error all over the earth."

JAMES MADISON: Author of our Constitution and Bill of Rights. "A just government instituted to perpetuate liberty, does not need the church or the clergy. During almost 15 centuries the legal establishment of Christianity has been on trial. What have been its fruits? These are the fruits in all places: pride and indolence in the clergy...ignorance and servility in the laity...and in both clergy and laity superstition, bigotry and persecution." Madison passionately objected to state supported chaplains in Congress and the military, as well as the exemption of churches from taxation. And rightly so. They should be taxed.

JOHN ADAMS: "The doctrine of the divinity of Jesus has made a convenient cover for absurdity." Adams signed the Treaty of Tripoli, which states that the United States is not in any sense founded on the Christian religion. Episcopalian minister Bird Wilson, in a sermon of October 1831, summed up the religion of our founding presidents in these words: "Among all of our Presidents, from Washington downward, not one was a professor of Christianity."

ABRAHAM LINCOLN: Not a founding president but a giant who shared exactly the same religious views: quote: "Christianity is not my religion and the bible is not my book. I have never united myself in any church because I could never give assent to the long, complicated statements of Christian doctrine and dogma." Lincoln never joined any church and was never baptized, looking upon it as superstition. His wife said: "my husband is not a Christian, but is a spiritual man I think." The most magnificent Pulitzer-Prize biography of this giant is Carl Sandburg's "Abraham Lincoln." And as Sandburg put it: "His views were such as would place him entirely outside of Christianity."

Thomas Jefferson put in one succinct sentence what they all believed. "The day will come when the mystical generation of Jesus, by a supreme being as his father in the womb of a virgin, will be classed with the fable of the generation of Minerva in the brain of Jupiter" (Letter to John Adams, April 11, 1823).

Why are these facts of American history not being taught in our High Schools? What forces are at work in our society to keep historical truth from our young people? We get all hot and sweaty about censoring movies and television. A far, far more lethal virus that is at work is the censorship of the religious views of our first six presidents, our Founding Fathers. Why is this not being taught? Why is your minister not telling you about it, assuming he is historically literate?

The genius Goethe said it best: "Nothing is more terrifying than...ignorance in action."

– William Edelen

339

Religious Coercion and Liberty

For decades, both conservative and progressive Supreme Court Justices have recognized that one of the most important ways in which our Constitution protects religious liberty is by requiring government to stay truly neutral toward religion. A Scalia-Thomas Supreme Court, however, would eradicate that protection. In a 1992 dissent joined by Justices Thomas, White, and Chief Justice Rehnquist, Scalia wrote that the First Amendment does not require government neutrality towards religion (*Lee v. Weisman*). They argued, instead, that the government may promote prayer and religion, as long as it stops short of specifically favoring a particular sect or legally coercing participation in or payment for religious activity. On the current Court, only two more votes are needed to make this radical view a reality.

The consequences of turning this Scalia-Thomas view into the law of the land would be devastating. Schools could mandate "captive audience" prayer at graduations, in classrooms and at any other school activity, as long as they did not favor only one sectarian point of view, as Scalia, Thomas, and Rehnquist argued in dissenting from the Court's ruling that school-sponsored "student-led" prayer at high school football games was unconstitutional in *Santa Fe Independent School District v. Doe* (2000). Young students could be told to bow their heads in vocal or silent prayer and, if they disagree, they could be told that they are not good citizens. States could require the teaching of religious creationism along with evolution, as Scalia urged in his dissent in *Edwards v. Aguillard* (1987), or could mandate anti-evolution disclaimers in textbooks, as suggested by Scalia, Thomas, and Rehnquist in dissenting from the denial of review in *Tangipahoa Parish Board of Educ. v. Freiler* (2000). Police officers, judges, drill sergeants and others in positions of authority over adults could also foist their own religious views on captive audiences of adults. The familiar principle that government cannot take action that is intended to, or does in fact, promote religion would be eliminated, as Scalia and Thomas suggested in a 1993 concurring opinion (*Lamb's Chapel v. Center Moriches Union Free School District*).

Justices Scalia's and Thomas' writings about government involvement in religion evidence complete disrespect for the legitimate rights and interests of people who are not religious or are members of minority faiths. In *Lee v. Weisman*, they scoffed at the harm to religious liberty and freedom of conscience that resulted from imposing captive audience graduation prayer. Indeed, they noted that attendance was not required at the graduation ceremony at issue in Weisman and that therefore there was no "penalty" involved in forgoing the ceremony altogether. The cavalier suggestion that children and families who oppose government-imposed prayer could simply skip graduation utterly fails to recognize the fundamental importance to the overwhelming majority of students and their families of this time-honored rite of passage.

Both *Edwards v. Agullard* and *Church of Lukumi Babalu Aye, Inc. v. City of Hialeah* (1993) reveal an additional threat that a Scalia-Thomas majority would pose to religious liberty. Scalia's writings in these cases demonstrate a radical view toward many religion cases and argue that an analysis of legislative intent should play absolutely no role in the adjudication of First Amendment cases. This Scalia position would pave the way for laws that, while neutral in their wording, are blatantly motivated by intent to promote religion. Justice Thomas has taken an even more radical view, asserting that the Establishment Clause does not apply to state and local governments at all, and that individuals have no right whatsoever to religious neutrality other than concerning the federal government, contradicting decades of Supreme Court precedent.

Ironically, despite their rejection of true neutrality towards religion in cases like Weisman in order to permit government promotion of religion, Scalia and Thomas have embraced a different version of neutrality in arguing that government should be able to fund even pervasively religious institutions with compelled taxpayer dollars. Although a narrow 5-4 majority including Scalia and Thomas permitted the use of taxpayer-funded school vouchers in religious schools in *Zelman v. Simmons-Harris* (2002) where genuine and independent parental choice is found to occur, Scalia and Thomas would go even further. In a plurality opinion with two other justices in *Mitchell v. Heims* (2000), Scalia and Thomas suggested that virtually any government aid to religious schools is permissible, as long as the material provided is not religious and it is provided equally to non-religious schools. Although this view has been rejected by five justices, Scalia and Thomas clearly adhere to it. For example, as the dissenting voice from a denial of certiorari in a 1999 case, Justice Thomas wrote in favor of abolishing the prohibition against supporting pervasively sectarian organizations with public funds (*Columbia Union College v. Clark*). One more Justice like Scalia and Thomas would likely authorize direct government funding of sectarian religious social services and schools, and authorize spending public dollars on activities with an explicitly religious purpose or content. Indeed, a Scalia-Thomas Court would force a state to subsidize those training for the clergy because the state offers college scholarships for secular subjects (*Locke v. Davey*). A Scalia-Thomas Court would even allow school district or municipal lines to be drawn so as to permit one religious sect to predominate (*Board of Education of Kiryas Joel Village School District v. Grumet*, 1994).

Finally, Justice Scalia would even allow tax exemptions for religious books and periodicals — even if non-religious publications were denied the same benefit. In 1989, Scalia dissented from a majority holding that it was unconstitutional for the government to provide a tax exemption for religious periodicals where similar exemptions were not allowed for non-sectarian publications and the exemption served no secular purpose. Even though the Texas law in question explicitly discriminated in favor of religious publications and effectively increased taxes on secular publishers by exempting religious ones, Scalia claimed that the law did not improperly favor religion (*Texas Monthly, Inc. v. Bullock*). In short, a Scalia-Thomas Supreme Court would abolish religious liberty and church-state separation as we know it.

– From People for the American Way
www.pfaw.org

A key priority of the fat right that would be achieved under a Scalia-Thomas Court would be the dismantling of the wall between church and state, so carefully and deliberately erected by the Founders to protect religious liberty for all Americans.

Reversal of *Lee v. Weisman* (1992) and *Santa Fe Independent School Dist. v. Doe* (2000) would eliminate true government neutrality toward religion and authorize government-sponsored prayer at graduation and other public school events.

Reversal of *Board Education of Kiryas Joel Village School District v. Grumet* (1994) would authorize drawing of school district lines to permit one religious sect to predominate.

Extension of *Mitchell v. Helms* (2000) would permit virtually any government aid given to public schools and social service programs to be granted directly to pervasively religious schools, churches, and other religious institutions.

Thomas stakes out a particularly extreme position in the religious liberty arena, arguing that the establishment cause of the First Amendment does not apply to state and local governments at all. In other words, Thomas sees no constitutional barrier to a state declaring an official religion and treating people differently under state law based on their religious beliefs. We certainly do not need any more justices who share the interpretation of the Constitution.

– from People For the American Way

Televangelists

Questions about the pronouncements we hear from the pulpit and on radio and television programs demand attention. When we get evasion instead of answers, we have reasons to suspect that deception not elucidation is the principal raison d'être of religion. We see that much of what religious leaders teach us about gods and morality is contradictory, evasive, self-serving, and amounts to thinly veiled coercion. The exhortation, garrulity, bombast, and drivel that is increasingly replacing calm, reasoned, and meaningful dissertation disturb us. In a world that insists on rational explanations, religious seem less sure of the fantasy and fustian they pass off as fact and perspicacity. The desperation in the harangues of pulpiteers is becoming more and more evident as they lose the battle for credibility.

In Their Own Words...

Pat Robertson

If Christian people work together, they can succeed during this decade in winning back control of the institutions that have been taken from them over the past 70 years. Expect confrontations that will be not only unpleasant but at times physically bloody...This decade will not be for the faint of heart, but the resolute. Institutions will be plunged into wrenching change. We will be living through one of the most tumultuous periods of human history. When it is over, I am convinced God's people will emerge victorious.

We at the Christian Coalition are raising an army who cares. We are training people to be effective — to be elected to school boards, to city councils, to state legislatures, and to key positions in political parties...By the end of this decade, if we work and give and organize and train, THE CHRISTIAN COALITION WILL BE THE MOST POWERFUL POLITICAL ORGANIZATION IN AMERICA.

A Supreme Court ruling is not the Law of the United States. The law of the United Sates is the Constitution, treaties made in accordance with the Constitution, and laws duly enacted by the Congress and signed by the president. And any of those things I would uphold totally with all of my strength, whether I agreed with them or not...I am bound by the laws of the United States and all 50 states...[but] I am not bound by any case or any court to which I myself am not a party...I don't think the Congress of the United States is subservient to the courts…They can ignore a Supreme Court ruling if they so choose.

We have a court that has essentially stuck its finger in God's eye and said we're going to legislate you out of the schools. We're going to take your commandments from off the courthouse steps in various states. We're not going to let little children read the commandments of God. We're not going to let the Bible be read, no prayer in our schools. We have insulted God at the highest levels of our government. And then we say, 'Why does this happen?' Well, why it's happening is that God Almighty is lifting his protection from us.

– Robertson explaining on his "700 Club" cable TV program why the terrorist attacks of September 11, 2001 had occurred two days earlier.

I think George Bush is going to win in a walk. I really believe that I'm hearing from the Lord it's going to be like a blowout election of 2004. It's shaping up that way. The Lord has just blessed him…I mean, he could make terrible mistakes and comes out of it. It doesn't make any difference what he does, good or bad. God picks him up because he's a man of prayer and God's blessing him.

The Constitution of the United States, for instance, is a marvelous document for self-government by the Christian people. But the minute you turn the document into the hands of non-Christian people and atheistic people they can use it to destroy the very foundation of our society. And that's what's been happening.

Individual Christians are the only ones really — and Jewish people, those who trust God of Abraham, Isaac, and Jacob — are the only ones that are qualified to have the reign, because hopefully, they will be governed by God and submit to Him

I never said that in my life…I never said only Christians and Jews. I never said that.

– Robertson in *Time Magazine*, after having been confronted regarding his statement on "The 700 Club" January 11, 1985.

When I said during my presidential bid that I would only bring Christians and Jews into the government, I hit a firestorm. "What do you mean?" the media challenged me. "You're not going to bring atheists into the government? How dare you maintain that those who believe in the Judeo-Christian values are better qualified to govern America than Hindus and Muslims?" My simple answer is, "Yes, they are."

If anybody understood what Hindus really believe, there would be no doubt that they have no business administering government policies in a country that favors freedom and equality…Can you imagine having the Ayatollah Ruhollah Khomeini as defense minister, or Mahatma Gandhi as minister of health, education, and welfare? The Hindu and Buddhist idea of karma and the Muslim idea of kismet, or fate condemn the poor and the disabled to their suffering…It's the will of Allah. These beliefs are nothing but abject fatalism, and they would devastate the social gains this nation has made if they were ever put into practice.

It is interesting, that termites don't build things, and the great builders of our nation almost to a man have been Christians, because Christians have the desire to build something. He is motivated by love of man and God, so he builds. The people who have come into [our] institutions [today] are primarily termites. They are into destroying institutions that have been built by Christians, whether it is universities, governments, our own traditions, that we have... The termites are in charge now, and that is not the way it ought to be, and the time has arrived for a godly fumigation.

I know it sounds somewhat Machiavellian and evil, to think that you could send a squad in to take out somebody like Osama bin Laden, or to take out the head of North Korea, but isn't it better to do something like that, to take out Milosevic, to take out Saddam Hussein, rather than to spend billions of dollars on a war that harms innocent civilians and destroys the infrastructure of a country?

The feminist agenda is not about equal rights for women. It is about a socialist, anti-family political movement that encourages women to leave their husbands, kill their children, practice witchcraft, destroy capitalism, and become lesbians.

[Planned Parenthood] is teaching kids to fornicate, teaching people to have adultery, every kind of bestiality, homosexuality, lesbianism — everything that the Bible condemns.

I know this is painful for the ladies to hear, but if you get married, you have accepted the headship of a man, your husband. Christ is the head of the household and the husband is the head of the wife, and that's the way it is, period.

These girls are not stupid. If you want to pay them five hundred, six hundred, seven hundred, eight hundred dollars a month, or whatever it is, to have a baby, they'll have babies. And if they'll stop paying them, they'll stop having babies. It's that simple. It's not heartless, it's not cruel, it's an intelligent use of money.

If the widespread practice of homosexuality will bring about the destruction of your nation, if it will bring about terrorist bombs, if it'll bring about earthquakes, tornadoes and possibly a meteor, it isn't necessarily something we ought to open our arms to.

I would warn Orlando that you're right in the way of some serious hurricanes, and I don't think I'd be waving those flags in God's face if I were you.

– Robertson on "The 700 Club" August 6, 1998, regarding the occasion of the Orlando, Florida, Gay Pride Festival 1998.

Many observers say that AIDS is the hammer and gun of the homosexual movement, an effective vehicle to propel the homosexual agenda throughout every phase of our society.

It's one thing to say, "We have rights to jobs…we have rights to be left alone in out little corner of the world to do our thing." It's an entirely different thing to say, well, "We're not only going to go into the schools and we're going to take your children and your grandchildren and turn them into homosexuals." Now that's wrong.

I think "one man, one vote," just unrestricted democracy, would not be wise. There needs to be some kind of protection for the minority which the white people represent now, a minority, and they need and have a right to demand a protection of their rights.

– Robertson on "The 700 Club" March 18, 1992, suggesting that South African white people's votes ought to count more than other votes because they are in the minority.

To see Americans become followers of Islam is nothing short of insanity…The Islamic people, the Arabs, were the ones who captured Africans, put them in slavery, and sent them to America as slaves. Why would the people in America want to embrace the religion of slavers.

People For the American Way were founded by the creator of Archie Bunker. Do we want Archie Bunker determining what the United States Senate votes for?

How can there be peace when drunkards, drug dealers, communists, atheists, New Age worshippers of Satan, secular humanists, oppressive dictators, greedy money changers, revolutionary assassins, adulterers, and homosexuals are on top?

I'd like to say to the good citizens of Dover: If there is a disaster in your area, don't turn to God. You just rejected him from your city.

God is tolerant and loving, but we can't keep sticking our finger in his eye forever. If they have future problems in Dover, I recommend they call on Charles Darwin. Maybe he can help them.

The wars of extermination have given a lot of people trouble unless they understand fully what was going on. The people in the land of Palestine were very wicked. They were given over to idolatry. They sacrificed their children. They had all kinds of abominable sex practices. They were having sex apparently with animals. They were having sex men with men and women with women. They were committing adultery and fornication. They were serving idols. As I say, they were offering their children up, and they were forsaking God.

God told the Israelites to kill them all: men, women and children; to destroy them. And that seems like a terrible thing to do. Is it or isn't it? Well, let us assume that there were two thousand of them or ten thousand of them living in the land, or whatever number, I don't have the exact number, but pick a number. And God said, "Kill them all." Well, that would seem hard, wouldn't it? But that would be 10,000 people who probably would go to hell. But if they stayed and reproduced, in thirty, forty or fifty or sixty or a hundred more years there could conceivably be...ten thousand would grow to a hundred, a hundred thousand conceivably could grow to a million, and there would be a million people who would have to spend an eternity in Hell! And it is far more merciful to take away a few than to see in the future a hundred years down the road, and say, "Well, I'll have to take away a million people, that will be forever apart from God because the abomination is there." It's like a contagion. God saw that there was no cure for it. It wasn't going to change, and all they would do is cause trouble for the Israelites and pull the Israelites away from God and prevent the truth of God from reaching the earth. And so God in love — and that was a loving thing — took away a small number that he might not have to take away a large number.

You know, I don't know about this doctrine of assassination, but if he (Hugo Chavez) thinks we're trying to assassinate him, I think that we really ought to go ahead and do it. It's a whole lot cheaper than starting a war...and I don't think any oil shipments will stop.

Reverend Jerry Falwell

If you're not a born-again Christian, you're a failure as a human being.

I had a student ask me, "Could the savior you believe in save Osama bin Laden?" Of course, we know the blood of Jesus Christ can save him, and then he must be executed.

I hope I live to see the day when, as in the early days of our country, we won't have any public schools. The churches will have taken them over again and Christians will be running them. What a happy day that will be!

The idea that religion and politics don't mix was invented by the Devil to keep Christians from running their own country.

If we are going to save America and evangelize the world, we cannot accommodate secular philosophies that are diametrically opposed to Christian truth...We need to pull out all the stops to recruit and train 25 million Americans to become informed pro-moral activists whose voices can be heard in the halls of Congress.

It appears that America's anti-Biblical feminist movement is at last dying, thank God, and is possibly being replaced by a Christ-centered men's movement which may become the foundation for a desperately needed national spiritual awakening.

There is no separation of church and state. Modern U.S. Supreme Courts have raped the Constitution and raped the Christian faith and raped the churches by misinterpreting what the Founders had in mind in the First Amendment to the Constitution.

The Bible is the inerrant...word of the living God. It is absolutely infallible, without error in all matters pertaining to faith and practice, as well as in areas such as geography, science, history, etc.

But these things speak evil of those things, verse 10 [reading from Jude] which they know not: but what they know naturally, as brute beasts, in those things they corrupt themselves. Look at the Metropolitan Community Church today, the gay church, almost accepted into the World Council of Churches. Almost, the vote was against them. But they will try again and again until they get in, and the tragedy is that they would get one vote. Because they are spoken of here in Jude as being brute beasts, that is going to the baser lust of the flesh to live immorally, and so Jude describes this as apostasy. But thank God this vile and satanic system will one day be utterly annihilated and there'll be a celebration in heaven.

Grown men should not be having sex with prostitutes unless they are married to them.

We're fighting against humanism, we're fighting against liberalism...we are fighting against all the systems of Satan that are destroying our nation today... our battle is with Satan himself.

AIDS is the wrath of a just God against homosexuals. To oppose it would be like an Israelite jumping in the Red Sea to save one of Pharaoh's charioteers.

You'll be riding along in an automobile. You'll be the driver perhaps. You're a Christian. There'll be several people in the automobile with you, maybe someone who is not a Christian. When the trumpet sounds you and the other born-again believers in that automobile will be instantly caught away — you will disappear, leaving behind only your clothes and physical things that cannot inherit eternal life. That unsaved person or persons in the automobile will suddenly be startled to find the car suddenly somewhere crashes...Other cars on the highway driven by believers will suddenly be out of control and stark pandemonium will occur on...every highway in the world where Christians are caught away from the driver's wheel.

Pat Robertson and Jerry Falwell

Falwell: *What we saw on Tuesday, as terrible as it is, could be miniscule if, in fact, God continues to lift the curtain and allow the enemies of America to give us probably what we deserve.*

Robertson: *Well, Jerry, that's my feeling. I think we've just seen the antechamber to terror, we haven't begun to see what they can do to the major population.*

Falwell: *The ACLU has got to take a lot of blame for this. And I know I'll hear from them for this, but throwing God...successfully with the help of the federal court system...throwing God out of the public square, out of the schools, the* *abortionists have got to bear some burden for this because God will not be mocked and when we destroy 40 million little innocent babies, we make God mad...I really believe that the pagans and the abortionists and the feminists and the gays and the lesbians who are actively trying to make that an alternative lifestyle, the ACLU, People for the American Way, all of them who try to secularize America...I point the thing in their face and say you helped this happen.*

Robertson: *I totally concur, and the problem is we've adopted that agenda at the highest levels of our government, and so we're responsible as a free society for what the top people do, and the top people, of course, is the court system.*

Falwell: *Pat, did you notice yesterday that the ACLU and all the Christ-haters, the People for the American Way, NOW, etc., were totally disregarded by the Democrats and the Republicans in both houses of Congress, as they went out on the steps and called out to God in prayer and sang 'God bless America' and said, let the ACLU be hanged. In other words, when the nation is on its knees, the only normal and natural and spiritual thing to do is what we ought to be doing all the time, calling on God.*

Paul Crouch

(Paul and Jan Crouch own the Trinity Broadcasting Network (TBN), the platform of the Word of Faith movement which promotes Jesus and his apostles as wealthy men. They claim that their viewer's donations to them are actually investments, which God will repay 100 fold.)

He [God] doesn't even draw a distinction between Himself and us...You know what else that's settled, then, tonight? This hue and cry and controversy that has been spawned by the Devil to try and bring dissension within the body of Christ that we are gods. I am a little god!...I have His name. I'm one with Him. I'm in covenant relation. I am a little god! Critics, be gone! If you have been healed or saved or blessed through TBN and have not contributed to (the) station, you are robbing God and will lose your reward in heaven.

...that old rotten Sandedrin crowd (i.e., those who oppose the "unity movement" for doctrinal reasons — for instance, those who allege the incompatibility of Catholic and evangelical theology), twice dead, plucked up by the roots... they're damned and on their way to hell and I don't think there's any redemption for them...

...the hypocrites, the heresy hunters that want to find a little mote of illegal doctrine in some Christian's eyes...when they've got a whole forest in their own lives...I say, to hell with you! Get out of my life! Get out of the way! Quit blockin'

God's bridges (of ecumenism)! I'm tired of this!

There's a spiritual application here…I want to say to all you Scribes, Pharisees, heresy hunters, all of you that are going around pickin' little bits of doctrinal error out of everybody's eyes and dividin' the Body of Christ…get out of God's way, stop blockin' God's bridges (of unity), or God's goin' to shoot you if I don't…

…let Him sort out all this doctrinal doodoo! I refuse to argue any longer with any of you out there! Don't even call me if you want to argue…Get out of my life! I don't want to talk to you…I don't want to see your ugly face!

God, we proclaim death to anything or anyone that will lift a hand against this network and this ministry that belongs to You, God. It is your work, it is Your idea, it is Your property, it is Your airwaves, it is Your world, and we proclaim death to anything that would stand in the way of God's great voice of proclamation to the whole world. In the Name of Jesus, and all the people said Amen!"

A few days ago, Jan and I were discussing the awesome growth and expansion of TBN and she asked me: "What will be the future of TBN, if Jesus tarries and we go licon home to heaven?"

– From the cover of a TBN brochure titled "Estate Planning"

Benny Hinn

I know deep in my soul something supernatural is going to happen in Nairobi Kenya. Paul and Jan are coming to Nairobi with me, but Paul, we may very well come back with footage of Jesus appearing on the platform. You know that the Lord appeared in Romania recently and there's a video of it, where the Lord appeared in there back of a church and you see Him on video walking down the aisle, Yea. Paul do you remember when I came on TBN years ago I showed you a clip of the Lord appearing in our church in Orlando on the balcony on the wall? Yea you remember that.

The Lord also tells me to tell you, in mid '90s, about '94 or '95, no later than that, God will destroy the homosexual community of America. But He will not destroy it with what many minds have thought Him to be. He will destroy it with fire. And many will turn and be saved, and many will rebel and be destroyed.

The Spirit of God tells me, an earthquake will hit the East Coast of America and destroy much in the '90s. Not one place will be safe from earthquakes in the '90s. These who have known earthquakes will know it. People I feel the Spirit all over me [speaks in 'tongues'].

The Spirit tells me, Fidel Castro will die in the '90s. Oh my. Some will try to kill him and they will not succeed. But there will come a change in his physical health, and he will not stay in power. And Cuba will be visited of God. I will visit Cuba. Oh. Oh. Holy Spirit do you mean he'll die physically? What do you mean, Holy Spirit? Tell me please. My. Oh. Holy Spirit just said to me, it could be worse than any death you can imagine. There's some question in my spirit on what kind of death the Lord means. I'm not sure. I see him. Uh. I see Cas, I, I see Castro bent over behind bars. I don't know what that means.

God the Father, ladies and gentleman, is a person and He is a triune being by Himself, separate from the Son and the Holy Ghost. See, God the Father is a person, God the Son is a person, God the Holy Ghost is a person; but each one of them is a triune being by himself. If I can shock you and maybe I should, there's nine of them! What did you say? Let me explain. God the Father, ladies and gentlemen, is a person with his own personal spirit, with his own personal soul and his own personal spirit body. You say, I never heard that! Well, you think you are in church to hear things you heard for the last fifty years?

It's closer to you than the air you breath. I've walked in that world. I've seen things you would never be able to understand. Paul, do you believe that I am a man of God? Do you? How long have you known me? Am I crazy? Can I tell you something? I've never shared this. Never! I was in prayer one day and a man appeared in front of me. For two days in a row, twice, one day and the next day. I saw this man in my room. It frightened me at first. When you enter into this world of prayer it starts with the mind where you're so accustomed to the things around you, then you enter into a spiritual thickness and wealth where nothing bothers you, nothing frightens you. Angels don't surprise you anymore with their appearance because you've been already tasting and been feeling and you been living in an atmosphere. Do you understand that? You are not shocked by anything. There appeared to me a man. He was about six feet two. Old man, white beard. His face was somewhat thin, but very bold. Eyes, crystal blue. He had on a white garment. On his head was like a shawl. He looked like a priest. But every part of Him glistened like crystal. And I spoke out and I said, Lord, who is this man I see? I know you might think I lost my mind, but the Lord said, Elijah the prophet! Do you know when that happened? That happened days before the anointing on my life doubled. Literally! The ministries' anointing doubled after that.

Jimmy Swaggart

The Media is ruled by Satan. But yet I wonder if many Christians fully understand that. Also, will they believe what the media says, considering that its aim is to steal, kill and destroy?

Sex education in our schools is promoting incest.

Evolution is a bankrupt speculative philosophy, not a scientific fact. Only a spiritually bankrupt society could ever believe it…only atheists could accept this Satanic theory.

Jim Bakker

I sorrowfully acknowledge that seven years ago...I was wickedly manipulated by treacherous former friends and colleagues who victimized me with the help of a female confederate. They conspired to betray me into a sexual encounter at a time of great stress in my marital life. I was set up as a part of a scheme to co-opt me and obtain some advantage for themselves over me in connection with their hope for a position in the ministry.

Oral Roberts

I felt an overwhelming holy presence all around me. When I opened my eyes, there He stood...some 900 feet tall, looking at me...He stood a full 300 feet taller than the 600-foot-tall City of Faith. There I was face to face with Jesus Christ, the Son of the living God, I have only seen Jesus once before, but here I was face to face with the King of kings. He reached down, put his hands under the City of Faith, lifted it, and said to me: "See how easy it is for me to lift it!"

Sources: www.positiveatheism.org; politicalhumor.about.com; www.geocities.com; www.imdb.com; www.brainyquote.com; The 700 Club

Hell Houses

A Hell House is a type of a haunted house organized by Christian Churches during the Halloween season when regular haunted houses are going on everywhere. Customers often mistakenly enter a Hell House and don't realize they have done so until after they have already paid an admission and walked partially through the Christian horror scenes. Some of the scenes are:

- A ritual satanic sacrifice.
- Cruel masochistic doctors performing a bloody abortion on a young screaming girl.
- Gays and lesbians victims being tortured in hell by demons.
- A married man being seduced by his vixen of a secretary after arguing with his wife.
- A teenager being pressured by evil witches to murder his classmates.
- Hasidic Jews being tortured in Hell by demons.
- A reenactment of Cassie Bernall being gunned down at the Columbine High School massacre. The killers ask if she believes in God and shoot her when she answers "yes." Although this never actually took place, Christian talk-show hosts and writers suggest it did.
- A ground zero scene after 911.

The end of a Hell House is usually a typical heaven scene with Jesus, clouds and angels. After being frightened by the threat of burning in Hell for all of eternity; customers are asked to repent and accept Jesus Christ as their lord and savior.

– Sources: www.religioustolerance.org; www.atheists.org;
www.landoverbaptist.org

Environmental Armageddon

In this past election several million good and decent citizens went to the polls believing in the rapture index. That's right — the rapture index.

Google it and you will find that the bestselling books in America today are the twelve volumes of the left-behind series written by the Christian fundamentalist and religious right warrior, Timothy LaHaye. These true believers subscribe to a fantastical theology concocted in the nineteenth century by a couple of immigrant preachers who took disparate passages from the Bible and wove them into a narrative that has captivated the imagination of millions of Americans.

Its outline is rather simple, if bizarre (the British writer George Monbiot recently did a brilliant dissection of it and I am indebted to him for adding to my own understanding). Once Israel has occupied the rest of its 'biblical lands,' legions of the antichrist will attack it, triggering a final showdown in the valley of Armageddon.

As the Jews who have not been converted are burned, the Messiah will return for the rapture. True believers will be lifted out of their clothes and transported to heaven where, seated next to the right hand of God, they will watch their political and religious opponents suffer plagues of boils, sores, locusts and frogs during the several years of tribulation that follow.

I'm not making this up. Like Monbiot, I've read the literature. I've reported on these people, following some of them from Texas to the West Bank. They are sincere, serious, and polite as they tell you they feel called to help bring the rapture on as fulfillment of biblical prophecy. That's why they have declared solidarity with Israel and the Jewish settlements and backed up their support with money and volunteers. It's why the invasion of Iraq for them was a warm-up act, predicted in the Book of Revelation where four angels 'which are bound in the great river Euphrates will be released to slay the third part of man.' A war with Islam in the Middle East is not something to be feared, but welcomed — an essential conflagration on the road to redemption. The last time I Googled it, the rapture index stood at 144 — just one point below the critical threshold when the whole thing will blow, the Son of God will return, the righteous will enter heaven, and sinners will be condemned to eternal hellfire.

So what does this mean for public policy and the environment? Go to Grist to read a remarkable work of reporting by the journalist Glenn Scherer, "The Road to Environmental Apocalypse." Read it and you will see how millions of Christian fundamentalists may believe that environmental destruction is not only to be disregarded but actually welcomed–even hastened–as a sign of the coming apocalypse.

As Grist makes clear, we're not talking about a handful of fringe lawmakers who hold or are beholden to these beliefs. Nearly half the U.S. Congress before the recent election — 231 legislators in total — more since the election–are backed by the Religious Right.

Forty-five Senators and 186 members of the 108th Congress earned 80 to 100 percent approval ratings from the three most influential Christian right advocacy groups. They include Senator Majority Leader Bill Frist, Assistant Majority Leader Mitch McConnell, Conference Chair Rick Santorum of Pennsylvania, Policy Chair Jon Kyl of Arizona, House Speaker Dennis Hastert, and Majority Whip Roy Blunt. The only Democrat to score 100 percent with the Christian Coalition was Senator Zell Miller of Georgia, who recently quoted from the biblical book of Amos on the Senate floor: "The days will come, sayeth the Lord God, that I will send a famine in the land." He seemed to be relishing the thought.

And why not? There's a constituency for it. A 2002 Time/CNN poll found that 59 percent of Americans believe that the prophecies found in the Book of Revelation are going to come true. Nearly one-quarter think the Bible predicted the 9/11 attacks. Drive across the country with your radio tuned to the more than 1,600 Christian radio stations or in the motel turn to some of the 250 Christian TV stations and you can hear some of this end-time gospel. And you will come to understand why people under the spell of such potent prophecies "cannot be expected," as Grist put it, "to worry about the environment." Why care about the earth when the droughts, floods, famine and pestilence brought by ecological collapse are signs of the apocalypse foretold in the Bible? Why care about global climate change when you and yours will be rescued in the rapture? And why care about converting from oil to solar when the same God who performed the miracle of the loaves and fishes can whip up a few billion barrels of light crude with a word?

Because these people believe that until Christ does return, the Lord will provide.

One of their texts is a high school history book, *America's Providential History*. You'll find there these words: "the secular or socialist has a limited resource mentality and views the world as a pie...that needs to be cut up so everyone can get a piece." However, "[t]he Christian knows that the potential in God is unlimited and that there is no shortage of resources in God's earth...while many secularists view the world as overpopulated, Christians know that God has made the earth sufficiently large with plenty of resources to accommodate all of the people." No wonder Karl Rove goes around the White House whistling that militant hymn, "Onward Christian Soldiers." He turned out millions of the foot soldiers on November 2, including many who have made the apocalypse a powerful driving force in modern American politics.

I can see in the look on your faces just how hard it is for the journalist to report a story like this with any credibility. So let me put it on a personal level. I myself don't know how to be in this world without expecting a confident future and getting up every morning to do what I can to bring it about. So I have always been an optimist. Now, however, I think of my friend on Wall Street whom I once asked: "What do you think of the market?" "I'm optimistic," he answered. "Then why do you look so worried? And he answered: "Because I am not sure my optimism is justified."

I'm not, either. Once upon a time I agreed with the Eric Chivian and the Center for Health and the Global Environment that people will protect the natural environment when they realize its importance to their health and to the health and lives of their children. Now I am not so sure. It's not that I don't want to believe that — it's just that I read the news and connect the dots.

I read that the administrator of the U.S. Environmental Protection Agency has declared the election a mandate for President Bush on the environment. This for an administration:

> • That wants to rewrite the Clean Air Act, the Clean Water Act and the Endangered Species Act protecting rare plant and animal species and their habitats, as well as the National Environmental Policy Act that requires the government to judge beforehand if actions might damage natural resources.
> • That wants to relax pollution limits for ozone. Eliminate vehicle tailpipe inspections. And ease pollution standards for cars, sports utility vehicles and diesel-powered big trucks and heavy equipment.
> • That wants a new international audit law to allow corporations to keep certain information about environmental problems secret from the public.
> • That wants to drop all its New-Source Review suits against polluting coal-fired power plans and weaken consent decrees reached earlier with coal companies.
> • That wants to open the Arctic Wildlife Refuge to drilling and increase drilling in Padre Island National Seashore, the longest stretch of undeveloped barrier island in the world and the last great coastal wild land in America.

I read the news just this week and learned how the Environmental Protection Agency had planned to spend nine million dollars — $2 million of it from the administration's friends at the American Chemistry Council — to pay poor families to continue to use pesticides in their homes. These pesticides have been linked to neurological damage in children, but instead of ordering an end to their use, the government and the industry were going to offer the families $970 each, as well as a camcorder and children's clothing, to serve as guinea pigs for the study.

I read all this in the news.

I read the news just last night and learned that the administration's friends at the International Policy Network, which is supported by ExxonMobil and others of like mind, have issued a new report that climate change is "a myth, sea levels are not rising, scientists who believe catastrophe is possible are an embarrassment."

I not only read the news but the fine print of the recent appropriations bill passed by Congress, with the obscure (and obscene) riders attached to it: a clause removing all endangered species protections from pesticides; language prohibiting judicial review for a forest in Oregon; a waiver of environmental review for grazing permits on public lands; a rider pressed by developers to weaken protection for crucial habitats in California.

– Excerpt from Bill Moyer's acceptance speech made on Dec. 1, 2004 in New York, when the Center for Health and the Global Environment at Harvard Medical School presented him with its fourth annual Global Environment Citizen Award.

The Ends

Prophecies have been with us for centuries, even before Jesus and Christianity. The overall success rate of predictions is miserable, even with re-writes and re-dating.

In Matt. Xvi. 28, for example, Jesus says; "Truly I say unto you, there are some standing here who shall not taste of death, till they see the Son of man coming in his kingdom." This implies that the time of the fulfillment of these hopes was not thought of by Jesus and his disciples as at all remote. It means that Jesus promised the fulfillment of all Messianic hopes before the end of the existing generation. Most Christians were already very surprised that Christ hadn't returned within the first decade or so after his resurrection. They decided that the End had been deferred to allow more time to baptize more people before the last judgment.

Failed End of the World Predictions

• Approx. 60: The Epistles of Paul of Tarsus imply that Jesus would return during his lifetime and the Rapture would begin.

• Approx. 90: Saint Clement predicted that the world would end this year.

• 500: Based on the dimensions of Noah's ark, a Roman priest and theologian in the second and third centuries, predicted Christ would return in A.D. 500, based on the dimensions of Noah's ark.

• January 1, 1000: This year has gone down as one of the most heightened periods of hysteria over the return of Christ. Many European Christians had predicted the world would end on this date. As the date grew closer, Christians waged war against some of the Pagans in the north. This was an effort to convert them before Jesus' got here. During concluding months of 999 AD, everyone was on his best behavior; worldly goods were sold and given to the poor; crops were left unplanted; and criminals were set free from jails.

• 1033: When Jesus didn't come back in 1000, a new fervor developed about this date.

• 1147: Gerard of Poehlde claimed that the millennium had started in 306 C.E. during Constantine's reign. This recalculated Jesus' return to be in 1306 C.E.

• 1205: Joachim of Fiore predicted that King Richard of England would defeat the Antichrist who was already loose in the world.

• 1284: Pope Innocent III added 666 years onto the date the Islam was founded and came up with this date.

• 1346: One-third of Europe died from the black plague. Christian authorities had been killing off all of the cats, believing they were used by witches as familiars. This caused the rat population to flourish. The fleas from the rats spread the plague.

• 1533: Melchior Hoffman predicted that New Jerusalem would be established in Strasbourg, Germany upon Jesus' return this year.

• 1669: Between the years 1669 to 1690, 20,000 of The Old Believers in Russia burned themselves to death because they believed that the world was ending and they didn't want the Antichrist to get them.

• 1689: Seventeenth-century Baptist leader Benjamin Keach predicted that Armageddon was this year.

• 1792: Many Shaker movement followers predicted this date as the end of the world.

• 1814: Joanna Southcott announced that she would bring the second coming of Jesus Christ, by means of a virgin birth. She began to gain weight and did appear pregnant. The time for the birth came and went. She died shortly afterwards. Her body was autopsied and revealed that she had experienced a false pregnancy.

• 1830: Sear Margaret McDonald predicted that Robert Owen would be revealed as the Antichrist. Owen helped found New Harmony, IN.

• March 21, 1843: The Millerite movement founder, William Miller predicted that Jesus second coming was this year.

• October 22, 1844: When Miller missed the first date, he set a new one which is now referred to as "The Great Disappointment." Again, many Christians gave up all of their belongings, quit their jobs and waited for Christ.

• 1850: Seven Day Adventist Ellen White, founder of the movement, predicted many dates as the last one. This year she wrote: "My accompanying angel said, 'Time is almost finished. Get ready, get ready, get ready.' …now time is almost finished…and what we have been years learning, they will have to learn in a few months."

• 1856 or later: Ellen White's last prediction was about her fellow attendees at a SDA conference; "I was shown the company present at the Conference. Said the angel: 'Some food for worms, some subjects of the seven last plagues, some will be alive and remain upon the earth to be translated at the coming of Jesus."

• 1890: Mormon Church founder and leader, Joseph Smith heard a voice. He wrote of it:

> I was once praying very earnestly to know the time of the coming of the Son of Man, when I heard a voice repeat the following: 'Joseph, my son, if thou livest until thou are eighty-five years old, thou shalt see the face of the Son of Man; therefore let this suffice, and trouble me no more on this matter.'
> I was left thus, without being able to decide whether this coming referred to the beginning of the millennium or to some previous appearing, or whether I

should die and thus see his face. I believe the coming of the Son of Man will not be any sooner than that time.

This would have been 1890.

• 1891: On February 14, 1835, Joseph Smith called a meeting of church leaders. He said that God had commanded it so he could make the announcement that Jesus would return within 56 years.

• 1914, 1915, 1918, 1920, 1925, 1941, 1975 and 1994, etc.: All end times dates set by the Watchtower Society or its members. These were based on various interpretations from the Book of Daniel, Chapter 4 combined with some silly arithmetic.

• 1936: The Worldwide Church of God leader Herbert W. Armstrong predicted this year for the second coming. When that didn't happen, he set the date for 1975.

• 1948: The state of Israel was established. Many Christians predicted this to be the beginning of the Rapture.

• 1957: Mihran Ask was quoted in *The Watchtower* magazine: "Sometime between April 16 and 23, 1957, Armageddon will sweep the world! Millions of persons will perish in its flames and the land will be scorched."

• 1970s: The Children of God's founder, Moses David had predicted that all life in the United States would end after a comet hit the earth in the mid 1970s.

• 1972: *Atlantic* magazine wrote, "Herbert W. Armstrong's empire suffered a serious blow when the end failed to begin in January of 1972, as Armstrong had predicted, thus bringing hardship to many people who had given most of their assets to the church in the expectation of going to Petra, where such worldly possessions would be useless."

• 1975: Another famous Jehovah's Witness prediction date.

• 1978: Pastor Chuck Smith, of Calvary Chapel in Costa Mesa, CA, predicted the Jesus' return in 1981.

• 1980: The Baha'i World Faith Group leader, Leland Jensen leader predicted a nuclear disaster would take place setting off twenty years of war and strife. The new millennium would bring in God's Kingdom on earth.

• 1981: Christian Identity leader, Arnold Murray of the Shepherd's Chapel predicted that the Antichrist would be on Earth by 1981. He made a later prediction that the Battle of Armageddon would be in June of 1989.

• 1982: Pat Robertson predicted publicly that the world would end in the fall of this year.

• 1986: Moses David from "The Children of God" faith group made a prediction that Russia would defeat Israel and the United States in the Battle of Armageddon this year. Communism would dominate the earth and then Jesus would return.

• 1988: In Hal Lindsey's book, *The Late, Great Planet Earth*, he predicted that the Rapture would be one 40 years after the the state of Israel was established.

• October 11, 1988: NASA scientist, Edgar Whisenaut, published a best-selling book, *88 Reasons Why the Rapture Will Occur in 1988*.

• About 1990: Peter Ruckman analyzed the Bible and computed the rapture date would be sometime around 1990.

• 2000: Our favorite failed prediction of the end of the world made by just about everyone.

– Sources: www.religioustolerance.org and *The Date Setters Diary*

Killer Jesus

Will Jesus return to Earth and destroy all non-Christians? According to the latest of the *Left Behind* fiction thrillers, *Glorious Appearing*, Jesus will merely raise his hand and they will be swallowed into the bowels of the Earth, being crushed as it closes. Is this really what a peaceful, non-judging savior would do? Genocide; Ethnic-cleansing?

These "made for TV" Hollywood novels have been translated into thirty-three different languages and have sold over 50 million copies. *The Left Behind Series* also offers best-selling children's books and other related products which encapsulate a growing industry which is similar to that of the *Star Wars Trilogy*. The authors are proud to boast that "over 3000 people have become believers through reading the series." Their website bio also quotes, "*Left Behind* is designed to fulfill the greater goal of assisting you on your spiritual journey." Is the goal of Christianity to destroy all non-Christians or to spread God's love for peaceful co-existence?

According to American laws, Freedom of Speech is our God given right (not to mention constitutional right) and these fiction novels were written in America. The USA, being a melting pot of cultures and religion, is supposed to be a safe haven, where people can practice their faiths and politics freely. At this point in time, some of these faiths and beliefs are frowned upon or even outlawed. Imagine if a series of books were written by a Muslim, Jew or African-American, describing the glorious obliteration of anyone not sharing the same beliefs they have. Would this be a best seller or would it be banned by the religious right? Would these authors be celebrated or persecuted? How would our children answer these questions?

Even though *Left Behind* is fiction, a large number of readers accept the storyline as fact. This is validated by the number of readers who became believers. If some of the readers become believers, then those believers become haters. Do these books breed ignorance and hatred? Do they insinuate they Muslims and all people of other faiths are evil? Is the Dalai Lama Satan himself? Would he ever write such nonsense?

Today, we Americans live in a society gripped by fear. This fear is perpetuated by our media and the threat of terrorism. This fear creates a growing suspicion between neighbors and friends. Do we really need another bestseller that promotes religious intolerance? I believe Jesus, Allah, Yahweh or any God would preach tolerance and love at this time.

– Chad Cooper

A poster depicting Jesus Christ as a Che Guevara-style revolutionary has been launched by Christians to entice more people into church.

The slogan: "Meek. Mild. As if. Discover the Real Jesus."

– BBC News Online, regarding a new campaign to recast the traditional gentle image of Jesus Christ in Britain's mainstream Christian churches.

When fact is stranger and more dangerous than fiction, it is time to act. Action through education and reason can make the only true difference.

Can fundamentalist and religious beliefs ultimately lead to sudden death for mankind? The answer is definitely, yes. But even more unsettling is the slow form of suffocation that mankind is suffering — brought on by non-discernment, religious illiteracy, institutionalized myth — and non-action by those who have it all figured out...

– Tim C. Leedom, Excerpt from *The Main Man*

The Jesus Landing Pad

It was an e-mail we weren't meant to see. Not for our eyes were the notes that showed White House staffers taking two-hour meetings with Christian fundamentalists, where they passed off bogus social science on gay marriage as if it were holy writ and issued fiery warnings that "the Presidents [sic] Administration and current Government is engaged in cultural, economical, and social struggle on every level" — this to a group whose representative in Israel believed herself to have been attacked by witchcraft unleashed by proximity to a volume of Harry Potter. Most of all, apparently, we're not supposed to know the National Security Council's top Middle East aide consults with apocalyptic Christians eager to ensure American policy on Israel conforms with their sectarian doomsday scenarios.

But now we know.

"Everything that you're discussing is information you're not supposed to have," barked Pentecostal minister Robert G. Upton when asked about the off-the-record briefing his delegation received on March 25. Details of that meeting appear in a confidential memo signed by Upton and obtained by the *Voice*.

The e-mailed meeting summary reveals NSC Near East and North African Affairs director Elliott Abrams sitting down with the Apostolic Congress and massaging their theological concerns. Claiming to be "the Christian Voice in the Nation's Capital," the members vociferously oppose the idea of a Palestinian state. They fear an Israeli withdrawal from Gaza might enable just that, and they object on the grounds that all of Old Testament Israel belongs to the Jews. Until Israel is intact and Solomon's temple rebuilt, they believe, Christ won't come back to earth.

Abrams attempted to assuage their concerns by stating that "the Gaza Strip had no significant Biblical influence such as Joseph's tomb or Rachel's tomb and therefore is a piece of land that can be sacrificed for the cause of peace."

Three weeks after the confab, President George W. Bush reversed longstanding U.S. policy, endorsing Israeli sovereignty over parts of the West Bank in exchange for Israel's disengagement from the Gaza Strip.

In an interview with the *Voice*, Upton denied having written the document, though it was sent out from an e-mail account of one of his staffers and bears the organization's seal, which is nearly identical to the Great Seal of the United States. Its idiosyncratic grammar and punctuation tics also closely match those of texts on the Apostolic Congress's website, and Upton verified key details it recounted, including the number of participants in the meeting ("45 ministers including wives") and its conclusion "with a heart-moving send-off of the President in his Presidential helicopter."

Upton refused to confirm further details.

Affiliated with the United Pentecostal Church, the Apostolic Congress is part of an important and disciplined political constituency courted by recent Republican administrations. As a subset of the broader Christian Zionist movement, it has a lengthy history of opposition to any proposal that will not result in what it calls a "one-state solution" in Israel.

The White House's association with the congress, which has just posted a new staffer in Israel who may be running afoul of Israel's strict anti-missionary laws, also raises diplomatic concerns.

The staffer, Kim Hadassah Johnson, wrote in a report obtained by the *Voice*, "We are establishing the Meet the Need Fund in Israel, 'MNFI'...The fund will be an Interest Free Loan Fund that will enable us to loan funds to new believers (others upon application) who need assistance. They will have the opportunity to repay the loan (although it will not be mandatory)." When that language was read to Moshe Fox, minister for public and interreligious affairs at the Israeli Embassy in Washington, he responded, "It sounds against the law which prohibits any kind of money or material [inducement] to make people convert to another religion. That's what it sounds like." (Fox's judgment was e-mailed to Johnson, who did not return a request for comment.)

The Apostolic Congress dates its origins to 1981, when, according to its website, "Brother Stan Wachtstetter was able to open the door to Apostolic Christians into the White House." Apostolics, a sect of Pentecostals, claim legitimacy as the heirs of the original church because they, as the 12 apostles supposedly did, baptize converts in the name of Jesus, not in the name of the Father, Son, and Holy Spirit. Ronald Reagan bore theological affinities with such Christians because of his belief that the world would end in a fiery Armageddon. Reagan himself referenced this belief explicitly a half-dozen times during his presidency.

While the language of apocalyptic Christianity is absent from George W. Bush's speeches, he has proven eager to work with apocalyptics — a point of pride for Upton. "We're in constant contact with the White House," he boasts. "I'm briefed at least once a week via telephone briefings...I was there about two weeks ago...At that time we met with the president."

Last spring, after President Bush announced his Road Map plan for peace in the Middle East, the Apostolic Congress co-sponsored an effort with the Jewish group Americans for a Safe Israel that placed billboards in 23 cities with a quotation from Genesis ("Unto thy offspring will I give this land") and the message, "Pray that President Bush Honors God's Covenant with Israel. Call the White House with this message." It then provided the White House phone number and the Apostolic Congress' Web address.

In the interview with the *Voice*, Pastor Upton claimed personal responsibility for directing 50,000 postcards to the White House opposing the Road Map, which aims to create a Palestinian state. "I'm in total disagreement with any form of Palestinian state," Upton said. "Within a two-week period, getting 50,000 postcards saying the exact same thing from places all over the country, that resonated with the White House. That really caused [President Bush] to backpedal on the Road Map."

When I sought to confirm Upton's account of the meeting with the White House, I was directed to National Security Council spokesman Frederick Jones, whose initial response upon being read a list of the names of White House staffers present was a curt, "You know half the people you just mentioned are Jewish?"

When asked for comment on top White House staffers meeting with representatives of an organization that may be breaking Israeli law, Jones responded, "Why would the White House comment on that?"

When asked whose job it is in the administration to study the Bible to discern what parts of Israel were or weren't acceptable sacrifices for peace, Jones said that his previous statements had been off-the-record.

When Pastor Upton was asked to explain why the group's website describes the Apostolic Congress as "the Christian Voice in the nation's capital," instead of simply a Christian voice in the nation's capital, he responded, "There has been a real lack of leadership in having someone emerge as a Christian voice, someone who doesn't speak for the right, someone who doesn't speak for the left, but someone who speaks for the people, and someone who speaks from a theocratical perspective."

When his words were repeated back to him to make sure he had said a "theocratical" perspective, not a "theological" perspective, he said, "Exactly. Exactly. We want to know what God would have us say or what God would have us do in every issue."

The Middle East was not the only issue discussed at the March 25 meeting. James Wilkinson, deputy national security advisor for communications, spoke first and is characterized as stating that the 9-11 Commission "is portraying those who have given their all to protect this nation as 'weak on terrorism,' that 99 percent of all the men and women protecting us in this fight against terrorism are career citizens," and offered the example of Frances Town-send, deputy national security adviser for combating terrorism, "who sacrificed Christmas to do a 'security video' conference."

Tim Goeglein, deputy director of public liaison and the White House's point man with evangelical Christians, moderated, and he also spoke on the issue of same-sex marriage. According to the memo, he asked the rhetorical questions: "What will happen to our country if that actually happens? What do those pushing such hope to gain?" His answer: "They want to change America." How so? He quoted the research of Hoover Institute senior fellow

Stanley Kurtz, who holds that since gay marriage was legalized in Scandinavia, marriage itself has virtually ceased to exist. (In fact, since Sweden instituted a registered-partnership law for same-sex couples in the mid '90s, there has been no overall change in the marriage and divorce rates there.)

It is Matt Schlapp, White House political director and Karl Rove's chief lieutenant, who was paraphrased as stating "that the Presidents Administration and current Government is engaged in cultural, economical, and social struggle on every level."

Also present at the meeting was Kristen Silverberg, deputy assistant to the president for domestic policy. (None of the participants responded to interview requests.)

The meeting was closed by Goeglein, who was asked, "What can we do to assist in this fight for these issues and our nations [sic] foundation and values?" and who reportedly responded, "Pray, pray, pray, pray."

The Apostolic Congress' representative in Israel, Kim Johnson, is ethnically Jewish, keeps kosher, and holds herself to the sumptuary standards of Orthodox Jewish women, so as to better blend in to her surroundings.

In one letter home obtained by the Voice she notes that many of the Apostolic Christians she works with in Israel are Filipino women "married to Jewish men — who on occasion accompany their wives to meetings. We are planning to start a fellowship with this select group where we can meet for dinners and get to know one another. Please Pray for the timing and formation of such." Elsewhere she talks of a discussion with someone "on the pitfalls and aggravations of Christians who missionize Jews." She works often among the Jewish poor — the kind of people who might be interested in interest-free loans — and is thrilled to "meet the outcasts of this Land — how wonderful because they are in the in-casts for His Kingdom."

An ecstatic figure who from her own reports appears to operate at the edge of sanity ("Two of the three nights in my apartment I have been attacked by a hair raising spirit of fear," she writes, noting the sublet contained a Harry Potter book; "at this time I am associating it with witchcraft"), Johnson has also met with Knesset member Gila Gamliel. (Gamliel did not respond to interview requests.) She also boasted of an imminent meeting with a "Knesset leader."

"At this point and for all future mails it is important for me to note that this country has very stiff anti-missionary laws," she warns the followers back home. "[D]iscretion is required in all mails. This is particularly important to understand when people write mails or ask about organization efforts regarding such."

Her boss, Pastor Upton, displays a photograph on the Apostolic Congress website of a meeting between himself and Beny Elon, Prime Minister Sharon's tourism minister, famous in Israel for his advocacy of the expulsion of Palestinians from Israeli-controlled lands.

His spokesman in the U.S., Ronn Torassian, affirmed that "Minister Elon knows Mr. Upton well," but when asked whether he is aware that Mr. Upton's staffer may be breaking Israel's anti-missionary laws, snapped: "It's not something he's interested in discussing with *The Village Voice.*"

In addition to its work in Israel, the Apostolic Congress is part of the increasingly Christian public face of pro-Israel activities in the United States. Don Wagner, author of the book Anxious for Armageddon, has been studying Christian Zionism for 15 years, and believes that the current hard-line pro-Israel movement in the U.S. is "predominantly gentile." Often, devotees work in concert with Jewish groups like Americans for a Safe Israel, or AFSI, which set up a mostly Christian Committee for a One-State Solution as the sponsor of last year's billboard campaign. The committee's board included, in addition to Upton, such evangelical luminaries as Gary Bauer and E.E. "Ed" McAteer of the Religious Roundtable.

AFSI's executive director, Helen Freedman, confirms the increasingly Christian cast of her coalition. "We have many good Jews, of course," she says, "but they're in the minority." She adds, "The liberal Jew is unable to believe the Arab when he says his goal is to Islamize the West…But I believe it. And evangelical Christians believe it." Of Jews who might otherwise support her group's view of Jews' divine right to Israel, she laments, "They're embarrassed about quoting the Bible, about referring to the Covenant, about talking about the Promised Land."

Pastor Upton is not embarrassed, and Helen Freedman is proud of her association with him. She is wistful when asked if she, like Upton, has been able to finagle a meeting with the president. "Pastor Upton is the head of a whole Apostolic Congress," she laments. "It's a nationwide group of evangelicals."

Upton has something Freedman covets: a voting bloc.

She laughs off concerns that, for Christian Zionists, actual Jews living in Israel serve as mere props for their end-time scenario: "We have a different conception of what [the end of the world] will be like…Whoever is right will rejoice, and whoever was wrong will say, 'Whoops!'"

She's not worried, either, about evangelical anti-Semitism: "I don't think it exists," she says. She does say, however, that it would concern her if she learned the Apostolic Congress had a representative in Israel trying to win converts: "If we discovered that people were trying to convert Jews to Christianity, we would be very upset."

Kim Johnson doesn't call it converting Jews to Christianity. She calls it "Circumcision of the Heart" — a spiritual circumcision Jews must undergo because, she writes in paraphrase of Jeremiah, chapter 9, "God will destroy all the uncircumcised nations along with the House of Israel, because the House of Israel is uncircumcised in the heart…[I]t is through the Gospel…that men's hearts are circumcised."

Apostolics believe that only 144,000 Jews who have not, prior to the Second Coming of Christ, acknowledged Jesus as the Messiah will be saved in the end times. Though even for those who do not believe in this literal interpretation of the Bible — or for anyone who lives in Israel, or who cares about Israel, or whose security might be affected by a widespread conflagration in the Middle East, which is everyone — the scriptural prophecies of the Christian Zionists should be the least of their worries.

Instead, we should be worried about self-fulfilling prophecies. "Biblically," stated one South Carolina minister in support of the anti-Road Map billboard campaign, "there's always going to be a war."

Don Wagner, an evangelical, worries that in the Republican Party, people who believe this "are dominating the discourse now, in an election year." He calls the attempt to yoke Scripture to current events "a modern heresy, with cultish proportions.

"I mean, it's appalling," he rails on. "And it also shows how marginalized mainstream Christian thinking, and the majority of evangelical thought, have become."

It demonstrates, he says, "the absolute convergence of the neoconservatives with the Christian Zionists and the pro-Israel lobby, driving U.S. Mideast policy."

The problem is not that George W. Bush is discussing policy with people who press right-wing solutions to achieve peace in the Middle East, or with devout Christians. It is that he is discussing policy with Christians who might not care about peace at all — at least until the rapture.

The Jewish pro-Israel lobby, in the interests of peace for those living in the present, might want to consider a disengagement.

– Rick Perlstein

Rick Perlstein is former chief national political correspondent for *The Village Voice* and author of *Before the Storm: Barry Goldwater and the Unmaking of the American Consensus.*

“ *President Bush said to all of us: 'I'm driven with a mission from God. God would tell me, "George, go and fight those terrorists in Afghanistan." And I did, and then God would tell me, "George, go and end the tyranny in Iraq ..." And I did. And now, again, I feel God's words coming to me, "Go get the Palestinians their state and get the Israelis their security, and get peace in the Middle East." And by God I'm gonna do it.'* ”

Palestinian Foreign Minister, Nabil Shaath

“ *Americans should have a clear understanding about why the religious right believes that Israel should be supported and defended unconditionally by the west: Christians believe seriously that they will go to heaven and physically escape death when Jesus returns to usher in the Rapture. This easy way out can only occur if the State of Israel does exist, according to their doctrine. If Israel was taken off the map, this fantasy would have to be abandoned.* ”

Tim C. Leedom

" *You do not want a President who believes that Jesus is coming soon! Believing in the Second Coming of Jesus has caused people to do very stupid things.* "

Bob Minick

How Fundamentalism Promotes Ignorance

Fundamentalism almost invariably has a problem with science. Science is the process of starting with the evidence and proceeding to the conclusion that best fits the evidence, regardless of what that conclusion may be.

Fundamentalism, on the other hand, starts with a conclusion and searches for evidence to support that conclusion.

Anyone who has ever been wrong knows that the latter is no way to find the truth, because it presumes the searcher has the truth to begin with, which of course may or may not be the case.

But this doesn't stop the fundamentalist; the very premise of fundamentalism presumes to start with the truth, and all the fundamentalist lacks is evidence. This false science has even become an industry in such organizations as the Institute for Creation Science, the Family Research Council, etc. There are many other examples, and from many religions besides just Christianity.

– Scott Bidstrup

IX

Archaeology and Science:
The Death Blow to Christianity

Some Specific Reasons Why Many Scientists Disbelieve Creation Science and a Literal Interpretation of Genesis

Two major competing models of the Earth's past exist. New Earth creation scientists generally conclude that:

• God created all of the species during a short period of time, perhaps about 4004 B.C.E., and certainly not before 10,000 B.C.E.

• God created all of the species of bacteria, primitive one-celled creatures, trilobites, dinosaurs, humans, etc. within a few days of each other. Just as *The Flintstones* cartoon shows, humans and dinosaurs wandered about the earth together.

• During the 40 days of rain and the approximately nine months of drainage of Noah's flood, all of the land animals outside the ark were drowned. Various deposits were formed with sediment and the bodies of dead animals; their remains became fossils, embedded in rock layers.

Most scientists believe that a very different sequence of events happened:

• That a primitive, one-celled life form came into existence by some series of natural processes, billions of years ago. Scientists are currently only dimly aware of the nature of these processes.

• Billions of years later, this primitive life form had evolved into more complex species (e.g. trilobites), even as the primitive life forms became extinct.

• Later species evolved into Dinosaurs hundreds of millions of years ago. They died out, probably because of extreme environmental changes brought about by a massive collision of an asteroid with the Earth. But new species that evolved from the dinosaurs and other species that were on earth with the dinosaurs continued to evolve.

• Homo sapiens, Neanderthals, and some of the higher apes appeared much more recently, and shared a common ancestor. Neanderthals became extinct.

• All during this extinction of old species and arrival of new species, individual animals died. A very small fraction of those with hard shells or a skeleton became converted to fossils and were embedded in rocks.

• Most scientists do not believe that any world-wide flood has occurred. There are serious questions about where all the water came from and went.

Some reasons why many scientists believe Genesis to be inaccurate:

There are additional indicators why many scientists believe that the order of creation described in Genesis could not have happened.

- Some plants rely upon birds and ants for propagation. If plants were created on Day 3, and birds and ants were created on Day 5 and 6, and if each Genesis "day" is equal to 1000 or more real years (as some creation scientists believe), then some plants would have had to survive without propagation for thousands of years. To other creation scientists who believe that a "day" in Genesis is literally 24 hours, then this does not present a problem.

- The fossil record clearly shows that land animals developed before birds. But the Genesis account indicates the reverse.

Scientists have found many other indicators that other parts of the book of Genesis are in error. Some examples are:

- Theologians have generally agreed that the Bible teaches that the earth is less than 10,000 years of age. However, in Wyoming, the Green River Formation shows that varves — a 260-meter thick formation made from annual layers of sediment — were laid down for the past 2 million years. Three Ice core samples have been taken in Greenland that show 40,000 annual layers of ice. In each case, one detectable layer of sediment or ice is laid down each year.

- The Bible said that Noah loaded the entire ark with two (or seven) from each species within a 24-hour day. This would have required him to have taken into the vessel, classified and stored 480 species per second.

- Noah took his wife, three sons, and three daughters-in-law into the ark. Each person would have had to sort, house, look after, feed, water, and remove the excrement from about 5 million animals each day.

- Noah is said to have built an all-wooden arc about 450 feet long. Long wooden ships, some as long as 300 feet, have actually been built, but they required extensive metal reinforcing — an option not available to Noah. And they leaked badly, requiring either a large crew or mechanically driven pumps to remove water from the hold. Motor driven pumps were not available in those days, and there were not enough humans on the arc to manually pump the water.

- Many animals can only survive in certain small regions of the earth where the food supply and temperatures are ideal. These species could not have left their homeland, moved through jungle and desert in order to reach the arc; they would not have survived the journey.

- There was no mechanism whereby animals found only in North America, South America, and Australia could cross oceans and arrive at the arc.

• When there are fewer than about 40 members to a species, extinction is inevitable, even when massive human intervention occurs. After the flood there would have been only 2 or 7 members to each species; they would not have survived.

• The Bible states that the Tower of Babel was constructed 110 to 150 years after the flood. One might ask how could the 3 fertile female human survivors of the flood (Noah's daughters in law) produce such a large number of descendants within 6 generations?

• There is no indication of a worldwide flood in ancient Egyptian, Indus or Chinese writings, temples, pyramids, sculptures, etc., which existed at the time of Noah. Yet, if the flood really did occur, then all of the world's early civilizations would have been completely destroyed. The entire population of the world would have consisted of 8 people, in the vicinity of the ark. It would have taken millennia for humanity to become re-established in China and elsewhere. Also, they would have developed a very different culture from the pre-flood society. The archaeological record in Egypt would show a sudden change from ancient Egyptian artifacts, to no signs of civilization, to ancient Israelite culture after the time of the flood. The archaeological record in China would show a sudden change from ancient Chinese artifacts, to no signs of civilization, to ancient Israelite culture after the time of the flood. And so on. But the archaeological record shows that the various cultures were not interrupted; they continued to develop throughout the period when the flood is supposed to have happened. For example, the Egyptian "Old Kingdom" covered the era from 2649 B.C.E. to 2134 B.C.E., the 3rd to the 8th dynasty. In particular, the fifth dynasty covered the interval 2465 to 2323 B.C.E., straddling the time when religious conservatives believe that the flood happened.

• One might ask how would the fish survive? Some fish require fresh water, some brackish water and some salt water. If sufficient water were added to the oceans so that the level rose above that of the highest mountains, then the salinity of the oceans would drastically change. There would have been a mass die-off of fish species; only a few tolerant ocean fish would have survived. The salt content of all the fresh water lakes in the world would drastically increase, causing a die-off of numerous fish species found only in fresh water. None of this happened, except in one small area of the world: the Black Sea circa 5600 B.C.E. This is believed by many scientists to be the source of the world-wide flood myth of ancient Babylonian that was adopted by the ancient Jewish writers who wrote the Bible.

– Bruce A Robinson, Ontario Consultants on Religious Tolerance,
www.religioustolerance.org

The Seed of Ysiraal

Only one mention of the people of Israel occurs by name on all the monuments of Egypt. This was discovered a few years since by Professor Petrie on a stele erected by the King Merenptah II. Not that there is any possibility of identifying these with the Israelites of the biblical exodus. The "people of Ysiraal" on the monument belong to those who were amongst the confederated Nine Bows, the marauders, North Africans, the Kheta, the Canaanites, the Northern Syrians, and others with whom they are classed.

> Every one that was a marauder hath been subdued by the King Merenptah, who gives life like the sun-god every day.

This inscription gives an account of the Libyan campaign, and concludes with the following description of the triumph of King Merenptah:

> Chiefs bend down, saying, Peace to thee; not one of the Nine Bows raises his head. Vanquished are the Tahennu (North Africans); the Khita (Hittites) are quieted; ravaged is Pa-kanana (Kanun) with all violence; taken is Askadni (Askelon?); seized is Kazmel; Yenu (Yanoh) of the Syrians is made as though it had not existed; the people of Ysiraal is spoiled — it hath no seed (left); Syria has become as widows of Egypt; all lands together are in peace (Petrie, *Contemp. Review*, May, 1896).

The people of Ysiraal (Israel) are here included, together with the Syrians, and amongst the confederated "Nine Bows" who made continual incursions into Egypt as invaders and marauders, and who are spoken of as having been exterminated. Hence it is said, "The people of Ysiraal is spoiled; it hath no seed." But there is nothing whatever in the inscription of King Merenptah corresponding to or corroborative of the biblical story of the Israelites in the land of Egypt or their exodus into the land of Canaan.

The campaign against the Libyan confederacy had been undertaken by Merenptah, who, according to the inscription, was born as the destined means of revenging the invasion of Egypt by the Nine Bow barbarians. In proclaiming the triumph of the monarch the inscription says,

> Every one that was a marauder hath been subdued by the King Merenptah.

The people of Ysiraal in this inscription are identified by the Pharaoh with the nomads of the Edomite Shasu or shepherds, and are classed by him with the confederate marauders who invaded Egypt with the Libu, and were defeated with huge slaughter at the battle of Procepis (Pa-ar-shep, which is also recorded on the monuments). They were a tribe or totemic community of cattle-keepers, one of "the tribes of the Shasu from the land of Aduma" who went down into Egypt in search of grazing ground to find sustenance for their herds in the eastern region of the Delta.

At this very time, when the people of Ysiraal and their seed were being "wiped out" or annihilated as the Israelites in Syria, there was an exodus of the Edomite Shasu which has been pressed into the service of false theory on behalf of biblical "history." These tribes had considered the eastern region of the Delta, as far as Zoan, to be their own possession, until they were driven out by Seti I. Now they bestirred themselves anew, under Meneptah II (Merenptah), but "in a manner alike peaceful and loyal."

> As faithful subjects of Egypt, they asked for a passage through the border fortress of Khetam in the land of Thuku in order that they might find sustenance for themselves and their herds in the rich pasture-lands of the lake districts about the city of Pa-Tum (Brugsch, *Egypt under the Pharaohs*, Eng. tr., one vol., p. 317).

An Egyptian official makes the following report on the subject. He says:

> Another matter for the satisfaction of my master's heart: we have carried into effect the passage of the tribes of the Shasu from the land of Aduma (Edom) from the fortress (Khetam) of Merenptah-Hetephima, which is situated in Thuku (Succoth), to the lakes of the city Pa-Tum, of Merenptah-Hetephima, which are situated in the land of Thuku, in order to feed themselves and to feed their herds on the possessions of Pharaoh, who is there a beneficent sun for all peoples. In the year 8 . . . Sut, I caused them to be conducted (according to the list of the days on which the fortress was opened for their passage) (Brugsch, citing Pap. Anastasi; 6).

Merenptah also had his royal seat in the city of Ramses. Here we meet with the field of Zoan and the store-cities of Pithom and Ramses which have been imported into the second book of Moses, and futile efforts have been made to show that this record corroborated the biblical version of the exodus. But in this exodus we find the Shasu or shepherds are peaceful and loyal people, faithful subjects of the Pharaoh, who are politely conducted from the land of Edom through the fortress (Khetam) to the lake-country of Succoth (or Thuku), the first encampment assigned to the Israelites, where they would find abundance of food and fodder for themselves and their flocks and herds instead of wandering in the wilderness for forty years, according to the other story.

At the same time, or thereabouts, the people of Ysiraal in Syria were cut up root and branch by Merenptah. The passage through the land of Thuku,

Hebrew Succoth, here described is apparently the route adopted by those who converted the "coming forth" from Amenta into the biblical exodus from Egypt, and it tends to affiliate the cattle-keepers in the land of Goshen to the nomadic tribes of the Edomite Shasu (Gen. XLVI. 32). But we shall not overtake the children of Israel as an ethnological entity on this line of route, nor as the people who perish by the million in the wilderness of sand that formed the land of graves in the desert domain of Sekari. For that we shall have to "turn back" and encamp before Pi-ha-hiroth, and pass through the mouth of the cleft into the wilderness of Amenta. But it is useless trying any further to confuse the Jewish Exodus with the mythical "coming forth" from the Lower Egypt of Amenta, with intent to reestablish a falsely-bottomed history.

The eruption of the Libyans and their confederated invaders in the time of Merenptah is a matter of historic fact. That they were vanquished and driven back by Merenptah is equally historical. They at least made no triumphant exodus from Egypt as 600,000 fighting men, for they never got there, but were fatally defeated on the borders of the land. The only people, then, known by the name of Israel to the Egyptian monuments are the people of Ysiraal who had their very seed destroyed, as claimed by the Pharaoh beloved of Ptah. These can be identified as a North Syrian contingent of fighting men who had joined the Libyans, or the old confederation of the Nine Bows, in their attacks on Egypt, and were hunted back in wreck and ruin, if not entirely destroyed, by Merenptah, the so-called "Pharaoh of the Exodus." Thus, if these were the same people as those of the Hebrew Exodus, the deliverance of the Israelites from Egypt would be turned into the deliverance of Egypt itself from the Libyan confederacy of raiding barbarians amongst whom the Israelites were a hardly distinguishable unit.

What then was "the seed of Israel" as an ethnological entity in the eyes of Merenptah, or the writer of his inscription? They fought as mercenaries and marauders for the Libyan king, who had made war on Egypt collectively, and were driven backward all together in one common, overwhelming rout. They came and went, and left no record of their past. Israel in Syria was not Israel in Egypt. Israel in Egypt is not an ethnical entity, but the children of Ra in the Lower Egypt of Amenta, who are entirely mythical.

– Gerald Massey,
Excerpt from *Ancient Egypt: The Light of the World*

In *The Bible Unearthed*, Israel Finkelstein and Neil Asher Silverman theorize that early books of the Bible weren't written until the seventh century B.C.E., which is hundreds of years after the lives of the patriarchs, the Exodus from Egypt, and the conquest of Canaan were said to have transpired.

The truth is that virtually every modern archeologist who has investigated the story of the Exodus, with very few exceptions, agrees that the way the Bible describes the Exodus is not the way it happened, if it happened at all.

– From a sermon delivered by Rabbi David Wolpe

People who try to find scientific explanations for the splitting of the Red Sea are missing the boat in understanding how ancient literature often mixed mythic ideas with historical recollections. That wasn't considered lying or deceit; it was a way to get ideas across.

– Carol Meyers, a professor specializing in biblical studies and Archeology at Duke University, source: Teresa Watanabe, *Los Angeles Times*

In the thirteenth century B.C.E., the likely date of the entry of the Israelites into Canaan, Jericho was an unfortified village. In other words, the familiar account was most likely embroidered upon in later tellings. The Jordan River valley in which Jericho lies sits on a major rift, or geological fault zone. One explanation for the river stopping is that both events were earthquake-induced. However, there is no archeological evidence of those tumbled walls at Jericho.

For evidence of how old war stories get embellished and overlaid with notions of "divine intervention," one needn't look too far in the ancient Mediterranean neighborhood. At about the same general historic time period that Joshua may have been leading the loose confederation of Israelite tribes into Canaan, there was along running battle between a loose confederation tribes and the inhabitants of another fortified town on the coast of what is now Turkey. This extended but otherwise historically insignificant battle fought over "Illium" around 1193 B.C.E. was transformed into a much bigger story. Transmitted orally, like the Bible stories, it was finally written down more than three hundred years later in 850 B.C.E. by a poet we call "Homer" and is titled *The Iliad* and its sequel is *The Odyssey*.

– Kenneth C. Davis,
Excerpt from *Don't Know Much About the Bible*, Publisher: William Morrow

Locating Jesus in Time, Space and Archaeology

Within fifty years after Jesus' death, Christian writers began to try to anchor his life in time and space. By this time, Paul was dead and his expectations that Jesus would soon return and establish his kingdom had not been fulfilled. Roman soldiers had destroyed the Jewish temple in Jerusalem and had wiped out the Jewish Essene community at Qumran. Masada, the last Jewish holdout against the Romans, had fallen under a brilliant Roman assault. It was clear that to survive, Judaism and its offspring, Christianity, would have to redirect their thinking and their missions.

In his letters, which are the earliest New Testament writings, Paul paid scant heed to Jesus' life-story. Whether he made more of Jesus' biography in his public lectures cannot be known. Nor is it possible to ascertain that stories about Jesus' life may have circulated among Jesus' followers. Sometime after the year 70 of the Common Era (C.E.), the Gospel of Mark was written. (Some sources claim a date as early as 55 C.E. for Mark.) This writer opened his account with an adult Jesus arriving at the Jordan River for baptism by John the Baptizer. He related nothing of Jesus' birth or childhood.

When Was Jesus Born?

The Gospels of Matthew and Luke display greater interest in an expanded life story of Jesus. These documents, which seem to have been written some ten years after Mark, used Mark as a basis for their writings, but added separate accounts of Jesus' birth and infancy. The Gospel of Matthew claimed that Jesus was born in Bethlehem during the reign of King Herod the Great and that to protect the infant Jesus from the monarch's soldiers, the family fled to Egypt and returned to Palestine only after Herod had died. According to the Jewish historian Josephus, Herod died following a lunar eclipse.

Modern astronomers inform us that such eclipses which would be visible in Palestine occurred on March 14, in 4 B.C.E. and on January 10 in 1 B.C.E. Therefore, depending upon which eclipse is meant, Herod died in either 4 B.C.E. or 1 B.C.E. and Jesus would therefore be born either before 4 B.C.E. or 1 B.C.E. These dates provide little or no help in fixing a time for Jesus' birth in history. On the basis of information in the Gospel of Matthew we simply cannot know when Jesus was born.

The Gospel of Luke (1:5) also noted that Jesus was born during Herod's reign. The writer linked the birth story to a world-wide census instigated by Caesar Augustus (Gaius Octavius) who ruled between 30 B.C.E. and 14 C.E., at the time when Cyrenius (P. Sulpicius Quirinius) was governor of Syria. From a number of sources, we know that Quirinius was governor between the years 6-7 C.E. Because Luke 2:2 noted that this was the first enrollment (apographe), some scholars have conjectured that Quirinius may have been responsible for more than one census.

They suggest that perhaps the 6-7 C.E. census that we know of was the second census and perhaps Quirinius had been governor at an earlier time. There is a gap in the known list of governors that falls between 3-2 B.C.E., so perhaps Quirinius was the governor whose name is missing between these dates. This would harmonize the Matthean and Lukan accounts so that it could be estimated that Jesus was born between 3 and 2 B.C.E. The theory is forced. Whenever one must rely on a series of "maybes" and "perhapses" that rise out of lack of good evidence, it is time to become uneasy. In any event, the separate and different accounts in the Gospels do not provide any real help in establishing Jesus' birth date.

Where Was Jesus Born?

Both Matthew and Luke stated that Jesus was born in Bethlehem. Matthew's Gospel (2:3-6) sought to make Jesus' birthplace a fulfillment of a prophecy found in the book of Micah (5:2):

> But you, O Bethlehem Ephrathah, who are little to be among the clans of Judah, from you shall come forth one who is to be ruler in Israel, whose origin is from old, from ancient days.

This particular passage is one of several similar passages added to the original writings of the prophet Micah. The contributor was not someone who lived during the prophet's lifetime in the eighth century B.C.E., but was a sixth-century B.C.E. editor. While the Jews were in exile in Babylon, some of them dreamed of the restoration of Judah under a monarch from the lineage of David — perhaps from the royal Hebrew family that was captive in Babylon. This addition to the work of Micah echoes that dream. Although the prophecy had nothing to do with Jesus, the writer of Matthew reinterpreted it and tried to make it apply to Jesus.

A conservative Christian colleague once said, "Isn't it wonderful that the Holy Spirit could give the passage one meaning in the sixth century and a whole new meaning in the first century!" This I call the "double-bounce" theory of biblical interpretation. The colleague admitted that the same Holy Spirit might give still another meaning to the passage in a later time (the theory would then become "triple-bounce!"). The statement in Micah had nothing to do with Jesus' birth and the use of the prophecy represents the intent of the writer of Matthew to prove that Jesus was the long-awaited Jewish messiah.

There is in Bethlehem a Church of the Nativity, built, so local guides will tell you, over the very grotto where Jesus was born. In fact, a star set in the floor of a niche is said to mark the very spot where the baby is supposed to have rested. Over the centuries, hundreds of thousands of pilgrims have worshipped in this church and at this spot in the belief that this was Jesus' birthplace. Could they all have been in error, or could this really be the place where Jesus was born? Matthew and Luke disagree on the locale of the birthplace in Bethlehem. Matthew wrote of wise men visiting the infant Jesus in a house which was, presumably, the place where he was born (2:11). By the middle of the second century C.E., Jesus' birthplace was identified as a cave — a not unreasonable assumption inasmuch as caves were, and still are, used to house animals in that region.

Most modern scholars believe that Jesus was born in Nazareth, not in Bethlehem. The birth stories are pious fiction or legends composed by Christian writers to demonstrate that Jesus fulfilled Jewish expectations and Jewish prophecy concerning the coming of a messiah. Therefore, references to governmental figures are designed to locate Jesus in time, and the identification of the birth cave and the subsequent erection of a shrine over the cave constitute efforts to locate Jesus in space. The needs of worshippers are met, insofar as through visits to this sacred space they feel that they are able to come into some sort of intimate contact with the founder of their faith system. The work of archaeologists casts doubt on the tradition and the sites.

Childhood and Youth

As the Jesus story in the gospels progresses, Matthew and Luke come into conflict According to the Matthew tradition, Joseph, Mary and Jesus fled to Egypt to avoid Herod's soldiers (2:13-15). Luke, on the other hand, wrote that Jesus was circumcised and then taken to Jerusalem for purification rites before the family returned to Nazareth (2:21-39). There was a time when the church was able to produce Jesus' foreskin as a tangible artifact of the circumcision, but I have been unable to learn what has happened to that precious bit of infant skin in more recent times.

There seems to be little doubt that Jesus grew up in Nazareth in Galilee as the son of the local carpenter, Joseph. Archaeological and historical research into the history of Nazareth indicates that although it was inhabited as early as Neanderthal times (c. 70,000-35,000 B.C.E.), in Roman times it housed only a small Jewish community — a village so small and so insignificant that it was ignored in first-century C.E. geographical references.

Therefore, the Church of the Annunciation, which commemorates the place where the angel Gabriel informed the Virgin Mary that she was to be divinely impregnated when the Holy Spirit would "come upon" her and "overshadow" her (Luke 1:35), is an early Byzantine structure, probably built during the fifth century C.E. All of the other locales (and there are several), which pilgrims to Nazareth are told are associated with Jesus' life, are late inventions and have nothing to do with Jesus. Perhaps the only authentic relic of the past that might be associated with Jesus is "Ain Myriam," the one local spring from which water has been flowing for centuries.

Ministry

So far, excavations associated with sites listed in Christian scriptures as those visited by Jesus have produced nothing that sheds any direct light upon his life. This is particularly true when we look at the environs of Jerusalem. Of course, the Mount of Olives is still there, virtually peppered with sacred spots.

There are the ruins of the Eleona Church where Jesus is supposed to have instructed his disciples about the end of the world; there is the Church of the Lord's Prayer, where Jesus is supposed to have taught his disciples to pray; there is the Mosque of the Ascension, formerly the Church of the Ascension, marking the very spot from which Jesus made his ascension into heaven; there is the Franciscan chapel Dominus Flevit where Jesus is said to have wept over Jerusalem; there are the Church of Mary Magdalene, the Garden of Gethsemane Church, the Grotto of the Betrayal where Judas betrayed Jesus; the Tomb of the Virgin Mary where her body rested before ascending to heaven; and finally the entrance to Jerusalem and Via Dolorosa — the way of sorrows or the way of the cross.

Each site commemorates some Gospel account concerning Jesus' life. None of the locales have any basis in fact. All are separated from Jesus' time by hundreds of years. They are nothing more than structures built to commemorate Gospel stories but without historical bases for their location.

Within the city of Jerusalem, the site of the ancient Jewish temple is covered by the magnificent mosque Harem es-Sharif — the sacred enclave — and other Muslim shrines. We can learn nothing of the Jewish temple in Jesus' time from this locale, except perhaps that the Western wall, where pious Jews still weep over the destruction of the Temple in 70 C.E., remains as a testimonial to the kind of protective walls that once surrounded the structure. Excavations within and around the walled city of Jerusalem provide information about the ancient city, but not about the temple proper nor about Jesus.

The streets that Jesus may have walked are not those where today's faithful Christians carry wooden crosses, observe the stations of the cross and try to ignore souvenir merchants with their olive wood artifacts. The streets of Jesus' day are 10 to 15 or more feet below present walkways, and there is no way of determining whether the way of the pilgrims corresponds to Jesus' reputed journey with the cross.

There is a bit of exposed pavement known as the Lithostratos that has been exposed by excavation in the church built by the Sisters of Sion. The stones appear to have been part of the Praetorium or courtyard of the Antonia — the fortress tower named by King Herod to please Mark Antony. Portions of that same courtyard have been found in excavations under the Convent of the Flagellation and the Greek Orthodox Convent, On the basis of these finds it has been suggested that the Lithosratos covered an area of some 1,500 square meters. It is quite possible that Jesus stood somewhere on this pavement when he was judged by Pilate.

Crucifixion

The Via Dolorosa leads to the Church of the Holy Sepulchre which houses both the place of the crucifixion and Jesus' burial site. The site of crucifixion was called "Golgotha," the place of the skull (Matt. 27:33; Mark 15:22; Luke 23:33; John 19:17). It was located "near the city" (John 19:20) and outside the city, according to Hebrews 13:12. Certainly the burial place would be outside the city walls and probably the place of execution would be too.

It is recorded that when Hadrian visited Jerusalem, he erected a sanctuary to the Roman god Jupiter on the site of the Jewish temple which had remained a desolate ruin since its destruction in 70 C.E. Many view Hadrian's act as an act of desecration, and perhaps it was. On the other hand, it is well known to historians and archaeologists that holy places tend to retain their sacredness and magical power.

However, Hadrian did bar the Jews from Jerusalem, no doubt in part as a reaction to the revolt by Jews (114-117 C.E.) that had shaken Rome's eastern empire just before Hadrian became emperor and also to the Bar-Cochba revolt (132 C.E.) which occurred after he assumed the throne. He did erect a shrine to Jupiter on the holy mountain of Gerazim which was sacred to the Samaritans and he did erect a temple to Venus on Golgotha. It is quite likely that his motivation was, in part, to humiliate the Jews, to desecrate their holy places, and to demonstrate the superiority of the Roman deities over those of the subject people.

Early Christians may have retained some memory of the place where the crucifixion occurred, although their concerns appear to have been focused less on the past and on Jesus' personal history and more on the expected return of Jesus. Perhaps Hadrian deliberately built the Venus temple on a place sacred to Christians, but it was not until Jerusalem became a Christian city when it was conquered in 325 C.E. that Golgotha became a Christian shrine. By this time Venus had been worshipped at the site for nearly 200 years.

Constantine ordered the Venus shrine destroyed, and during the demolition an empty tomb that was supposed to be that of Jesus was "discovered." How it was determined that this was the tomb of Jesus is not recorded, but it should be noted that empty tombs abound in Palestine and most archaeologists have looked into dozens of them. By 335 C.E., the church that now forms the foundation for the present-day Church of the Holy Sepulchre was erected, although only fragments of that early structure remain.

Wondrous discoveries were supposed to have been made at the tomb site. Queen Helena had a dream in which the hiding place of the cross was disclosed. Sure enough, while the queen sat nearby, workers probed a pit and three crosses were found. At this point, I prefer to let the great American writer, Mark Twain, tell the story as he learned it when he traveled to Palestine in 1867. He published it in *The Innocents Abroad* in 1869.

> Here, also a marble slab marks the place where St. Helena, the mother of the Emperor Constantine, found the crosses about three hundred years after the Crucifixion. According to the legend, this great discovery elicited extravagant demonstrations of joy. But they were of short duration. The question intruded itself: "Which bore the blessed Savior, and which the thieves?" To be in doubt in so mighty a matter as this — to be uncertain which one to adore — was a grievous misfortune. It turned the public joy to sorrow. But when lived there a holy priest who could not set so simple a trouble as this to rest? One of these soon hit upon a plan that would be a certain test. A noble lady lay very ill in Jerusalem. The wise priests ordered that the three crosses be taken to her bedside one at a time. It was done. When her eyes fell upon the first one, she uttered a scream that was heard beyond the Damascus Gate, and even upon the Mount of Olives, it was said, and then fell back into a deadly swoon. They recovered her and brought in the second cross. Instantly she went into fearful convulsions, and it was with the greatest difficulty that six strong men could hold her. They were afraid, now, to bring in the third cross. They began to fear they had fallen upon the wrong crosses, and that the true cross was not with this number at all.
>
> However, as the woman seemed likely to die with the convulsions that were tearing her, they concluded that the third could do no more than put her out of her misery with a happy dispatch. So they brought it, and behold, a miracle! The woman sprang from her bed, smiling and joyful, and perfectly restored to health. When we listen to evidence like this, we cannot but believe. We would be ashamed to doubt, and properly, too. Even the very part of Jerusalem where this all occurred is there yet. So there is really no room for doubt.

But who would have dared to chop the sacred cross into the thousands of fragments that are enshrined in Roman Catholic churches throughout the world? If one is to believe that the fragments are truly those from the cross on which Jesus died, then the cross must have been destroyed. More objective scholars suggest that the bits of wood may have been gathered from around the site of the Church of the Holy Sepulchre. In that case, they could just as well have been fragments from the wood of the demolished shrine sacred to Venus.

There have been challenges to the Church of the Holy Sepulchre. One is the so-called Garden Tomb which is located outside the present Turkish walls of Jerusalem. Apparently, those who prefer the Garden Tomb do so because the Church of the Holy Sepulchre lies within the present walls of the ancient city. Through archaeological research, we think we now know the course of the ancient walls, and if the tracing is correct, the Church of the Holy Sepulchre definitely lies outside the ancient city walls even though it is located within the present Turkish walls.

In other words, the location of the Church of the Holy Sepulchre is not an unlikely place for the burial. The Garden Tomb is a late selection and is accepted as authentic only by those millions who follow fundamentalist media preachers. During Passover-Easter season, we see the televangelists standing beside what they term the "true tomb," that is, the Garden Tomb. No present-day scholar attributes any validity to their claims. The so-called Garden Tomb was discovered in 1867. The tomb was probably cut into the rock during the early Byzantine period in the fourth or fifth centuries CE and has nothing to do with the time of Jesus. And, of course, there is no proof that the tomb in the Church of the Holy Sepulchre was that of Jesus.

Perhaps the most dramatic claims are those concerning an artifact known as the "Shroud of Turin" that some believe was associated with Jesus' burial. Few readers of the popular press know that during the fourteenth century there were several shrouds, each of which claimed to be the one that enveloped Jesus' body at the time of burial. Pseudo-scientific claims for the authenticity of the Turin shroud produced dramatic terms to explain the body image, including "radiation scorch" resulting from "bursts of radiant energy," whatever those terms meant. Carbon-14 dating has demonstrated that the Shroud is a fourteenth-century forgery and is one of many such deliberately created relics produced in the same period, all designed to attract pilgrims to specific shrines to enhance and increase the status and financial income of the local church.

Shrines and Symbols

I have no quarrel with those who visit sacred places for the renewal and deepening of their faith. I can appreciate the fact that since the establishment of the Church of the Nativity and the Church of the Holy Sepulchre in the fourth century, millions of Christians have made pilgrimages to these sites and have paid homage to their beliefs. I can also understand the ways in which those who go to these shrines today can feel a linkage to the hundreds of thousands of others who have preceded them over the centuries. But to make a pilgrimage that links one to a Christian fellowship that extends back through time and that deepens one's commitment to the highest values and ethics of the Christian faith is quite different from visiting these shrines in the belief that the spots are sacred because they have had some actual physical association with Jesus.

To hear and watch pre-Easter advertisements by fundamentalist ministers who seek to persuade the uninformed to join them in a trip to Jerusalem to visit, among other places, the Garden Tomb which they state is the authentic tomb of Jesus, insults my intelligence, promotes ignorance and discards the best results of conscientious modern historical and archaeological scholarship.

As an educator in the humanities, as one committed to seeking to help produce a culturally literate society and committed to educating students and the public in the best understanding of the past, I am frustrated by the ignorance of history and science in so many of my audiences. Many participants come from solid liberal churches and from good high schools and colleges. Unfortunately, in these institutions, the findings of the best biblical scholarship are ignored or watered down, and as a result faith tends to replace reason.

Jesus is an important figure in western thought, but the Jesus that seems to matter most is the Jesus of religious fiction, the so-called "Christ of faith." As a symbol, Jesus can be an inspirer of the finest ethical traditions that humans have developed. What must be clearly maintained is the fact that we are dealing with a faith symbol and that the historical Jesus has been lost in the mist of time. The Christ of faith is a creation of religious believers who have taken the historical figure and clothed it in mythological swaddling bands in the same way that ancient Egyptians took Osiris, who may have been a historical figure, and mythologized him. Osiris was then clothed in the garments of divinity, and sacred spots associated with his fictionalized life were sanctified and became holy.

Conclusion

Our problem, as I see it, is two-fold. The first part is associated with the greed of towns, cities, churches and parishes, that seek to bring tourists and pilgrims to their shrines. They beckon to men and women who spend time gawking at places that may have little to do with what their guides are telling them.

The second problem lies with the educated clergy and teachers in our western world. For whatever reasons, perhaps fear of parishioners, fear of being challenged, fear of controversy, they fail to educate their parishioners and their students by making available the best evidence we have of the past. Of course there are pressure groups, largely composed of fundamentalists, who constantly threaten those of us who do not teach or accept their particular interpretation of the Bible, of Jesus or of life itself. When we, who are committed to the best information and evidence that our research can produce, fail to challenge their assumptions, when we fail to set forth our best evidence, when we bow to the pressure from these special groups and remain silent, we fail in our highest calling as teachers, leaders, thinkers and rationalists and betray our personal sense of integrity.

We can locate Jesus in a general way in time during the first century C.E. He may have been born in any one of the few years before the start of the Common Era. He died during the time of Pontius Pilate (26-36 C.E.), perhaps in the year 29 or 30. We can locate Jesus vaguely in space, but the locales now associated with him are questionable. We cannot locate him archaeologically, because so far, archaeologists have found only what at best might be termed tangential evidence. We can recreate dimensions of the world in which he lived but, outside of the Christian scriptures, we cannot locate him historically within that world.

– Gerald A. Larue

Gerald Larue is an emeritus professor of biblical history and archaeology, University of Southern California, and chairs the Committee for the Scientific Examination of Religion. He is the author of numerous books.

> *" The exact contrary of what is generally believed is often the truth. "*

Jean de la Bruyere

Bone-Box No Proof of Jesus

In the week of October 21, 2002, headlines around the world screamed that evidence of Jesus Christ had been found in the form of an ossuary, or bone-box, supposedly once containing the bones of "James, son of Joseph, brother of Jesus," as was inscribed on the box in Aramaic. The original scholar who reported this spectacular find, the Sorbonne's biblical expert Andre Lemaire, "born a Catholic," concluded it was "very probable" that the inscription referred to Jesus of Nazareth, i.e., Jesus Christ. The ossuary, therefore, would supposedly be that of the biblical "James the Just," who is referred to as Jesus' "brother" at Matthew 13:55 and Galatians 1:19. Naturally, Christian apologists and fanatics rubbed their hands together, and gleefully and smugly bombarded nonbelievers with the news via email. But was there really some wondrous "new proof" of Jesus that would set the record straight once and for all, or was it all another bit of faithful flotsam?

In actuality, it seems to be time once again for the world's religious handlers to pull out another holy relic in order to bolster up the flagging faith. Such shenanigans have been behind the incessant news releases regarding the Shroud of Turin (a more bogus relic there never was), the recent "depiction" of what Jesus would have looked like (a Neanderthal), and the never-ending slew of books concerning the "real Jesus," who invariably resembles the authors of said books. To those who have been around a while and have developed a jaundiced eye, this latest "find" is yet more of the same "evidence."

The original *Biblical Archaeology Review* article that scooped this story was blatant and injudicious in its pronouncements, flatly stating that "This container [ossuary] provides the only New Testament-era mention of the central figure of Christianity and is the first-ever archaeological discovery to corroborate Biblical references to Jesus."

Hillary Mayell, writing for the *National Geographic* (10/21/02), said, "Researchers may have uncovered the first archaeological evidence that refers to Jesus as an actual person and identifies James, the first leader of the Christian church, as his brother."

The article on MSNBC's website regarding the ossuary stated, "No physical artifact from the first century related to him has been discovered and verified."

CNN's Jeordan Legon, in an article entitled, "Scholars: Oldest Evidence of Jesus?" writes, "While most scholars agree that Jesus existed, no physical evidence from the first century has ever been conclusively tied with his life."

Newsweek's Kenneth Woodward opens his article, "A Clue to Jesus?" (11/4/02) by stating:

> Although Jesus of Nazareth is a universally recognized figure, no one has ever found any evidence for his existence apart from texts.

Rossella Lorenzi's article in *Discovery News* is entitled "First Proof of Jesus Found?" This title allows for a couple of interpretations, including that the bone box is the earliest evidence yet discovered. However, in the initial sentence Lorenzi says, "The first archaeological evidence of Jesus' existence has come to light..." and she repeats that "the new find would be the first archaeological discovery to corroborate Biblical references to Jesus," indicating the proper interpretation of the headline to be that there was no prior evidence.

Moreover, Dan Rahimi, the "director of collections" for the museum where it is being housed, stated, "A lot of people accept the reality of Jesus as a historical figure but don't accept him as Christ, and to use the words 'before Christ' is really quite ethnocentric of European Christians..." The article reporting this comment also relates, "Even the date of Jesus' own birth has been disputed for centuries, with many scholars asserting it took place between 4 and 7 B.C., in the autumn months."

On their face value, such headlines and comments imply that there has never been any other proof of Jesus ever found. Such an assertion is quite astounding, considering that Jesus Christ was supposedly a man who shook up the world and purportedly has been supernaturally in charge of the cosmos for the past 2,000 years! What these remarks regarding the "only New Testament-era mention," "first-ever archaeological discovery," "first archaeological evidence," "oldest evidence," and "first proof" reflect is that there has previously been no direct evidence that Jesus Christ ever existed. Moreover, the comment that "a lot of people accept the reality of Jesus as a historical figure" implies that many people recognize this dearth of evidence and do not accept him as "historical figure." In addition, the admission that Jesus's birth date is basically unknown further undermines his "historical reality."

– Acharya S

Excerpt from essay, www.truthbeknown.com

Bone Box Linked to Jesus is a Fake

June 19, 2003: The stone box which many hoped would provide the oldest evidence for the life of Jesus was declared a fake by investigating archaeologists.

"The inscription appears new, written in modernity by someone attempting to reproduce ancient written characters." The inscriptions, possibly inscribed in two separate stages, are not authentic."

– From a statement issued by Israel's Antiquities Authority

Top Selling Items to Crusaders:

- Holy Grail
- Lance of Longinus
- The Turin Shroud
- The Veil of Veronica
- The Holy Manger
- The Swaddling Clothes (for baby Jesus)
- The Holy Stairs Which Jesus Walked Up
- The Scourging Post where Jesus was whipped
- Pieces of the True Cross
- The Holy Nails
- The Seamless Robe
- The Title (Nailed above Jesus' Head)
- The Crown of Thorns
- The Blood of Christ
- Skull of John the Baptist (Younger and Older)
- Christ's Eyelashes
- The Very Finger which Doubting Thomas had poked into the side of His Lord
- Baby Jesus' foreskin

Note: some of these items are still available today

Relics

The "Constantine Christianity" which was invented between the years 312 and 337 A.D., was made up of a broad coalition of the disaffected, ignorant, poor, and "the disposed from Religions, and conquered lands. Constantine was the true Machiavellian — manipulating a group made up of early Christian priests, once persecuted and tortured by the Roman and pagan worshippers. He darkly created enemies for them to fight and unite against. He promised them a place in heaven by killing heretics and non-believers. The results were horrific. Over the following centuries, millions of Muslims, Jews and villagers were slaughtered by followers of the faith.

Thus, the march across Europe and the mid-east began. He also needed a cause. He seized on the recovery of mythical objects from the story of Jesus including the Holy Grail, which was purportedly used at the "Last Supper," and a counterfeit "Lance of Longinus" was carried in subsequent crusades by unknowing believers. The Lance that pierced Jesus was later discovered to have been manufactured five to eight centuries after the alleged crucifixion of Jesus.

Many other artifacts from the life and death of Jesus became popular souvenirs much like pennants, caps and baseballs sold as originals many times over from the World Series.

Catholic Church Perpetuating
Another Religious Hoax?

In Trier, Germany, credulous believers are "flocking" to that city's cathedral in hopes of seeing yet another religious artifact being attributed to one "Jesus Christ." Four thousand of the faithful attended the special mass which kicks off the month-long mystical shindig featuring the "Holy Coat of Trier," a brown robe which some insist was worn by J.C. during his trek to Golgatha and his crucifixion. The garment has been modified a bit over the decades — it now has decorative sections made from silk and a cotton-blend known as taffeta, and in the nineteenth century it was immersed in a rubber solution to preserve it. Reuters news service said that this latter procedure would make it difficult, if not impossible, for carbon dating and other tests which might be useful in establishing the age of this Christic Coat.

Even though the veracity of the "Holy Coat of Trier" depends mostly on legend and blind faith, church and tourism officials are plowing ahead with the celebration. "The local diocese plans to make the most of the pilgrimage with a range of associated events," notes Reuters. The event comes at a time when the German government is spending considerable money promoting tourism around that country's religious events and buildings, including an anniversary for Martin Luther. The "Holy Coat" has been a big box-office draw in years past, too; the diocese organized similar events in 1933 and 1959, attracting a total then of nearly 4,000,000 people.

Just Another Fake?

Church officials are often oblique concerning claims made about relics and other religious artifacts, especially since the debacle over the "Shroud of Turin." After extensive scientific examination, most researchers concluded that the Shroud — purported to be the burial cloth of Jesus Christ — was not consistent with material which had been made twenty or so centuries ago.

Others pointed out that the "miraculous" imagery which seemed to have been projected onto the Shroud was achieved through techniques and materials which are well known.

The "Holy Coat of Trier" has an equally dubious origin. The book *Forgery in Christianity* by Joseph Wheliss (Louisville, 1930) discusses religious fakery, noting: "The possession of the seamless garment of Christ is claimed by the Cathedral of Trier and by the parish church of Argenteuil; the former claims that the relic was sent by the Empress St. Helena, basing their claim on a document sent by Pope Sylvester to the Church of Trier, but this cannot be considered genuine...The relic itself offers no reason to doubt it genuineness. Plenary indulgences were granted to all pilgrims who should visit the cathedral of Trier at the time of the exposition of the Holy Coat, which was to take place every seven years..."

Supporters of the "Holy Coat" echo Wheliss's claim that it was linked to the Empress Helena. She becomes an important link, though, in the story of the garment and some more blatant religious frauds, including the "true cross" upon which the Christian messiah was allegedly crucified. Charles Mackay, author of the insightful book *Extraordinary Popular Delusions and the Madness of Crowds* (London, 1841, Richard Bentley) mentions Helena in his chapter titled "Relics."

> The reliquism of modern times dates its origin from the centuries immediately preceding (sic) the Crusades...The greatest favourite was the wood of the true cross...It is generally asserted, in the traditions of the Romish Church, that the Empress Helen, the mother of Constantine the Great, first discovered the veritable "true cross" in her pilgrimage to Jerusalem. The Emperor Theodosius made a present of the greater part of it to St. Ambrose, Bishop of Milan, by whom it was studded with precious stones, and deposited in the principle church of that city. It was carried away by the Huns, by whom it was burnt, after they had extracted the valuable jewels it contained.

Mackay notes that fragments of the "true cross" periodically appeared, enough so that "if collected together in one place, (would) have been sufficient to have built a cathedral."

Of these fragments, he added: "Happy was the sinner who could get a sight of one of them; happier he who possessed one!" and "Annual pilgrimages were made to the shrines that contained them, and considerable revenues collected from the devotees."

Mackay and other authors have noted the popularity of "relics" with credulous, un-critical religious believers. Some examples include tears shed by J.C., drops of blood from Jesus or Mary, breast milk from Mary, even hair and toenail fragments which, says Mackay, "were sold at extravagant prices."

> Many a nail, cut from the filthy foot of some unscrupulous ecclesiastic, was sold at a diamond's price, within six months after its severance from its parent toe, upon the supposition that it had once belonged to a saint or an apostle.

Another religious artifact hauled away by Empress Helen were the "Holy Stairs" which supposedly once graced the private home of Pontius Pilate. Mackay says:

They are said to be the steps which Jesus ascended and descended when brought
into the presence of the Roman governor. They are held in the greatest veneration at Rome...the knees of the faithful must alone touch them in ascending or
descending, and that only after the pilgrims have reverentially kissed them.

Helena was also responsible for the construction of both the Church of
the Holy Sepulcher and the Church of the Nativity. These mark the alleged
burial and birth places of the Messiah.

Are any of these artifacts truly authentic? Probably not. Helena's pilgrimage to Jerusalem took place in 325 C.E.; the sale of "relics" was already a
thriving business for the unscrupulous. Copies of the same "real" item were
sold to numerous buyers. There was even the grisly trafficking in human
bones which were said to belong to the "Holy Innocents," those children allegedly massacred by King Herod in his attempt to kill the infant messiah.
Figures on the number of "Holy Innocents" range from 14,000 to as many as
144,000, assuring a nearly-perpetual source of bones for the satisfaction of
relic enthusiasts.

Texts considered sacred even by Christians fail to give any provenance or
documentary support that the artifacts claimed as genuine by Empress (St.)
Helena are truly authentic. Matthew 27:35 states "And they crucified him,
and parted his garments, casting lots..."

A Variant of "Grail" Lore?

The legend surrounding the "Holy Coat" is of the same folklore as that
which eventually fostered the story about the "Holy Grail." Indeed, the "holy
coat" garment in Matthew disappears, and the story of the Joseph of Arimathea quickly appears. By verse 57, Matthew tells how this man obtained
the body of the messiah from Pilate and buried it in a tomb — later immor-
talized by Helena's Church of the Holy Sepulchre in Jerusalem. In non-bibli-
cal legend, though, Joseph ends up with the cup mentioned by Matthew back
in chapter 22, verse 27; like the cross, and the "Holy Coat" and the tomb, the
cup passed into mythic history in the form of the "Holy Grail," and the tales
about King Arthur. Joseph transported the cup, according to the legend, all
the way to Glastonbury in southwestern Britain; from there, the tale was further embellished by the monks at the nearby Abbey of Glastonbury.

And More About Helena...

Aside from being a frenetic collector of religious relics of questionable
authenticity, Helena (later made a "saint" by the Vatican) was the mother of
Constantine the Great, who did much to make Christianity the official religion of the post-pagan Roman Empire. One of his ambitious projects was to

re-build the old city of Jerusalem, where successive layers of religious temples to various gods had been constructed over the centuries. He began by tearing down the temple built for the worship of Jupiter; underneath was a small cave with a ledge and a large rock nearby. For zealous Christians of the time, including Helena, that was "proof" that they had found the tomb of the messiah constructed by Joseph of Arimathea. According to historian John Romer in his book *Testament*, the discovery of this "holy of holies" was "an identification based, like Christianity itself, on faith."

Meanwhile, the aged Helena arrives in Jerusalem on her pilgrimage with numerous other believers. Romer describes how: "Aided by the equally aged Bishop Marcarius, using prayers, dreams and diligent questioning, Helena discovered the True Cross of Jesus, with Pilate's wooden label still beside it… most of the sacred wood was shipped back to Constantinople; since those days it has been distributed in thousands of splinters throughout Christendom. After carefully measuring all of these fragments that he could find, a French divine the nineteenth century concluded that their combined volume would not amount to sufficient wood on which to crucify a man! But such rationalism, however well intentioned, belies the relics' true power…"

Indeed, the "true power" of scraps of wood, drops of water or blood and other religious relics, is not that they are true in any historical or physical sense, but that they are believed. Many continued to accept the authenticity of the Shroud of Turin, despite considerable scientific evidence that it could not have existed at the time Jesus Christ is said to have lived; others would "believe" in the verisimilitude of the "Holy Coat of Trier" if exacting scientific examination showed that it also was a fake.

– AANEWS, from: american.aethiests, aanews@listserv.atheists.org

The Crown of Thorns

The wreath set upon Jesus' head in mockery of a king's crown is of a class of artifacts called liturgical relics — objects or mementos connected with a holy person or a saint, or the body or a body part of such an individual People have venerated liturgical relics through time — feverishly in the first millennium since Christ, and even to some extent today — as being imbued with healing powers or having particular emanations owing to their association with a holy person.

– Harvey Rachlin,
Excerpt from *Lucy's Bones, Sacred Stones & Einstein's Brain*

Ecce Homo by Quentin Massys, ca. 1520

Presently, at least two crowns exist without thorns, which were said to have been broken off and distributed throughout the centuries. At various times, thorn counts have been as high as 700.

Spear of Destiny

The Spear that pierced Jesus' side when he was dying on the cross is called The Spear of Destiny. It is also known as the Holy Lance, The Lance of Longinus and Spear of Longinus.

According to Christian legend, possessing the spear has determined victory in several prominent world battles throughout the ages. It has been in the hands of some of the most dominant leaders in history such as Constantine, Justinian, Otto the Great and Adolph Hitler, who all believed in its supernatural power.

The Spear of Destiny

In truth, there are many purported spears or lances in existence. The spear that was kept by the Holy Roman Emperors now sits in a museum located in Vienna, Austria. Recent metallurgy dates it no earlier than the seventh century C.E. It is the sort of weapon which would commonly have been issued to Roman infantry, but there is no telling how many were made during the reign of the Roman Empire. There is a piece of metal in it which has been identified by hopefuls as a crucifixion nail (the *crucifixion* nail), but it has been altered.

Holy Chalice

In Christian legend and belief the holy chalice is the vessel which Jesus used at the last supper as a wine goblet. It is not mentioned in any account in canonic New Testament nor in any early non canonic literature, leading most anthropologists and historians to dismiss it as a fictional piece used to authenticate early stories and legends. Unfortunately the quest for the recovery of the chalice which is also identified as the Holy Grail has lead to the un-merciful slaughter by crusaders and other religious zealots throughout history.

There is a silver gilt chalice at The Cloisters, part of the Metropolitan Museum of Art in New York City which was made at Antioch, early in the sixth century. It was first recovered just prior to World War I and was celebrated as "The Holy Chalice," although the museum refers to this title as "ambitious."

Illustration by Arthur Rackham, 1917

X

New Takes, New Consequences

Witches

The Witch Trials primarily took place in Europe from about 1450 to the middle of the eighteenth century. At that time, accusations of malicious, harmful Satanic witchcraft were taken quite seriously. The victims of these charges were usually, but not exclusively women. Older women who lived alone were typical suspects.

Scholarly estimates about the numbers of people tortured, imprisoned and sometimes executed range between 150,000 to over 1,000,000. Most agree that at least 40,000 were killed and some claim that count is no less than 100,000. The trials were most common in England, France, Scotland, Italy, and Germany; they also occurred in Scandinavia, Spain and Ireland to a lesser degree, however the outcomes could be just as horrific

In Colonial America, the most noted Witch Trials were held in Salem, Massachusetts in 1692.

Exodus 22, 17 or 18

The entire sentence in Hebrew consists of 3 words:
Exodus 22: 17 or 18
The translation of each word is as follows:
    hebrew word meaning "sorcerer" = sorcerer
    hebrew word meaning "no, not" = no, not
    hebrew word meaning "resurrection, revival" = resurrection, revival

What then is the best translation into English? The King James Version translates it as, "Thou shalt not suffer a witch to live." This fit King James' agenda. He believed that witches were "raising storms against his ships," as he wrote in *Newes from Scotland* (1592). He also wrote a tract called *Daemonologie* (1597), and was actively persecuting witches, so his prejudices are clear.

Moreover, several arguments can be made against his translation. There is no evidence that witches were known to the writers of Exodus. To them a sorcerer would likely have referred to a magician of the Egyptian court from which they had just escaped. Exodus 7:11 refers to Pharaoh's "sorcerers," using the same word in Hebrew. There King James does not translate the Hebrew as "witches," probably because "Pharaoh's witches" would have been too obvious an anachronism.

Those ancient Egyptian priests practiced embalming, and legend suggests they claimed to be able to raise the dead, although they were forbidden to do so. Thus it makes sense that the writer of Exodus 22: 18 would have been refuting this claim. Hence we suggest, "A sorcerer cannot raise the dead," as a plausible translation.

However, the context of the line, coming in a series of lines listing punishments, suggests another translation, "A sorcerer shall not be resurrected." Which would imply that only Yahweh (Jehovah) had the power to resurrect, and the punishment for those who thought they could raise the dead, was that they themselves would not be resurrected. To combine the both senses, "A sorcerer cannot raise the dead, neither will he be raised from the dead by the Jehovah."

– Flash Light, Webmaster for www.polytheism.org

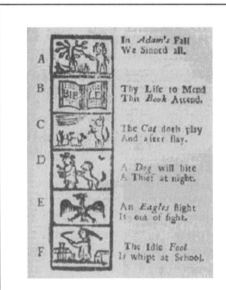

The Puritan Theocracy: In the *New England Primer*, the lesson for the letter "A" began in typical fashion: "In Adam's Fall, We Sinned All."

Hermes vs. Puritans

The contemporary social arena of the United States is characterized by a cacophony of competing voices, all claiming to be the authentic, the true voice of this country. On the left of the socio-political spectrum, we hear many voices heavily colored by late nineteenth- and early twentieth- century European thoughts. I am referring here primarily to the dialectical materialism of Marx and Engels in its several variants, some amplified by Lenin. Marxist thought has become well-nigh normative for the American left.

On the opposite end of the spectrum we find a frequently confused mélange of nineteenth century Protestant fundamentalist Christianity, liberally mixed with the economic outlook of the Industrial Revolution. As the Left talks of concern for the disadvantaged and other human values, so the Right dwells on tradition and family values, by which it means anything from the work ethic of the last century to sexual repression and the bashing of almost anyone who disagrees with these positions.

Who or what, then, is the true American? Who speaks for America? Does the land of the free and home of the brave, the land of opportunity, the nation of the Statue of Liberty, have an authentic voice? Or, is the cacophony of voices we hear the only voice of this land and this culture?

In my view there are three Americas. The first is ancient, or "Shamanic America" (discussed in another chapter in my book). The second is "Hermetic America," and the third is "Puritan America," which in most respects has acted as the opposing force to Hermetic America.

To gain an understanding of Hermetic America, we need to go back a considerable distance in history, to the Alexandrian period of late antiquity. At this time, the Greek god Hermes, son of Zeus, messenger of the gods and patron of communications and commerce, became fused archetypally with the god-form of the Egyptian god Thoth, lord of mind, scribe of the gods and patron of transformation. The result was the splendid mystery system of gnosis, closely related in spirit to the schools of Christian Gnosticism. A large and deeply inspiring body of mystical literature came into existence, all attributed poetically to Hermes-Thoth and designed to facilitate the spiritual insight, transformation, and ultimate liberation of the human soul.

The hermetic renaissance was in full swing when Columbus came to America. It flourished in England at the time of Elizabeth I, and thus the immediate ethnic and cultural parent-country of North America became thoroughly "hermeticized" at the very time when England was beginning her colonial expansion in the world.

Thus hermetic and neo-hermetic currents were rapidly transplanted from England to America and were frequently rein¬forced by the emigration to the New World of European esotericists of a hermetic orientation, such as German Rosicrucians from Central Europe. From Lord Francis Bacon, the Elizabethan scholar and hermetic wise man, to Johannes Kepler, the German astronomer and wizard, and beyond, esoteric influences, largely of hermetic origin, were brought to bear on the newly founded colonies of North America.

By the time of the American Revolution, the hermetic renaissance was fused to a considerable extent with the originally French movement of the enlightenment. Thus the normative leadership of the American Revolution, particularly its intellectual wing led and exemplified by Benjamin Franklin, was thoroughly imbued with the spirit of the hermetic enlightenment.

The founders of the American republic proceeded to create a model government, hitherto unheard of in history, a republic founded on the philosophy of the hermetic enlightenment and expressing, with certain modifications made necessary by the different historical era, the wisdom of the Corpus Hermeticum and other hermetic books.

This is how Hermes came to America, and this is how we can state today, perhaps to the discomfort of some, that the chief inspirer of the American republic was not Moses or Jesus, and even less Saint Augustine or Saint Thomas Aquinas, but rather Hermes Trismegistus of old. Hermes, who survived among the alchemists, magicians, Rosicrucians, esoteric Freemasons and the French enlightenment philosophers, crossed the Atlantic on his winged sandals and stood with his caduceus in the first assemblies of the Continental Congress.

There is no doubt that mystical, hermeticized freemasonry played a great role in the eighteenth-century establishment of a hermetic republic on the far side of the Atlantic. The emissary of the revolutionary colonists to France, Benjamin Franklin, was an ardent Freemason who established close links with leading members of that fraternity at the Lodge of the Nine Sisters in France.

Hermetic America

The question now arises: What was the content of this hermetic teaching that was transmitted to the early leadership of the American republic by various circles of the hermetic-Rosicrucian-Masonic enlightenment? To answer this question, I begin with a shorthand account, or abbreviated summary, of those points of the hermetic transmission that have a direct bearing on the founding of the American republic.

The first of the important principles brought into the fabric of the new commonwealth from the hermetic enlightenment was the separation of church and state. This principle was unheard of in any part of the world or in any government at the time of the founding of the United States. Under the Constitution, no longer was there an established faith. By law the government completely disengaged itself from the business of religion. The most that religious minorities could expect from other governments up to this time was "tolerance." This meant that, while maintaining an officially established state religion, the authorities would nevertheless patiently endure (tolerate means "to endure" in Latin) the exercise of a different religion on the part of some.

The prototype of tolerant monarchs was no doubt Frederick the Great, who uttered the famous words, "Let everyone be saved after his own fashion," but who still maintained the established Lutheran Church of Prussia. The founders of the American republic clearly went beyond that.

The popularly advanced theory accounting for the separation of church and state in America is that, since there were several religions present and flourishing in the colonies, it was best to make religion a private matter and thus diffuse potential sectarian dissension. However, in view of the hermetic influences that were brought to bear on the founders, it might be assumed that this was not the only reason for their attitude. The hermetic enlightenment as a whole was not interested merely in the absence of religious strife; rather, it felt that there was something profoundly wrong with the theologies of all existing religious denominations in the culture, and that for this reason, none of them ought to be supported. The issue was not that one did not know which of the religions was right, but rather that one knew, or at least suspected, that all of them were wrong.

One of the major disagreements between the hermetic enlightenment on the one hand and the various denominations of Christianity and Judaism on the other concerned the God concept. All denominations of Christendom at that time, as well as followers of Judaism, were adherents of theism, a belief in a personal God, creator, maintainer, and judge of the world, who is personally involved in the management of creation at every moment of time. In the eyes of the hermetic thinkers of the enlightenment, this concept had shown itself to have not only theoretical flaws, but also to be responsible for certain practical ills, such as the divine right of rulers, the presence of religious law within the fabric of society, and many more.

If God was actively involved in all the affairs of the world and of humans, it was easy to envision that this same God instituted the existing governmental and social structure and that the state ought to enforce God's ordinances in order to please Him. By their separation of church and state, we can infer that the founders of the United States were not in favor of such a God.

The men and women of the enlightenment were usually not theists, but deists. Deists accepted a Supreme Being as the ultimate origin and the final destiny of all beings and of the universe, but they were convinced that this

Godhead did not actively manage the universe or interfere in the affairs of humankind. Theirs was the "Alien God" of the hermeticists and Gnostics, also known at times as Deus Absconditus, "the God who has gone away."

(Esotericists of various schools and historical periods shared in this conviction. The aforementioned late nineteenth-century figure of the esoteric revival, H. P. Blavatsky, was extremely emphatic in her denial of a theistic concept of God. The heterodox religious views of many of the founding fathers were not only a matter of privately held conviction: Benjamin Franklin even wrote a liturgy for a new religion based on deistic, hermetic principles, and sent a copy of it to Jean Jacques Rousseau, who accepted it with pleasure and presumably with approval.)

The second distinctively hermetic feature of the American republic was the three-branch theory of government. Although it is not very well known, the United States became and remained in effect a constitutional, elective monarchy, wherein the monarch (named, or misnamed, "president") has far broader powers than the present constitutional monarchs of Europe. At the time the Constitution was framed there was even serious debate that the president ought to have the title "Serene Highness," indicating the monarchial character of the office.

Another important consideration is the source of the legitimacy of government. In the prevailing arrangement in Europe at the time, it was understood that the source of legitimacy was the will or grace of God. However, the founders of American government decided that the will of the people, or "the just consent of the governed," made a government legitimate. Here we find the hermetic principles powerfully at work again. Ever since Alexandrian Egypt, hermetic teachings have always given prominence to the god-like power and dignity of the human soul. The human soul is not a mere creation of God, but rather is divine in origin and in its essential nature, and as such cannot be forever subjected to external authority.

The human was constituted as someone who causes events to occur and not as someone who is the passive recipient of the effects of an external divine will. As free agents, citizens may contract with each other to form associations such as state and nation and are not destined to remain subjects of rulers who are foisted on them. The social contract theory of Montesquieu also served as one of the inspirations for this feature of American government.

Finally, one must consider the hermetic principle, more than any other, came to permeate not only American government but the entire history of the United States. The hermetic vision of existence declares that life is a process, not a fixed condition. Because of this, life cannot be managed, but rather must be permitted to function. In this vision, government is like a master of the alchemical art, who guards and oversees the process, but does not interfere with it. The less the government interferes with the life process of the body politic, the better.

If citizens are free to move about, to keep their earnings, to take up trades and professions and engage in business as they choose, the process works. Thus, politically, religiously, socially, and economically, the existing forces, rather like the alchemical salt, sulfur, and mercury, freely interact with each other, the result is growth, transformation, and the unfolding of countless, latent potentials of a beneficent nature. The guiding principle of this process is not the petty, obsessive, and tyrannical Old Testament God, but rather Hermes, shepherd of the forces of being, the facilitator and wise alchemical transformer of all things.

Puritan America

In contrast to the hermetic spirit, however, is another element in American life, which from the very beginning was different from and indeed antagonistic toward the hermetic enlightenment. This opposing idea was Puritanism, or the Calvinist Protestant form of Christianity. In many ways Puritanism became an entire lifestyle, a powerful force, influencing public life throughout American history.

The puritans were transplanted from England, following in the footsteps of John Calvin, the theocratic tyrant of Geneva, who was known to put people into prison for such "crimes" as dancing. Inspired by Calvin's disciple, John Knox, the ranting scourge of Scotland, English puritans had become the cause of much anguish in their home country. Some of them came to America in 1630, close on the heels of the Pilgrims, who were not puritans and who had arrived in 1620.

Oliver Cromwell, whose associates cruelly executed King Charles I, instituted a pious dictatorship in which Christmas was outlawed and merry old England was stripped of virtually all color and beauty. This cruel and boring regime was eventually replaced by the restored monarchy of the House of Stuart, and Cromwell's puritan friends were increasingly subjected to the ire of just about everybody. Many of them decided to sail over the Atlantic, to join their fellows in Massachusetts.

The puritans are remembered in sentimentalized literature and art as a harmless sort of immigrant folk, and are confused with the Pilgrims, who sought religious freedom denied to them in their homeland. However, the truth is that the puritans had denied similar freedom to so many for so long that they were driven out of their homeland as a punishment for very real misdeeds. They soon distinguished themselves in the New World by hanging not a few alleged witches, and this at a time when that curious practice was already nonexistent elsewhere. Looking to more recent times, we note that the Dutch puritans who settled South Africa became the inventors and perpetuators of apartheid. An altogether unpleasant record, one might say.

Unfortunately, matters did not rest there. Puritan ideology exercised an uncanny influence on practically all of American Protestantism (and, one must admit, on much of Irish-dominated, Jansenist American Catholicism also). Not only the direst extensions of the Calvinist tradition, such as the Presbyterian and Reformed churches, but innumerable other ecclesiastical bodies have become saturated with Calvinist ideas and with puritan values and life-style.

In innumerable ways, the United States became a very Calvinist country, more so than Switzerland, Scotland, and Holland, the original strongholds of this faith. Deism and the hermetic world view appealed to the cultural elite, while Puritanism, originally ensconced in New England, spread its principles (modified at times) to the broad masses and to every state. Whether Jacksonian Democrat or Lincolnian Republican, the "Common Man" of American history always had at least a partially Calvinist element in his character.

Four features of Calvinism (or Puritanism) need to be emphasized here. The first is that the God-image of Calvinism is Old Testament in the extreme. Luther was the reformer representing Christ, Calvin the one representing Yehovah. It has been wisely noted by C. G. Jung and others that the God whom people worship places his signature on their psyches. The God-image of the Calvinists is radically at odds with the deism of the founders of the republic, and its influence has been characterized by harshness, vengefulness, and cold-hearted cruelty. (It must be remembered that Calvin and his associates did not avail themselves of the refined and softened theology of later rabbinical Judaism, in which this God-image underwent salutary modifications. Calvin's God came straight out of the Old Testament and out of his projections placed upon the same.)

The second point is that Calvinism is by nature and history theocratic in orientation. Pious dictatorship had been very much a part of the history of this religion. The petty, intolerant, and obsessive image of its God was mirrored in the public conduct and policy of its members. Early American history bears abundant testimony to the Calvinist desire to control public as well as private life. Witches were hanged, and sinners were placed in the pillory or branded with a scarlet letter as part of this syndrome. A fairly direct line runs from Cotton Mather and his clerical judges to such modern movements as the Moral Majority. Clearly, the hermetic principle of the separation of church and state was never seriously endorsed by the Calvinist mentality.

A prominent feature of Calvinist belief is the doctrine of predestination. While originating in abstract theology, this doctrine came to be universally interpreted to mean that those following the Calvinist ethic were the new "chosen people." Material wealth and success were regarded as the signal hallmarks of divine favor accorded to those predestined for salvation. From this it followed that Calvinists, and those influenced by them, became ambitious, success-oriented, and often ruthless.

Euphemistically, this attitude was submerged under the innocuous term "the work ethic," ostensibly a wholesome, decent, and virile creed, which at the same time carried an enormous shadow. This feature of Calvinism soon joined in an unholy alliance with the capitalism born of the industrial revolution. The robber baron, the unscrupulous business person of our culture, is not a hermetic but a Calvinistic figure. Thus, from early times onward, the Calvinist or puritan spirit countermanded and minimized many of the great advantages the hermetic spirit had bestowed on America. This tendency has not ceased even today.

Finally, Puritanism is in fact what we colloquially mean by the term. It is characterized by extreme moralizing in respect to personal life and conduct, conjoined with considerable laxity when moral principles are applied to politics or business. It implies a joyless, dour attitude toward the pleasurable side of human life on the surface, compensated by fierce greed and a lust for power underneath. (A poignant jest has it that a Calvinist preacher declared ice cream must have been invented by the devil because it tastes so good. Along the same line, H.L. Mencken defined Puritanism as "the haunting fear that someone somewhere may be happy.") Depth psychology reveals that this kind of obsessive, repressed life-style holds great dangers for the psyches of those who adopt it. At the time of his first visit to the United States, Jung spoke of this matter in an interview printed in *New York Times* of September 29, 1912:

> When I see so much refinement and so much sentiment as I see in America, I look for an equal amount of brutality. The pair of opposites — you find them everywhere. I find the greatest self-control in the world among the Americans — and I search for its cause…I find a great deal of prudery. I ask, what is the cause and I discover brutality. Prudery is always the cover for brutality. It is necessary — it makes life possible until you discover the brute and take real control of it. When you do that in America, then you will be the most feeling, the most temperamental, the most fully developed people in the world.

The natural result of a lack of self-knowledge is the exercise of a repressive and judgmental will. Those who do not know themselves must ever try to control themselves, without knowing whom or what they are attempting to control. The Calvinistic moral attitude is the direct antithesis of the gnosis represented by Jung. Prudery, repression, and artificial rules for moral behavior serve only to hide (at times to fortify) dangerous instinctual forces and psychological complexes in the unconscious. Thus Jung foresaw many of the future dilemmas of American culture.

Defending Our Hermetic Heritage

From this vantage point it is clear that the principal features of hermetic America and puritan America have differences which are portentous and still very much with us. A profound and seemingly irreconcilable conflict rends the soul of America in two. While in some subtle way, this conflict may also be envisioned as an alchemical process, it is still incumbent upon those who perceive the hermetic heritage of this country to try to defend it and save it from being engulfed by its opposite. Only by recalling and supporting the hermetic qualities of the American vision will the beneficent alchemical operation envisioned by the founders be permitted to do its work.

What then should be the course of action? First, let us recognize the existence of the conflict and consciously understand and articulate its nature and significance. In the legend of the grail-hero Parsifal, the hero encounters the wounded fisher king Amfortas, and asks a simple question: "What ails thee, uncle?" If, like Parsifal, we ask the right question, we too may become the healers of the kingdom. What ails our culture more than any other illness is the continuing, insidious, and perilous conflict between the original hermetic archetypal matrix of the republic on the one hand, and the puritan complex on the other. Crime, economic woes, blunders in foreign policy, the human failings of statesmen: all of these are symptoms of the greater, underlying conflict. Will the hermetic vision prevail? Or will the encroachments of an archaic, unconscious religiosity, and of a gravely flawed world view and life-style based on them, drive the American people and culture farther and farther away from the goals envisioned by the founders of this nation?

Finally, we need to take our stand and begin vigilantly to sift the hermetic wheat from the puritan chaff in contemporary public life. Conservatives ought not to allow themselves to be taken in by slogans and ideas that are not truly conservative at all. What sane individual could envision Dr. Franklin storming clinics where abortions might be performed? Could Thomas Jefferson sanction the government interfering with the most private activities of citizens in their homes? These men, like other sensible persons everywhere, knew freedom to be one and undivided; they knew that people are either free privately as well as in public, or they are not free at all.

Liberals ought to cease seeking remedy for all ills in more government, manipulation, and interference. The passing of large numbers of laws, as Lao Tse recognized, leads to greater lawlessness; the increase of regulations increases confusion and unruliness. Governments do not exist to manage and regulate the lives of citizens but to ensure a setting in which the inherent powers and talents of persons can develop and flourish. Every good government in history has been small in size, restrained in the exercise of power, and kept at a distance when it concerned the personal, economic, and political freedoms and privacy of people. The advancement of commendable causes ought not to be used as an excuse to increase government and to dwarf the freedom and initiative of individuals.

Hermetic America contains the remedy for the ills that have befallen us in this age. The remedy is freedom. With freedom, the alchemy of the spirit corrects the flaws of culture and rectifies the excesses of civilization.

– Stephan A. Hoeller, Ph.D.

Stephan A. Hoeller, Ph.D. *is a Gnostic and Jungian scholar whose fourth book,* Freedom: The Alchemy of a Voluntary Society, *was published by Quest Books in June 1992.*

> *Toward no crimes have men shown themselves so cold-bloodedly cruel as in punishing differences of belief.*

James Russell Lowell

To Those Who Are
Investigating "Mormonism"

If you are investigating Mormonism (the "Church of Jesus Christ of Latter-day Saints" or "LDS Church"), you are probably studying it in private meetings in your home with missionaries from that church. Here are some of the key things that they are probably telling you:

Mormonism began in 1820 when a teenage boy in western New York named Joseph Smith was spurred by a Christian revival where he lived to pray to God for guidance as to which church was true. In answer to his prayers he was visited by God the Father and God the Son, two separate beings, who told him to join no church because all the churches at that time were false, and that he, Joseph, would bring forth the true church. This event is called "The First Vision."

In 1823 Joseph had another heavenly visitation, in which an angel named Moroni told him of a sacred history written by ancient Hebrews in America, engraved in an Egyptian dialect on tablets of gold and buried in a nearby hill. Joseph was told it was the history of the ancient peoples of America, and that Joseph would be the instrument for bringing this record to the knowledge of the world. Joseph obtained these gold plates from the angel in 1827, and translated them into English by the spirit of God and the use of a sacred instrument accompanying the plates called the "Urim and Thummim." The translation was published in 1830 as The Book of Mormon, now revered by Mormons as scripture, along with the Bible.

The Book of Mormon is a religious and secular history of the inhabitants of the Western Hemisphere from about 2200 B.C. to about 421 A.D. It tells the reader that the American Indians are descended from three groups of immigrants who were led by God from their original homes in the Near East to America. One group came from the Tower of Babel, and two other groups came from Jerusalem just before the Babylonian Captivity, about 600 B.C. They were led by prophets of God who had the gospel of Jesus Christ, which is thus preserved in their history, the Book of Mormon. Many of the descendants of these immigrants were Christians, even before Christ was born in Palestine, but many were unbelievers. Believers and unbelievers fought many wars, the last of which left only degenerate unbelievers as survivors, who are the ancestors of the American Indians. The most important event during this long history was the visit of Jesus Christ to America, after his crucifixion, when he ministered to (and converted) all the inhabitants.

Joseph Smith was directed by revelation from God to reestablish ("restore") the true church, which he did in 1830. He was visited several times by heavenly messengers, who ordained him to the true priesthood. He continued to have revelations from God to guide the church and to give more knowledge of the Gospel. Many of these revelations are published in the Doctrine and Covenants, accepted by Mormons as scripture, along with the Bible and the Book of Mormon.

Joseph Smith and his followers were continually persecuted for their religious beliefs, and driven from New York State to Ohio, then to Missouri, then to Illinois, where Joseph Smith was murdered in 1844 by a mob, a martyr to his beliefs. The church was then led by Brigham Young, Joseph's successor, to Utah, where the Mormons settled successfully.

The LDS church is led today by the successors of Joseph Smith. The present president of the church is a "prophet, seer and revelator" just as Joseph Smith was, and guides the members of the church through revelations and guidance from God.

The modern LDS church is the only true church, as restored by God through Joseph Smith. Other churches, derived from the early Christian church, are in apostasy because their leaders corrupted the scriptures, changed the ordinances of the original church, and often led corrupt lives, thus losing their authority.

By accepting baptism into the LDS church you take the first step necessary toward your salvation and your ultimate entrance into the Kingdom of Heaven (the "Celestial Kingdom").

What the Missionaries Will Not Tell You

Until recently, the missionaries were required to present Mormonism in six "discussions," which were a series of memorized sales talks. They are now encouraged simply to "follow the spirit" in their presentations. The basic message and approach, however, is still essentially the same.

Here is a summary of important facts about the Mormon church, its doctrine, and its history that the missionaries will probably not tell you. We are not suggesting that they are intentionally deceiving you — most of the young Mormons serving missions for the church are not well educated in the history of the church or in modern critical studies of the church. They probably do not know the all the facts themselves. They have been trained, however, to give investigators "milk before meat," that is, to postpone revealing anything at all that might make an investigator hesitant, even if it is true. But you should be aware of these facts before you commit yourself.

Each of the following facts has been substantiated by thorough historical scholarship. And this list is by no means exhaustive!

The "First Vision" story in the form presented to you was unknown until 1838, eighteen years after its alleged occurrence and almost ten years after Smith had begun his missionary efforts. The oldest (but quite different) version of the vision is in Smith's own handwriting, dating from about 1832 (still at least eleven years afterwards), and says that only one personage, Jesus Christ, appeared to him. It also mentions nothing about a revival. It also contradicts the later account as to whether Smith had already decided that no church was true. Still a third version of this event is recorded as a recollection in Smith's diary, fifteen years after the alleged vision, where one unidentified "personage" appeared, then another, with a message implying that neither was the Son. They were accompanied by many "angels," which are not mentioned in the official version you have been told about. Which version is correct, if any? Why was this event, now said by the church to be so important, unknown for so long?

Careful study of the religious history of the locale where Smith lived in 1820 casts doubt on whether there actually was such an extensive revival that year as Smith and his family later described as associated with the "First Vision." The revivals in 1817 and 1824 better fit what Smith described later.

In 1828, eight years after he supposedly had been told by God himself to join no church, Smith applied for membership in a local Methodist church. Other members of his family had joined the Presbyterians.

Contemporaries of Smith consistently described him as something of a confidence man, whose chief source of income was hiring out to local farmers to help them find buried treasure by the use of folk magic and "seer stones." Smith was actually tried in 1826 on a charge of "Money-digging." It is interesting that none of his critics seemed to be aware of his claim to have been visited by God in 1820, even though in his 1838 account he claimed that he had suffered "great persecution" for telling people of his vision.

The only persons who claimed to have actually seen the gold plates were eleven close friends of Smith (many of them related to each other). Their testimonies are printed in the front of every copy of the Book of Mormon. No disinterested third party was ever allowed to examine them. They were retrieved by the angel at some unrecorded point. Most of the witnesses later abandoned Smith and left his movement. Smith then called them "liars."

Smith produced most of the "translation" not by reading the plates through the Urim and Thummim (described as a pair of sacred spectacles), but by gazing at the same "seer stone" he had used for treasure hunting. He would place the stone into his hat, and then cover his face with it. For much of the time he was dictating, the gold plates were not even present, but in a hiding place.

The detailed history and civilization described in the Book of Mormon does not correspond to anything found by archaeologists anywhere in the Americas. The Book of Mormon describes a civilization lasting for a thousand years, covering both North and South America, which was familiar with horses, elephants, cattle, sheep, wheat, barley, steel, wheeled vehicles, shipbuilding, sails, coins, and other elements of Old World culture. But no trace of any of these supposedly very common things has ever been found in the Americas of that period. Nor does the Book of Mormon mention many of the features of the civilizations which really did exist at that time in the Americas. The LDS church has spent millions of dollars over many years trying to prove through archaeological research that the Book of Mormon is an accurate historical record, but they have failed to produce any convincing pre-Columbian archeological evidence supporting the Book of Mormon story. In addition, whereas the Book of Mormon presents the picture of a relatively homogeneous people, with a single language and communication between distant parts of the Americas, the pre-Columbian history of the Americas shows the opposite: widely disparate racial types (almost entirely east Asian — definitely not Semitic, as proven by recent DNA studies), and many unrelated native languages, none of which are even remotely related to Hebrew or Egyptian.

The people of the Book of Mormon were supposedly devout Jews observing the Law of Moses, but in the Book of Mormon there is almost no trace of their observance of Mosaic law or even an accurate knowledge of it.

Although Joseph Smith said that God had pronounced the completed translation of the plates as published in 1830 "correct," many changes have been made in later editions. Besides thousands of corrections of poor grammar and awkward wording in the 1830 edition, other changes have been made to reflect subsequent changes in some of the fundamental doctrine of the church. For example, an early change in wording modified the 1830 edition's acceptance of the doctrine of the Trinity, thus allowing Smith to introduce his later doctrine of multiple gods. A more recent change (1981) replaced "white" with "pure," apparently to reflect the change in the church's stance on the "curse" of the black race.

Joseph Smith said that the Book of Mormon contained the "fullness of the gospel." However, its teaching on many doctrinal subjects has been ignored or contradicted by the present LDS church, and many doctrines now said by the church to be essential are not even mentioned there. Examples are the church's position on the nature of God, the Virgin Birth, the Trinity, polygamy, Hell, priesthood, secret organizations, the nature of Heaven and salvation, temples, proxy ordinances for the dead, and many other matters.

Many of the basic historical notions found in the Book of Mormon had appeared in print already in 1825, just two years before Smith began producing the Book of Mormon, in a book called *View of the Hebrews*, by Ethan Smith (no relation) and published just a few miles from where Joseph Smith lived. A careful study of this obscure book led one LDS church official (the historian B.H. Roberts, 1857-1933) to confess that the evidence tended to show that the Book of Mormon was not an ancient record, but concocted by Joseph Smith himself, based on ideas he had read in the earlier book.

Although Mormons claim that God is guiding the LDS church through its president (who has the title "prophet, seer and revelator"), the successive "prophets" have repeatedly either led the church into undertakings that were dismal failures or failed to see approaching disaster. To mention only a few: the Kirtland Bank, the United Order, the gathering of Zion to Missouri, the Zion's Camp expedition, polygamy, the Desert Alphabet. A recent example is the successful hoax perpetrated on the church by manuscript dealer Mark Hofmann in the 1980s. He succeeded in selling the church thousands of dollars worth of manuscripts which he had forged. The church and its "prophet, seer and revelator" accepted them as genuine historical documents. The church leaders learned the truth not from God, through revelation, but from non-Mormon experts and the police, after Hofmann was arrested for two murders he committed to cover up his hoax. This scandal was reported nationwide.

The secret temple ritual (the "endowment") was introduced by Smith in May, 1842, just two months after he had been initiated into Freemasonry. The LDS temple ritual closely resembles the Masonic ritual of that day. Smith explained that the Masons had corrupted the ancient (God-given) ritual by changing it and removing parts of it, and that he was restoring it to its "pure" and "original" (and complete) form, as revealed to him by God. In the years since, the LDS church has made many fundamental changes in the "pure and original" ritual as "restored" by Smith, mostly by removing major parts of it. Many doctrines which were once taught by the LDS church, and held to be fundamental, essential and "eternal," have been abandoned. Whether we feel that the church was correct in abandoning them is not the point; rather, the point is that a church claiming to be the church of God takes one "everlasting" position at one time and the opposite position at another, all the time claiming to be proclaiming the word of God. Some examples are:

- The Adam-God doctrine (Adam is God the Father)
- The United Order (all property of church members is to be held in common, with title in the church)
- Plural Marriage (polygamy; a man must have more than one wife to attain the highest degree of heaven)
- The Curse of Cain (the black race is not entitled to hold God's priesthood because it is cursed; this doctrine was not abandoned until 1978)
- Blood Atonement (some sins — apostasy, adultery, murder, interracial marriage — must be atoned for by the shedding of the sinner's blood, preferably by someone appointed to do so by church authorities).

All of these doctrines were proclaimed by the reigning prophet to be the Word of God, "eternal," "everlasting," to govern the church "forevermore." All have been abandoned by the present church.

Joseph Smith's early revelations were collected and first published in 1833 in the Book of Commandments. God (as recorded in the Doctrine and Covenants Sections 1 and 67) supposedly testified by revelation that the revelations as published were true and correct. Because the Book of Commandments did not receive wide distribution (most copies were destroyed by angry opponents of the Mormons in Missouri, where it was published), they were republished — with additional revelations — as the Doctrine and Covenants in 1835 in Kirtland, Ohio. However, many of the revelations as published in Kirtland differed fundamentally from their versions as originally given. The changes generally gave more power and authority to Smith, and justified changes he was making in church organization and theology. The question naturally arises as to why revelations which God had pronounced correct needed to be revised.

Joseph Smith claimed to be a "translator" by the power of God. In addition to the Book of Mormon, he made several other "translations."

The Book of Abraham, from Egyptian papyrus scrolls which came into his possession in 1835. He stated that the scrolls were written by the biblical Abraham "by his own hand." Smith's translation is now accepted as scripture by the LDS church, as part of its Pearl of Great Price. Smith also produced an "Egyptian Grammar" based on his translation. Modern scholars of ancient Egyptian agree that the scrolls are common Egyptian funeral scrolls, entirely pagan in nature, having nothing to do with Abraham, and from a period 2000 years later than Abraham. The "Grammar" has been said by Egyptologists to prove that Smith had no notion of the Egyptian language. It is pure fantasy: he made it up.

The "Inspired Revision" of the King James Bible. Smith was commanded by God to retranslate the Bible because the existing translations contained errors. He completed his translation in 1833, but the church still uses the King James Version.

The "Kinderhook Plates," a group of six metal plates with strange engraved characters, unearthed in 1843 near Kinderhook, Illinois, and examined by Smith, who began a "translation" of them. He never completed the translation, but he identified the plates as an "ancient record," and translated enough to identify the author as a descendant of Pharaoh. Local farmers later confessed that they had manufactured, engraved and buried the plates themselves as a hoax. They had apparently copied the characters from a Chinese tea box.

Joseph Smith claimed to be a "prophet." He frequently prophesied future events "by the power of God." Many of these prophecies are recorded in the LDS scripture Doctrine and Covenants. Almost none have been fulfilled, and many cannot now be fulfilled because the deeds to be done by the persons named were never done and those persons are now dead. Many prophecies included dates for their fulfillment, and those dates are now long past, the events never having occurred.

Joseph Smith died not as a martyr, but in a gun battle in which he fired a number of shots. He was in jail at the time, under arrest for having ordered the destruction of a Nauvoo newspaper which dared to print an exposure (which was true) of his secret sexual liaisons. At that time he had announced his candidacy for the presidency of the United States, set up a secret government, and secretly had himself crowned "King of the Kingdom of God."

Since the founding of the church down to the present day the church leaders have not hesitated to lie, to falsify documents, to rewrite or suppress history, or to do whatever is necessary to protect the image of the church. Many Mormon historians have been excommunicated from the church for publishing their findings on the truth of Mormon history.

Mormonism includes many other unusual doctrines which you will probably not be told about until you have been in the church for a long time. These doctrines are not revealed to investigators or new converts because those people are not yet considered ready to have more than "milk" as doctrine. The Mormons also probably realize that if investigators knew of these unusual teachings they would not join the church. In addition to those mentioned elsewhere in this article, the following are noteworthy:

- God was once a man like us.
- God has a tangible body of flesh and bone.
- God lives on a planet near the star Kolob.
- God ("Heavenly Father") has at least one wife, our "Mother in Heaven," but she is so holy that we are not to discuss her nor pray to her.
- We can become like God and rule over our own universe.
- There are many gods, ruling over their own worlds.
- Jesus and Satan ("Lucifer") are brothers, and they are our brothers — we are all spirit children of Heavenly Father
- Jesus Christ was conceived by God the Father by having sex with Mary, who was temporarily his wife.
- We should not pray to Jesus, nor try to feel a personal relationship with him.
- "God" ("Jehovah") in the Old Testament is the being named Jesus in the New Testament.
- In the highest degree of the celestial kingdom some men will have more than one wife.
- Before coming to this earth we lived as spirits in a "pre-existence," during which we were tested; our position in this life (whether born to Mormons or savages, or in America or Africa) is our reward or punishment for our obedience in that life.
- Dark skin is a curse from God, the result of our sin, or the sin of our ancestors. If sufficiently righteous, a dark-skinned person will become light-skinned.
- The Garden of Eden was in Missouri. All humanity before the Great Flood lived in the western hemisphere. The Ark transported Noah and the other survivors to the eastern hemisphere.

Your Life as a Mormon

If you should decide to become a member of the LDS church, you should be aware of what your life in the church will be like. Although you will find yourself warmly accepted by a lively community of healthy, active and generally supportive people, many of whom are very happy in Mormonism and could not imagine their lives without it, there is another side:

You will be continually reminded that to enter the highest degree of heaven (the "Celestial Kingdom"), you will have to go through the endowment ceremony in the temple and have your marriage to your Mormon spouse "sealed." (If your spouse is not Mormon, or if you are not married, you cannot enter the highest degree of heaven.) To get permission to have these ceremonies performed in the temple, you must prove yourself to be a faithful and obedient member of the church and do everything commanded by the church authorities, from the Prophet down to the local level. You will have to undergo a personal "worthiness" interview with the local church authorities inquiring into your private life and your religious and social activities.

You will be expected to donate at least ten percent of your income to the church as tithing. Other donations will be expected as the need arises. You will never see an accounting of how this money is spent, or how much the church receives, or anything at all about its financial condition; the church keeps its finances secret, even from its members.

You will be expected to give up the use of alcohol, tobacco, coffee, and tea.

You will be expected to fulfill any work assignment given to you. These assignments may be teaching, record keeping, janitorial work, cannery or farm work, helping in the Sunday nursery — any job that needs to be done. Each task you perform successfully will make you eligible for others, with more responsibility and more demands upon your time. The members who perform these jobs, even those involving sensitive pastoral counseling, receive no formal training whatsoever (there is no paid, trained clergy). You will be told that God has called you to your assignments. Many Mormons find much of their spare time taken up with church work, trying to fulfill the numerous assignments that have been given them.

You will be expected to be unquestioningly obedient to church authorities in whatever they might tell you to do. "Follow the Brethren" is the slogan, and it means to follow without doubt or question. Discussion of whether a decree from above is correct is discouraged. You will be expected to have faith that the leaders cannot possibly lead you astray. Even if they should tell you something which contradicts what a previous prophet may have said, you will be told "A living prophet takes precedence over a dead prophet."

You will be able to "vote" on those who have been called to positions of authority over you, but the voting will be by the show of hands in a public meeting. Only one candidate for each office will be voted on (the one "called by God"). The voting is therefore almost always unanimous in favor of the candidate.

You will be advised not to read any material which is "not faith-promoting," that is, which may be critical or questioning of the church or its leaders, or which might place the church or its leaders in an unfavorable light.

You will be advised not to associate with "apostates," that is, former Mormons. (You will be asked in your "worthiness" interview about this.)

If you are unmarried, you will be encouraged to marry a good Mormon as soon as possible. When you do marry, in a wedding ceremony in the temple, your non-Mormon family members and friends will not be allowed to attend the ceremony, because only "worthy" Mormons are allowed to enter the temple.

If you are homosexual, you will be pressured to abandon this "evil" aspect of your nature. If you do not, you will probably not be fully accepted by other church members. If you do not remain celibate, you may be excommunicated.

If you are a male over 12 years of age and "worthy" (that is, if you are obedient, attend meetings, do not masturbate, etc.), you will be ordained to one of the levels of priesthood, and, if you continue to be faithful and obedient, you will gradually advance through the priesthood ranks. If you are female, you will receive the benefits of priesthood authority only indirectly, through your Mormon father or your Mormon husband. The role of the Mormon woman is to be a wife and mother and to obey and honor her priest husband (or father).

If you prove yourself to be faithful, hard working and obedient, you will eventually be considered worthy to "receive your endowment" in a Mormon temple. You will not be told in advance exactly what to expect in this lengthy ceremony, except that the details of the ritual are secret (Mormons prefer to say they are just "sacred," but they treat them as though they are secret). As part of that ceremony you will be required to swear a number of oaths, the penalty for violation of which is no longer stated but until 1990 was death by various bloody methods, such as having your throat slit from ear to ear. You will be given the secret signs and passwords which are required to enter heaven. After receiving the endowment you will be required to wear a special undergarment at all times.

If you should ever decide that you made a mistake in joining the church and then leave it, you will probably find (judging from the experiences of others who have done so) that many of your Mormon friends will abandon and shun you. If you are unable to convince your family members to leave the church with you, you will find that the church has broken up your family and your relationship with them may never recover.

Consider very carefully before you commit yourself, and remember that any doubts you may have now will likely only increase.

Examine carefully both sides of the Mormon story. Listen to the stories of those who have been through an unhappy Mormon experience, not just those Mormons who may speak glowingly of life in the church.

The Mormon missionaries are often charming and enthusiastic. They have an attractive story to tell. At first it sounds wonderful. But remember the old saying, "If it sounds too good to be true, it probably is!" Be careful not to fall into the trap of believing something simply because you want it to be true. Mormons may tell you that those who criticize the church are lying, misquoting and distorting. If you examine the sources used by the critics, however, you will discover that most of their source material is from official or semi-official Mormon writings. You, too, should examine those sources.

To get more information about the other side of Mormonism, or to see the evidence supporting any of our statements about the church, feel free to contact us. Our only aim is to make sure that you hear both sides. We promise not to preach at you, but only to provide you with facts to balance the Mormon story.

– Richard Packham, Founder of the Ex-Mormon Foundation,
www.exmormon.org

A typical LDS temple will represent a castle or a palace.

Polygamy in the U.S.

The term "Fundamentalist" in religious context refers to extreme and often overzealous followers of the basic tenants of a religion. The Mainstream Mormon Church of Utah is of the belief that there is no such thing as a true "Fundamentalist Mormon," as they are going against the church by living a polygamous lifestyle. Extreme followers of the Mormon Church, who for the sake of this discussion I will refer to as Fundamentalists, believe in a different point of view. They believe that they are following the original teachings of Joseph Smith, the man who founded the Mormon Church. Joseph Smith himself was a polygamist, though the issue was still being hotly debated by him and his wife at the time if his death. Mormonism is founded on the belief that God communicates directly with his followers, though in actual practice his words only hold validity when they come through men. Joseph Smith claimed that polygamy would not feel so good if God did not want it that way. So does a fundamentalist follow what was taught at the beginning of the religion's birth, or do they go by what was last said by the religion's founder, whose words inspired the following in the first place?

Some Mormons believe there were practical reasons for polygamy in the beginning, as polygamy was founded during the slow journey west toward Utah in the early part of the 1800s. Before finally settling in Salt Lake City, the Latter Day Saints attempted to take up residence in already settled towns. The Mormons were large in numbers and adopted a policy of refusing to do business with any nonbeliever. They invariably encountered resistance, which led to the Mormonism's famous history of religious persecution. Since there was much fighting going on during this time, women were often widowed. Polygamy may have been a helpful solution to the problem of single-parent households on the American frontier. According to Fundamentalist doctrines, the women are regarded as being inferior to the men, and all should be in polygamous marriages. A man must take three brides to reach the highest level of the celestial kingdom in the afterlife. Young teenage girls are married off to men who are old enough to be their fathers and sometimes even old enough to be their grandfathers. Current critics of polygamy point out that it is no coincidence that the men are endlessly able to satisfy their sexual desires and always with the most young and often desirable members of the opposite sex. Here the young women become unwilling brides and as a result are raped repeatedly. The young men in the community are sometimes victimized as well, in that they may end up being pushed out of the community so that they do not become competition to the older men. Even when they want to go along with the doctrines of their religion, they are told to get their own wives from the outside. This being a difficult thing to ask of any young woman from other parts of the country, they are left with nobody to marry unless they leave the community. Probably the worst thing about the situation is the oppression involved in women's lives. They are expected to have a baby every year and are often denied medical treatment, relying instead on prayer. "Painkillers are forbidden during deliveries. Stillborn children are routinely buried in back yards, their mothers often denying they were ever pregnant" according to Lu Ann Kingston of Bountiful, another predominantly polygamous community in Utah. Intensive prayer and 40-day fasts are used to rid the body of illness.

There are many reasons for which this practice continues, despite the fact that the young women live in a free country and, in theory, should be able to leave if they choose to. The reasons are varied and complex, often requiring an in-depth look at human nature, as well as Stockholm-Syndrome often associated with kidnapping victims. The people who practice Mormon Fundamentalism are also by design a very private group, and to discuss their situation with outsiders can involve self-incrimination. Another factor may be the inability to communicate with the outside, because even though they may speak the same language as the rest of the country, they may be coming from such a vastly different place that there may be no room for understanding. As the towns have no television and limited access to media, it would go against their beliefs (and comforts) to allow an outsider to come in and gain a full, in-depth perspective of the inside of their lifestyle. So far nobody has done this, and the few members who will give interviews do so only in private and in fear of bringing trouble upon themselves.

First, there is a type of shock that people go through when they are let out of a situation in which their every move was monitored. This enigma has been explored when discussing people who were let out of prison or let out of the military. It can be a very frightening experience to go from a strict world full of boundaries to a world in which there are almost none at all. Even years after her escape from Hildale-Colorado City, Sarah Cooke still finds the independence "unnerving. It's scary, there are almost no rules." They also may be forced to suffer the loss of their family. They might never see their siblings, cousins, moms and friends again if they leave them behind. This alone may be incentive enough for a woman to stay. She would very possibly leave misery only to live the rest of her life in a different kind of misery.

Girls are frequently taken out of school in eighth grade. In an even more controlling move, Hildale-Colorado City community leader Warren Jeffs declared last year that the children are to be taken out of schools and home schooled. His intention was to give the state less say in the community's handling of children, despite the fact that the schools functioned more like a bible school anyway. Lack of education gives the women less of a chance to make informed and objective decisions about their lives. Their ability to express themselves and articulate their situation is limited as well, even if they do know that they want something different out of life than what is being forced upon them. A lack of basic education may deprive them of laying the foundation for constructing a life for themselves based on their own decisions.

Further complicating things is the fact that some girls actually desire to be in polygamous marriages. They will talk about how their plans for the future include a house with a room for the husband, a room for the first wife, a room for the second wife, and so on. This may be the result of having their belief system embedded in them so thoroughly that they set their goals around a limited and prescribed set of parameters. Their decision-making process may also tainted by their having lacked attention from their fathers in their childhood. More specifically, they may be considered to have almost no father, as they may share a dad with several dozen other children. They may already be comfortable with competing for the attention of the men in their lives, having, again, known no other way of life. There are signs around the house that dictate the Mormon Fundamentalist doctrine of "Be sweet, no matter what." These signs are reported to be in every household. The failure to follow the beliefs of their family may simply be felt by the individual as personal failure. Praise and approval are gained only by eagerly doing as they are told, and without question, no matter what it is that they are being asked to do. This can result in a kind of disassociation from one's own self, in which she perceives her unhappiness at a distance and does not consider it to be something that she can or should attempt to seek a solution to. Discouragement can be very powerful and lasting. These effects can be seen when a person is kidnapped, and in a very short time is turned into almost a weapon against his or her own self, in that she will not take opportunities to escape when they are presented. These ideas were widely explored when in June of 2002 a fourteen-year-old girl by the name of Elizabeth Smart was kidnapped by a homeless polygamist and his wife and was held captive for nine months. She had several opportunities to escape, but did not take the opportunities. If one is to look at this effect on a person who is a part of normal society, one can only imagine what it is like to be raised from birth to only accept the confines of the world they are born into.

A strong sense of spirituality can also be a weakness for a girl, and sometimes a boy, in a polygamous community. If he or she believes in heaven and hell and believes in what she reads in the spiritual literature she is given, then she is also to believe that she will go to hell if she refuses to go along with an arranged marriage. She is to believe that if she does not yield to any demands her husband might make of her, she is sinning. In one situation, a man continually coerced his wife into sex acts that she had resistance to. He convinced her for years that if his sexual needs were not being met and he was forced to go outside of the marriage then the sin of adultery would be on her head. These circumstances can lead to a very unusual situation in which the man is brought up to believe that he must consummate the marriage on the wedding night. If his new bride is unwilling to participate, he is forced to decide between sinning and breaking the law. If he doesn't force her into sex, he is sinning, but if he forces her then he is hurting the woman he has just made marital vows to. He is also committing a crime. Furthermore, he is committing a sin if he does not enter into polygamous marriages. There is also a consistent "us and them" feeling about the rest of the world beyond the borders of the community, as the rest of the world is said to be a product of evil, in which sin is abundant. Brainwashing techniques are likely to be easy when they are carried out on young, isolated and uneducated girls. In one example of the dialogue used to persuade already believing and faithful church members, a member of the Hildale-Colorado City who chose to remain anonymous said, "Satan has been jealous of God since day one. Satan wants to rule. He doesn't want God to rule, so he tricks weak people into apostatizing and going over to the other side."

Fear of punishment plays a strong role in convincing girls to stay in their communities as well. They can and will be hunted down by members of their community, and in extreme cases dragged back to their home and punished with belt lashings. The most well-documented cases of women escaping polygamy involve their attempts to escape resulting in such severe physical abuse that they are black and blue and bloody. One woman, Flora Jessop, made it all the way to a gas station only to have her father and uncle catch up with her and take her back home. Women in these situations often face the choice between being put in a mental institution and going along with their arranged marriage, the latter choice being the only one that has any benefits to it.

Even in cases in which the parents are also against their daughter's arranged marriage, the church can retaliate. The church in Hildale-Colorado City owns almost all of the land in the community. The United Effort Plan, or UEP, is the legal name of the financial trust that holds ownership of all of the church's assets, including most of the land in the two towns. The UEP has been known to evict people for not obeying the word of the Church's leader, which carries the same weight as the law. If a couple refuses to give up their daughter to a person she has been assigned to, they face excommunication from the church. This can result in the loss of their home, even if they built it with their own means. The church simply bulldozes their home if and when they are successful in extracting the residents. Excommunication is like a form of death for a person whose community is so entangled with the church. They suddenly find themselves unable to talk to their own family members and neighbors, isolated and alone in their own hometown.

The chief and often misunderstood reason for the community's existence below radar lies in its history. A 1953 police raid on the town was so unsuccessful that it eventually backfired. Law enforcement officials came in during the pre-dawn hours of July 26th and arrested the majority of the community and put the children in foster homes. The church members were defended by civil rights activists when photos were subsequently published of children being ripped from their mothers' arms. These photos were highly publicized, and despite a *Time Magazine* article which published only neutral photos of the raid, the more emotive images had already burned themselves into the memory of the public. The raid is thought to have ruined the political career of then Governor Howard Pyle, who arranged the raid, and the community was left almost entirely alone until the mid-nineties. Even recently the District Attorney, who convicted a man of sex offense crimes within his polygamous marriage to a teenage girl, was not reelected. Many of the citizens of Arizona and Utah descend from polygamists and do not think ill of polygamy enough to prosecute people for it.

Basic geography has had an enormous role in the isolation of Colorado City and Hildale. An area known as "The Strip," the part of Arizona that is home to Colorado City is in the remote northwest corner of the state. It is protected from the rest of the state by The Grand Canyon, a canyon that no bridge could ever span. To the north there are massive cliffs common to that part of the country. To the east and west are large and unpopulated expanses of arid desert. The nearest town, Fredonia, population 1,036, is the second largest town on the strip. Residents of Hildale-Colorado City, originally known simply as Short Creek, began populating the area in the 1920's when Mormons wanted to be free to continue practicing Joseph Smith's principles.

It is difficult to imagine what life is like for a woman in this community. She is probably relatively comfortable as long as she does not go against the grain. There is plenty of opportunity for the women to bond with each other, in situations where jealousy is not present. If a person has never fully been allowed to think for herself, then she may not know what she is missing. Often an issue is only raised when a girl has a marriage arranged with someone she dislikes, such as a perverted uncle who has been leering at her since she was a little girl. Another circumstance that could potentially cause a problem is when a young woman falls in love with another young man, and is not only forbidden to be with that man, but is forced to marry someone she has no feelings for at all. The community leader appoints the marriage under the veil of God having decided it. God usually tells him to keep the more attractive ones for himself. With convictions beginning to go through, such as that of polygamist Tom Green, things are looking up for the women. Mr. Green was convicted of having sex with a minor when it was discovered that one of his wives was only thirteen when he first impregnated her. Mr. Green toured the television talk-show circuit following a revelation from God to do so.

He talked openly about his lifestyle and past, and incriminated himself in the process. Mr. Green not only married his thirteen-year-old stepdaughter, but his "spiritual wives" have been living off of welfare and defrauding the Government. Such activity is known as "bleeding the beast," and is condoned under the theory that they will eventually be persecuted for their lifestyles and they are seeking retribution in advance.

Attempts are being made to put in a rescue type station so that women have somewhere to turn to if they want to leave. In these situations, young women in the communities are being labeled "at risk" if they fit a specific profile; their body is beginning to develop and/or they are approaching the age of fourteen. A satellite sheriff station is proposed to be built twenty miles outside of the town limits. This would be a place where women can go to and be protected should they desire to escape the fate of being forced into polygamy. The station would include agencies such as the Child Protective Services and the Attorney General's Office. Attempts are also being made at passing laws that would more closely govern polygamous activities, such as more strict penalties for sex with minors. A law enacted by the 2003 Legislature created the new crime of child bigamy: marrying a second wife who is under the age of 18. These new laws are enacted with young polygamy brides in mind. Until then, they are in "God's" hands.

– Corrina Murdy

Joseph Smith had an estimated 33 wives.

Nation of Islam

Also known as "Farrakhanism" after its founder, Louis Farrakhan, the NOI has become synonymous with militant Black Power in America. Going further than the Iranian Ayatollah Khomeini's proclamation that America and the West is "the Great Satan," NOI members suggest that all White men are devils created by the evil scientist "Yakub," six thousand years ago. Thus the Nation of Islam wishes to segregate Caucasians and Negroes, bringing about a global apartheid.

Not only is the NOI a racist religion, it is also not Islamic. NOI followers are not committed to prayer or the Hajj, perhaps due to Malcolm X's experiences on his own pilgrimage to Mecca, a journey on which he discovered to his utter horror that Islam was founded by Arabs, not black people.

Moreover, that it is a global religion with congregation members from every colour and nationality on Earth. Of course, once he came back to America and began to tell Black people the truth about Islam he was apparently murdered by the NOI, of which he was a founding member.

The Nation of Islam is quite strict about its Black power philosophy, certainly as a result of the abuses of the Negro race by the White. However, abuses and oppression are not good enough reasons for perverting the truth. Although Bilal, a Black slave set free by Mohammad, was the first person ever to call Muslims to prayer ("adhan"), Islam was not a Black religion at the time. Africans already had thousands of different animist religions and magical beliefs, and were regarded as infidels ("Kaffirs") by Muslim Arabs.

Desiring to prove Black superiority over Caucasians, NOI preachers often quote the Egyptians as being the first great civilization on Earth. Yet they refrain from also mentioning the Chinese civilization, the Mycenaeans, the Minoans and the Trojans. Moreover, it is not the Egyptians whom are rightfully and accurately credited as "inventing" civilization, rather it was the Sumerians, around 4000 to 3000 years B.C.E. So if racial superiority is to be measured by who was civilized first, the award should go to the races of the Near and Middle East, perhaps even modern-day Iraqis.

NOI also forgets to mention that it was not the White man whom invented mass slavery but the Black man, if Egyptians are indeed to be classed as such.

Aside from the historical opinions of the NOI being flawed, their understanding of Islam itself is prone to much error. Louis Farrakhan regards the Qur'an as being written for Elijah Muhammad, the true prophet of Islam — a man who more correctly made a profit out of religion, rather than being an actual prophet.

Farrakhan's other beliefs include the strange notion that 1) God came to Earth in July 1930 in the form of W. Fard Muhammad. 2) That Ezekiel's throne chariot of "Merkabah" will one day come to Earth as a giant UFO, killing White men and Jews in the process. And 3) that he has himself twice traveled to Mexico in a UFO.

Although Farrakhan was banned from entering Britain in 2001, the UK government may reverse its decision once a landing strip for UFOs is built.

– Rich Stanit, Excerpt from *Religion Must Die*,
Published by The Book Tree, www.thebooktree.com

Wallace Fard Muhammad

Wallace Fard Muhammad (1877-1834?) was the original founder of the Nation of Islam (NOI). Its first mosque was in Detroit. He preached his interpretation of Islam there for three years and then disappeared without a trace in 1934. At the time, many rumors circulated that his successor and student Eli Poole (who had changed his name to Elijah Muhammad) had killed him.

Fard had several known aliases: Wali Farad, Farrad Mohammed, W.D. Fard, and F. Mohammed Ali. The NOI refers to him only as Master Fard Muhammad.

FBI photograph of Wallace Dodd Ford

FBI records show that Fard Muhammad and one Wallace Dodd Ford, are the same person. They possess fingerprints and photographs of both men to prove this. Ford, who is also known as Wallace Dodd, was born February 25, 1891, to mixed Euro-

NOI's acknowledged photograph of Wallace Fard Muhammad.

pean and Polynesian parents. He was either born in New Zealand. He came to the U.S. sometime in the early 1920s. He was arrested and convicted on drug offenses, and even served three years in San Quentin between 1926 and 1929.

Elijah Muhammad dismissed the FBI's claims as part of a smear campaign. He said publicly that Fard was the living God and that he hadn't disappeared at all; he had gone to Mecca. He made this statement about his teacher in his book, *Message to the Blackman*:

Allah (God) came to us from the Holy City Mecca, Arabia, in 1930. He used the name Wallace D. Fard, often signing it W.D. Fard. In the third year (1933), He signed His name W.F. Muhammad, which stands for Wallace Fard Muhammad. He came alone. He began teaching us the knowledge of ourselves, of God and the devil, of the measurement of the earth, of other planets, and of the civilizations of some of the planets other than earth.

A Brief History of the Church
of Scientology

L. Ron Hubbard established the Church of Scientology in 1954 against the following backdrop: He had dropped out of college with failing grades. Although he would later claim a distinguished wartime naval career, Hubbard in fact never saw combat and left the U.S. Navy petitioning the Veterans Administration for psychiatric care. Two bigamous marriages failed. He found success writing pulp/science fiction, but as he declared in the late 1940s: "Writing for a penny a word is ridiculous. If a man really wants to make a million dollars, the best way would be to start his own religion."

Hubbard took up ritual magic, the occult and hypnosis, giving demonstrations of hypnosis in 1948 and writing to his literary agent about a therapy system he was working on that had tremendous promotional and sales potential. Piecing together hypnotic techniques, Freudian theories, Buddhist concepts and elements of other philosophies and practices, Hubbard came up with Dianetics. He published *Dianetics: The Modern Science of Mental Health* in 1950.

In Dianetic practice the "patient," working with a partner called an "auditor" recalls past painful experiences in reverse chronological sequence, supposedly erasing their negative effects and attaining a state called "clear," allegedly free from all ills. The auditor carefully records any intimate revelations, including sexual or criminal activities and marital or family troubles; these records are kept on file.

Hubbard represented Dianetics as a mental health therapy. He asserted that it was scientifically based and developed through careful research, and his use of the word "patient" suggests that he anticipated acceptance of Dianetics by the medical profession. But he never produced copies of any research protocol. Dianetics was opposed immediately by the American Medical Association and the American Psychological Association, the latter recommending that its members limit use of Dianetic techniques to investigation only, until Hubbard's claimed results could be corroborated.

The public, however, made the book a bestseller, and it seemed that Hubbard's ship had come in. He created the Hubbard Dianetic Research Foundation to promulgate his theories and techniques.

With auditors repeatedly asking patients in trance state to recall "earlier similar incidents," patients began to report past lifetime experiences. Hubbard incorporated belief in past lives into his evolving ideology, discussing the concept in his second Dianetics book, *Science of Survival*.

The Hubbard Foundation began to collapse as the initial Dianetics craze wore off, and Hubbard's new-found emphasis on past lives exacerbated tensions with the Foundation's financial partners. By 1952 Hubbard was penniless and had lost control of Dianetics.

Scientology is Born

Hubbard became interested in a type of lie detector called the "electropsychometer" that he believed would yield better results in auditing. He obtained a franchise for this device, which he renamed the Hubbard Electrometer, or E-meter. He began calling patients "pre-clears" and "within six weeks had created a new subject apparently out of thin air."

Hubbard called his new subject Scientology and in introducing it, he claimed to have discovered the human soul.vWhereas Dianetics had addressed the body, Scientology involved freeing souls (which Hubbard called "thetans") from supposed entrapment in the physical or material world and restoring their alleged supernatural powers.

Hubbard established a headquarters in Phoenix, Arizona, awarded himself the degree of D.Scn. (Doctor of Scientology) and in May 1952 incorporated the Hubbard Association of Scientologists International under the personal control of himself and his third wife, Mary Sue. The AMA meanwhile continued its opposition to Dianetics and Scientology.

In 1953 Hubbard regained control of Dianetics after a protracted legal battle and incorporated the Church of Scientology, Church of American Science and Church of Spiritual Engineering. In 1954 he incorporated the Church of Scientology of California, which became the mother church. In 1956 the church was granted US federal tax-exempt status.

In 1957, passing himself off as a nuclear physicist, Hubbard gave a series of lectures in London on "nuclear radiation and health," promoting a vitamin compound which he claimed cured both "radiation sickness" and cancer. Also that year the CIA began a file on him.

Hubbard repeatedly wrote to the FBI with complaints of Communist and Nazi persecution. The Bureau considered him a mental case, but kept a file on him and would later, as his organization grew, investigate him actively… abusively, Scientologists maintain.

International Expansion

In 1959 Hubbard moved to England and bought Saint Hill Mansion in Sussex, from which he would direct international operations and expansion of the CoS until 1967. The 1960s saw the introduction of "Ethics" procedures, which include harsh punishments (even for children) and the "discon-nection" policy, which requires Scientologists to sever ties with family and friends critical of Scientology.

Although the essentials of Scientology had been thoroughly presented early on, Hubbard turned out a steady stream of books and audio tapes that are aggressively marketed to his followers. He created systems of "Security Checks" in which members are interrogated to ensure loyalty and extract confessions. He produced reams of policy directives on subjects varying from Scientology "tech" (technology) to church management to approved cleaning solvents to his own recipe for baby formula; all these missives are considered by CoS members to be sacred scripture.

In the late 1960s Hubbard released the "upper levels." Scientologists who had spent hundreds or thousands of hours vainly pursuing often-promised supernatural abilities were guaranteed that these procedures would finally deliver on the promise. Based on a science-fiction-like story taking place millions of years ago and involving a cruel Galactic despot named Xenu and his evil minions (elsewhere identified as present-day Christian clergy and psychiatrists), the upper levels are kept secret until a member is deemed ready to receive them. The estimated cost from beginning Scientology cours-es through completion of the upper levels is today $300,000 - $500,000 in US dollars.

In 1967 the IRS stripped Scientology's mother church of its tax-exempt status. With his organization coming under increasing scrutiny from a va-riety of governments and tax woes abounding, Hubbard wrote his famous "Fair Game" law, which states that anyone named an enemy of Scientology "may be tricked, sued, lied to or destroyed." A year later, he would issue a directive canceling use of the term, "Fair Game," (due to negative publicity) but making plain that attacks on Scientology's perceived enemies were to continue.

In mid-1967 Hubbard bought three ships and put to sea with a small cadre of followers. Styling himself "the Commodore," he spent the next sev-eral years wandering the Atlantic, pursued by imaginary Reds and Nazis and attended by "Commodore's Messengers," teenaged girls dressed in white hot pants who waited on him hand and foot, bathing and dressing him and even catching the ash from his cigarettes. He had frequent screaming tantrums and instituted brutal punishments such as incarceration in the ship's filthy chain-locker for days or weeks at a time and "overboarding," in which errant crew members were blindfolded, bound and thrown overboard, dropping up to 40 feet into the cold sea and hoping not to hit the side of the ship with its razor-sharp barnacles on the way down. These punishments applied to children as well as to adults.

Hubbard made bungling attempts to take over Morocco and Rhodesia and was banned from further entry into Britain. He began the Sea Organization (SO), whose members wear pseudo-naval uniforms, adopt naval ranks, sign billion year contracts and are pressured to have abortions when they become pregnant because children are perceived as interfering with their SO obligations. Hubbard created the infamously abusive Rehabilitation Project Force as a special punishment for SO members who fail to follow orders, make mistakes or fall short of production goals.

Going Religious

During the early 1970s the IRS "proved that Hubbard was skimming millions of dollars from the church, laundering the money through dummy corporations in Panama and stashing it in Swiss bank accounts. Moreover, church members stole IRS documents, filed false tax returns and harassed the agency's employees."

A U.S. federal court in 1971 ruled that Hubbard's medical claims were bogus and that E-meter auditing could not be called a scientific treatment. The CoS responded by "going fully religious, seeking First Amendment protection...counselors started sporting clerical collars. Chapels were built, franchises became 'missions,' fees became 'fixed donations,' and Hubbard's comic-book cosmology became 'sacred scriptures.'"

After years of running the Scientology organization from aboard his flagship, the Apollo, in 1975 Hubbard bought the Fort Harrison Hotel and a former bank building in downtown Clearwater, Florida under the name United Churches of Florida, to hide Scientology's connection. He moved his crew to Clearwater, establishing the Flagship Land Base, a.k.a. "Flag."

While the Church of Scientology continued to expand, its private intelligence agency known as the Guardian's Office (GO) ran cloak-and-dagger operations against the mayor of Clearwater, various governmental agencies and anyone else perceived as in their way.

Hubbard had established the GO in 1966 for internal and external security purposes. The GO's purview included attacking critics, keeping members in line and silencing defectors. GO agents "stole medical files, sent out anonymous smear letters, framed critics for criminal acts, blackmailed, bugged and burgled opponents, and infiltrated government offices stealing thousands of files...Critics were to be driven to breakdown or harassed into silence." Eventually, in the early 1980s, eleven GO officials, including Hubbard's wife, were imprisoned following a massive bugging and burgling operation against government offices across the U.S. that Hubbard had personally created and code-named "Operation Snow White." Hubbard himself was named as an uninvited co-conspirator but escaped justice because no one could find him.

Almost from the beginning, Hubbard had been in trouble with the law.

In 1951 the New Jersey Board of Medical Examiners brought proceedings against him for teaching medicine without a license; he fled to Los Angeles to escape prosecution. His organizations were repeatedly charged with practicing medicine without a license; E-meters and vitamin compounds were seized. The FDA accused Scientology of falsely claiming the E-meter could cure medical ailments and all E-meters were required to carry labels disavowing such claims.

At various times, Hubbard (and/or the church) was investigated by the US Justice Department, the FBI, FDA, CIA, IRS, NSA, Bureau of Customs, DEA, DOD, the Secret Service, the US Post Office, INS, BATF, Department of Labor, police departments of various US cities as well as Interpol and a host of other governmental agencies worldwide. Hubbard was convicted in absentia of fraud in France. The Church of Scientology was convicted of breach of the public trust and infiltration of government offices in Canada. Scientology was banned by the state of Victoria, Australia. Hubbard attributed all these events to widespread plotting by Russian communists, neo-fascists, bankers, the media, the IRS, Christian clergy, fiendish extraterrestrials and the psychiatric profession, which he considered his arch enemy.

– Andreas Heldal-Lund,
from *Operation Clambake*, www.xenu.net

Xenu

According to Hubbard, 75 million years ago, there was a confederation of 76 planets, including Earth. The "Galactic Confederation" (the title comes from the science fiction of E.E. 'Doc' Smith), was ruled by Xenu (also called "Xemu" by Hubbard). Over-population had become a serious problem, which Xenu resolved by murdering many of the inhabitants of the Confederation. Hubbard estimated that the 76 planets averaged 178 billion people each. The people were killed and the thetans (or spirits) gathered, frozen in a mixture of glycol and alcohol, and brought to Earth where they were placed near volcanoes which were exploded with hydrogen bombs. The thetans were gathered on "electronic ribbons," packaged together as clusters and given 36 days of implanting, to render them servile and incapable of decision. A cluster is a collection of body thetans containing a leader and an "alternate" leader. The cluster conceives itself to be an individual. According to OT 3, everyone on Earth is in fact a collection of such clusters (Hubbard says that each person doing OT 3 will find "hundreds" of body thetans — many victims of this course believe that they find millions).

On OT 3, the individual finds "body thetans" by locating any sensation of pressure or mass in his or her body. This is addressed "telepathically" as a cluster, and taken through the cluster-making incident of 75 million years ago. Once this is done, the individual body thetans should be available to be taken through either the same incident or the incident of entry into this universe. This is called "incident one," and supposedly occurred four quadrillion years ago. This incident is described in the materials as: "Loud snap — waves of light — chariot comes out, turns left and right — cherub comes out — blows horn, comes close — shattering series of snaps — cherub fades back (retreats) — blackness dumped on thetan." Most scientologists are unaware of the true definition of "cherub."

The Scientologist spends days or years dealing with "body thetans" (I have known two people who "audited" this procedure almost every day for eleven years). Scientology materials of different dates assert that at the end of OT 3 the individual will be "stably exterior" (from his body out of his head, it might be rephrased), free from "overwhelm" (i.e., nothing will ever overwhelm him emotionally again), and have total recall of his entire round of incarnations from four quadrillion years ago to the present. Secret materials seen only by those selling the course give the "end phenomenon" as a "big win" urging that the person be put onto the next course — where they pay by the hour — quickly.

Anyone who encounters this material without having undertaken Scientology courses up to OT 2 will supposedly die from pneumonia.

OT 3 is of course in substantial disagreement with conventional geology. Geologists hold that almost all of the volcanoes listed by Hubbard and both Hawaii and Los Palmas came into being far more recently than 75 million years ago. On a simple point of logic, it seems strange that none of these volcanoes was damaged by the explosion of the hydrogen bombs. Hubbard was taking barbiturates and drinking heavily when he wrote this material, according to letters he wrote at the time which are kept from scientologists by the management of Scientology.

– Jon Atack

Dangerous Leaders

Jim Jones

The American born preacher, James Warren "Jim" Jones (May 13, 1931–November 18-19(?), 1978) was the founder of the Peoples Temple Church. Jones led his followers to the jungles of Guyana where they became his virtual prisoners. His devotees were convinced that he was God. They drank poisonous Kool-aid on November 18, 1978 as he advised and in some cases, forced them to do. Nine-hundred and fourteen women, children and men died a horrible death. Jim went with them…he committed suicide with a shotgun.

David Koresh

The Branch Davidians gained much attention in 1993 with their standoff at the Mt. Carmel center near Waco, Texas. The group is an extreme sect of the Seventh Day Adventist Church which has a history of failed prophecy and total intolerance of other religions. David Koresh, the sect's self anointed leader, maintained a high profile with guns and confrontation. The FBI and BATF soon became involved, leading a fiery ending to their standoff. The standoff was promoted by Koresh and his followers who were now calling themselves "the Students of the Seven Seals" instead of Branch Davidians. Eighty-two Davidians died in the flames, most likely set by the followers. 26 of the deceased were children, along with Koresh himself and his female "wives."

XI

Revelations

What is it to be the New Mythology?

We live today — thank God! — in a secular state, governed by human beings (with all their inevitable faults) according to principles of law that are still developing and have originated not from Jerusalem, but from Rome.

The concept of the state is yielding rapidly at this hour to the concept of the ecumene, i.e., the whole inhabited earth; and if nothing else unites us, the ecological crisis will. There is no need any more for those locally binding, sociopolitically bounded, differing forms of religion which have held men separate in the past, giving to God the things that are Caesar's and to Caesar the things that are God's.

"God is an intelligible sphere whose center is everywhere and circumference nowhere." So we are told in a little twelfth-century book known as *The Book of the Twenty-four Philosophers*. Each of us — whoever and wherever he may be — is then the center, and within him, whether he knows it or not, is that Mind at Large, the laws of which are the laws not only of all minds but of all space as well. For we are the children of this beautiful planet that we have lately seen photographed from the moon.

We were not delivered into this planet by some god, but have come forth from it. We are its eyes and mind, its seeing and its thinking. And the earth, together with its sun, this light around which it flies like a moth, came forth, we are told, from a nebula; and that nebula, in turn, from space. So that we are the mind, ultimately, of space. No wonder, then, if its laws and ours are the same! Likewise, our depths are the depths of space, whence all those gods sprang that men's minds in the past projected onto animals and plants, onto hills and streams, the planets in their courses, and their own peculiar social observances.

Our mythology now is to be of infinite space and its light, which is without as well as within. Like moths, we are caught in the spell of its allure, flying to it outward, to the moon and beyond, and flying to it inward. On our planet itself all dividing horizons have been shattered. We can no longer hold our loves at home and project our aggressions elsewhere; for on this spaceship Earth there is no "elsewhere" any more. And no mythology that continues to speak or teach of "elsewheres" and "outsiders" meets the requirement of this hour.

And so to return to our opening question: What is to be the new mythology?

It is — and will forever be, as long as our human race exists — the old, everlasting, perennial mythology, in its "subjective sense," addressed to the waking of individuals in the knowledge of themselves, not simply as egos fighting for place on the surface of this beautiful planet, but equally as centers of Mind at Large — each in his own way at one with all, and with no horizons.

– Joseph Campbell: educator, author, and editor
Excerpt from *Myths To Live By*, Viking Press, 1972

Humanism, the Hope for Mankind

John F. Kennedy said in 1962 during the Cuban missile crisis that "God's work on earth, is surely our own." His comments were prompted in part by the worldwide terror brought on by the impending showdown between the United States and the U.S.S.R., a showdown that could have spelled the end of the world as we know it. Fortunately cooler heads prevailed; unfortunately no lessons or the wrong lessons were learned.

Both the Soviet Union and the United States staggered away and immediately in the next year started a massive build-up of offensive and defensive weapons of mass destruction. The more moderate and 'alternate' solution leaders were removed from the world scene; Kennedy at the hands of a gunman while the Soviet leader was removed by a coup. This left two ideologues fighting not for the betterment of the race, but for their dominance of Christian democracy on the one hand versus godless communism on the other. Left in the middle was the rest of the world, seemingly powerless, while the two giants of political dogma and military might wrestled on, misspending billions of dollars on weapons, while ignorance and poverty spread.

This snapshot of history is not unique. A quick read of history shows that the two most deadly plagues in history are wars and dogmatic thought...the most destructive being religion. When war and religion join forces, the world creates orphans. No area of the world has been spared from this plague. The mid east which has been the cradle of religion...supposedly the birthplace of the "prince of peace," ironically is the cradle or origin of most wars. The Jews v. the Christians, Islam v. the Hindus, everyone against everyone else, all in the name of God, their exclusive God! This infection has spread to all corners of the world, including our country. When land became real estate and the American Natives were labeled "Godless heretics" by the Mother Church and the puritans, the complete theft of America became more digestible for the participants and their offspring who now live here. A special name was given to it...Manifest Destiny.

The Crusades financed and fought by England and the Catholic Church has been reduced to over 800 books. But the lessons of history have not been learned, thus sadly we are doomed to repeat them. Our current crisis in the mid east is a case in point. We have simplified our hatred by labeling our enemies in an invaded country as 'godless', 'evil,' and anti-democratic. The enemy is a faceless one...a faceless one on purpose; undemocratic and non-Christian. We now have justified our actions to ourselves and others. We now have free rein: same story, different book.

Thus we creep into the twenty-first century with the same baggage that we have had for the last 20 centuries. Dehumanizing military solutions and labels of 'infidel', 'heretic', and 'Satan' put into the mass media for all to hear and react to; business as usual. The choice that non-religious humanists have now is to play the game of getting alternate thought and new thinking into the mainstream. There is no other choice. We live in the global village which is molded by spin, infomercials, spatial repetition. The humanist voice is seldom heard. The voice that says "we are all painted by the same brush," that we are all on the spaceship earth and have no choice but to live in peace.

All very well and good: As much as we want to think that "'60s speak" is going to free the world, it may not on its own. The mass media is the battle front for the hearts and minds of the world. The "alternate" model must be shown to have had adherents, who were successful, and who made a difference with a humanistic approach to brotherhood and solutions for differences. The goal of this media display is twofold. Identify the benefits of peace and non interference of toxic religions and their limited ancient beliefs.

This is a tall order. Since life is a stage, we must put a face on our ideal. We must identify a group of people who have made and difference, and would have made more of a difference if they had not be taken from us. In other words 'martyrs.' The Church used this very successfully through history. Almost every revolution has had one...from Thomas Paine to Martin Luther King, Jr. Sadly the humanists have more than we can think of. Most without religious dogma, most with the common good in mind must who said to the world "let us explore those things that unite us, not dwell on the things that divide us."

The list includes all races and circumstances. The list should show the world that the alternative to war, harsh rhetoric, stereotyping, violence and sanctions is more beneficial than the fundamentalist course. In a simple child's story one of the characters simply states that the way to have fewer enemies is to have more friends. The adult list of 'alternate solutions' is impressive and sad at the same time. There is an adage that says a person does not die if his or her ideals are lived or spoken by another. The legacy of the humanist family must be dramatized, or humankind we be the next victim to violence and mindless religion and hate.

Martin Luther King, Jr., Gandhi, Mary Dyer, Cesar Chavez, Robert F. Kennedy, John F. Kennedy, Chief Joseph, Rachel Corrie, Anwar Sadat, Yitzhak Rabin, Dag Hammarsjold, T. Makiguchi, John Lennon, George Helm, Abraham Lincoln, Oscar Romero, the everyman hero Wang of Tiananmen Square, Imre Nagy and the Hofer brothers; each a martyr in his own right; each with an alternative; each with a relevant drama. Wouldn't the world be better off today if violence hadn't cut their lives short? The embers of these great humanists must be played out, not left on a reference shelf in a New England library. These lives must be center stage, in the global village, for as social critic Marshall McCullen said "the media is the massage [message]."

Humanists must enter this arena, or be forced into oblivion by the Fox Televisions and Pat Robertsons of the world. All the resources of the splintered humanist groups must be capitalized and move forward into the world media stage. The prescription for growth and influence is simple. The plan is simple. But as Alan Watts said, "Action is the only truth."

– Kelsey M. Leedom

Wisdom from Ingersoll

➤ A believer is a bird in a cage. A freethinker is an eagle parting the clouds with tireless wing.

➤ I want no heaven for which I must give my reason; no happiness in exchange for my liberty; and no immortality that demands the surrender of my individuality.

➤ Banish me from Eden when you will; but first let me eat of the fruit of the tree of knowledge.

➤ The man who invented the telescope found out more about heaven than the closed eyes of prayer ever discovered.

➤ Fear paints pictures of ghosts and hangs them in the gallery of ignorance.

➤ Superstition is, always has been, and forever will be, the foe of progress, the enemy of education and the assassin of freedom.

➤ Liberty is my religion.

➤ No one pretends that Shakespeare was inspired, and yet all the writers of the books of the Old Testament put together could not have produced *Hamlet*.

➤ Religion can never reform mankind because religion is slavery.

➤ Theology is not what we know about God, but what we do not know about Nature.

➤ If a man would follow, today, the teachings of the Old Testament, he would be a criminal. If he would strictly follow the teachings of the New, he would be insane.

➤ When I speak of God, I mean that god who prevented man from putting forth his hand and taking also the fruit of the tree of life that he might live forever; of that god who multiplied the agonies of women, increased the weary toil of man, and in his anger drowned a world — of that god whose altars reeked with human blood, who butchered babes, violated maidens, enslaved men and filled the earth with cruelty and crime; of that god who made heaven for the few, hell for the many, and who will gloat forever and ever upon the writhing of the lost and damned.

➤ I believe in the fireside. I believe in the democracy of home. I believe in the Republicanism of the family. I believe in liberty, equality, and love.

– Robert G. Ingersoll, 1833-1899

Our appreciation to Steven Kropko from Atheists United, P. O. Box 5329, Sherman Oaks, CA 91413 for these quotations.

Chief Seattle Speaks

How can you buy or sell the sky, the warmth of the land? The idea is strange to us. If we do not own the freshness of the air and sparkle of the water, how can you buy them?

Every part of this earth is sacred to my people. Every shining pine needle, every sandy shore, every mist in the dark woods, every clearing and humming insect is holy in the memory and experience of my people. The sap which courses through the trees carries the memories of the red man.

The white man's dead forget the country of their birth when they go to walk among the stars. Our dead never forget this beautiful earth, for it is the mother of the red man. We are part of the earth and it is part of us. The perfumed flowers are our sisters; the deer, the horse, the great eagle, these are our brothers. The rocky crests, the juices in the meadows, the body heat of the pony, and man — all belong to the same family. So, when the Great Chief in Washington sends word that he wishes to buy land, he asks much of us. The Great Chief sends word he will reserve us a place so that we can live comfortably to ourselves.

He will be our father and we will be his children. So we will consider your offer to buy our land. But it will not be easy. For this land is sacred to us. This shining water that moves in the streams and rivers is not just water but the blood of our ancestors. If we sell you land, you must remember that it is sacred, and you must teach your children that it is sacred and that each ghostly reflection in the clear water of the lakes tells of events and memories in the life of my people. The water's murmur is the voice of my father's father.

The rivers are our brothers, they quench our thirst. The rivers carry our canoes, and feed our children. If we sell you our land, you must remember, and teach your children, that the rivers are our brothers, and yours, and you must henceforth give the rivers the kindness you would give any brother.

We know that the white man does not understand our ways. One portion of land is the same to him as the next, for he is a stranger who comes in the night and takes from the land whatever he needs.

The earth is not his brother, but his enemy, and when he has conquered it, he moves on. He leaves his father's graves behind, and he does not care. He kidnaps the earth from his children, and he does not care. His father's grave, and his children's birthright, are forgotten. He treats his mother, the earth, and his brother, the sky, as things to be bought, plundered, sold like sheep or bright beads. His appetite will devour the earth and leave behind only a desert.

I do not know. Our ways are different from your ways. The sight of your cities pains the eyes of the red man. But perhaps it is because the red man is a savage and does not understand.

There is no quiet place in the white man's cities. No place to hear the unfurling of leaves in spring, or the rustle of an insect's wings. But perhaps it is because I am a savage and do not understand. The clatter only seems to insult the ears. And what is there to life if a man cannot hear the lonely cry of the whippoorwill or the arguments of the frogs around a pond at night? I am a red man and do not understand. The Indian prefers the soft sound of the wind darting over the face of a pond, and the smell of the wind itself, cleaned by a midday rain, or scented with the pinion pine.

The air is precious to the red man, for all things share the same breath — the beast, the tree, the man, they all share the same breath. The white man does not seem to notice the air he breathes. Like a man dying for many days, he is numb to the stench. But if we sell you our land, you must remember that the air is precious to us, that the air shares its spirit with all the life it supports. The wind that gave our grandfather his first breath also receives his last sigh. And if we sell you our land, you must keep it apart and sacred, as a place where even the white man can go to taste the wind that is sweetened by the meadow's flowers.

So we will consider your offer to buy our land. If we decide to accept, I will make one condition: The white man must treat the beasts of this land as his brothers.

I am a savage and I do not understand any other way. I've seen a thousand rotting buffaloes on the prairie, left by the white man who shot them from a passing train. I am a savage and I do not understand how the smoking iron horse can be more important than the buffalo that we kill only to stay alive.

What is man without the beasts? If all the beasts were gone, man would die from a great loneliness of spirit. For whatever happens to the beasts, soon happens to man. All things are connected.

You must teach your children that the ground beneath their feet is the ashes of your grandfathers. So that they will respect the land, tell your children that the earth is rich with the lives of our kin. Teach your children what we have taught our children, that the earth is our mother. Whatever befalls the earth befalls the sons of the earth. If men spit upon the ground, they spit upon themselves.

This we know: The earth does not belong to man; man belongs to the earth. This we know. All things are connected like the blood which unites one family. All things are connected. Whatever befalls the earth befalls the sons of the earth. Man did not weave the web of life: he is merely a strand in it. Whatever he does to the web, he does to himself.

Even the white man, whose God walks and talks with him as friend to friend, cannot be exempt from the common destiny. We may be brothers after all. We shall see. One thing we know, which the white man may one day discover, our God is the same God. You may think now that you own Him as you wish to own our land; but you cannot. He is the God of man, and His compassion is equal for the red man and the white. This earth is precious to Him, and to harm the earth is to heap contempt on its Creator.

The whites too shall pass; perhaps sooner than all other tribes. Contaminate your bed, and you will one night suffocate in your own waste. But in your perishing you will shine brightly, fired by the strength of God who brought you to this land and for some special purpose gave you dominion over this land and over the red man. That destiny is a mystery to us, for we do not understand when the buffalo are all slaughtered, the wild horses are tamed, the secret corners of the forest heavy with scent of many men, and the view of the ripe hills blotted by talking wires.

Where is the thicket? Gone.

Where is the eagle? Gone.

The end of living and the beginning of survival.

– Chief Seattle

A Call for a New Reformation

In the sixteenth century the Christian Church, which had been the source of much of the stability of the western world, entered a period of internal and violent upheaval. In time this upheaval came to be called the Protestant Reformation, but during the violence itself, it was referred to by many less attractive adjectives. The institution that called itself the body of Christ broke first into debate, then acrimony, then violence and counter-violence and finally into open warfare between Protestant Christians and Catholic Christians. It produced the Hundred Years War and the conflict between England and Spain that came to a climax in the destruction of the Spanish Armada in 1588. That destruction was widely interpreted as a defeat for the Catholic God of Spain at the hands of the Protestant God of England.

Yet, when looking at that ecclesiastical conflict from the vantage point of more than four hundred years, there is surprise at how insignificant were the theological issues dividing the two sides. Neither side was debating such core teachings of Christianity as the doctrine of the Holy Trinity, Jesus as the incarnate son of God, the reality of heaven and hell, the place of the cross in the plan of salvation or the role of such sacraments as Baptism and Communion. These rather were faith assertions held in common.

Of course this conflict was not without theological issues, though they seem quite trivial in retrospect. Protestant Christians and Catholic Christians disagreed, for example, about whether salvation was achieved by faith alone, as Luther contended, or whether faith without works was dead as the Vatican, quoting the Epistle of James, argued. There was also debate over the proper use of scripture and the role of ordination. Despite the hostile appellations of "heretic" hurled at Protestants and "anti-Christ" hurled at Catholics, anyone viewing this debate from the vantage point of this century would see that, while an acrimonious and unpleasant fight, it was nonetheless a fight that pitted Christian believers against Christian believers. The Reformation was not an attempt to reformulate the Christian faith for a new era. It was rather a battle over issues of Church order. The time had not arrived in which Christians would be required to rethink the basic and identifying marks of Christianity itself.

It is my conviction that such a moment is facing the Christian world today. The very heart and soul of Christianity will be the content of this reformation. The debate which has been building for centuries has now erupted into public view. All the past ecclesiastical efforts to keep it at bay or deny its reality have surely failed and will continue to do so. The need for a new theological reformation began when Copernicus and Galileo removed this planet from its previous supposed location at the center of the universe, where human life was thought to bask under the constant attention of a humanly defined parental deity. That revolution in thought produced an angle of vision radically different from the one in which the Bible was written and through which the primary theological tenets of the Christian faith were formed.

Before that opening salvo of revolution had been absorbed, Sir Isaac Newton, who charted the mathematically fixed physical laws of the universe, weighed into the debate. After Newton the Church found itself in a world in which the concepts of magic, miracle, and divine intervention as explanations of anything, could no longer be offered with intellectual integrity. Once more people were forced to enter into and to embrace a reality vastly different from the one employed in the traditional language of their faith tradition.

Next came Charles Darwin who related human life to the world of biology more significantly than anyone had heretofore imagined. He also confronted the human consciousness with concepts diametrically opposed to the traditional Christian world view. The Bible began with the assumption that God had created a finished and perfect world from which human beings had fallen away in an act of cosmic rebellion. Original sin was the reality in which all life was presumed to live. Darwin postulated instead an unfinished and thus imperfect creation out of which human life was still evolving. Human beings did not fall from perfection into sin as the Church had taught for centuries; we were evolving, and indeed are still evolving, into higher levels of consciousness. Thus the basic myth of Christianity that interpreted Jesus as a divine emissary who came to rescue the victims of the fall from the results of their original sin became inoperative. So did the interpretation of the cross of Calvary as the moment of divine sacrifice when the ransom for sin was paid. Established Christianity clearly wobbled under the impact of Darwin's insights, but Christian leaders pretended that if Darwin could not be defeated, he could at least be ignored. It was a vain hope.

Darwin was followed by Sigmund Freud who analyzed the symbols of Christianity and found in them manifestations of a deep-seated infantile neurosis. The God understood as a father figure, who guided ultimate personal decisions, answered our prayers, and promised rewards and punishment based upon our behavior was not designed to call anyone into maturity. This view of God issued rather into either a religious mentality of passive dependency or an aggressive secular rejection of all things religious. After Freud, it was not surprising to see Christianity degenerate into an increasingly shrill biblical fundamentalism where thinking was not encouraged and preconceived pious answers were readily given, but where neither genuine questions nor maturity were allowed or encouraged. As Christianity moved more and more in this direction, contemporary people, who think with modern minds, began to be repelled and to drop out of their faith commitments into the Church Alumni Association. Between these two poles of mindless fundamentalism and empty secularism are found the mainline churches of Christendom, both Catholic and Protestant. They are declining numerically, seem lost theologically, are concerned more about unity than truth, and are wondering why boredom is what people experience inside church walls. The renewal of Christianity will not come from fundamentalism, secularism or the irrelevant mainline tradition. If there is nothing more than this on the horizon then I see no future for the enterprise we call the Christian faith.

My sense is that history has come to a point where only one thing will save this venerable faith tradition at this critical time in Christian history, and that is a new Reformation far more radical than Christianity has ever before known and that this Reformation must deal with the very substance of that faith. This Reformation will recognize that the pre-modern concepts in which Christianity has traditionally been carried will never again speak to the post-modern world we now inhabit. This Reformation will be about the very life and death of Christianity. Because it goes to the heart of how Christianity is to be understood, it will dwarf in intensity the Reformation of the sixteenth century. It will not be concerned about authority, ecclesiastical polity, valid ordinations and valid sacraments. It will be rather a Reformation that will examine the very nature of the Christian faith itself. It will ask whether or not this ancient religious system can be refocused and re-articulated so as to continue living in this increasingly non-religious world.

Martin Luther ignited the Reformation of the sixteenth century by nailing to the door of the church in Wittenberg in 1517 the *95 Theses* that he wished to debate. I will publish this challenge to Christianity in The Voice. I will post my theses on the Internet and send copies with invitations to debate them to the recognized Christian leaders of the world. My theses are far smaller in number than were those of Martin Luther, but they are far more threatening theologically. The issues to which I now call the Christians of the world to debate are these:

> 1. Theism, as a way of defining God, is dead. So most theological God-talk is today meaningless. A new way to speak of God must be found.
> 2. Since God can no longer be conceived in theistic terms, it becomes nonsensical to seek to understand Jesus as the incarnation of the theistic deity. So the Christology of the ages is bankrupt.
> 3. The biblical story of the perfect and finished creation from which human beings fell into sin is pre-Darwinian mythology and post-Darwinian nonsense.
> 4. The virgin birth, understood as literal biology, makes Christ's divinity, as traditionally understood, impossible.
> 5. The miracle stories of the New Testament can no longer be interpreted in a post-Newtonian world as supernatural events performed by an incarnate deity.

6. The view of the cross as the sacrifice for the sins of the world is a barbarian idea based on primitive concepts of God and must be dismissed.

7. Resurrection is an action of God. Jesus was raised into the meaning of God. It therefore cannot be a physical resuscitation occurring inside human history.

8. The story of the Ascension assumed a three-tiered universe and is therefore not capable of being translated into the concepts of a post-Copernican space age.

9. There is no external, objective, revealed standard writ in scripture or on tablets of stone that will govern our ethical behavior for all time.

10. Prayer cannot be a request made to a theistic deity to act in human history in a particular way.

11. The hope for life after death must be separated forever from the behavior control mentality of reward and punishment. The Church must abandon, therefore, its reliance on guilt as a motivator of behavior.

12. All human beings bear God's image and must be respected for what each person is. Therefore, no external description of one's being, whether based on race, ethnicity, gender or sexual orientation, can properly be used as the basis for either rejection or discrimination.

So I set these theses today before the Christian world and I stand ready to debate each of them as we prepare to enter the third millennium.

– John S. Spong

Satyagraha
The Martyrs of Peace

Peace has been the most elusive state of affairs in history. Ironically, the religious formula that has been thrust on the world and mouthed by leaders with secondary agendas has lead to more hate and killing in God's name. Several cases in point are the murders of pacifists and advocates of peace over the last three centuries. Twenty of our more notable advocates of peace, justice and equality have been cut down by religious zealots rationalizing their actions in a religious context. Many of the assassins were waiting on the return of the prince of peace, the divine Inman from his cave, Krishna's justice, Zionism's revenge or the Catholic conversion of the heathen.

Satyagraha
The Martyrs of Peace

Yitzhak Rabin

Prime Minister of Israel; "Solider for Peace" — Nobel Prize Recipient in 1990s; murdered at peace demonstration celebrating treaties with Palestinians and Israelis.

Abraham Lincoln

Freed the slaves; planned a peaceful Reconstruction "with malice toward none…." after Civil War; assassinated at Ford Theater in April 1865 at the hands of a racist assassin.

Dag Hammarskjöld

Second Secretary of United Nations; Nobel Peace Prize winner in 1961; life ended on U.N. peace mission in Africa in 1960 in suspicious air crash.

Anwar Sadat

President of Egypt; Nobel Prize Winner; signed Camp David Accords with President Jimmy Carter and Israel; killed by Islamic extremist terrorists in public ceremony.

Imre Igy

Imprisoned-Premier of Hungary after 1956 "Revolt" for freedom and socialist democracy; imprisoned for 2 years; executed in 1958 by Soviets after secret trial.

Robert F. Kennedy

United States Senator and leading Peace Candidate for the Presidency in 1968; Attorney General; strong supporter of civil rights and civil disobedience; died June 6,1968 after winning California Presidential primary by Arab assassin.

John F. Kennedy

35th President of the United States; signed historic test-ban treaty; founder of the Peace Corps; strong supporter of civil rights movement; an advocate of peaceful development abroad; killed in presidential motorcade in Dallas, TX by political extremists.

Medgar Evers

Civil Rights worker in the South with Martin Luther King, Jr.'s Freedom Rides and nonviolence; died during peaceful march in 1963.

Wen

"Lone, unknown" peaceful Chinese protestor in Tiananmen Square uprising; known to the world for his bravery in standing in front of a tank; never seen again.

Mary Dyer

Quaker in Boston, seventeenth century; martyr for peaceful protest for religious tolerance; Quaker in Boston seventeenth century; martyr for peaceful co-existence and religious tolerance; hung by the Catholic Church.

George Helm

Hawaiian "O'Hana" activist; musician; protestor for Hawaiian Island rights and peaceful land use; mysteriously disappeared while paddling to island military site.

Tsunesaburo Makiguchi

Buddhist Pacifist and WWII protestor; died in prison in 1944 at the hands of Emperor in Japan; founder of Soka Education.

Chief Joseph

Nez Perce Chief of Peace in Northwestern U.S. in the late 1800s; "deported" from his ancestral lands, and treatied reservation; sent to Oklahoma prison to die.

Martin Luther King, Jr.

Advocate of civil disobedience and civil rights; Nobel Peace Prize winner; in August 1964, gave famous "I have a dream…" speech in Washington D.C.; assassinated during labor dispute and civil rights demonstration by racist malcontent on April 4, 1968.

John Lennon

Beatle; musician; advocate of peace through his songs in life, such as "Imagine"; murdered in New York City in the early 1980s by disgruntled Christian fan.

Mohandas Gandhi

"Father of Civil Disobedience" and creator of democracy in India; killed by radical fellow Hindu in 1947.

Oscar Romero

El Salvadoran Archbishop; leading proponent of liberation theology and non-violence in war-torn El Salvador; died at the hands of death squads in 1980; The Vatican has opened the process of Beatification: the first step toward Sainthood.

Michael Hofner

American immigrant in the early 1900s; conscientious objector to WWI — jailed, beaten, and imprisoned at Alcatraz and Leavenworth; model for popular peace song "Great Mandella"; died at the end of WWI.

Rachel Corrie

American Human Rights Advocate killed in Palestine protecting Arab Doctor's home from Israeli bulldozer.

Caesar Chavez

Early organizer of Mexican Farmer-Workers in California; fasted, beaten, jailed; an advocate of civil disobedience and non-violence; died of natural causes at age of 66.

What We Must Do

We want to stand upon our own feet and look fair and square at the world — its good facts, its bad facts, its beauties, and its ugliness; see the world as it is and be not afraid of it. Conquer the world by intelligence and not merely by being slavishly subdued by the terror that comes from it. The whole conception of God is a conception derived from the ancient Oriental despotisms. It is a conception quite unworthy of free men. When you hear people in church debasing themselves and saying that they are miserable sinners, and all the rest of it, it seems contemptible and not worthy of self-respecting human beings. We ought to stand up and look the world frankly in the face. We ought to make the best we can of the world, and if it is not so good as we wish, after all it will still be better than what these others have made of it in all these ages. A good world needs knowledge, kindliness, and courage; it does not need a regretful hankering after the past or a fettering of the free intelligence by the words uttered long ago by ignorant men. It needs a fearless outlook and a free intelligence. It needs hope for the future, not looking back all the time toward a past that is dead, which we trust will be far surpassed by the future that our intelligence can create.

– Bertrand Russell

Our Challenge

In 1993 when I was starting to gather information for *The Book Your Church Doesn't Want You to Read*, I decided to test the leaders of different religious denominations on their knowledge of Holy Books. The informal test was very simple. I took 50 sayings from various holy texts of the world religions. Included in this 'pop' quiz were scriptures from Hinduism, Zoroastrianism, Judaism, Buddhism, Taoism, Christianity, Islam, Shintoism, and Native American books of wisdom.

The challenge to these men of god was this:
1. Identify the sayings that come from your religion.
2. Tell me where these other holy scriptures come from.

The ministers, priests, preachers, reverends, clerics, monks, rabbis failed miserably in both sections. The highest score was 56 percent on both sections; Most scores were less than 50 percent!

Here is the test...with the answers. Take the test and decide for yourself if there is really any difference between these faiths. Without a doubt, there is a creator of force far beyond our comprehension. One thing is for sure; the man made gods, whatever their names are; Yahweh, Jehovah, Isis, Buddha, Krishna, Allah, Amaterasu, Lao Tzu, or Zarathushtra; they separate us and keep the world in darkness.

1. In everything, do to others what you would you would have then do to you, for this sums up the law and the prophets.

Christianity, Matthew 7.12

2. Not one of you have faith unless you love others, what you love for yourself.

Islam, Hadith of Bukhari

3. You should not behave towards others in a way which is disagreeable to yourself.

Hinduism, Mahabharata Parva 113.8

4. Be the disciples of Aaron-one that loves peace that loves mankind, and brings them nigh to the law.

Judaism, Abot 1.12

5. Love thy neighbor as yourself.

Judaism, Leviticus 19.18

6. Love the world as your own self: then you can truly care for all things.

Taoism, Tao Te Ching 13

7. The believer, men and women are protecting friends of another: they enjoin the right and forbid the wrong.

Islam, Qur'an 9.71

8. When you give to the needy, do not announce it with trumpets...do not let your left hand know what your right hand is doing.

Christianity, Matthew 6.2-3

9. There is a man who gives his charity and he conceals it so much so that his left hand does not know what his right hand spends.

Islam, Hadith of Bukhari

10. When help is given by weighing the recipients need and not the donor's reward, its goodness is greater than the sea.

Hinduism, Tirukkural 226

11. In good deeds, pure heart lays real religion.

Shinto, Genchi Kato

12. Everyone has a goal to which they turn so vie with one another in good works.

Islam, Qur'an 2.148

13. The highest good is like water; water gives life to ten thousand things and does not strive.

Taoism, Tao Te Ching 8

14. Love does no harm to its neighbor therefore love is the fulfillment of the law.

Christianity, Romans 13.10

15. Hurt no one so that no one may hurt you. Remember that you will indeed meet your lord and that he will indeed reckon your deeds.

Islam, Hajj Khutba [farewell address of Prophet Mohammed]

16. You should not murder.

Judaism, Exodus 20.13

17. As for those who seemed to be important-whatever they were makes no difference to me: god does not judge by external appearances.

Christianity, Galatians 2.6

18. God does not look to your faces and your wealth but he looks at your heart and to your deeds.

Islam, Hadith of Muslim

19. Do not consider appearances or height…people look at the outward appearance, but the lord looks at the heart.

Judaism, 1 Samuel 16.7

20. Let me take the speck out of your eye, when all the time there is a plank in your own eye?

Christianity, Matthew 7.2-4

21. When you focus on the faults of others, your perceptions soon become distorted, increasing your own imperfections.

Buddhism, Dhammapada 252-253

22. If people would see their own faults as they would see the faults of others truly evil would come to an end in this world.

Hinduism, Tirukkural 190

23. The best deed of a great person is to forgive and forget.

Shiite, Hahjul Balagha, saying 201

24. Forgive your brother and sister from your heart.

Christianity, Matthew 18.35

25. For whom does god pardon uniquity? For the one who pardons transgression in others.

Judaism, Rosh Hashanah 17.A

26. If there is cause to hate someone, the cause of love has just begun.

Woolf proverb, Senegal

27. Love your enemies, do good to those who hate you, bless those who curse you, pray for those who mistreat you.

Christianity, Luke 6.27-28

28. Requite evil with good, and the one is your enemy will become your dearest friend.

Islam, Qur'an 41.34

29. Hate is not conquered by hate: hate is conquered by love. This is a law eternal.

Buddhism, Dhammapada

30. Return love for hate.

Taoism, Tao Te Ching 63

31. God said " Resemble me: just as I repay good for evil so do you also repay good for evil."

Judaism Exodus, Rabbah 26.2

32. It is no longer good enough to cry peace; we must act peace, live peace and live in peace.

Native American Proverb, Shenandoah

33. Seek peace and pursue it.

Judaism, Psalm 34.14

34. Who regards self as the world may accept the world.

Taoism, Tao Te Ching 13

35. It makes no difference as to the name of God, since love is the real God of all the world.

Apache Proverb

36. To be attached to a certain view and to look down upon others' view as inferior-this the wise call a fetter.

Buddhism, Sutta Nipata 789

37. Like the bee, gathering honey from different flowers, the wise accept the essence of different scriptures and see only the good in all religions.

Hinduism, Bhagavata Purana 11.3

38. The problem with clinging to a single doctrine is that it plunders the Way.

Confucianism, Mencius V11 A. 26

39. Whoever wants to become great among you must be a servant.

Christianity, Matthew 20.25-26

40. Anyone whom God has given the authority of ruling some people, and who does not look after them in an honest manner, will never feel even the smell of Paradise.

Islam, Hadth of Bukhari

41. It is not the strength of arms that gives success to rulers, but their rule and its uprightness.

Hinduism, Tirukkaral 546

42. Blessed are the pure in heart, for they shall see God.

Matthew 5.8

43. All you who come before me, hoping to attain the accomplishments of your desires, pray with hearts pure from falsehood, clean within and without, reflecting the truth like a mirror.

Shinto, Oracle of Temmangu

44. The seal of God is truth.

Judaism, Shabbat 55

45. Stolen food never satisfies hunger.

Native American, Omaha proverb

46. You shall not take each others' money illicitly, nor shall you bribe the officials to deprive others of some of their rights illicitly, while you know.

Islam Qur'an 2.188

47. You shall not steal.

Judaism, Exodus 20.15

48. There are no bigger fools than those who have acquired much learning and preach the same to others but who do not control themselves.

Hinduism, Tirukkural 834

49. Say little and do much.

Judaism, The Fathers According to Rabbi Nathan xx111.1

50. The wise don't talk, they act.

Taoism, Tao Ching 17

51. So long as you remain unknowing that your body is a thing borrowed, you can understand nothing at all.

Tenrikyo Ofudesaki 111.137

52. Our citizenship is in heaven.

Christianity, Philippians 3.20

53. Be in the world as if you were a stranger or a traveler.

Islam, Forty Hadith of an-Nawawi 40

54. The dust returns to the ground it came from, and the spirit returns to God who gave it.

Judaism, Ecclesiastes 12.7

55. The soul's connection with the body is just that of a bird's with the eggshell. The bird leaves it joyfully in the air.

Hinduism, Tirukkural 338

56. Nothing is real but the eternal. Nothing will last but the Eternal.

Sikhism, Guru Granth, Japuji 1, p. 1

57. Truth knows neither birth nor death; it has no beginning and no end.

Buddhism, Gospel of Buddha 2.10

58. In the beginning was the Word, and the word was with God and the Word was God.

Christianity, John 1 1-3

59. I [wisdom] was appointed from eternity, from the beginning, before the world began.

Judaism, Proverbs 8.2

60. The truth is that which is received from Heaven. By nature it is the way it is and can not be changed.

Taoism, Chuang Tzu 31

61. Search and you will find: knock and the door will be opened to you.

Christianity, Matthew 7.7

62. If anyone comes to me walking, I will come to him running.

Islam, Allah Hadith of Muslim

63. When you search for me, you will find me, if you seek me with all your heart.

Judaism, Jeremiah 29.13

64. The spirit himself testifies with our spirit that we are all God's children,

Christianity, Romans 8.16

65. I am returning to my Father and your Father, and to my God and your God.

Christianity, John 20.17

66. All creatures are Allah's children.

Islam, Hadith of Baihaqi

67. I am the father of this universe, the mother...I am that which is and that which is not.

Hinduism, Bhagavad-Gita 9.18

68. Call upon your Lord humbly and in secret.

Qur'an 7.55

69. When you pray, go into your room, close the door and pray to your Father, who is unseen. Then your Father will reward you.

Christianity, Matthew 6.5

70. Take time to worship the unnamable.

Taoism, Hua Hu Ching 81

71. Are not all angels ministering spirits sent to serve those who will inherit salvation?

Christianity, Hebrews 1.14

72. Praise be to Allah...the maker of the angels, messengers flying on wings.

Islam, Qur'an 35.1

73. The heavenly beings day and night for the sake of the Law constantly guard and protect them.

Buddhism, Lotus Sutra, chapter 14

74. If you make the Most High your dwelling…he will command the angels concerning you, to guard you in all your ways.

Judaism, Psalm 91.9,11

75. The body is the field of action…as you plant, so will you harvest.

Sikhism. Guru Granth Sahib, Gauri Var, p. 308

76. You reap what you sow…

Christianity, Galatians 6.7-8

77. Good is the reward for those who do good in this world.

Islam, Qur'an 39.10.

78. Whoever sows righteousness reaps a sure reward.

Judaism, Proverbs 11.18

79. Evil will recoil on those who plot evil.

Islam, Qur'an 35.43

80. The wages of sin is death.

Christianity, Romans 6.2

81. He is the only Path to life eternal…He is the bridge supreme which leads to immorality.

Hinduism, Svetasvatara Upanishad 6.15,19

82. You are the light of the world.

Christianity, Matthew 5.14

83. Be as a lamp unto to them that walk in darkness…

Bahai Faith. Gleanings from the Writings of Baha'u'll'ah

84. Those who believe, their light will gleam before them and on their right hands.

Islam, Qur'an 66.8

85. Use your own light and return to the source of light. This is called practicing eternity.

Taoism, Tao Te Ching 52

86. In regard to evil be infants, but in your thinking be adults.

Christianity, 1 Corinthians 14.20

87. Do not accept any information, unless you verify it for yourself. I have given you the hearing, the eyesight, and the brain, and you are responsible for using them.

Islam, Qur'an 17.36

88. Do not believe in anything simply because you have heard it...Do not believe in anything simply because it is found written in your religious books.

Buddhism, Anguttara-nikaya, Kalama Sutra

89. Mortals, forests, blades of grass, animals and birds all meditate on you.

Sikhism, Guru Granth Sahib, Asa Chhant, p. 45

90. Oh, how I love your law. I meditate on it all day long.

Christianity, Psalm 119.97

91. Prayer is when you speak to God; meditation is when God speaks to you.

Zen Buddhist saying

92. If you can empty your mind of all thoughts your heart will embrace the tranquility of peace. Returning to the source is tranquility.

Taoism, Tao Te Ching 16

93. It does not require many words to speak the truth.

Chief Joseph, Nez Perce

94. Those who consider themselves religious but do not keep a tight rein on their tongues, they deceive themselves and their religion is worthless.

Christianity, James 1.26

95. Better than a thousand meaningless words is one word of deep meaning which when heard will bring peace.

Buddhism, Dhammapada 1

96. Those who know do not talk. Those who talk do not know.

Taoism, Tao Te Ching 56

97. Abstain from fleshly lusts, which war against the soul.

Christianity, 1 Peter 2.11

98. Do you know what most commonly brings people to hell? It is two hollow things: the mouth and the private parts.

Islam, Hadith of Tirimidhi

99. What good will it be for you if you gain the whole world, yet forfeit your soul?

Christianity, Matthew 16.26

100. The wise wear common clothes and carry the jewels in their hearts.

Taoism, Tao Te Ching 70

– Sources: *Holy Books of the World, One Heart* edited by Bonnie Louise Kuchler

Acknowledgments

Sincere thanks to the James Hervey Johnson Charitable Educational Trust for their financial assistance throughout the years. Also for the invaluable teamwork of the Truthseeker Company in the formatting of *The Book Your Church Doesn't Want You to Read*. Also, the many scholars who selflessly gave their time and advice; including Steve Allen and Jordan Maxwell. A special thanks to Dr. Alan A. Snow who passed on last year. His scholarship, generosity and brilliance will be missed. In the arena of critical thought and humanism few could equal his intellectual capacity. Another special thanks to our technical editor, Cheryl Griffith for patiently bringing us into the twenty-first century. Sincere gratitude goes out to Chad Cooper. This book could never have been completed without his support. Special mention has to be made to the innumerable supporters, booksellers and website hosts who in many cases stood firm to get *The Book* into the mainstream when it was not popular to do so. Their foresight helped to make *The Book* a best-seller…and will I trust make this expanded version equally successful. And the most important for last, my co-editor, Maria Murdy who has put countless hours in to create, edit and launch the new edition. Without her, *The Book* would not be a reality.

Appendix

Appendix A

Partial List of Freethinkers

- John Adams – U.S. President, promoter and signer of the Declaration of Independence
- Samuel Adams – Moving spirit in the Boston Tea Party, signer of the Declaration of Independence
- Ethan Allen – Hero in the Revolutionary War; wrote *Reason the Only Oracle of Man*
- Steve Allen – Author, humorist, and entertainer
- Isaac Asimov – Leading science fiction author and Humanist, past president American Humanist Association
- Clara Barton – Founder of the American Red Cross Society
- Frank L. Baum – Writer, author of Oz books
- Alexander Graham Bell – Inventor of the telephone
- D.M. Bennett – Founder in 1873 and first editor of Truth Seeker, a freethought magazine
- Samuel Beckett – Irish author
- Marlon Brando – Movie actor; specialized in morally intense roles
- Giordano Bruno – Philosopher, monk, burned at the stake in 1600
- Luther Burbank – Horticulturist and plant breeder
- Albert Camus – Essayist, novelist, short-story writer, playwright, journalist
- Rachel Carson – Environmentalist, author of *The Silent Spring*
- Norman Cousins – Editor, *Saturday Review*
- Clarence Darrow – Lawyer
- Charles Robert Darwin – English naturalist, author of *Origin of Species*
- Charles Dickens – Novelist
- Frederick Douglass – Abolitionist
- Thomas Alva Edison – Inventor
- Charles W. Eliot – President of Harvard for 40 years
- Benjamin Franklin – American writer, statesman, and inventor
- Sigmund Freud – Austrian neurologist
- Betty Friedan – Author of *Feminine Mystique*
- Erich Fromm – Psychoanalyst and author of *The Sane Society*
- Robert Frost – American poet
- Galileo Galilei — Astronomer, physicist, "Eppur Si Muove!"
- Annie Laurie Gaylor – Editor of *Freethought Today*, author, lecturer, and speaker for women's rights
- Horace Greeley – Founder *New York Tribune*
- Armand Hammer – American industrialist, secular philanthropist, past president of Occidental Petroleum
- Oliver Wendell Holmes – American physician and author
- Aldous Huxley – English critic and novelist

- Immanuel Kant – German philosopher, considered by some to be one of the greatest of modem thinkers
- Rudyard Kipling – English author
- Paul Kurtz – Prof. Philosophy at State U. of NY; editor, publisher
- Norman Lear – Television producer, produced "All In The Family" Founder of People For the American Way
- James Madison – U.S. President and youngest of the Founding Fathers helped bring about ratification of the Constitution and passage of the Bill of Rights
- Horace Mann – American Educator
- Henry Miller – American writer
- Friedrich Nietzsche – Philosophical pioneer; anti-Christian
- Florence Nightingale – English nurse, philanthropist
- Thomas Paine – Writer and political theorist; the mind behind the American Revolution and the Declaration of Independence
- Linus Pauling – Nobel Peace Prize winner, chemist
- Pablo Picasso – Spanish painter, sculptor
- Ayn Rand – American writer, Objectivist philosopher
- Bertrand Russell – English philosopher, mathematician, writer
- Carl Sagan – Astronomer, scientist, writer, TV host
- William Shakespeare – English playwright and poet
- George Bernard Shaw – English-Irish playwright
- Upton Sinclair – American writer
- B.F. Skinner – Behaviorist, psychologist, signed 1973 Humanist Manifesto
- Mark Twain – American author, humorist
- Gore Vidal – American author, movie and TV personality
- Walt Whitman – American poet, true inheritor of Emersonian principles

Appendix B

Illustrations and Photos

Origins of Religion
1. Statue of the Tauroctony in the Vatican Museum; courtesy of Dr. Alan Albert Snow
2. Detail from The Aztec Temple of Quetzalcoatl, in the Ancient city of Teotihuacán, near Mexico City; courtesy of Chad Cooper
3. Ahura Mazda; Detail from Zoroastrian Temple in Iran; courtesy of Dr. Alan Albert Snow
4. Horus; Detail from an Egyptian tomb painting in Egypt; courtesy of Dr. Alan Albert Snow
5. Clockwise from left:
    a. Ancient Aztec priest with crown detail.
    b. Christ detail.
    c. Statue of Liberty detail.
    d. Scepter
    All courtesy of Jordan Maxwell, www.jordanmaxwell.com
6. Stained glass simulation; courtesy of Cheryl Dunivan
7. "Aquarius" by Jehoshaphat Aspin, from *A Familiar Treatise on Astronomy*, Published by Samuel Leigh, 1825
8. Jesus/Pharoah; courtesy of Cheryl Dunivan
9. Thomas Jefferson portrait; from The Harry S. Truman Library; one of eleven Presidential Libraries administered by the National Archives and Records Administration
10. Statue of Roman Isis, Capitoline Museum: Hall of the Galatian; courtesy of Dr. Alan Albert Snow

Worldwide Religions
11. Dome of the Rock, Israel; www.istockphoto.com
12. Muslim woman; API Worldwide Photo
13. Star of David; by Nancy Melton
14. Map of Palestine/ Israel; Central Intelligence Agency's World Factbook

The Bible
15. Gideon Logo reproduction; courtesy of Cheryl Dunivan
16. Thomas Paine at the age of 55; Engraved in London, by William Sharp, 1792, from an oil painting by George Romney R.A.
17. Bible photo; Tim C. Leedom

The Dead Sea Scrolls and The Gnostic Gospels

18. Calendar of the Zodiac; courtesy of Cheryl Dunivan
19. Scroll photo; courtesy of Stephan A. Hoeller, www.gnosis.org

Jesus

20. Cimabue; 1268, at San Domenico Church in Arezzo, Tuscany
21. Zeus statue head; courtesy of Robert Ellsworth
22. Jesus with cross statue, atop St. Peter's Basilica, Vatican City; courtesy of Dr. Alan Albert Snow
23. Christ Pantocrator icon from St. Catherine's Monastery in Egypt; courtesy of Dr. Alan Albert Snow
24. "The Last Supper" by Leonardo da Vinci, 1495–1498; mural in the refectory of the convent of Santa Maria delle Grazie in Milan, Italy
25. Church of Saint-Pierre Moissac, France, South Portal; courtesy of Dr. Alan Albert Snow
26. Mary; courtesy of Robert Ellsworth
27. Devaki and Krishna; by Edward Moor, from Hindu Pantheon, Published by Edward Moor in 1910
28. Christ/ Krishna; courtesy of Cheryl Dunivan
29. Chi Rho; courtesy of Cheryl Dunivan

Doctrine

30. Triune God; courtesy of Cheryl Dunivan
31. "After Jesus, The Triumph of Christianity" The Reader's Digest Inc.; Illustrated by Chris Majadini
32. "The Inscription over Hell-Gate" by William Blake ca.1824–27, Inferno 3: 1–20, Tate Gallery London; purchased with the assistance of a special grant from the National Gallery and donations from the National Art Collections Fund, Lord Duveen and others, and presented through the National Art Collections Fund 1919
33. Beelzebub statue; Tim C. Leedom
34. Satan; drawn by Gustave Dore, in John Milton's *Paradise Lost*, originally published by Cassell, Petter, and Galpin, 1866
35. Impaled Savior; courtesy of Cheryl Dunivan
36. Mushroom Priest; from *The History of Costume*, published by Braun & Schneider, 1861

The Catholic Church

37. Statue of Diocletian and Maximian; photos courtesy of Kenneth Humphreys, www.jesusneverexisted.com
38. Joan of Arc Illustration from *The Book of Days*, by Robert Chambers, W. & R. Chambers, Ltd, 1906
39. "Giordano Bruno" by Christian Bartholméss, 1846, Paris: Librairie Philosophique de Ladrange, frontispiece
40. Pope Paul VI and John F. Kennedy; Associated Press Photo
41. Native Americans Statue; Tim C. Leedom

42. Father Serra Statue; Tim C. Leedom
43. Nazi Pope; West German Government archive photos
44. Virgin Mary Grilled Cheese, www.ebay.com
45. St. John Vianney Chapel, Balboa Island, CA; by Tim C. Leedom

Fundamentalism
46. Kansas Sign; courtesy of Sam Trent
47. Columns; courtesy of People for the American Way, www.pfaw.org
48. Jesus Poster; courtesy of Sam Trent

Archaeology and Science
49. The ossuary, or bone-box; courtesy of Biblical Archaeology Society
50. "Ecce Homo" by Quentin Massys, 1520, at Doge's Palace, Venice
51. "Le Coup De Lance" by Peter Paul Rubens, 1620, at the Royal Museum of Fine Arts (Koninklijk Museum voor Schone Kunsten), Antwerp
52. "How at the Castle of Corbin a Maiden Bare in the Sangreal and Foretold the Achievements of Galahad" by Arthur Rackham, from *The Romance of King Arthur and His Knights of the Round Table*, by Alfred W Pollard, Weathervane Books, 1917

New Takes, New Consequences
53. 1533 account of the execution of a witch; from the Baden State Museum, Wikipedia.org
54. "Lesson from The New England Primer" by Benjamin Harris, 1683
55. Mormon Temple in Utah; Tim C. Leedom
56. Joseph Smith portrait; courtesy of Rethinking Mormonism, www.i4m.com
57. Wallace Dodd Ford; FBI photograph, http://foia.fbi.gov/fard/fard1.pdf
58. Wallace Fard Muhammad; photo presented to the public by Elijah Muhammad

Revelations
59. "Satyagraha, The Martyrs of Peace" painted by Tom Owens, created by Tim C. Leedom

Appendix C

Bibliography

About.com Encyclopedia. http://66.102.7.104/search?q=cache:WnQnFTVqkp0J:experts.about.com/e/e/ex/Exorcism.htm.

Acharya S. *The Christ Conspiracy*, Adventures Unlimited Press, 1999, www.truthbeknown.com.

Achtemeier, Paul. *In Inspiration of Scripture: Problems and Proposals,* Westminster John Knox Press, 1980.

ACFnewsource; Muslim PR, October 9, 2001, http://66.102.7.104/search?q=cache:0 eRYZ3lmcJoJ:www.acfnewsource.org/general/muslim.

Allegro, John. *The Sacred Mushrooms and the Cross*, Doubleday, 1970.

Ally, Shabir. *Al-Attique Int'l Islamic Publications*, www.islamway.com/english/images/library/contradictions.htm, 1998.

Al Qur'an, 650 C.E.

American Atheists, AA News, www.skepticfiles.org/american/aanes121.htm, April 24, 1996.

Analects, 500 B.C.

Anderson, Max. *The Polygamy Story: Fact and Fiction,* Salt Lake City: Publishers Press, 1979.

A News Center; quoted from *Washington Times*; February 27, 2006, http://www.angelfire.com/stars/promotions/Nov5Mar6.html.

Anti-Defamation League; U.N. World Conference Against Racism; www.adl.org, 2001, http://www.adl.org/durban/zionism.asp.

"Arabia, History of," *Encyclopedia Britannica, Inc.* 1979, p 1049.

Arellano, Gustavo. "Pope John Paul II: A Moral, Abject Failure When It Mattered," *OC Weekly*, Vol. 10 No. 31, April 8, 2005.

Armstrong, Karen. *Holy War*, Anchor; 2nd edition 2001.

Armstrong, Karen. *Muhammad*, HarperSanFrancisco; 1993.

Atack, Jon. "Xenu," 1996, http://www.xs4all.nl/~kspaink/cos/essays/atack_ot3.html.

Atheistsunited.org. "Robert G. Ingersoll quotes," www.atheistsunited.org/newsletters/AU-05-03.pdf+robert+ingersoll+quote&hl=en&gl=us&ct=clnk&cd=2

Atheists.org; Church Groups operating Halloween Hell Hoaxes, www.atheists.org/flash.line/hallow2.htm, October 24, 1999

Aust, Jerold and John Ross Schroeder. "Who and What is Hamas?" *The Good News Magazine*, March 2006, http://www.goodnewsmag.org/magazine.

Ballou, Robert O. *World Bible*, Penguin, 1977.

Barker, Dan. "What do you Really Know about the Bible?" fff.org, http://www.ffrf.org/quiz/banswers.php.

Barna Organization Poll; George Gallup & Jem Castelli, Macmillan Publishing Co., Dec. 1994.

BBC News Online; 1999, http://66.102.7.104/search?q=cache:me6sIYct6ycJ:news.bbc.co.uk/1/hi/uk/2491.

Beadle, J.H. *Life in Utah*, Philadelphia, PA.: National Publishing Company, 1870.

Bidstrup, Scott. "The Bible and Christianity - The Historical Origins," 2001; http://www.bidstrup.com/bible.htm.

Bidstrup, Scott. "Why Fundamentalism is Wrong," 2001; http://www.bidstrup.com/religion.htm.

Blaine, Barbara of Chicago. The Survivors' Network of those Abused by Priests Founder and President; statement "Female Victims of Clergy Abuse," Press Conference Presentation, December 1, 2005.

Blaine, Barbara. "Old Myths, New Myths," www.snapnetwork.org/op_ed/oped_index.htm, February 27, 2004.

Bradley, Martha Sonntag. *Kidnapped from that Land: The Government Raids on the Polygamists of Short Creek*, Salt Lake City: University of Utah Press, 1993.

Brainyquote.com; Televangelist quotes, http://www.brainyquote.com/quotes/authors/p/pat_robertson.html.

Butcher, Tim. *News Telegraph*, Israeli hawks circle Iran's N-plants, 12/08/2005, http://www.telegraph.co.uk/news/main.jhtm.

Campbell, Joseph. *Myths to Live By*, Viking Press, 1972.

Carroll, Robert Todd. *The Skeptic's Dictionary*. Wiley: August 15, 2003.

Catholic Encyclopedia, The. Volume X, Robert Appleton Company, 1911.

Chief Seattle. "Chief Seattle Speaks," *Seattle Times*, October, 1887.

Churchward, Albert. *Book of Religion*, Dutton & Company, 1924.

CNN.com, 2004, http://www.cnn.com/2004/WORLD/europe/11/02/netherlands.filmmaker.

Cooke, Jeremy. "School Trains Suicide Bombers," BBC News, 18 July, 2001, http://news.bbc.co.uk/1/hi/world/middle_east/1446003.stm.

Coon, Carleton S., *Smithsonian*, Washington D.C., 1944, p 398.

Cooper, Chad. "Killer Jesus," Presentation for Artwalk night, June 2005.

Date Setters Diary; failed return dates, http://www.raptureready.com/rr-date-setters.html.

Davis, Kenneth C. *Don't Know Much About the Bible*, William Morrow, 2001.

Doane, T.W. *Bible Myths and Their Parallels in Other Religions*, University Books, 1882.

Dolan, Chester. *Religion on Trial*, Mopah Publications, 2000.

Doyle, Thomas. "The Thomas Doyle Memo Part 3; #22," Memo written to his superiors in the Catholic Church, 1985.

Easton, Karyn. "Virgin Visions," 2002 http://www.paranormality.com/virgin_visions.html.

Edelen, William. *Spirit Dance*, William Edelen Publishing, www.williamedelen.com, 1988

Edelen, William. *Earthrise*, William Edelen Publishing, www.williamedelen.com, 1998.

Eisenman, Dr. Robert H. "Rehabilitating Judas Iscariot," January 23, 2006, http://www.huffingtonpost.com/robert-eisenman/rehabilitating-judas_b_14335.html.

Ellerbe; Helen. *The Dark Side of Christian History*, San Rafael: Morningstar Books, 1995

Errico, Rocco A. *Let There Be Light, The Seven Keys*. DeVorss & Company, 1994.

Evans, Michael D. *The American Prophecies*, Faith Words, 2004.

Flash Light. "Exodus 22: 17 or 18," Webmaster for www.polytheism.org.

Frank, Mitch. *Understanding the Holy Land*, Penguin Books, April 2005.

Friedman, George and foxnews.com. "Israel Prepares Massive Blow Against Palestinians," August 09, 2001, http://www.foxnews.com/story/0,2933,31209,00.html.

Froiseth, Jennie Anderson. *The Women of Mormonism: The Story of Polygamy*, Detroit, Michigan: C.G.G. Paine, 1886.

Funk, Robert W., Roy W. Hoover, and the Jesus Seminar. *The Five Gospels: The Search for the Authentic Words of Jesus*, HarperSanFrancisco; 1997.

geocities.com; Televangelist quotes, http://www.geocities.com/CapitolHill/7027/quotes.html.

Gibson, David; www.beliefnet.com, "America's Favorite Unopened Text," 12/07/2000, http://www.beliefnet.com/story/57/story_5746_1.html.

Gibson, Jano. "Vatican Exorcist Warns of Harry Potter," *The Sydney Morning Herald*, March 3, 2006, http://www.smh.com.au/news/unusual-tales/vatican-exorcist-warns-of-harry-potter/2006/03/03.

Goeringer, Conrad. "The Vatican Bank Scandal," http://www.americanatheist.org/pope99/calvi.html.

Golding, Shmuel. "Biblical Polemics in Jerusalem," The Jerusalem Institute of Biblical Polemics, Israel Jerusalem, Spring, 1990, p. 11-19.

Graham, Billy. "Of Angels, Devils and Messages From God," *Time Magazine*, Nov. 15, 1993, http://www.time.com/time/magazine/printout/0,8816,979587,00.html.

Graves, Kersey. *The World's Sixteen Crucified Saviors*, Truth Seeker Co., 1875.

Guardian Unlimited. "Virgins? What Virgins?" January 12, 2002, http://www.guardian.co.uk/saturday_review/story.

Hancock, Kaziah May. *Prisons of the Mind*. Utah: Desert Blossom Publishing, 1987.

Heldal-Lund, Andreas. "A Brief History of the Church of Scientology," Operation Clambake, http://www.xenu.net/archive/infopack/8.htm.

Hedges, Chris. "The Christian Right and the Rise of American Fascism," Nov 2004, http://www.theocracywatch.org/chris_hedges_nov24_04.htm.

Hoeller, Stephan A., Ph.D. *Freedom: The Alchemy of a Voluntary Society*, Quest Books, 1992.

Holy Bible, The. ca. 100 to 200 C.E.[?]

Humphreys, Kenneth. *Jesus Never Existed*, Iconoclast Press, 2005.

imdb.com; Televangelist quotes, http://www.imdb.com/title/tt0149408.

Ingersoll, Robert Green. *The Foundations of Faith*, C.P. Farrell, Ingersoll Publishers, 1895

Israel's Antiquities Authority. "Final Report of the Examining Committees for the Yehoash Inscription and James Ossuary," March 2003, http://www.antiquities.org.il/article_Item_eng.asp.

James, J. Courtenay. *The Language of Palestine and Adjacent Regions*, Edinburgh, T. & T. Clark, 1920.

Jefferson, Thomas. "Letter to Nephew Peter Carr, August 10, 1787," *The Writings of Thomas Jefferson*, New York Library Of America, 1994.

jihadwatch.org; "Fallujah adopts Taliban theocracy," June 04, 2004, http://www.jihadwatch.org/archives/2004/06/002124print.html.

Khan, Riaz. The Associated Press, 2006, http://66.102.7.104/search?q=cache:ejW-Rk5-UlAJ:www.amren.com/mtnews/archives/2006/02/cleric.

Katz, Yaakov. "Extremists Boast They Cursed Sharon," *Jerusalem Post*, Jan. 6, 2006, http://www.jpost.com/servlet/Satellite?cid.

Krakauer, Jon. *Under The Banner of Heaven*, New York: Doubleday, 2003.

Konig, Yakov. Neturei Karta UK; at the meeting on the crisis in the Middle East, March 2004, House of Commons, London, England, http://www.nkusa.org/activities/speeches/London30Mar04.cfm.

Kuchler, Bonnie Louise. *One Heart*, Marlowe & Company, 2004.

Laub, Karin. "'End-timers' focus on Jerusalem," April 22, 1998, http://www.dispatch.co.za/1998/04/22/editoria/JERUSALEM.HTM.

Land Over Baptist. "Hell House Feature," 2003, http://www.landoverbaptist.org/news0903/hellhouse.html.

Langborgh, Eric. "'Functional Atheist' Directs Theology at Catholic Boston College?" *Accuracy in Academia's Campus Report*, http://www.academia.org/campus_reports/2000/october_2000_3.html.

Larue, Gerald A. "Humanism and Christmas," The Truth Seeker Journal, Fall, 1990, p. 38-40.

Leedom, Kelsey M. "Humanism, the Hope for Mankind," St. Margaret's Episcopal School, March 2005.

Leedom, Tim C. *The Main Man*, Manoa Valley Publishing Co., 1999.

Loyd, Anthony. "Tomb of the Unknown Assassin Reveals Mission to Kill Rushdie," Times Online, June 08, 2005, http://www.timesonline.co.uk/article/0,,3-1645223,00.html.

Massey, Gerald. *Ancient Egypt: The Light of the World*, T. Fisher Unwin, Adelphi Terrace, 1907.

Maxwell Jordan. *The Naked Truth*, video series; www.jordanmaxwell.com.

Mbachu, Dulue. "Anti-Muslim Riot in Nigeria Turns Deadly," Breitbart.com/AP, February 21, 2006, http://www.wwrn.org/article.php?idd=20533&sec=46&cont=3

McCabe, Joseph. *Popes and Their Church*, Watts, 1953.

Messiahpage.com. "Why Jesus Didn't Qualify," http://messiahpage.com/htmldocs/whynotj.html.

Miles, Austin. *Don't Call Me Brother*, Prometheus Books, 1989.

Miles, Austin. *Setting the Captives Free*, Prometheus Books, 1990.

Monaghan, Patricia. *The New Book of Goddesses and Heroines*, Llewellyn Publications, 2001.

Moyer, Bill. Acceptance speech for Global Environment Citizen Award, December 2004, http://www.truthout.org/docs_04/120504G.shtml.

Murdy, Corrina. "Polygamy in the U.S." Long Beach State University, 2004.

Nihon Gi, 712 C.E.

Owens, Lance S. "An Introduction to Gnosticism and The Nag Hammadi Library," The Gnosis Archive website, http://www.gnosis.org/naghamm/nhlintro.html.

Packham, Richard, Founder of the Ex-Mormon Foundation. "To Those Who are Investigating Mormonism," May 14, 2005, http://www.exmormon.org/tract2.htm.

Paine, Thomas. *The Age of Reason*, Philadelphia, 1795, p 11-12.

Pali Cannon, *Theravada*, 246 B.C.

Pearlman, Moshe and Yaacov Yannai. *Historical Sites in Israel*, Chartwell Books, Secaucus, 1978.

People for the American Way. "The Good Book Taught Wrong," http://www.pfaw.org/pfaw/general/default.aspx?oid=1345.

People for the American Way. "Religious Coercion and Liberty," 2005, http://www.pfaw.org/pfaw/general/default.aspx?oid=11156.

Perlstein, Rick. "The Jesus Landing Pad," *Village Voice*, May 18th, 2004, http://www.villagevoice.com/news/0420,perlstein,53582,1.html.

politicalhumor.about.com; Televangelist quotes, http://politicalhumor.about.com/od/funnyquotes/a/patrobertson.htm.

"Polygamy under siege," *The Economist* (US), Article A6398467 Jan 30, 1988 v306 n7535 p 20(2).

Portable World Bible, The. Viking Press, 1939.

positiveatheism.org; Televangelist quotes, Cedric Whitman Quote, http://www.positiveatheism.org/hist/quotes/scar_b.htm.

Rachlin, Harvey. *Lucy's Bones, Sacred Stones & Einstein's Brain*, Henry Holt & Company, February 2000.

Remsburg, John E. *The Bible*, Truth Seeker Company, 1905.

Remsburg; John E.; *The Christ*. The Truth Seeker Company, 1909.

Renan, Ernest. *Nouvelles études d' histoire Religieuse*, 1851.

Rivera, Jose Ignacio. "Father Serra and the Skeletons of Genocide," Doctoral Thesis, University of California Berkeley, 1991.

Robinson, Bruce A. "64 Failed End-of-the-World Predictions Before 1990," Ontario Consultants on Religious Tolerance, http://www.religioustolerance.org/end_wrl2.htm.

Robinson, Bruce A. "Some Specific Reasons Why Many Scientists Disbelieve In Creation Science and a Literal Interpretation of Genesis," Ontario Consultants on Religious Tolerance, http://www.religioustolerance.org/ev_proof1.htm.

Robinson, Bruce A; Ontario Consultants on Religious Tolerance, Basic Information on Various Religions Chart http://www.religioustolerance.org/worldrel.htm

Russell, Bertrand. Lecture "Why I Am Not A Christian," South London, National Secular Society, 1927.

Schaefer, Franz. "The Unofficial Opus Dei FAQ," http://www.mond.at/opus.dei/opus.dei.uo.faq.html

Schonfield, Hugh J. *The Passover Plot*, Element Books Ltd, 1998

Singer, Rabbi Tovi. "Crucifixion/Resurrection Chart," 1998, http://www.outreachjudaism.org/crucifix.html

Solomon, Dorothy Allred. *Predators, Prey, and Other Kinfolk: Growing Up In Polygamy*, New York: W.W. Norton, 2003.

Sykes, Egerton. *Everyman's Dictionary of Non-Classical Mythology*, J.M. Dent & Sons Ltd; Rev Edition, 1977.

Shamir, Israel. "Genocidal Depopulation: The Deir Yassin Massacre," *The Barnes Review*, October 2002.

Sharlet, Jeff. "God's Senator," *Rolling Stone*, Jan 25, 2006.

Shashaa, Esam. "A Brief History of Palestine," http://www.palestinehistory.com/history.htm.

Silberman, Neil Asher and Israel Finkelstein. *The Bible Unearthed*, Free Press; 2002.

Simpson, Wayne. "Ten False Messiahs", 2000, http://jasher.com/Messiahs.htm.

Smith, Warren Allen. *Who's Who in Hell*, Barricade Books, 1993.

Snow, Dr. Alan Albert. "Astrology in the Dead Sea Scrolls," *The Book Your Church Doesn't Want You To Read*, Kendall Hunt Publishing Company, August, 1993.

Spong, Bishop John Shelby; Rescuing the Bible from Fundamentalism, HarperSan-Francisco; 1992.

Spong, Bishop John Shelby. *Why Christianity Must Change or Die*, HarperSanFrancisco, 1999.

Stanit, Rich. *Religion Must Die*, The Book Tree, 2006, www.thebooktree.com.

Stannard, David E. *The American Holocaust*, Oxford University Press, 1992.

Swindler, Adrian C. "The Trinity: An Absurdity Borrowed From Paganism," *The Truth Seeker Journal*, Fall, 1992, p 30-31.

Talmud, 1200 B.C.

Tao Te Ching, 1000 B.C.

Teeple, Howard M. *The Noah's Ark Nonsense,* The Religion and Ethics Institute, Inc., 1978

Thiering, Dr. Barbara. "The Dead Sea Scrolls and Christianity" http://www.pesherof-christ.infinitesoulutions.com/ Webmaster Dylan Stephens.

Tice, Paul. *Triumph of the Human Spirit*, The Book Tree, 1999.

Till, Farrell. "A Problem for Biblical Inerrancy," *The Skeptical Review*, Spring, 1991, p 18-26.

Veda, 1000-500 B.C.

Vermes, G. *The Dead Sea Scrolls in English*, Penguin Books, 1987

Veiga, Alex. "JDL Activist Linked to California Bomb Plot Killed in Prison," November 5, 2005, http://www.sfgate.com/cgi-bin/article.

Voss, Carl Herman Voss. *Living Religions of the World*, Prometheus Books, 1977.

Walker, Barbara G. *Women's Encyclopedia of Myth*, Harper, 1983.

Watanabe, Teresa. "Doubting the Story of Exodus," *Los Angeles Times*, April 13, 2001, http://www.raceandhistory.com/historicalviews/doubtingexodus.htm.

Watchtower, The; Watch Tower Bible and Tract Society of Pennsylvania, December 15, 1990.

Wikipedia.org; quote about Beelzebub, http://en.wikipedia.org/wiki/Beelzebub.

Wine, Sherwin T. "Jewish Humanism," *Macha*r, March 1992, p 6-10.

World Encyclopedia, The. Oxford University Press, October 2001.

If you enjoyed

THE BOOK YOUR CHURCH*
DOESN'T WANT YOU TO READ

please check out…

FLOCK OF DODOS

Behind Modern Creationism, Intelligent Design
& the Easter Bunny

by Barrett Brown & Jon P. Alston, Ph.D.

Praise for **FLOCK OF DODOS**:

"*Flock of Dodos* is in the great tradition of debunkers with a sense of humor, from Thomas
Paine to Mark Twain."

– Alan Dershowitz

"Simultaneously smart, insightful, and hilarious! Eventhough refuting creationism is like
shooting tiny Noah's Arks in a barrel, Brown and Alston dissect the movement with a wholly
unique wit and perspective. The best book I've read in years."

– Bob Cesca, The Huffington Post

"Here's the problem with America's born-again wackos: only a gifted comic is capable of
describing them, but no one with a sense of humor can stomach being around them. That's
why there are so few books like *Flock of Dodos*. With their painstaking attention to historical
detail and amusingly violent writing style, Brown and Alston have given the religious right
exactly the righteous, merciless fragging it deserves. I wish I could tie James Dobson down
and make him eat every page."

– Matt Taibbi, *Rolling Stone* magazine

"Jesus Christ and lesbian monkeys in the same book. Brilliant. 'Smart' and 'funny' in the
same book. Genius."

– Cenk Uyger, "The Young Turks," Air America Radio

Available online and at bookstores nationally.

i